CARI

CHALI

Care in the Community:

Challenge and Demonstration

MARTIN KNAPP
PAUL CAMBRIDGE
CORINNE THOMASON
JENNIFER BEECHAM
CAROLINE ALLEN
ROBIN DARTON

ASHGATE

First published in Great Britain in 1992

Ashgate
Ashgate Publishing Limited
Gower House
Croft Road
Aldershot
Hants GU11 3HR
England

Ashgate Publishing Company
Old Post Road
Brookfield
Vermont 05036
U.S.A.

A CIP catalogue record for this book is available from the British Library and the US Library of Congress.

ISBN 1 85742 071 3 (Hardback)
ISBN 1 85742 069 1 (Paperback)

Typeset at the PSSRU, University of Kent at Canterbury

Printed and bound in Great Britain by
Billing and Sons Limited, Worcester.

Contents

List of tables

List of figures

Preface

In 1983 the Personal Social Services Research Unit, University of Kent at Canterbury, was invited by the then Department of Health and Social Security to promote, monitor and evaluate the Care in the Community Demonstration Programme. £15 million (£25 million at today's prices) had been allocated by the Department to support a programme of pilot projects that would help long-stay hospital residents resettle in the community. This book describes the programme and comprehensively reports its evaluation.

We have worked together on the evaluation since 1987, and with former colleagues Roger Hampson, Ken Judge and Judy Renshaw since 1984. The PSSRU research team needed to work very closely with staff in the 28 pilot projects, and with over 1,000 hospital residents and community care clients, over a period of several years. Without the cooperation, patience and enthusiasm of project staff and clients, our work would certainly not have been possible. The DHSS contributed helpfully at key stages of the analysis and writing. At various times, Catherine Drury, Andrew Fenyo, Liz Garside, Kerry Gordon, Eriko Gould, Lesley Hayes, Lucy Holley, Deborah Scott and Karen Traske helped establish our database and interpret our data. Jenny Kirby and Debbie Munslow assisted with interviewing. Over the years, a number of secretaries supported our research, and we particularly thank Lesley Banks, Jenny Conway, Sarah Conyers, Moira Forth, Glenys Harrison, Rebecca Robson, Anne Walker, Jackie Waller and Maureen Weir. Melanie Henwood made some useful comments on our penultimate draft, David Challis took over the research management of one project within the programme with considerable success, Ian Leedham undertook his PhD research in two areas and offered invaluable advice, and Bleddyn Davies provided leadership in his inimitable way. Jane Dennett coped magnificently with all the editorial tasks, and produced the camera-ready copy.

The six authors take responsibility for the contents of the book, the analyses of the data and the interpretation of findings. Clearly however, without the baseline established by our former colleagues, the support of clients and staff, and the financial assistance of the DHSS, we would not have been able to complete this book. We record our considerable gratitude to all concerned.

We dedicate this book to the people who moved from hospital to the community under the auspices of the Care in the Community programme, and to the many other people undergoing similar experiences today.

Martin Knapp, Paul Cambridge, Corinne Thomason,
Jeni Beecham, Caroline Allen, Robin Darton
Canterbury, December 1991

Part I: Policy and background

1 A developing context

Care in the community is not new. As an informal, localised, family-centred means to support people with long-term needs it obviously pre-dates formal, institutional and congregate care arrangements. Community care support has long been offered to people with most mental health problems, physical disabilities, learning difficulties or age-related needs, notwithstanding shame, concealment and neglect by a few families. As a loosely-structured system of collectively-funded services delivered to people living outside hospitals, community care has been a feature of British health and welfare policy at least since the eighteenth century. Community care itself may not be new, but as an administrative function and pre-eminent policy goal it is a recent phenomenon. For the first time, 'community care' is an identifiable concept or process, the focus of political debate, legislation, purposive funding, professional training and research enquiry, rather than an unsung, ill-defined and fragmented care residual remaining after residential, hospital and day care have been attended to.

During the 1980s community care rarely left the policy agenda. Indeed, the period sandwiched between the Department of Health and Social Security (DHSS) consultative document on the subject issued in July 1981, and the announcement exactly nine years later of the phased implementation of the *National Health Service and Community Care Act 1990* saw unprecedented attention lavished on community care. Over the same period the circumstances of community care also altered dramatically, with the accelerated rundown and closure of some hospitals, the growth of informal care and recognition of its inequitable burden, the pouring of social security money into residential and nursing homes in the voluntary and private sectors, and experimentation with various forms of case (or care) management.

At the start of the decade, as now, community care was a priority policy:

> Most people who need long-term care can and should be looked after in the community. This is what most of them want for themselves and what those responsible for their care believe to be best (DHSS, 1981a, para. 1.1).

Yet, at that time, government assumptions did not match the perceptions of a majority of health and social care professionals; and government preferences for change did not meet professional and public concerns. Broadly speaking, the desirability of community care as a policy often contrasted with reservations about its operation in practice. By 1990, after billions of words had been devoted to the debate, government ministers were looking less than wholly committed to the policies fashioned from the Griffiths report and its antecedents, and delayed full implementation of the 1990 Act. With the Secretary of State blaming the unpreparedness of local authorities, and most local authorities blaming government anxiety about the consequences of community care reorganisation and funding for the poll tax, community care appeared to become a less desirable or less urgent policy. By this time, of course, many of the central planks of the legislation – the support for carers, the transfer of some responsibilities and funds to local authorities, the encouragement of client choice, the drawing up of community care plans, and the introduction of case management – were attracting the approbation of care professionals, health and local authority members, carers, care users and their advocates. For perhaps the first time, community care had well-defined expectations – planned and tailored packages of services delivered to people with assessed needs, in cognisance of people's preferences, funded with these needs and preferences in mind, complete with built-in resource monitoring and quality assurance. That at least remains the hope. If the reality proves to be only half as good, community care will still be in a radically different and generally better position than ten years earlier.

Had it not been for the runaway social security bill for residential and nursing home care, and the untested assumption that closing hospitals would save millions of pounds of taxpayers' money, it is arguable that the 1990 community care reforms would not have happened. Over the 1980s, in part a consequence of the emphases at the start of the decade, community care moved from loosely-formulated professional concern to an ever-present item on the political, public policy and administrative agenda. By dint of the very controversy surrounding the government's early manoeuvres in community care – the relaxation of social security funding, the emphasis on the family, the vision of local authorities as enabling bodies – community care inevitably became a political issue. Social and long-term health care do not account for a particularly large slice of public expenditure, nor directly impinge upon the lives of most citizens. They therefore command disproportionately high media profiles. Most media attention during the 1980s latched onto the 'closure of the asylums' and the summary despatch of homeless residents onto the streets, and the plight of Britain's hidden army of unpaid informal carers. But would these equal opportunities' questions, the homeless people on London's streets, and the haphazard distribution of services have brought about a community care policy of the kind that developed over the 1980s without the financial pressures on government?

The 'new managerialism' and the heightened cost-consciousness of the decade – which included the insistence upon monitoring and value-for-money auditing, and the promotion of accountability for public money – helped to transform the delivery of community care into an administrative function. The roles of local and health authorities, and the links between them, were formalised and institutionalised through, in turn, new mechanisms for joint planning, joint financing and joint purchasing. Community care is now infused with the language of administration and commerce – contracts, consortia, trusts, purchaser/provider separation, business plans, care management, accountability, quality assurance, and so on.

As the locus of concern and influence shifted, it became clear that, outside the family (and to a degree outside the ranks of social work, nursing and medicine), comparatively little was known about the workings of community care, and still less about its impacts on clients, their families, or the wider community. At the start of the 1980s community care policies were bolstered by the optimism and rhetoric of policy-makers, and buffeted by the practical preoccupations and prejudices of care professionals. Indeed, community care remained predominantly within the professional sphere, with case-specific and anecdotal evidence often accepted as sufficient to swing the argument one way or the other. With one or two notable exceptions, rarely was a policy or practice proposal confronted with evidence. For example, although few viewed permanent hospital residence as appropriate or best for people with long-term needs for support, it was difficult to assemble convincing information on the comparative advantages of different community care settings or approaches. Debate was often based on tangentially relevant research, and seemingly dominated by anecdote.

The Care in the Community demonstration programme

The Care in the Community demonstration programme was launched by the DHSS against this background. The DHSS provided funding for a number of pilot projects to assist long-stay hospital residents move to community living settings. It was expected that projects would demonstrate both the good and not-so-good sides of community care. By supporting projects for people with mental health problems, learning difficulties (mental handicaps), physical disabilities, or age-related needs, and by funding some very different community care arrangements, the DHSS sought to gather experience from a variety of circumstances and contexts. £25 million (at 1991 prices) was set aside for the programme from joint finance budgets, spread over four years. Applications for grant aid to support projects were invited from local and health authorities and voluntary organisations. Each project application was required to set out plans for the *joint* planning and coordination of health and social services. The programme was confined to England. Twenty-eight projects each received central government funding for three years. Overall, two-thirds of the DHSS grant funding was expected to support revenue expenditure and the remainder capital.

It was expressly intended that the programme would pilot different ways of organising and delivering community care. To ensure that the pilot experiences were illuminated and disseminated, the Personal Social Services Research Unit (PSSRU), University of Kent at Canterbury, was commissioned to promote, monitor and evaluate the programme. This book offers a comprehensive account of the evaluation findings. The evaluation reveals how community living was preferred to hospital by most of the people experiencing it, and was superior on other counts. It was not prohibitively expensive. But by no means everything in the Care in the Community garden was rosy: pilot projects encountered resourcing and political difficulties, and by no means every client thrived.

The evidence accumulated from the programme offers important information about the development of community alternatives to hospital. Because no single model of community care was laid down, a plurality of styles emerged in pursuit of overlapping but not identical sets of objectives. Some projects sought to include very dependent long-stay hospital residents, some sought to return people to their area of origin, some built particular staff training programmes into their plans, some organised their services around particular ideologies such as normalisation, and so on. The projects combined statutory and voluntary responsibilities in different ways. They were built on different service foundations, inherited and developed different macro- and micro-organisational arrangements, and supplemented DHSS programme grant aid with various local resources. Contrasting styles of care delivery were selected. Clients' preferences were taken on board with greater or lesser enthusiasm. The *de facto* definition of 'community' included almost any accommodation other than (long-term) hospital residence – from independent living to residential homes – combined with a range of support services and activities, mostly coordinated through some form of case management structure. Project scale ranged from three clients in two of the projects to over 100 in another. Some services were geographically concentrated and others dispersed.

A common view about demonstration programmes is that their special nature divorces them from the reality of mainstream activity. This is always a possibility, but we believe there are fundamental lessons from the Care in the Community programme which transcend interpretational problems. Some of those lessons have already exerted their influence on the *Caring for People* White Paper (see Cm 849, 1989, para. 3.3.3). It must not be forgotten that although the Care in the Community projects *were* special, primarily because they had the time, money and space to develop something new, they always had to plan and organise their activities with future local funding and agency location in mind, and in accord with existing service organisation and delivery structures. Thus they could not pursue excellence with disregard for costs, nor could they establish themselves as local policy mavericks. There is no doubt, however, that central funding enabled relatively smooth integration with mainstream services.

The structure of the book

This book is organised into four parts. The first part introduces the pilot projects and clients, briefly describing national and local policy contexts (Chapter 2), and sets out the objectives of both programme and individual projects (Chapter 3). Chapter 4 offers an account of the research methodology which shapes the remainder of the book. The second part concentrates on the *process* of community care, with chapters on financing, accommodation and service use, staffing, case management and joint working. The third part of the book is more conventionally evaluative, with a twin focus on outcomes and costs. The client groups covered by the Care in the Community programme are considered in turn. Finally, the book examines the policy and practice implications of the programme.

2 The demonstration programme in policy context

The 1983 Care in the Community Circular

When the DHSS issued its Care in the Community Circular in 1983, community care was a much less clearly defined or prescribed social or health care option than it is today. There were, for example, only sketchily-drawn equivalents to the joint planning, case coordination, funding, inspection and monitoring requirements introduced by the *National Health Service and Community Care Act 1990*. Community care policy, as set out in the Circular and the *Health and Social Services and Social Security Adjudication Act* of the same year, was built on an earlier consultative document (DHSS, 1981a). It offered only the broadest of frameworks. Like the early stages of a jigsaw, the edges were in place and a few key pieces were correctly located, but the picture remained for local agencies to complete. Local and health authorities had considerable latitude to shape community care as they saw fit – or *not* to complete the jigsaw if they so wished. Some enabling legislation and guidelines were contained in a series of reports over 40 years, offering a skeletal structure within which incremental improvements to organisation and funding could be achieved at local level. The introduction of joint consultative committees in 1974 and joint finance in 1976 were two such developments which produced a wide range of responses across the country. Neither was sufficiently attractive for local or health authorities to set a comprehensive community care programme in place.

The 1983 Circular introduced new arrangements for health authorities to transfer funds to local authorities and voluntary organisations in order to stimulate the movement of hospital residents to the community. In addition, the Circular announced a pilot programme to demonstrate different ways to assist people to move from hospital into high-quality community support settings. A substantial slice of joint finance money was used to fund the pilot programme. Applications for funding under the programme were invited from statutory bodies. Voluntary organisations could make joint applications with health or local authorities. In all, 28 projects were funded by the DHSS between 1984 and 1988, each for three years.

In an earlier book, *Care in the Community: The First Steps*, we described the background to the 1983 Care in the Community Circular and the pilot programme, and included a detailed account of each project, as well as some of the difficulties and successes in the early stages of implementation (Renshaw et al., 1988). We will not, therefore, repeat an account of the gestation of the Care in the Community projects but will set them in context by identifying the main policy and ideological planks upon which the programme was built: the development of community care, the rundown of hospital provision, the promotion of joint working between health and social services agencies, the pursuit of value for money, the mixing of the service economy, and the more recent emphasis on user preference and choice. These six themes are considered in this chapter at national and programme level, and appear again in Chapter 3 when we return to the pilot projects. First we describe the basic features of the programme.

The demonstration programme

In seeking general and transferable lessons for the development of community care and the rundown or closure of long-stay hospitals, the DHSS chose to cover a cross-section of traditional client groups.

> First and foremost, proposals for projects should be for moving long-stay hospital patients into the community. In addition a reasonable spread of projects is looked for, both geographically and among client groups (DHSS, 1983, Annex E, para. 3).

The result was 11 projects for people with learning difficulties (mental handicaps), eight for people with mental health problems, one for young people with multiple disabilities, one for physically disabled adults and seven for elderly people with physical frailty or mental health problems (see Table 2.1). It was not intended that the particular needs that arise from different disabilities should be smothered under a single blanket; rather, it was hoped that insights gained in one project would prove relevant to others, and to community services in general.

We describe in the next chapter how projects aimed to enable people with a range of needs and abilities to move into the community. In general, project clients were less dependent than the typical long-stay population of England's hospitals, but more dependent than most people already living in the community. Many had been in hospital most of their lives (see Chapter 5 for descriptions of programme clients). Many projects were working with hospitals which had not started rundown or closure programmes before the Care in the Community programme.

The pilot projects chose many different residential and day support arrangements. There were residential homes, sheltered housing facilities, hostels, staffed group homes, core and cluster networks (with the facility for users to move progressively to more independent living), supported lodgings and home care (foster) placements, as well as independent living. Service orientation and care philosophy were not laid down by the DHSS, although good practices (such as case management and normalisation) were encouraged. Generally, it was not the intention to impose particular service models on projects, although the 1983 Circular did offer guidance on some matters (DHSS, 1983, Annex E):

Table 2.1
The pilot projects

For people with learning difficulties		
Bolton	Calderdale	Camden
Derby	Islington	Kidderminster
Liverpool	Maidstone	Somerset
Torbay	Warwick	
For young people with multiple disabilities		
Cambridge		
For people with mental health problems		
Brent	Buckinghamshire	Chichester
Greenwich	Waltham Forest	Warrington
West Berkshire	West Lancashire	
For people with physical disabilities		
Glossop		
For elderly people with physical frailty		
Coventry	Darlington	Winchester
For elderly people with mental health problems		
Camberwell	Hillingdon	St Helens
West Cumbria		

- Projects should meet the specific needs of the hospital residents being transferred, undertaking prior assessment of their needs.
- Projects were able to provide both residential and other forms of care, for example support services, education and leisure activities to allow people with learning difficulties to move from hospital into ordinary housing, or supported accommodation (such as unstaffed group homes or adult fostering).
- Projects for people with mental health problems were urged to aim to help those who did not need to be in hospital find suitable accommodation and support, according to individual needs, and to offer support to families.
- Where residential provision was planned, projects were encouraged to provide small homely units, although this need not exclude adaptations of existing local authority or voluntary organisation premises.
- Siting of facilities, whether residential or day, should try to ensure easy access to the same health, education and social services, shops and transport as are normally available to other people living in the community.
- The Circular noted that a number of potentially relevant models of care already existed, for the Department wanted to encourage the replication of

tried and tested services as well as innovative approaches. It was felt, however, that plans for residential provision should avoid the creation of institutions. Small group living units which emphasised community links were clearly preferred.
- Integrated care delivery was important. Support schemes linking sheltered housing with packages of domiciliary care were among the options illustrated by the Circular.
- Housing associations and voluntary organisations were noted as having their part to play, although there was nothing like the endorsement of a mixed economy of care of the kind found in the 1989 community care White Paper.

Although the Circular pushed particular practices, unitary solutions – in an area in which most people were still unsure of the best direction for change – were obviously inappropriate.

Funding and timescales

Applications for support under the programme had to address a number of criteria laid down by the DHSS. They had to formulate plans for effective joint working between health and social services authorities and for some form of case management for individual clients, they had to target services on long-stay hospital residents and demonstrate an awareness of broader objectives, and they had to explain how they intended to develop funding strategies for the newly-established services once the three-year programme ended. Projects also had to open their doors to regular monitoring, evaluation and publicity.

Central funding for up to 100 per cent of the capital and revenue costs of a project could be sought, although a majority applied for and received a smaller proportion. Thirteen projects were funded from 1984 to 1987, and 15 from 1985 to 1988. The processes of application, negotiation and selection of projects are described in *The First Steps* (Renshaw et al., 1988, chap. 3).

The balance between capital and revenue allocations varied enormously, partly reflecting the types of resources projects sought to develop (facility-based or domiciliary support, new build or conversion, and so on), and partly the mix of funds secured from other sources (statutory bodies, voluntary agencies, social security coffers, the Housing Corporation). Revenue allocations were greater than capital for most projects. All of the grant was expended on capital in Torbay, and the capital proportion exceeded two-thirds in Chichester, Glossop, Maidstone and St Helens. For the Coventry, Hillingdon and Kidderminster projects, the full grant was allocated to revenue expenditure, and for Bolton, Brent, Camden, Darlington, Derby, Liverpool and Winchester revenue accounted for over 90 per cent. Some projects were later able to use revenue funding for capital, and vice versa.

Demonstration

Demonstration and revelation were fundamental to the programme. Ministers wished to encourage a programme of pilot projects to explore and evaluate different approaches to moving people and resources into the community (DHSS, 1983, para. 11). Each project aimed to establish and demonstrate effective delivery in its local context. One of the intentions of a demonstration programme is the promotion of organisational change from within, through implementation of new management and care practice. This may be more appropriate than radical policy changes introduced externally (and universally) and at short notice. While innovative, in practice some projects were one-off and sometimes isolated developments, and some had as much if not more impact *outside* their locales than within them. A few went too far and became marginalised. Others were part of wider strategies for hospital closure and wider service reorientations.

Dissemination

The benefits of demonstration are lost if they are not disseminated to a wider audience. Dissemination was written in as a specific objective. Early in the course of the programme, the DHSS sponsored the production of a video (*Back to the Community*) and organised a series of seminars in London from 1983 until 1986. The PSSRU continued dissemination with two series of seminars in 1987 and 1989, and published nine issues of the *Care in the Community Newsletter* and an edited volume of papers (Cambridge and Knapp, 1988). These activities ran alongside conferences and other support and exchange activities for the projects. Among other benefits, this helped to exchange information and reduce the isolation of staff working in the new services.

Evaluation

One condition of programme funding was that projects allow access for evaluation by the PSSRU, and perhaps by others. The design and the tools of our evaluation were selected with one eye on their relevance for the information needs of projects. A case review form was designed with both practice and research users in mind. Schedules employed in hospital for assessment and selection of clients were sometimes also helpful for planning community accommodation. There was also need for routine monitoring of client moves out of hospital, the development of accommodation and organisation of staff resources, in addition to the slightly more distanced evaluation of outcomes, costs and processes.

The shell of the evaluation was sketched in the Care in the Community Circular, with emphasis on outcomes for clients, costs and processes. In designing our research we were aware of the broad policy themes which ran through the Circular and the 1981 Consultative Document on which it was based. Many of these themes are taken up in the 1990 Act, and although we now consider them in more detail in relation to their impact on the programme, we shall resist commenting on the new reforms until the final chapter. The relevant legislative and other landmarks over the period are summarised in Table 2.2.

Table 2.2
Community care landmarks

1957	Royal Commission reports
1959	Mental Health Act
1961	Enoch Powell, Minister of Health, announces rundown of psychiatric hospitals
1962	Hospital Plan, setting out rundown targets
1963	White Paper on *Health and Welfare* published
1971	Publication of *Better Services for the Mentally Handicapped*
1974	Joint Consultative Committees established
1975	DHSS publishes *Better Services for the Mentally Ill*
1976	Joint finance introduced
1978	Publication of *A Happier Old Age*
1979	Royal Commission on the Health Service reports
	Jay Committee reports
1981	Publication of *Care in Action* and *Growing Older*
	Care in the Community consultative document circulated
1982	Comptroller and Auditor General reports on joint finance
	Financial Management Initiative launched by H.M. Treasury
1983	Public Accounts Committee reports
	Health and Social Services and Social Security (Adjudications) Act gets royal assent
	Care in the Community Circular published
1985	*Progress in Partnership* published
	House of Commons Select Committee on Social Services reports on *Community Care*
	Government's response to Select Committee
1986	Audit Commission publishes *Making a Reality of Community Care*
	Disabled Persons Act
1987	Firth Committee reports on public support for residential care
	National Audit Office reports
1988	Wagner Committee reports on residential care
	Sir Roy Griffiths reports
1989	*Caring for People* White Paper published
1990	*National Health Service and Community Care Act* gets royal assent
1991	First phase of community care reforms implemented

Hospital closure

Long before governments or local agencies were formulating community care policies, there were moves to run down hospital provision for people with mental health problems, learning difficulties and age-related needs. This long-running policy to reduce the reliance on hospital in-patient care for people with long-term needs was undoubtedly influential in prompting the demonstration programme in 1983.

The hospital rundown policy has been part medical preference, part public opinion and part 'hard political economy' (Korman and Glennerster, 1990, p.11), although it is not always easy to disentangle their respective influences. This is illustrated by looking at the hospital in-patient care of people with mental health problems.

Chlorpromazine, the first of the benzodiazepine anxiolytics, and other pharmaceutical developments in the 1950s, allowed the acceleration of the 'dehospitalisation' trend in the treatment and care of mental illness. One of the most commonly-quoted statistics is the peaking of the hospital in-patient population at 154,000 in 1954, but the *per capita* population may have peaked more than 30 years earlier (Goodwin, 1989), and 'all the techniques of rehabilitation and resettlement now accepted as good psychiatric practice were introduced ... well before the introduction of reserpine and chlorpromazine' (Wing, 1990, p.823).

The work of the Royal Commission on Lunacy and Mental Disorder during the 1920s led to the *1930 Mental Health Treatment Act*, which introduced voluntary admission (later informal admission) to mental hospitals. This open-door policy reduced the numbers of certified patients; custody was gradually replaced by treatment. Although admission rates to mental hospitals continued to grow, so too did discharge rates, with mean length of stay falling. Psychiatric wards appeared in general hospitals, industrial therapy was introduced, and out-patient services started to replace in-patient accommodation. There was growing recognition that people with mental health problems needed to maintain links outside hospitals if they were to progress and to be successfully rehabilitated, and realisation that physical and social environments of institutions had undesired, and perhaps iatrogenic effects upon the welfare and health of residents. This realisation is most obviously associated with a series of influential post-war publications, but is in fact not a peculiarly post-war perspective (Stanton and Schwartz, 1954; Belknap, 1956; Goffman, 1961; and in Britain, Barton, 1959; Freeman and Farndale, 1963; Morris, 1969; Wing and Brown, 1970). The associated development of therapeutic communities, halfway houses, hospital-hostel wards, community mental health centres and intensive support programmes are the more recent examples of this trend in professional preference, built on assumptions about more effective treatment or support away from the psychiatric hospital.

There were other influential changes. Over at least half a century public attitudes to mental health problems and learning difficulties appear to have become gradually more understanding, or perhaps it is just that greater indifference is generating less overt hostility. We return to this issue in Chapter 8, but whatever the true situation there is still a very long way to go before mental ill health is accepted as readily as physical ill health, or before people with learning difficulties are treated as ordinary citizens. Whether or not public opinion has changed over the years (Jones, 1981; Scull, 1984; Goodwin, 1989), policy decisions have sometimes been justified on the assumption that they *have*, helping to support proposals for hospital closure. The view that there is a need to incarcerate people with particular characteristics, in order to protect them from stigma and ridicule, and to protect the public from the disturbing spectacle of 'odd' behaviours is less readily propounded today. It would be a mistake to under-estimate the impact of public opinion and the non-medical professions in shaping services. One eminent psychiatrist recently commented that the move to close hospitals was

> supported by a motley group of civil libertarians, who maintained in the name of various creeds and ideologies that mental hospitals were effectively prisons, depriving their inmates of 'freedom' under an authoritarian medical regime from whose yoke discharge represented a release and a return to normal life (Shepherd, 1989, p.667).

This is a common theme. Two months later, again in the *British Medical Journal*, an editorial opined:

> A generation of sociologists convinced themselves that mental illness was a myth and the disabilities of those so labelled were largely a consequence of their incarceration and mistreatment (Kendell, 1989, p.1237).

Misplaced or not, these ideologies or myths, coupled with revelations of scandalous practices and conditions in various hospitals, starting with Ely in 1969 and continuing for some years (Martin, 1984; Wistow, 1985), in a period in which government ministers were sensitive to threats to civil liberties, ensured that limited action to close the hospitals ensued. The *Mental Health Act 1983* addressed many of these human rights issues.

Although the stark economic realities of maintaining the hospitals were brought home in the 1950s and 1960s, the physical decline of the predominantly Victorian hospital stock had presented problems somewhat earlier. In the early post-war years, with all their economic privations, it would have been perverse to inject substantial capital sums into institutions which were not regarded by all psychiatrists as efficacious in the treatment of mental illness or learning difficulty, or by public opinion as appropriate. The initial response was not to develop community care but to lament the shortage of beds, psychiatrists and nurses, and the poor condition of the hospital fabric. Capital allocations to mental hospitals increased over the 1950s, and financial incentives were offered to attract psychiatric nurses, but neither was sufficient to improve standards to an acceptable level. The cost of improving the mental hospitals was simply too great (Ministry of Health, 1962). A similar argument surfaced in the 1970s, propelled into the policy debate by fiscal crises and, subsequently, the 'value-for-money imperative'. This was the comparative cost argument: hospitals providing long-term care were believed to be more expensive than community services of comparable quality. Moreover, in this recent revival of the political-economic argument, there has been the additional attraction that many hospitals were sitting on prime building land.

In a 1961 speech about the 'isolated, majestic, imperious [hospitals], brooded over by the gigantic water tower and chimney combined, rising unmistakable and daunting out of the countryside', Enoch Powell, Minister of Health, announced the intention to halve the acute population of psychiatric hospitals in 15 years, and to work towards the eventual disappearance of the long-term (chronic) in-patient population. The former aim was virtually realised in the timescale envisaged, although the latter is taking longer to achieve. The 1975 White Paper, *Better Services for the Mentally Ill*, emphasised early recognition and prevention, and recommended the integration of support from families and community services (Cmnd 6233, 1975). This followed, and to a degree mirrored, the 1971 White Paper, *Better Services for the Mentally Handicapped* (Cmnd 4683), which was one of the first major policy documents to be focused on a single client group. Ten years later, *Care in Action* carried the clear message that closure plans should be introduced for some hospitals, phased over a ten-year period, and the *Care in the Community* consultative document of the same year set out proposals to encourage joint working and joint finance (DHSS, 1981a,b).

The numerous commentaries on the hospital rundown programme have criticised the government either for its failure to implement policy quickly enough, or for doing so too fast. Relatives of people in hospital or with long-term needs for care or support have argued vociferously that beds have closed precipitately. The slump in property prices and land values at the end of the 1980s halted some reprovision programmes, frustrating the plans of many health authorities, yet ministers are still urging them to speed up closures.

Community care

For many years community care was seen simply as getting people out of hospital. Quite what was to happen thereafter was not tackled thoroughly in official publications until the reports of the Audit Commission (1986) and Sir Roy Griffiths (1988). The 1971 White Paper, for instance, included rather unspecific strategies for the support of people with learning difficulties and their families, and only one of the five main policy objectives made recommendations for services in the community (see, for example, Wistow, 1985). Given that most community care is provided informally by relatives and neighbours, and most community care clients have never spent long periods in hospital, there is a case for arguing that a community care policy *per se* – that is a policy in which community care was the primary and not the residual aim, and in which service plans were not confined to formal residential and day care provision – did not arrive until the late 1980s, despite its permanent place in policy rhetoric. Even in relation to the care of former hospital residents outside informal care settings, as was the case in the demonstration programme, there were few policy guidelines to direct (or, indeed, constrain) projects.

Government's role in making community care policy has, until recently, looked more reactive than proactive. As Goodwin comments, the introduction of community care by the Ministry of Health in the 1950s 'was not so much generating a new and progressive policy as responding to changing circumstances' (Goodwin, 1989, p.45). Indeed, the reforms contained within the *Mental Health Act 1959*, like earlier government statements, sought to foster or establish, not community care for people with mental health problems, but 'treatment in the community'. These reforms were necessary to overcome problems already arising as a result of changes in professional practice and political-economic realities. Attempts to initiate a concerted, coherent and internally consistent community care policy were a long way off. 'Rather than simply constituting a reformist measure resulting from enlightened thinking, the community care policy in fact represented a response to a crisis of institutional care' (Goodwin, 1989, p.41).

Partly for this reason there is no clear definition of what community care *is* or what it can achieve. Bulmer (1987, chap. 1) identifies four different usages of the term. In its original usage it was 'care outside of large institutions', meaning anything other than the remote and massive asylums. A second meaning was the delivery of various professional services outside all hospitals, as in 'community nursing'. Third, it can connote care *by* the community (Bayley, 1973), principally via the involvement of voluntary agencies and families. Finally, community care has been used to describe provision which is as close to normality or ordinary living as possible. The last three definitions are still in use, generating obvious difficulties of interpretation. In this book, and in the Care in the Community programme, it is a variant of the second definition that is in play: community care is anything other than long-term residence in a hospital. Ambiguities remain, of course, as our experience revealed in working with different health authorities employing different definitions of hospital and discharge.

Community care was encouraged as a 'Good Thing', but not supported by financial incentive until the arrival of joint finance in the 1970s (see below), and then was fettered by so many disincentives and limitations as to lead the House of Commons Social Services Committee (1985, para. 21) to complain of 'under-financed and under-staffed' community provision. The history of community care was described as 'painfully slow progress towards timid goals' (Walker, 1982, p.16). The Care in the Community programme could thus initially have been seen as a quite adventurous experiment in service management, organisation and funding. Comparatively little research had been conducted on community care as an alternative to long-stay hospital residence, and because some aspects of the programme were successful it was not surprising that it should influence the 1989 *Caring for People* White Paper (Cm 849).

The development of community care as an explicit, internally consistent, comprehensive goal of public policy has until recently followed rather than shaped professional opinion and preferences. Like the hospital rundown policies of the past 40 years, it has been spurred on by economic forces. The 1975 White Paper posited that community care would be cheaper than hospital, although the 1981 consultative document was more circumspect. These views from central government were based on fairly comprehensive cost concepts, ranging over numerous services and agencies. A more partial or fragmented view of costs – such as a health authority calculating only its own expenditure implications of a hospital closure decision – would likely encourage over-enthusiastic support for such a policy. It was this and associated problems which the Audit Commission (1986) pointed to in its influential report. We return to the comparative cost and fragmented expenditure questions, examining the validity of the key assumptions in Part III, for this issue has been one of the more contentious in the community care debate.

Other criticisms of community care practice (and lack of policy) centred on the uncompensated, inequitable burdens placed on relatives and neighbours (and women in particular), the speed of hospital rundown in relation to the rate of development of community facilities, and the dumping and neglect of disabled and defenceless people without adequate assistance or personal resources. There was also, it was argued, insufficient recognition of a continuing need for asylum, not necessarily in 'large or isolated institutions ... [but] in a physical and psychological sense [perhaps] in the middle of a normal residential community' (House of Commons Social Services Committee, 1985, para. 26). Many of these recent criticisms of government policy started out as hypotheses constructed from observations of the mistakes that were made in the USA and parts of Italy when hospitals were emptied over-hastily (see, for example, Kirk and Therrein, 1975; Scull, 1984; Jones and Poletti, 1985, 1986; Torrey, 1988), although they are not unique to modern times (for example, see Titmuss, 1963; Brown et al., 1966; Jones, 1972). What many of the accounts of community care failure themselves fail to do is to distinguish between the discharge of long-stay hospital residents into the community and the diversion (or early discharge) of people who would previously have become in-patients (or stayed for longer). This was an unfortunate and slightly distracting oversight in the 1985 House of Commons Social Services Committee Report, for example, and continues to crop up.

It is perhaps surprising – although possibly revealing of the current climate of opinion in the UK – that such an ill-researched and poorly reasoned polemic [as Weller (1989)] can find its way into the prestigious columns of *Nature*. None can doubt Dr Weller's sincere desire to protect the long-term mentally ill from precipitate discharge from hospital and inadequate services in the community, but the way in which he plays 'fast and loose' with the figures is really very difficult to defend. ... Weller raises some important points, but his failure to distinguish between the needs of people who can now no longer get *in* to the psychiatric system, as opposed to the needs of the people who may have just been thrown out, seriously undermines his arguments (Shepherd, 1990, p.279).

These logical errors notwithstanding, the fundamentally correct point that, in the early 1980s and therefore around the time of the demonstration programme, 'community care [had] become a slogan, with all the weakness that implies' (House of Commons Social Services Committee, 1985, para. 8); it was not a rounded policy. It is perhaps no surprise, therefore, that a review of psychiatric research in the UK should conclude

The dangers of deinstitutionalisation *imperfectly implemented* are clear. Those discharged face the prospect of isolated, segregated, impoverished, and under-stimulated lives. They have a high likelihood of homelessness and recurrent admission ... In short, such discharged patients are at risk of multiple disadvantage and neglect (Thornicroft and Bebbington, 1989, p.749).

The italics in the above quote are ours, for with this emphasis we could almost take this conclusion as the prompt or composite null hypothesis for the evaluation of the demonstration programme. The inadequacy of much previous research, whether in psychiatry or in relation to other groups in need of long-term support, is a direct corollary of the inadequacy of policy – both were preoccupied for too long with the rundown of hospitals, making few concerted attempts to tackle the problem of developing good community care. Thornicroft and Bebbington rightly note that 'properly provided' community care can have beneficial effects on quality of life (and see Shepherd, 1990), but such an assertion was comparatively rare in the early 1980s.

The challenge for projects in 1984 was to deliver good quality community care in what was still a national policy vacuum, and in a climate of opinion (both informed and uninformed) which was not altogether friendly.

Joint working

The *Mental Health Act 1959* was influential in setting the agenda for joint working between health and social services. In relation to services for people with learning difficulties, the 1971 White Paper anticipated the expansion of local authority provision, aided by closer links with the health service. The Act and the White Paper advocated a major role for local authorities, but ignored the financial implications of providing care outside hospitals. Thus, although joint finance arrangements were introduced in the 1970s, and extended in 1983 by the introduction of dowries, it was not until the demonstration programme that specific, front-loaded, grant aid was made available for the development of community care.

Health and local authorities were statutorily obliged to collaborate from 1974 (as laid down in Circular HC(74)19). Joint consultative committees were set up, offering the opportunity to establish sound organisational bases for taking community care forward. Although it was realised that financial collaboration was essential if authorities were to work together effectively, the joint finance arrangements introduced in 1976 harboured too many disincentives to effect significant change in collaboration, and the view gained currency that joint working could be further encouraged by more radical financial transfers. At the same time, there was growing criticism that monies transferred from health to local authority budgets were not being adequately monitored by the NHS. The Comptroller and Auditor General's report of 1982 and the Public Accounts Committee report of 1983 both voiced this concern, and the National Audit Office took up the theme in its 1987 report.

One problem with the 1976 style of joint finance was that it offered little incentive for local authorities to develop community care, since financial transfers were of only limited duration. This was combined with the difficulty of reconciling the often different priorities of health and social services authorities. A related political problem in the early 1980s was the perception of many Labour-controlled local authorities that central government controlled the health authorities. 'The easy assumptions of collaboration and cooperation were no longer appropriate, if they ever were' (Korman and Glennerster, 1990, p.24). Into these hostile waters steamed the pilot projects, although changes to the joint finance rules introduced in the same DHSS Circular which launched the projects eased the tension somewhat. The 1981 Care in the Community consultative document had canvassed ways to remove the existing obstacles to the transfer of resources from health authorities to the personal social services. The 1983 Circular made perpetual transfers possible, introducing the long-term dowry when people moved out of hospital into community care. The amount of the dowry was for regional, or in some cases district, health authorities to agree in negotiation with local authorities and voluntary agencies, and based on current costs since they were to be financed from hospital savings. Quite a number of the clients of the demonstration programme moved to the community under dowry funding arrangements. We will consider the workings of the dowry and social security systems in Chapter 7.

The 1983 joint finance changes did not address all of the difficulties and disincentives. No capital funding was made available to help local authorities and voluntary organisations establish the new facilities needed by many of the more dependent people now moving from hospital. There was the difficulty of hospitals denuded of cash and resources when dowry or other transfers were pitched at average hospital cost level or otherwise failed to take account of the time needed to reduce overhead costs. Someone leaving hospital does not save the hospital the average cost of an in-patient case (marginal cost is less than average cost), and it is anyway common practice to rehabilitate people who are less dependent than the hospital average, and who therefore cost less to support (see Part III). A further problem was that the resource transfer followed rather than preceded the planning and initial implementation of the new community care facilities.

These were serious problems which needed to be addressed at the (macro) policy level and circumvented at the (micro) practice level. The pilot projects generally did not face these difficulties: they were able to apply for capital funding, their revenue allocations constituted the kind of double or bridging funding whose absence was causing denuding problems elsewhere, and the money was available before clients left hospital. These were considerable advantages, and there is no doubt that the success of the projects in helping people to move successfully from hospital to the community is in large measure due to the availability of sufficient funds at the right time for the right purposes. The invitation to apply for demonstration programme funding also made it clear that joint working was high on the policy agenda:

> Proposals for pilot projects will, like all developments following up the Care in the Community initiative, need to be developed jointly by the health and local authorities and, where appropriate, voluntary organisations, and endorsed by the JCC (DHSS, 1983, para. 11).

Projects were therefore expected not only to test new service models, but also to examine new approaches to joint working. The ways in which pilot projects did this are considered in Chapters 10 and 11.

The value-for-money imperative

One of the central research questions which the PSSRU was asked to address in the evaluation of the pilot projects concerned the relative cost-effectiveness of different forms of community care. It is uncommon to find social or health care policy or practice research today which does not have a cost dimension, however small or incidental, but this was less obviously the case in 1983. We have already noted how the political economy of hospital rundown and community care development accelerated some trends initiated on other grounds. The cost-effectiveness enquiry was therefore not an irrelevant or peripheral request. Moreover, the 'value-for-money imperative' was fast pushing its way through central and local government. It is wholly appropriate to explore the resource implications of policy changes alongside the impact on, for example, clients and carers; the difficulty which we faced in the evaluation, and which projects faced in their areas, was that the value-for-money imperative might dominate or divert attention from effectiveness.

The Financial Management Initiative was launched in 1982, encouraging in forceful terms the pursuit of the famous three Es of economy, effectiveness and efficiency. It was one of a number of steps taken by central government to promote value for money and financial accountability. The establishment of the Audit Commission, the transformation of the Social Work Service into the Social Services Inspectorate, various scrutinies of government data collections, as well as the tight constraints on public spending all contributed to a value-for-money ethos. Few people now dispute the objective of cost-effectiveness when properly defined to range comprehensively over costs and to include outcome assessment, but it is legitimate to protest and natural to be fearful when cost-effectiveness is mistaken to mean cheap or when it is pursued with disregard for other policy objectives. To take one example, the Department of the Environment made the tactical error of publishing two decidedly dubious reports by the old Audit Inspectorate (1983a,b) around the time the Audit Commission came into being, and the Commission made the mistake of using and defending these reports together with a third report published by the District Auditors (1981). Not one of these reports demonstrated proper awareness of the need for client outcomes to be considered, and each contained poor costings. With social care agencies sensitive to the danger of client welfare taking second place behind cost savings in service planning, the Commission immediately faced opposition to its attempts to raise efficiency. In its 1986 report, by contrast, the Commission was able to offer a thorough analysis of the economic and other problems associated with community care, and shift the focus of debate.

The 28 pilot projects had each started to work with hospitals and local agencies at a time when opposition to value-for-money auditing was at its peak. Although this did not generate research difficulties, it may have had some bearing on the reluctance of projects to build service utilisation information and financial control into case review and case management. Furthermore, the broad responsibilities for service coordination assumed by some projects made them hungry for detailed costs data. Many were organised or included provision by both statutory and voluntary organisations, and some included commercial sector services. They often worked with education and housing departments, and all were reliant to a degree on social security benefits. When later the Audit Commission (1986), Firth Committee (Firth, 1987), Wagner Committee (Wagner, 1988) and Sir Roy Griffiths (1988) reported, the costs issues came as no real surprise.

It must not be forgotten that cost is only half of cost-effectiveness. Client outcomes, the effectiveness of services in achieving identified client objectives, were not defined in the Circular or the earlier consultative document, but were abundantly clear. The implicit dimensionality ranged from tangible needs and achievements such as the need for, and provision of, high-quality shelter or adequate support, to higher needs (in a Maslovian sense) such as belongingness, esteem and self-actualisation. Also implicit was the aim not only to raise client well-being in community settings compared to hospital, but to strive for standards and qualities of life at least as good as those enjoyed by other citizens.

We will see in the next chapter that every project set client-level objectives, in varying detail, and our evaluation was organised around outcome assessment.

The span of different management arrangements, the diversity of service models and philosophies, and the plurality of local mixed economies offered by the projects provided an unusual opportunity to examine the relative cost-effectiveness of different community care arrangements.

The mixed economy

The promotion of competition on the assumption that it would enhance consumer choice and improve productive efficiency lay at the heart of Thatcherism, and the social policy changes of recent years bear witness to the pervasiveness of the application of that ideology. It was natural that the Care in the Community demonstration programme should be in step with the broader drift towards a more mixed economy. Of course, community care has always been characterised by pluralism – therein lay many of the difficulties identified by the Audit Commission (1986), Griffiths (1988) and others – and in fact the programme may even have been a small disappointment to the drier of Conservative backbenchers looking for social laboratories for market experiments in welfare. What the programme *did* do was to further explore certain avenues of the mixed economy, avenues to which Griffiths and the 1989 White Paper subsequently returned.

- It encouraged the involvement of the voluntary sector in the planning and management of projects. 'Voluntary organisations often play a key role in sustaining people in the community. If the fullest benefits of transferring patients from hospital to community care are to be realised, voluntary resources will have to be engaged at all levels, both when arrangements are being made for transfers and in the long-term provision of supporting services' (DHSS, 1983, para. 14).
- It required projects to introduce case management, and suggested devolution of budgets (what would now be described as the purchaser/provider split) to team or case level. As we describe in Chapter 10, the projects chose a variety of case management and keyworker styles, and tested variants of case review, staff autonomy, client advocacy and case accountability.
- It permitted an early form of joint purchasing by health and local authorities, for some of the projects were genuinely jointly directed.
- It created the space and offered the financial independence to some projects to employ what might almost be termed, in the market-speak of the 1990s, community care brokers or entrepreneurs. Such local autonomy is now being encouraged more generally. Some of the projects in the public sector were performing the kind of enabling role recently enshrined in legislation.

The pilot projects did not involve the private commercial welfare sector to any great degree, although privately rented housing was often used. The roles performed by the voluntary sector were wide-ranging, including acting as providers of day and residential care to complement or substitute for public sector provision, pressure groups and consumer representatives (see Chapter 11).

User choice

One final broad theme running through public policy in the 1980s which left a mark on many of the pilot projects was the emphasis on the user or consumer. At the start of the decade a junior DHSS minister was noting that:

> Community care policies are designed to provide a better quality of life for the consumer. The government is not looking to save money through these policies, but to use money more efficiently to achieve that aim; in commercial jargon, the customer comes first (Glenarther, 1986, pp.1-2).

By the end of the decade, the Secretary of State's Foreword to *Caring for People* declared that the aim was 'to promote choice as well as independence' (Cm 849, 1989, p.iii). In a well-behaved market, consumer power is the key to efficiency, but few people are under any illusions about the behaviour of unfettered markets for most social care services. Nevertheless, it is the government's view that giving the user choice within some form of internal or other market is inherently desirable. More generally, a natural corollary to the broad social aim to improve the responsiveness of support strategies to individual needs and preferences is to involve the service client. This is not *market consumerism* so much as *participative consumerism*, building relationships between providers and users 'on the explicit basis that people with special needs have a right to be consulted, feel valued, to have choice, to participate and have the opportunity to be accepted as integral members of the community' (Jowell, 1988, pp.20-21). Although clients of the demonstration programme could choose not to leave hospital (and we return to what this meant *in practice* later in the book), and were consulted and involved in decisions about their care programmes via case managers, choice was more limited than most projects would have liked. If there was only one staffed group home in the district or one day centre it was difficult to offer much real choice.

Client advocacy and consumerism made great strides during the 1980s, and a number of projects developed local initiatives to parallel the establishment of national organisations such as Advocacy Alliance and People First, and the general awareness raised by the passing of the *Disabled Persons Act 1986* (the advocacy clauses of which still remain unfunded). Later developments, such as the Birmingham Community Care Special Action Project, took consumerism forward (Jowell and Wistow, 1989). The rights of service users (and threats to them) are brought into sharp relief at a time of a major life-style change, such as a move from hospital to community. It is not that these issues are unimportant in hospital – quite the reverse – but the move to the community highlights the social and economic marginalisation of people with long-term care needs.

Consumerism can be embodied within individual programme planning and case management, even though these are second-best alternatives to independent advocacy. Chapter 10 will report how far this went within the pilot programme. If there is a drift towards large omnibus contracts between local authorities and monopoly-provider non-statutory agencies, the need for client-influenced case management, brokerage and advocacy will grow. Advocacy, including self-advocacy, and consumer participation more generally were to be found in many projects.

The six broad policy themes discussed here – hospital closure, community care, joint working, value for money, a mixed economy, and consumer choice – ran through the Care in the Community demonstration programme. They influenced the specification of local objectives at the outset, the adaptation of care programmes and other key features during each project's life-time, and the ease with which projects could move into mainstream provision thereafter. A programme as large as this one, and with so much attendant publicity, was likely to have some feedback influences on policy development, and we have already noted how some of the characteristics of the programme became national features subsequently (although we hesitate to draw any causal connections). We now turn to the projects and their local aims.

3 The pilot projects

Set in a common policy context and required to meet various criteria before funding was agreed, the 28 projects shared many features, despite covering a number of client groups, spanning a variety of care models and offering a diversity of service inputs. They intended to help a large number of people, of varying degrees of ability, move from hospital. They ranged in size from projects which involved more than 100 clients to those which catered for three people.

The aim of this chapter is to focus on the objectives set by projects *at the outset* in consultation with the DHSS, and to provide a preliminary examination of achievements, particularly as viewed by the projects themselves.

The projects

People with learning difficulties

Eleven of the 28 pilot projects were designed to support people with learning difficulties. Although the projects differed in many respects, and some departed considerably from previous models of care – Maidstone's devolved budgets within a case management system and Bolton's rural training scheme are examples – they shared at least two features characteristic of national developments in policy and practice for this client group. They all offered a service environment no longer dominated by health care and aligned closely with social care perspectives. Second, all projects claimed to be pursuing a policy of normalisation, and most succeeded. (We return to this later in the chapter.) The Camden project's use of the Independent Development Council's caring principles and Derby's guiding principles of service delivery were two examples of normalisation-influenced service orientations. Third, and a corollary of this second principle, each project tried to establish integrated accommodation within local communities. Five projects provided a range of accommodation from residential homes to independent living, one was based on hostel accommodation, two used staffed group homes, one a mixture of staffed and unstaffed group homes, and another independent accommodation only.

The *Bolton* Neighbourhood Network Scheme aimed to help 80 people leave five large hospitals to live in ordinary houses let to them by the local authority or housing associations, or with families under foster support or home care arrangements. It was jointly initiated and led by project coordinators from the health and social services, and included a comprehensive staff training programme. The scheme made extensive provision for day care by appointing education support tutors to draw up and implement individual learning programmes, and to help clients gain open access to ordinary adult education services at the local college of further education. A rural training scheme was created offering occupational alternatives such as gardening and farm work.

The *Calderdale* project planned to move 32 people from Fielden and Stansfield View Hospitals into staffed group homes in the area. The plans included provision of day care in a resource centre, a local college of further education and an adult training centre. The project contributed to the local hospital closure programme. The steering group for the project had parent representatives. Clients had volunteer befrienders to help them in their leisure activities.

The *Camden* LinC (Living in Camden) Scheme was set up with the intention of moving 17 people from St Lawrence's Hospital in Caterham back to Camden. The scheme was run and managed by CSMH (Camden Society for Mentally Handicapped People), a voluntary body, but had the full backing of statutory agencies, particularly the social services department. The project was able to tap into the housing and day care provision of CSMH. Clients had tenancy rights in a number of small flats and houses secured from the housing association. A life share programme was established, as was a (client) training project in the form of Applejacks Cafe just off Camden High Street.

In *Derby*, a project was set up to move 40 people from Aston Hall and Makeney Hospitals into their own homes in the city of Derby, using a range of housing types, some arranged through local housing associations. People leaving the hospitals were to be given the facility to move from one community placement to another as their needs changed. As far as possible, services were to be exactly as would have been provided for ordinary people and delivered to clients in their own homes, with specialist services provided only when needs could not be met elsewhere.

Eight people were expected to move from St Lawrence's, Leavesden, and Queen Elizabeth Hospitals, into shared or single flats in two houses provided by the housing department in the London Borough of *Islington*. Clients were initially to be supported by residential social workers, but the project was based on flexible support dependent on client needs, with the expectation that the workers would be withdrawn later as part of a rolling programme of reprovision. It was expected that volunteers would assist clients attending adult education classes.

The Dis-co (Discharge Coordination) project in *Kidderminster* planned to identify 33 people in Lea and Lea Castle Hospitals who could move into houses, hostels and group homes in various parts of Hereford and Worcester. A training house facility was to be an intermediate step into the community for some clients. Comprehensive day care provision was scheduled to include work experience, recreational skills and a variety of diversified day services. Day care instructors based at existing ATCs were to help provide day placements and work opportunities for clients. The scheme encouraged the development of an independent citizen advocacy scheme by securing separate funding.

The *Liverpool* project planned to move 12 people from Olive Mount Hospital to three fully staffed group homes in the community. Housing was the responsibility of Liverpool Housing Trust, with management by Mencap. Staff and case management arrangements were to be coordinated between the homes by a homes coordinator.

The *Maidstone* Care in the Community Project (MCCP) set out to facilitate the movement of 50 people from Lenham and Leybourne Grange Hospitals into a range of facilities in the Maidstone district. The project was part of the hospital closure programme for Lenham, the hospital closing in 1988. The project was to replicate the Kent Community Care Scheme for elderly people (Davies and Challis, 1986), which later became the county-wide service arrangement. Devolved budgeting was to allow each client to enter into a weekly support contract with their case manager. The scheme was one of the few to involve private sector residential care and rented housing. Day care was expected to be tailored to individual needs. Clients were encouraged to make their own decisions, and self-advocacy was promoted through training workshops.

In *Somerset*, the local authority-led project planned to move 45 people from Sandhill Park and Norah Fry Hospitals into core and cluster homes in Bridgwater and Yeovil. The service strategy was built on the expectation that clients would move to group homes after a period of rehabilitation and training. Core houses would be developed into resource centres for clients and staff, with local day centres providing support, training and social education. The project was part of a broader, county-wide strategy of similar developments.

The Park View Society, a voluntary body, was funded to establish a hostel in Newton Abbot for ten people from Hawkmoor Hospital. The *Torbay* project thus worked around a single residential facility. The care model was based on the success of a similar facility in Torbay, also run by the Society, for people with mental health problems. Although the project received some financial backing from the health authority, it set out to be almost exclusively funded from social security revenues, and was managed throughout by the voluntary organisation.

The *Warwick* project, a partnership between the county social services department and local Mencap societies, planned to move 44 clients from four hospitals (Chelmsley, Coleshill Hall, Weston and Abbeyfield) to core and cluster or hostel facilities. These were managed by Mencap and spread throughout the county. The project planned to tap into local authority day support, usually special education centres if these were available and appropriate for client needs.

Young people with multiple disabilities

One of the demonstration programme projects – in *Cambridge* – was set up to help young people with learning difficulties and physical disabilities to return to community settings from hospital. This small project worked with three adolescents who needed a considerable amount of support and care. The three clients were expected to move from Ida Darwin Hospital to an ordinary house in a residential area of the city. The original model was based on professional fostering arrangements, with additional staff providing organised support and relief. The clients were to continue attendance at a special school. The scheme was led by the district health authority, managed by the local authority social services department, and used housing provided by a housing association.

People with physical disabilities

The demonstration programme included the *Glossop* project for people with physical disabilities. Four self-contained, purpose-built flats were planned near the town centre, three of them for former hospital residents and the other for paid volunteer staff with primary responsibility for meeting the support needs of residents. Care would be provided round the clock, and residents would be fully involved in planning their own futures. The project was developed following suggestions by one disabled resident of Withington Hospital who later moved into one of the flats.

People with mental health problems

Eight projects in the programme were funded to assist people with mental health problems, all of them long-stay residents dependent on hospital in-patient services for some years. Like the clients with learning difficulties, they were most unlikely to have their own homes or relatives to return to. However, many of the projects aimed to embrace normalisation by choice of accommodation type and location. Four of the eight projects planned to provide a range of different accommodation types. Of the others, one chose a core and cluster model, two offered only ordinary housing (one staffed and the other unstaffed), and one opened a hostel. Three projects for this client group were managed by local authorities, two by health authorities, one by a consortium of agencies, and one by a voluntary organisation.

Brent Care in the Community Project aimed to provide rehabilitation training, housing and support for 60 people from Shenley Hospital. A range of different living environments, each variously supported by project staff, would allow clients to move as needs and preferences changed. A resource centre would provide an administrative base for staff and a setting for daytime and evening activities. The project was jointly led by Brent health and local authorities.

In *Buckinghamshire,* the project planned to move 65 people from St Johns Hospital, Aylesbury, to supported accommodation of different types across the county. The project was influenced by region-wide plans for mental health services for the whole of the Oxford RHA. A new 30-place day centre was to be opened, and peripatetic professional support was planned.

Thirty people were scheduled to move from Graylingwell Hospital to a core and cluster scheme in Bognor Regis, with facilities managed by housing associations. This was the *Chichester* project, which planned rehabilitation in hospital (in two designated wards), with occupational therapy provided in a community activity centre. The core house was designed to be a hostel for up to 11 relatively dependent people, with three unstaffed cluster houses for up to six more independent people. Psychiatric out-patient facilities and the day activity centre (managed by an occupational therapist) would be available for support and advice, the latter also functioning as a base for the community rehabilitation team. The Chichester project always planned to have a large proportion of health authority staff working in the community, with the hostel staffed predominantly by nurses.

The *Greenwich* project was funded to provide supported ordinary housing for 16 people from Bexley Hospital. Flexibility was planned by making available both staffed and unstaffed accommodation, with training and other support as necessary. All staff were employed by the local authority, and included project leader, occupational therapist and residential worker. Like most other projects, the staff team was employed to undertake the selection, assessment and initial training of residents before they left hospital, and to continue to organise and deliver support in the community.

The Mind project in *Waltham Forest* aimed to provide ordinary two-, three- or four-bedroomed housing for 18 people moving from Claybury Hospital in north-east London. The project planned its support around the principles of normalisation. Clients were not expected to pass through a rehabilitation or half-way stage, but would be given permanent homes with training and support for as long as necessary. Project workers employed by Mind would undertake most assessment and selection decisions, in accordance with residents' wishes. A day facility housing a cafe (managed by clients) was planned to be the coordinating link for the project, available to residents during the day, evenings, and weekends for training and leisure activities.

The *Warrington* project was organised around a 16-place hostel with 24-hour supervision, converted from a nurses' home (handed over to a housing association) near the town centre. Privacy and independence were to be fostered by splitting the hostel into four units each with four bedrooms and a lounge. Clients moved from Winwick and Delph Hospitals after a preparation programme. The project was managed by a voluntary consortium organisation, Warrington Community Care, which also provided other facilities in the area, including a day centre used by project clients. Funding was obtained from the European Community to open a workshop. The Waltham Forest and Warrington projects were the only mental health projects run by voluntary organisations.

In *West Berkshire,* the project planned to provide community care for 50 people from Fairmile Hospital by coordinating existing accommodation, employment and day support services run by health, social services and voluntary agencies in the Reading area. The project would comprise a staffed house as a permanent home for long-stay residents, a day facility for at least 35 people, and multidisciplinary staff teams in the community. An important local aim was to link the various local agencies already working to support people with mental health problems.

A system of services, including hostels, supported and independent flats, boarding houses and family placements, was proposed by the *West Lancashire* project to help 40 people move from Ormskirk General and Winwick Hospitals to Skelmersdale and Ormskirk. Clients would be supported by a rehabilitation officer and team of support staff who would help to find the most appropriate accommodation and daytime activities for individual clients, and provide flexible round-the-clock support.

Elderly people with physical frailty

Seven projects were funded by the DHSS to provide community care for elderly people, three for people with physically frailty and four for people with mental health problems, principally dementia. Although all of the projects were to help hospital residents move to the community, not all were part of hospital closure strategies. Their policy relevance came from their testing different community support packages.

In *Coventry,* 17 very dependent patients were to move from Gulson, High View, Walsgrave and Whitley Hospitals into a sheltered housing development with enhanced staffing. Seventeen other places in the same facility, funded by the local authority (and so not strictly part of the centrally-funded programme), would be available for less dependent people referred from the community. A range of support services and day care would be offered to clients on site.

In *Darlington* 62 people were to be supported in independent accommodation, either in their own homes or in housing provided by the project. A particular aim was to concentrate services on clients through one key individual – the home care assistant – trained to undertake domestic and personal care tasks, and provide support and advice to clients and their carers. Care would be coordinated by specialist case managers with control of individual budgets, and authority to choose the most suitable packages of care. Specialist therapists would be available, but the home care assistants were expected to be able to undertake basic therapeutic procedures, trained and supervised by the therapists. The Darlington scheme is described in more detailed by Challis et al. (1989).

Similar to Coventry, the *Winchester* project planned to provide sheltered housing with extra care. Two specialised sheltered housing schemes were to be opened in Winchester and Andover, with five places in each for very dependent people. Clients would be selected from St Paul's and St John's Hospitals, respectively. The scheme formed part of the local strategy, and although it was not expected to make an initial impact on hospital bed numbers, ward closures might follow when more patients had been transferred.

Elderly people with mental health problems

The four projects for elderly people with dementia or other mental health problems were designed to help reduce local demand for hospital places.

The *Camberwell* project intended to provide a residential home for 30 people moving from Cane Hill Hospital back to the local area. Age Concern Southwark was involved in project planning, and it was intended to consult with potential clients and their relatives. A psychogeriatric support team would be made available to Age Concern. Twenty people from Rainhill Hospital were expected to move into a purpose-built home in *St Helens*, with day care provided. The project would hopefully contribute to the rundown of the hospital. The Camberwell and St Helens projects faced more delays than others, principally because of problems with site acquisition and capital development, and were not fully operational until after our evaluation.

There was already a home care support service in *Hillingdon* working to prevent or delay admission to residential homes by elderly people living independently in the community. The pilot project was designed to enhance this service by providing refurbished extensions to residential homes, with extra staff to support residents, and home care to reduce community demand on residential places. The project was led by the local authority, with health authority cooperation.

In common with most projects for elderly people, the *West Cumbria* project aimed to move clients from a distant hospital back to their former locality. Eighteen people from various hospitals, one 50 miles away, would be accommodated in a local authority residential home. The home would have a high staff/resident ratio, with care programmes based on reality orientation and reminiscence therapy approaches to delay the onset of dementia.

Local project objectives

It is possible to get a rich description of the plans and intentions of the pilot projects from the original applications, which were produced after some discussion with other local agencies, the DHSS and the PSSRU. The final applications were therefore almost joint statements of intent. They were local specifications of ends, means and constraints. Table 3.1 reports the detail. Although some projects later altered their working objectives, we report the *original* intentions prompted by the 1983 Circular. Even after grouping similar objectives, more than 50 broad local aims are identifiable. The correspondence between local aims and broader national policy intentions is clear from the table. (The ordering and categorisation of objectives is ours.)

Some qualification is necessary. First, although we mainly relied on the explicit objectives set out in project applications, judgement was required about what could be reliably inferred from less explicit goals. Second, the very nature of the application process and the design of the form encouraged particular aims to surface. For instance, had there been a specific question on the application form about 'replication', there might have been more than eight projects citing this as an aim. Third, some objectives are linked and not mutually exclusive. Finally, projects chose to list different numbers of objectives, and our reduction and categorisation is, to a degree, subjective. With these qualifications in mind, it can be seen that the most common aims were the promotion of inter-agency cooperation in planning, multidisciplinary delivery of services, and accommodation of individual needs and preferences. Consultation with families was cited by 20 of the 28 projects. Although the type and level of provision were constrained by the availability of resources and although the pursuit of cost-effectiveness had a high profile at the time, cost-related aims were less frequently cited as compared to objectives concerning processes, values and client outcomes. The needs, expectations and perspectives of *individuals* rather than client groups or services were stressed throughout the programme.

We now consider seven loosely-grouped categories of objectives and projects' achievements. These measures of success are projects' own views. (The PSSRU measures of achievement are the topic of Parts II and III of this book.) We sent out an End of Project Questionnaire in June 1988, 15 months and three months respectively after the end of central funding for first- and second-round projects, and base some of what follows on responses.

Client characteristics

In the application for programme funding, each project specified the broad client group (people with learning difficulties, for example), the target number of movers, and perhaps some specification of client characteristics such as age, dependency and locality of origin. Ten projects set out to help 'more dependent' people move from hospital, and this emerged as an aim for some others as they developed. They were not concerned simply with rehabilitation of 'easy-

Table 3.1
Project objectives from original applications

	Whether objective is mentioned in original application[1,2]													
Project	A	B	C	D	E	F	G	H	I	J	K	L	M	N
Bolton		*	*	*	*	*	*		*	*			*	*
Calderdale	*	*	*	*	*	*	*			*	*	*	*	*
Camden	*	*	*	*	*	*	*	*	*	*	*		*	*
Derby		*		*	*	*	*		*	*	*			*
Islington		*	*	*	*	*				*	*	*	*	
Kidderminster		*	*	*	*	*	*	*	*	*				
Liverpool			*	*	*	*				*	*		*	*
Maidstone		*			*	*	*		*	*	*			*
Somerset		*	*	*		*	*	*		*	*	*		*
Torbay		*		*	*	*	*		*	*	*	*		*
Warwick			*		*			*		*	*			*
Cambridge		*	*	*	*	*				*	*		*	*
Glossop		*	*	*						*	*			
Brent		*	*	*	*		*		*	*	*	*		*
Bucks		*					*	*		*	*			*
Chichester	*	*	*		*		*			*	*			*
Greenwich	*			*			*	*		*	*	*	*	
Waltham Forest	*	*	*	*			*			*	*	*		*
Warrington				*			*	*		*				
West Berks	*		*			*	*				*			*
West Lancs		*	*	*	*	*	*	*	*	*	*	*		*
Coventry	*		*	*	*	*		*	*	*	*			*
Darlington		*	*	*	*	*	*			*	*	*		*
Winchester			*	*	*	*	*	*			*	*	*	
Camberwell			*		*		*	*		*	*			*
Hillingdon	*	*				*	*	*		*				
St Helens				*						*	*			*
West Cumbria		*		*		*								

1 Objectives cited by five or fewer projects are not included in this table, but are reported in the text. * indicates objective was mentioned.

2 The column heads are as follows: A = Help more severely dependent people; B = 'Holistic' approach; C = Monitor and review progress; D = Get as close to 'normal' life-style as possible; E = Comprehensive provision; F = Staff training valued; G = Offer flexible alternatives to hospital; H = Look beyond project to locality and future; I = Replicate success elsewhere; J = Accommodate individual needs; K = Consult with client; L = Client assessment of service as success criterion; M = Advocacy/individual rights; N = Consult with family

Table 3.1 (continued)

	Whether objective is mentioned in original application[2]													
Project	**O**	**P**	**Q**	**R**	**S**	**T**	**U**	**V**	**W**	**X**	**Y**	**Z**	**AA**	**BB**
Bolton	*	*	s	*	*	*						*	*	*
Calderdale	*	*	s	*	*	*		*	*	*		*		
Camden	*	*	p		*		*		*	*			*	
Derby	*	*	s		*	*					*			*
Islington	*	*	s	*	*			*	*			*	*	
Kidderminster	*			*	*	*		*	*	*	*			*
Liverpool		*	p	*	*	*						*	*	*
Maidstone	*			*	*	*			*					
Somerset	*	*	s	*	*	*	*	*		*	*			
Torbay	*	*	p		*	*			*		*	*		*
Warwick	*	*	s				*		*	*		*		
Cambridge	*	*	s		*	*		*	*			*		
Glossop	*		p						*			*		
Brent	*	*	s	*		*		*	*	*		*	*	*
Bucks	*	*	s	*					*					
Chichester	*	*	s	*	*				*			*		*
Greenwich		*	s	*	*				*	*	*	*		
Waltham Forest	*	*	p	*	*	*		*	*		*		*	
Warrington	*		p	*	*		*							
West Berks	*	*	s	*	*	*		*	*		*			
West Lancs	*	*	s	*		*	*		*	*	*			
Coventry	*	*	s	*				*	*	*		*	*	*
Darlington	*	*	s	*			*			*				
Winchester	*	*	s							*	*		*	
Camberwell	*	*	p	*					*		*			
Hillingdon	*	*	s	*				*		*	*	*		
St Helens	*	*	s						*		*			
West Cumbria	*	*	s				*					*		

Note 2 (continued)
O = Inter-agency cooperation; P = Multidisciplinary approach; Q = Voluntary sector role (s = supportive; p = prominent); R = Provide services according to need; S = Emphasis on occupation-related provision; T = Emphasis on social/recreational; U = Phase in provision/keep control on development; V = Use keyworker system; W = Detailed costings or cost projects; X = Explicit reference to costs/cost-effectiveness; Y = Transfer resources to community; Z = General improvement in client welfare; AA = Independence/self-determination; BB = Improve life satisfaction/quality of life.

to-place' residents, but endeavoured to help people who were more dependent than other hospital leavers at that time.

Many projects reported major differences between target characteristics and the characteristics of those clients who actually moved. In some cases this meant only minor adjustments to plans: the West Cumbria project, for example, was able to accommodate elderly clients who were more dependent than expected because they had already planned enhanced staffing in order to implement reality orientation, although this threatened the programme. In some projects the divergence between expectation and reality caused greater difficulties. The West Lancs project was unable to help the very dependent long-stay population which had originally been identified in Winwick Hospital, as the flexible range of supported and independent accommodation established proved inappropriate. With the agreement of the DHSS, plans were changed to offer a hostel with 24-hour support, with additional expenditure, for 'revolving door' rather than long-stay in-patients.

Generally, projects approached, and in one or two cases exceeded, their three-year targets for resettlement, but almost universally with less speed than anticipated. Difficulties with capital developments, staffing, hospital cooperation and community opposition were the principal causes (Renshaw et al., 1988). First-year targets proved particularly difficult to hit. Although the speed with which people move into community settings is only one of many objectives, this becomes relevant when funding for new services is partly dependent on closing and selling hospital sites.

Camden, Waltham Forest and Glossop targeted their services on younger people, and West Lancs and St Helens specifically aimed to accommodate people in their localities of origin (although others implicitly pursued this). Client turnover in the community was not mentioned.

Care principles and philosophies

We have already noted how community care policies around Britain have gravitated towards *normalisation.* The same was true within the demonstration programme. Most project plans were underpinned by service values which made reference to normalisation and ordinary life models, and all drew up plans concerning the orientation and quality of care. Normalisation is open to different interpretation, and there was inevitably divergence between planned orientation and what proved feasible in practice. (For example, Somerset moved towards normalisation over time. Bolton, Camden and Maidstone revised their service principles considerably. Waltham Forest and Warrington started with very different views about normalisation, and moved towards each other over time.)

Our evaluation included the assessment of achievements in the pursuit of some aspects of an ordinary life model. Our findings are reported in Chapter

8 and in Part III, and risk-taking, self-determination and choice are also explored in Chapter 10. Several projects reported difficulty in interpreting normalisation, or became bogged down by ideology. Some staff interpreted it naively as meaning that they should behave simply as friends to clients, rather than professionals. In one project there was a long-running conflict between those who wished to ensure that case management and service monitoring were conducted and those who wanted to abandon individual programme planning because it was not perceived to be 'normal'.

In the previous chapter we described how community care policy had for many years been consigned to a residual position. It was perhaps inevitable, though not defensible, that ideologies of Care in the Community should have been heavily influenced by perspectives of hospital provision. This in turn prompted some projects to draw up reactive philosophies of care, specified so as to contrast with dominant attitudes and practices prevailing in hospitals, or in parent community care agencies, and their full implications may not have been appreciated. Experience led to limited revision of aims, but the assumptions and preconceptions of other service providers had been challenged. It is obviously naive to build practice on a simple 'hospital bad, community good' perspective, which also makes it harder to see the failings of community care itself.

Fears about hostility towards people with mental health problems and learning difficulties were reflected in some of the objectives set by projects. (Bolton, Calderdale, Kidderminster and Greenwich explicitly noted this as an aim.) Changing societal attitudes was an ambitious aim, but projects reported satisfaction that they had been able to observe and perhaps themselves effect some improvement. Projects for people with learning difficulty, in particular, noted that there was less paternalism and more acceptance of people as adult citizens among, for example, GPs and dentists, bus drivers, shop assistants, and acquaintances in pubs.

Although judging whether philosophical objectives have been met is difficult, most projects were adamant that even loose aims were important for focusing discussion and setting goals. Even when projects realised they were over-optimistic at the outset, they reaffirmed their commitment to their ideals.

Consumerism

Public service consumers have historically exerted limited influence over service design and delivery decisions. By the standards of the 1990s, the *initial* consumerism objectives of many pilot projects look a little pale, but over the course of their development most consolidated client involvement, advocacy and representation at the service and case levels. From the beginning, all planned to respond to individual needs; but most also responded to individual wants. A common lament in responding to our End of Project Questionnaire was that they wished they had been more ambitious at the outset. We return to consumerism in Chapter 10.

Another commonly-stated aim was consultation with families. A number of projects involved families in the transition process from hospital to the community, or included relatives on their management groups in meaningful rather than token ways. It was not always easy to find relatives, although in some cases contacts were resumed after many years of isolation. In Waltham Forest, families were involved in service plans alongside Mind although, in practice, interest was limited. West Cumbria hoped to engage relatives and friends in reality orientation programmes, but several relatives found it easier to accommodate the client's confusion. Staff in more than one project faced the dilemma that they and a client supported the move out of hospital, but the client's family (who had not been in contact for some years, and who lived a considerable distance from both the hospital and the locality of origin) opposed the move. Such community placements invariably proved successful.

Joint working and agency mix

Joint working between health and social care agencies was a requirement of programme funding, and many projects saw central funding as a welcome opportunity to improve local inter-agency cooperation. Even when one agency dominated service lead or provision this was dependent upon good cooperation at the planning or service monitoring stages, as in Somerset and Brent for example. The involvement of the voluntary sector was encouraged, and all but two projects intended to do so, seven in a prominent role.

There were exceptions to the general success of joint working. Places on steering and management groups reserved for non-statutory agencies sometimes remained empty for the duration of central funding, or one agency 'captured' a project by taking key decisions without consultation, in one case by ignoring previous agreements about employment conditions. At least one health authority decided against involving the local authority in management of the project (although the local authority was admittedly also reluctant). The fragile alliance established in a couple of other projects was shattered once central funding ceased, in both cases because health authorities reneged on financial commitments. Local authority social services departments and voluntary agencies were not blameless either, in some instances riding roughshod over health authority interests and procedures. Such occurrences were rare but damaging.

Voluntary sector contributions were diverse (see Chapter 11). Project plans anticipated a dominant or prominent role for voluntary organisations in five cases, but elsewhere their expected involvement was only vaguely specified: 'the project will make full use of the voluntary sector' and 'housing associations will be used' were typical objectives. In the End of Project Questionnaire, projects made little reference to the voluntary sector. Projects which specifically set out to mix the economy of welfare hoped to challenge the preconceptions of statutory agencies, by demonstrating that multidisciplinary forums could work (Waltham Forest), or that housing associations could usefully link with public authorities to develop ordinary housing (Liverpool), or that cost-effective and efficient management was not the preserve of the public sector (Warwick and Warrington). The private sector was barely mentioned at any stage in the programme, and played no part in project management.

Service provision

Within each project's plans were one or two objectives broadly concerned with service provision such as provision according to need (specifically stated by 19 projects), occupation-related provision (16 projects), social and recreational activities (13) and the phasing of new provision into mainstream systems (7). Specific intentions included the provision of additional resource centres (Calderdale, Brent, Chichester, Greenwich, Waltham Forest) and to develop intermediate care facilities (Bolton and Darlington). DHSS grant money helped break inappropriate service patterns in some areas. New services were not necessarily innovative, but by freeing them from the constraints of existing resource allocation, inter-agency working or inter-department bargaining, projects could depart from conventional provision.

The Greenwich project realised its aim to provide an intensive home support service built by case managers and delivered by carefully trained and multi-skilled home care assistants. The aim to fill a gap in service provision was later recognised to have been over-ambitious, yet the gap was partially filled, which demonstrated feasibility and challenged local assumptions. The Kidderminster project achieved its aim of developing new forms of day and residential care, making optimum use of contributions from voluntary organisations and sources of finance from outside social services. These also provided extra resources for people already in the community. The intensive domiciliary support service planned for Darlington was fully operational, and case management with some decentralisation of budgets was successfully introduced in Darlington and Maidstone. With the exception of Camberwell and St Helens, all projects opened some or all capital facilities during the three-year pilot period, and even in these two projects services developed later on.

Cost-effectiveness

The cost-effectiveness objective which featured in the Care in the Community Circular was played down by some projects. This was not because projects denied its relevance, but because some saw little need to highlight an aim which already ran through – and, in 1984, threatened to dominate – policies and operational plans. Plans for detailed cost examinations or projections were noted by 18 projects, although only 12 made explicit reference to reducing the costs of care or improving cost-effectiveness. A similar number saw themselves as helping to shift resources from hospital to community. Two stated their intention to be self-financing within three years (Torbay and West Lancs). (The number of self-financing projects grew with the liberalisation of social security payments for residential care in the non-statutory sectors.) There is always tension between cost containment and improving client welfare, or establishing care practices such as ordinary life models. Some service systems proposed under the programme were known to be comparatively high-cost options compared to hospital or other community services, but projects were intent on examining whether they would also be comparatively high performers in relation to client welfare.

Two major resource problems surfaced. The first concerned staffing. Under-estimates of the support needs of people in the community (often the result of inaccurate hospital-based assessments, or lack of experience in developing and running community facilities) left a few projects operating with inadequate staffing levels. Related problems were the failure to budget for overtime, promotions and pay settlements. The second resource problem indirectly and temporarily helped deal with the first. Delays in starting or completing building work allowed projects to delay staff recruitment, and allowed savings to accrue in the early months of DHSS funding. However, capital costs then generally ran ahead of estimates. Inflation in building costs and house prices forced revisions to cost projections, with fixed budgets. This delayed rather than cancelled most community facility plans. Projects also under-estimated transport and depreciation costs.

In judging the generalisability of these experiences, it should be remembered that projects were often planned in a hurry to take advantage of the DHSS grant opportunities.

Client outcomes

Client outcome objectives are arguably the most critical, and it is therefore surprising to find only occasional explicit reference to them in the original applications. Fourteen projects aimed to bring about improvements in general client welfare, eight aimed to work on independence and self-determination, and eight set out to improve life satisfaction or quality of life. Other more specific objectives were also cited, including health, self-care skills, self-image, appearance, social interaction, integration, engagement and life expectancy. Nine projects made no reference to client outcome aims, although consumerism, normalisation and other process objectives were specified.

How did projects rate their own achievements? The End of Project Questionnaire gathered narrative descriptions of the effects on the lives of clients. We also asked projects to rank seven client-related outcomes in order of achievement (after consultation with key actors in the project or agency). Three projects felt unable to rank these achievements and five expressed reservations about their rankings. Table 3.2 therefore provides an inkling of projects' own impressions of client welfare achievements. Client group and programme averages are given in Table 3.3. For the programme as a whole, projects ranked their achievements in the following order: improvements in life satisfaction; greater personal freedom; appropriate personal presentation; use of community facilities and meeting people; greater engagement in activities; improved living skills; and fewer behaviour problems.

Nine projects ranked improvements in life satisfaction as their greatest achievement, 11 ranked personal freedom as most important, and rarely did these fall below second-rank order. Only in projects for people with mental health problems was improvement in life skills ranked highly. In Greenwich, the retrospective view from 1988 was the importance for clients to gain self-esteem and life satisfaction (in some cases resulting in improved skills). It was noted by more than one project that clients appeared to have *lost* some skills since moving to the community because of the relatively high emphasis placed on other aspects of life-style. (There is some confirmation of this from our outcome evaluation reported in Chapter 14, although changes do not reach statistical significance.) For the programme as a whole, achievements in reducing problems associated with behaviour were ranked lowest.

The narrative accounts of changes in client well-being and our continuing liaison with staff support the picture painted by these rankings and, more importantly, relate the story of the Care in the Community programme. They describe how some clients rated as immobile or wheelchair-bound in hospital are now walking. Others acquired speech after many years without verbal communication. Many have shown rekindled interest in events around them, making choices and expressing opinions. One woman visited friends in America after many years in hospital, and another is back in London after regaining contact with her family after many years in locked hospital wards and prison. Community care was seen by projects as an undoubted improvement on hospital.

There remained dissatisfaction with the level of independence achieved, and client life satisfaction and personal freedom were noted as needing more attention. Projects have been able to give clients more control over their lives, but find it difficult to offer yet more freedom because of staffing and societal constraints. Thus, while at the end of 1988 relatively few clients were leading completely independent lives, most had more independence than before and most were enjoying it. Another area of dissatisfaction related to in-patient hospital episodes. Because the most tangible indication of success was the

Table 3.2
Project perceptions of client outcome achievements

Projects and clients	*Rank order of achievement of client outcomes*[1,2]						
	SKILL	BEHAV	SATIS	ENGAG	COMM	PRES	FREE
Calderdale	5	7	1	4	3	6	2
Camden	3	7	1	5	4	6	2
Derby	6	7	2	5	3	4	1
Islington	4	6	1	3	2	5	7
Kidderminster	7	4	1	5	2	3	6
Liverpool	7	6	4	2	3	1	5
Maidstone	6	5	4	3	7	2	1
Somerset	4	4	1	4	1	4	1
Torbay	5	5	4	5	1	1	1
Warwick	4	6	2	5	3	7	1
Cambridge	7	6	2	3	3	1	5
Glossop	7	5	2	4	3	6	1
Brent	1	4	5	3	7	2	6
Bucks	3	6	2	5	3	7	1
Chichester	4	5	1	6	7	3	2
Greenwich	4	7	2	4	4	3	1
Waltham Forest	2	5	6	7	3	4	1
Warrington	7	5	1	2	2	5	2
West Lancs	3	7	2	6	3	3	1
Coventry	7	6	2	5	3	4	1
Darlington	6	7	1	5	4	2	3
Winchester	6	4	3	5	6	1	2
Hillingdon	6	2	1	4	5	3	7
St Helens	3	2	3	5	5	1	7
West Cumbria	5	7	3	4	6	1	2

1 The column heads indicate:
SKILL: achievement of adequate living skills (self-care, cooking, etc.)
BEHAV: fewer behaviour problems
SATIS: improvement in general satisfaction with life
ENGAG: greater engagement in activites
COMM: use of community facilities and meeting people
PRES: achievement of appropriate personal presentation (appearing better cared-for and 'normal')
FREE: greater degree of personal freedom and control over own life
2 Rank order: 1 = most important; 7 = least important.

Table 3.3
Project perceptions of client outcome achievements – client group and overall average rankings

Client group	*Rank order of achievement of client outcomes*[1,2]						
	SKILL	BEHAV	SATIS	ENGAG	COMM	PRES	FREE
Learning difficulties	6	7	1	5	3	4	2
Young people (mult. dis.)[3]	7	6	2	3	4	1	5
Physical disabilities[3]	7	5	2	4	3	6	1
Mental health problems	3	7	2	6	5	4	1
Elderly, physical frailty	7	6	1	5	4	3	2
Elderly, mental hlth probs	6	4	2	5	7	1	3
All projects[4]	6	7	1	5	4	3	2

1 The column heads are explained in the key to Table 3.2.
2 The rank numbers for client groups and all projects give the rank order of the averages of the appropriate project rankings: 1 = most important; 7 = least important.
3 One project only.
4 Bolton, Camberwell and West Berks did not give rankings and are therefore excluded.

movement of clients from hospital to supported community settings, later periods of in-patient treatment were sometimes regarded as 'failures'.

Given that it takes a long time to reverse the effects of many years of hospitalisation, the achievements observed by projects and revealed by our outcome analyses deserve congratulation.

Reassessing local objectives

To what extent have project objectives been achieved? With hindsight, were they realistic? With the benefit of experience, would projects choose different objectives were they to embark on a similar venture in the future? Projects were asked to respond to these questions.

The project perspectives are based on three or more years of service development, trying to implement plans and achieve immediate and long-term objectives. Much of this practical experience has been tapped during monitoring and evaluation (see, for example, Chapter 8), but for a realistic and balanced assessment it is also important to include project perspectives. An example comes from the Liverpool project, which aimed to provide 24-hour staff care which could be withdrawn as clients became more able and independent. As this did not happen, this particular objective was not achieved, but local experience and circumstances provided valuable lessons about the reality of setting such objectives, including the realisation that hospital-based assessments of likely ability in the community are unrealistic and unhelpful.

General achievements

- Twelve projects felt they had *achieved their overall objectives*. The response was qualified in some cases – 'although it is an ongoing process', 'substantially achieved them all', 'though not fully self-financing', 'against the odds' and 'despite poor resources'.
- Ten projects felt they had *partially achieved* their objectives. Four had not reached their target numbers of transfers, two felt they had not maximised satisfaction for all clients, and another two had not replicated 'ordinary' life-styles. Other sources of concern were: inadequate staffing resources, not involving family and friends, not achieving agency integration, not offering clients enough independence, and not establishing a planned core and cluster facility.
- Two projects were of the opinion that, overall, they had *not achieved* their objectives. In one case there was no further comment; in the other client isolation was still a problem.
- Two projects *were not able to say* what they had achieved; it was either 'too early' or the original criteria 'were not well enough defined to be sure'.

Given the small number of negative or uncommitted responses, the overall impression is favourable. Resource and time constraints often explained the inability to meet fully all the original success criteria, although their impact was felt in diverse ways. Relative lack of experience in planning and operating community care was responsible for some delays in acquiring and opening facilities. Difficulties with planning permission, fire and other regulations, builders, public relations and staff recruitment, resistance among hospital staff, and confusion in social security offices about entitlements were common (see Chapter 8). Some delays could be avoided if anticipated early enough, but in 1984 there was comparatively little experience to guide service managers. One consequence was that some projects effectively had only two years in which they were actively engaged in centrally-funded community care.

As part of the same retrospective overview, projects were also asked to rank their achievements in relation to 12 commonly-specified objectives for community care. These are process outcomes. The results are given in Table 3.4, with ranking 1 indicating the greatest achievement and 12 the least. These are not priority rankings of intentions, but orderings of success *as viewed by the projects themselves*. Client group and programme rankings are given in Table 3.5. These data simply give a general picture of how projects viewed the fruits of their labours. The three most important achievements were: successfully moving target clients into the community, adherence to principles and philosophy, and adequate housing provision. The least important related to cost-effectiveness, integrating services into the mainstream, and changing attitudes in the wider community.

The development of suitable rehabilitation techniques or facilities was not an important outcome for projects for elderly people but was ranked fourth

Table 3.4
Ranking of broad project achievements by project

	Areas of achievement[1,2]											
Project	**A**	**B**	**C**	**D**	**E**	**F**	**G**	**H**	**I**	**J**	**K**	**L**
Calderdale	3	8	4	5	7	9	2	6	1	12	10	11
Camden	2	5	3	8	4	10	9	1	6	12	11	7
Derby	3	10	7	12	6	11	1	5	4	8	9	2
Islington	1	10	7	4	6	12	9	2	8	11	5	3
Kidderminster	2	10	1	6	7	12	3	8	5	9	11	4
Liverpool	4	10	8	1	7	6	3	2	12	11	9	5
Maidstone	5	6	8	3	2	9	4	1	10	12	11	7
Somerset	4	2	7	8	3	10	6	1	9	12	11	5
Torbay	8	7	11	6	10	11	2	3	1	5	4	9
Warwick	3	6	5	4	10	11	9	2	1	12	8	7
Cambridge	3	5	11	5	7	9	8	1	2	12	10	4
Glossop	4	6	5	7	3	11	12	2	1	10	8	9
Brent	3	5	4	5	7	10	9	2	1	11	8	12
Bucks	3	2	6	7	8	4	5	9	10	12	1	11
Chichester	2	6	3	4	7	9	10	8	1	12	4	11
Greenwich	2	8	10	5	11	12	3	3	1	7	6	9
Waltham Forest	1	7	5	1	4	9	9	8	1	11	6	12
Warrington	2	5	8	3	7	12	6	11	1	9	4	10
West Lancs	1	1	1	1	1	1	1	1	1	12	11	10
Coventry	5	6	6	6	6	6	4	2	1	6	3	6
Darlington	11	12	9	10	8	7	1	6	5	3	2	4
Winchester	1	6	4	2	2	3	5	1	2	3	1	8
Hillingdon	12	8	11	2	4	7	6	5	1	10	3	9
St Helens	5	10	10	5	1	9	5	1	1	12	4	8
West Cumbria	12	9	8	4	1	6	2	3	11	5	10	7

1 The letters represent the following:
A: Adequate housing provision
B: Development of suitable rehabilitation facilities
C: Provision of appropriate day support services
D: Successful operational development of staff team
E: Application of appropriate assessments/reviews
F: Mainstreaming of project with other services
G: Demonstrating innovative service models
H: Adherence to principles and philosophies
I: Successfully moving target clients into community
J: Providing more cost-effective services than hospitals
K: Achieving successful joint working
L: Changing attitudes in the wider community
2 The ranks are: 1 = most important; 12 = least important.

Table 3.5
Ranking of broad project achievements by client group and for whole programme

	Areas of achievement[1,2]											
Client group	**A**	**B**	**C**	**D**	**E**	**F**	**G**	**H**	**I**	**J**	**K**	**L**
Learning difficulties	2	9	7	4	8	11	3	1	4	12	10	6
Young people (mult. dis.)[3]	3	6	11	5	7	9	8	1	2	12	10	4
Physical disabilities[3]	4	6	5	7	3	11	12	2	1	10	8	9
Mental health problems	1	4	5	3	9	10	8	7	2	11	6	12
Elderly, physical frailty	11	12	10	8	6	6	4	3	2	5	1	8
Elderly, mental hlth probs	9	12	11	4	1	6	3	2	5	9	8	6
All projects[4]	3	9	7	4	6	11	5	2	1	12	8	10

1 The key to the areas of achievement is:
A: Adequate housing provision
B: Development of suitable rehabilitation facilities
C: Provision of appropriate day support services
D: Successful operational development of staff team
E: Application of appropriate assessments/reviews
F: Mainstreaming of project with other services
G: Demonstrating innovative service models
H: Adherence to principles and philosophies
I: Successfully moving target clients into community
J: Providing more cost-effective services than hospitals
K: Achieving successful joint working
L: Changing attitudes in the wider community
2 The rank numbers for client groups and for all projects give the rank order of the averages of the appropriate project ratings. 1 = most important; 12 = least important.
3 One project only.
4 Excluding Bolton, Camberwell and West Berks.

by the projects for people with mental health problems. The provision of adequate housing was reported to be the most important achievement for projects for people with mental health problems and was ranked second by projects for people with learning difficulties. With the exception of Winchester, housing was seen to be relatively unimportant in projects for elderly people. By contrast, achieving cost-effectiveness and 'mainstreaming' were seen to be more important by projects for elderly people. In fact, there are many marked contrasts between the projects for elderly people and others, differences which are also mirrored in the broader evaluation reported in this book.

How realistic were the initial objectives?

Projects were asked if their original objectives were realistic.

- Fifteen of the 28 projects believed their original objectives *were* realistic. Of these, three felt that resources had been inadequate and three that they had not had enough development time. Two projects noted that it was important to have ideals.
- Nine projects viewed their objectives as unrealistic. Time-scales were too short (two projects) with a variety of service and resource constraints only becoming apparent after projects had been launched.
- The other six projects either gave no specific response, or did not know if the original project objectives were realistic.

Repeating the project

Finally we asked projects if they would choose the same objectives if they were to embark on a similar venture.

- Eighteen would alter their objectives very little. Five said they would keep the same objectives but approach them differently.
- Seven projects would make substantial alterations to their objectives, such as taking more notice of resource restrictions, or changing the *emphasis* of client-related objectives by being either more specific or less specific (one project each).
- Three projects gave no response or did not know.

From interpretation to implementation

Local objectives, not surprisingly, were influenced by the national agenda and the guidelines in the 1983 Circular. Nevertheless, local flavour was not lost. The programme was characterised by a wide span of objectives; some, like philosophy of care, featuring strongly throughout the programme. Projects interpreted the Circular in quite different ways, producing diverse models of practice. In reflecting on their achievements, some failures were identified on some counts, but most remained optimistic about their services and clients, and about community care policies generally. The tremendous enthusiasm, energy and commitment which characterised the early days of the demonstration programme may not have been so obvious or widespread by the end, but few projects lost sight of their original ideals. A strong sense of achievement emerges from this chapter and, while project perspectives are impressionistic and biased, it would be wrong to ignore them.

4 The evaluation methodology

The research agenda

The evaluation basis for a public policy preferring community care to hospital residence for people with long-term care needs is limited.

> The present ferment of change provides opportunities for weighing one kind of solution against another in order to determine which is more effective for meeting the particular problems of a particular community. If the alternative services are to be in place and shown to be working *before* large hospitals are closed, it is essential that multidisciplinary (including economic and administrative, as well as clinical and social) evaluation be undertaken at a local level and on a scale hitherto not considered. This is not only a matter for government departments (although there is an urgent need for initiative, guidance and sizeable central funding in order to start the process off), but for regional and district health and local authorities which, hitherto, have not been very active in this field. Only in this way will it be possible, over a decade or two, to meet the challenge (posed by the mental hospitals). The alternative is to muddle on as before with the result that services may actually become worse rather than better (Wing, 1986, p.47).

There is no shortage of argument about the fundamental right of people to live 'ordinary lives' in the community, and consequently – following this line of argument – it is unnecessary to have to 'prove' that it is more effective. This is not an acceptable stance for public agencies charged with balancing the conflicting preferences of different groups within society, and also charged with balancing the risks and the benefits of community care for people who need support in daily living. The demonstration programme, with its diversity and scale, offered an excellent opportunity to *evaluate* community care: 'It will be important to demonstrate methods which are both beneficial to the people concerned and cost-effective' (DHSS, 1983, para. 11). Research opportunities of this kind have their problems – every silver lining has its cloud – for the design and timing of the programme did not fit the ideal methodological approach, nor was the programme best positioned within national and local power structures to afford full research access.

The 1983 Circular put three items on the evaluation agenda: the costs of community care; the effects on people moving out of hospital; and the ways in which projects delivered community care. At the heart of the evaluation, therefore, was the examination of the circumstances in which cost-effective community care was provided to meet the needs of particular groups of former long-stay hospital residents.

The cost-effectiveness criterion meant what it said: a concern with both the resources needed for community care (the cost) and the outcomes for clients and others (the effectiveness). The purpose of this chapter is to describe the methodological framework within which the research was conducted.

Research questions

Beneath the overarching cost-effectiveness research objective is a set of associated questions which we explored during the course of the study.

- What were the Department of Health's objectives for the Care in the Community programme, and were they achieved? What were the objectives of individual pilot projects, and agencies sponsoring those projects, and were they achieved?
- Who were the people whose welfare the programme was designed to improve? What client characteristics were chosen by projects? What do the characteristics of people selected imply for generalisations outside the demonstration programme? What lives were residents leading before they moved to the community, and how did they view hospital residence?
- How did projects staff their community services? What were the characteristics of the staff employed? Did projects find certain people more suitable for community care? How were staff deployed, trained, supported and managed?
- How did projects implement the core tasks of case management? What arrangements were made concerning organisational and agency location, devolution of responsibilities and budgets, case review processes and client involvement?
- How and at what levels did projects establish joint working procedures? What service management systems were put into place, and how did they function? What benefits stem from pluralism?
- How were community services and systems financed? What roles did state benefits play, and what were the associated advantages and difficulties? How did projects use dowry payments?
- What were the costs of establishing community care, and how do they compare with hospital? Is community care affordable? Who bears the cost burden? Which client characteristics, care circumstances and other factors influenced costs?
- What were the client-specific objectives of the programme and of individual projects? What dimensions of client welfare changed by the move from hospital?
- What types of community care arrangement proved more successful than others? Was this related to client characteristics? For instance, is an 'ordinary life' model of care more successful than, say, a model centred on congregate care settings?
- What are the longer-term policy implications of the research findings and the experiences of projects? What are the policy and practice lessons?

Each set of questions is relevant to each client group. Each requires refinement before empirical testing. Although the questions are couched at a level of generality more relevant to the policy-maker than the clinician or social care practitioner, the process of refinement provides insights about community care which should be of broad interest. We cannot categorise the support or treatment regimes of different sub-systems, settings or care packages in sufficiently fine detail, for example, to be able to analyse small differences in style or mode of intervention, but we can describe the different case management, staff and joint working arrangements in 28 different systems, and we can examine the services set in place and utilised by clients. We are also able to examine whether the fears and concerns voiced about the closure of the long-stay hospitals – homelessness, destitution, imprisonment, behavioural problems, poor self-care skills, and so on – were justified. In short, the opportunity was created for a very comprehensive study of community care and hospital closure.

Promotion, monitoring and evaluation

The PSSRU was commissioned not only to evaluate, but also to promote and monitor, the programme of pilot projects. Indeed, evaluation was probably seen to be the least of the tasks by the DHSS in the initial specification of the commission, and the PSSRU team was small. The implications of the broad remit for the conduct of the evaluation need to be considered, and it is relevant to point out that the performance of activities other than evaluation had an influence on it – both as a distraction and as an added source of information.

Our research strategy was deliberately constructed at a level of generality which made it suitable for the programme as a whole, although it was slightly modified for individual projects and client groups while preserving core information flows. The strategy depended heavily on the interest and participation of project staff, who were consulted at various stages. Some research instruments were developed to be useful to projects themselves. The evaluation also had to dovetail with our monitoring of the programme.

The PSSRU's involvement began some months before the Minister of State announced the programme in March 1983. PSSRU staff initially had some influence on the orientation of the programme, but not in relation to specific service models. The Maidstone and Darlington projects explicitly built in elements of the successful Kent Community Care Scheme originally designed by Bleddyn Davies and David Challis of PSSRU, in collaboration with Nicolas Stacey, former director of social services in Kent (Challis and Davies, 1986; Davies and Challis, 1986). The PSSRU did not select the projects funded by the DHSS.

Distinguishing between evaluation, monitoring and promotion is not straightforward. Between late 1982 and early 1989 members of the research team made regular visits to each of the 28 projects to gather research data (evaluation), to help the DHSS keep abreast of developments (monitoring), to gather information for wider dissemination (promotion), and occasionally to offer advice to projects (none of the three commissioned tasks but important nonetheless). There may have been elements of all four tasks in one visit.

We can make a fairly general distinction between monitoring and evaluation as conducted in our work with the pilot projects. The information collected in *monitoring* is likely to be routinely available and necessary for project management and operation itself. In the annual reports and End of Project Questionnaire we imposed a degree of standardisation on such information. In interviewing case managers and in some instances advising projects on the design of case review forms (or similar), we formalised some of the client or case monitoring by projects. Monitoring information tends to be designed in order to meet practical and immediate needs. It is closer to what is often described as action research. *Evaluation*, by contrast, is generally based on a clearer theoretical framework from which hypotheses can be formulated. Monitoring activities gather information on broad trends and general features; evaluation is more concerned with the detail and its explanation. Monitoring is like consulting the Ordnance Survey map to check the contour lines or locate the village pub; evaluation requires a visit to the area to assess the view from the top of the hill or to sample the local hospitality. If you are not familiar with an area you are advised to do the former before the latter, and so it is that the monitoring activities informed the evaluation.

The competing demands of promotion and monitoring left their mark on the evaluation. We believe that the supportive role of the PSSRU and the exchange of information between projects reduced the likelihood of failure but heightened some evaluation difficulties. The evaluation is not simply a description of *what is*, but is an account of *what can be*: an account of successes and failures when services are organised in particular ways with particular levels of financial and other support. The evaluation extended beyond description to causal analysis, making demands well beyond routine monitoring. There is a further tension, since monitoring can imply policing (or auditing) of projects, and promotion can mean offering support and advice. Agreement was reached with the DHSS that the PSSRU would not adopt a policing role: we would not report details of a project to the Department without first consulting the project itself. We were also given relative latitude in our advisory activities, for example using a research grant from one part of the DHSS to advise projects on how to maximise social security benefits from another part of the DHSS. For a time, one project asked us not to broadcast their rather imaginative use of such benefits.

The production of welfare framework

In examining and measuring the effectiveness of a health or social care service or policy, the starting point is the set of objectives for service quality and impact upon clients. These are the *intermediate* and *final* objectives. The final objectives are ends in themselves; intermediate objectives are couched in terms of means to those ends. Final objectives are specified in terms of the effects of health or social care upon clients and their carers. Most health and social care interventions have a very general objective, such as the improvement of mental health, but almost always also aim to influence more than one facet of client welfare. (We use the term 'welfare' to refer to all relevant characteristics which may change as a result of intervention.) Objectives need to be specified in some detail. Providing mental health services where they are needed is really an intermediate objective, so too is offering a supportive, high-quality environment in a residential facility. These are means to achieve various desired changes in, for example, the self-care skills, behavioural characteristics, physical health and social integration of individual clients.

Deficiencies in respect of these objectives are related to *needs*. The precise definition and measurement of this decidedly glutinous concept is far from easy. For the present purposes it is not necessary for us to engage in debates about positive versus normative need concepts, or other issues (Davies, 1977; Knapp, 1984; Brewin et al., 1987). Improvements along the dimensions spanned by the objectives are the *outcomes* or effectiveness. This suggests a distinction between *intermediate outcomes* – the delivery of services, perhaps of a specified quality – and *final outcomes* – improvements in client welfare, perhaps by comparison to some reference or control group. There are few circumstances in which intermediate outcome indicators would be preferred to final, even allowing for the greater difficulties of measuring the latter.

We need to be sensible about the context within which we define, employ and interpret the measures of outcome. When we come to discuss client accommodation in the community, it needs to be recalled that homelessness was already a problem in some of Britain's cities, so that housing placement outcomes (conformity to ordinary life models, say) are partly exogenously determined (that is, they are in part influenced by policies, decisions and pressures outside the 'community care system'). Similarly, the high rates of unemployment in Britain make it even more difficult than usual for former long-term hospital residents to find paid work in the open labour market (that is, outside sheltered employment settings). Social security benefit levels are beyond the control of social and health care agencies, yet they determine the economic independence of clients. However, helping clients to get the benefits to which they are entitled *is* partly within the control of these agencies.

Service objectives are usually discussed by reference to a set of factors hypothesised or known to be related to outcome. A great deal of applied research in the mental health, learning difficulty and gerontology literatures is designed to test the impact on users of one or more service, or drug, or social situation. The most common study tests one explanatory factor at a time using an experimental design (random allocation) or quasi-experimental design (matching or standardisation) to control for extraneous influences and other potential explanatory factors (Challis and Darton, 1990). The range of factors with a potential influence on outcomes is broad. The personal characteristics, experiences and circumstances of clients will be of particular importance, but there are also the various social characteristics such as the quality of a care environment, and the availability of support and stimulation. Characteristics of the physical setting – such as the scale and structure of a facility, and the level of support from income maintenance programmes – would also need to be included in a list of possible determinants of levels of client welfare and outcomes.

The hypothesised determinants of or influences upon outcome may be termed the *inputs*, and fall into two groups. *Resource inputs* are the tangible resources such as staff, physical capital (including buildings and vehicles), provisions and other consumable items which go to create service packages and help achieve the desirable outcomes. Each of them has a *cost*, this being a shorthand term and summary measure for all these resource inputs. In contrast, the *non-resource inputs* are those determinants of final and intermediate outcomes which are neither physical nor tangible: they are embodied in the personalities, activities, attitudes and experiences of the principal actors in the care system or service. The non-resource inputs are distinguished from the resource inputs by virtue of their having no sensibly defined cost. (Because they exert an influence on outcomes but do not have a cost, a study of costs, outcomes or efficiency needs to include them, although inclusion remains rare. Some of the non-resource inputs are correlated with, and perhaps determined by, the resource inputs or costs, but others are determined outside the care system, and these need either to be comprehensively purged from an evaluation by rigorous design, or built into the analyses.) The resource and non-resource inputs include the 'intervening' or 'confounding' variables of an evaluation, although many – perhaps most – are of intrinsic interest in their own right. The 'Hawthorne effect' associated with a high-profile demonstration programme – people behave differently because they are being evaluated (Roethlisberger and Dickson, 1939) – is among the confounding factors which we will want to exclude.

This simple framework – illustrated in simplified form in Figure 4.1 – suggests that analogies can be drawn between health and social care processes and the economist's theory of production relations. It has been called the *production of welfare model* or framework (Davies and Knapp, 1981). The basic premise of the production of welfare approach is that final and intermediate outcomes are determined by the level and modes of combination of the resource and non-resource inputs. This approach allows us to structure and plan the Care in the Community evaluation so as to extract from a mass of

Figure 4.1
Production of welfare model

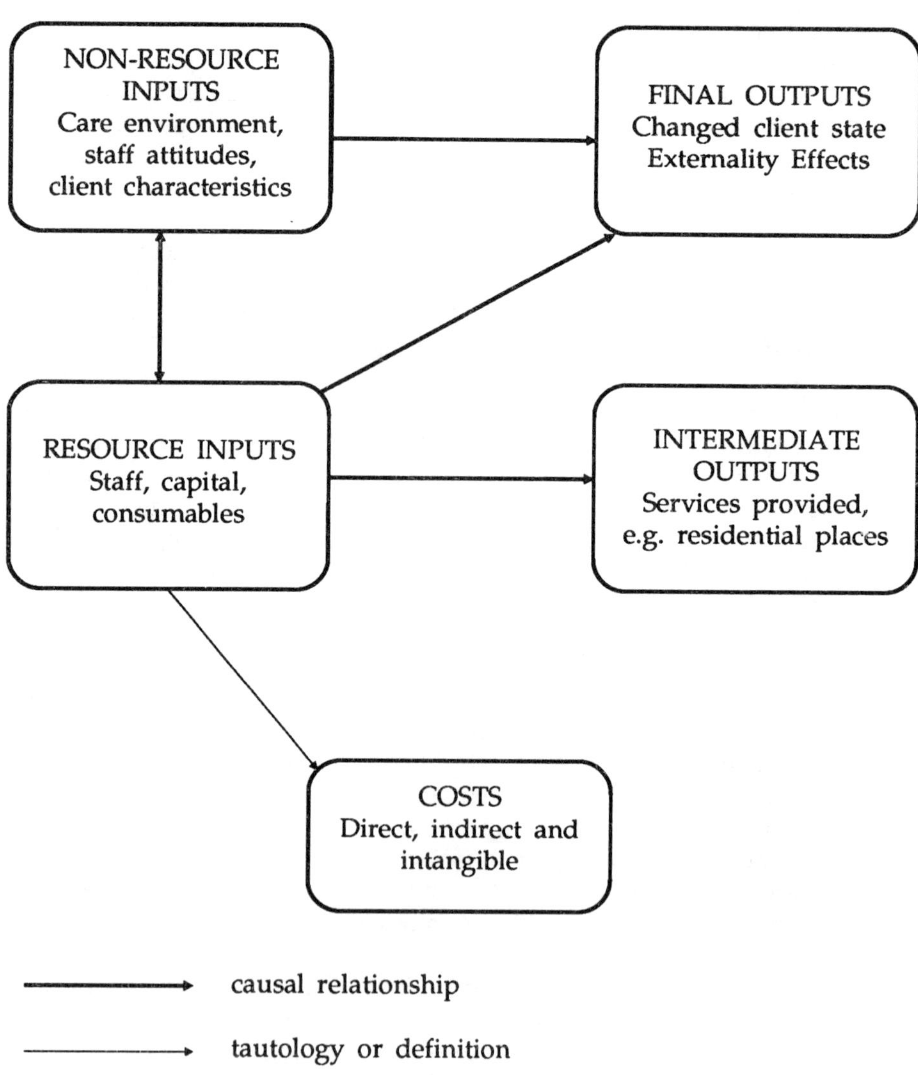

Source: Adapted from Davies and Knapp, 1981

information about projects, hospitals and clients the answers to our core research questions. It can provide the basis for a system model evaluation (Etzioni, 1960) or an experimental model (Campbell, 1957; Campbell and Stanley, 1963). It also gives us a framework with which to organise and locate previous empirical and theoretical work on community care, and health and social care more generally. (The first applications of the production of welfare approach were for the organisation and analysis of previous empirical research, and to guide secondary analyses of previously collected data. See Knapp, 1980, and Davies and Knapp, 1981. Later, the production of welfare framework provided the starting point for new data collections, most notably by Davies and Challis, 1986. See also Davies and Knapp, 1988a,b; and Knapp, 1984.)

In adopting such a theoretical perspective we most certainly do not suggest or imply that the support of people with mental health problems, physical disabilities, learning difficulties or age-related needs is one based predominantly on economic incentives, nor that it is mechanistic, nor do we seek to reduce the many inter-relationships between outcomes and costs (or inputs) to simple summary formulae. The influence and relevance of any one factor upon client or other outcomes depends on a combination of factors, the sequence in which they appear or are experienced, and the marginality of the stimulus which they bring to the care setting. We do not have the data to explore all such factors and influences here, but it is clear that any empirical study requires careful specification and complex analysis. As Szmukler concludes from a review of psychiatric research on alternatives to hospital:

> ... ultimate conclusions about the effectiveness of community service programmes may have to come about slowly and cumulatively, based on convergent findings from many individually less-than-ideal outcome studies. There are just too many variables to be taken into account for anything else to be possible (Szmukler, 1990, p.276; and see Creed et al., 1989 and Häfner and an der Heiden, 1989a).

We describe our measurement of client characteristics in Chapter 5 and the measurement of outcomes and costs in Chapters 12 to 15. Resource and non-resource inputs to the community care 'packages' for individual clients are the subject of Chapters 6 to 11. Outcomes or outputs are gauged by reference to judgements about client welfare, as far as possible in comparison with life in hospital. Many different approaches to measuring welfare have been developed, but there is some consensus as to which of a number of potential domains of outcome should be included. We used a set of measures relevant for all client groups included in the programme, as required by the DHSS, to allow inter-client group comparisons. This constrained our work, as we describe later. Client welfare was defined to move beyond symptomatology, ranging over:

- morale and life satisfaction
- skills and behaviour (including symptoms)
- social contacts
- daily activities

- personal presentation
- significant events
- life-style and living environment.

Assessment of the welfare of each client along each of these dimensions was attempted before they left hospital and again after approximately nine months in the community.

To aid understanding of outcome levels, to standardise for extraneous influences, and to 'explain' variations, we collected information on services received by clients, the physical and social environments characterising those services, the coordination of service packages, staffing levels and characteristics, and client background data (including skills, behaviour, diagnoses, and time in hospital). We built up a picture of each project from the services provided along three principal dimensions: accommodation, including physical and social environment or care regime; services received by individual clients; and information about staff training, experience, responsibilities and job satisfaction. From these service profiles, community services could be costed for individual clients, based on information about services used, whether provided by projects or obtained from elsewhere, and prices (or unit costs) based on accounts and related data. Service receipt information was collected at the same time as the follow-up client welfare information.

Research design

The design issues faced in any evaluation are complex, with contrasting views of events and experiences, the timing and breadth of the evaluation, the choice of instrumentation, the treatment of inter-personal comparisons, and the establishment of comparison groups being particular issues in need of resolution (cf. Pfeiffer, 1990). We now describe how we tackled these issues in designing the collection and interpretation of evidence.

It had to be decided *whose views* and *whose values* were to inform the evaluation. Consumerism was certainly one of the strong flavours of the 1980s, and from the outset we built user views into the methodology. An attempt was made to interview every client, preferably after careful preparation, and with privacy. (There were some communication problems, of course, as we will describe later.) With few exceptions, we did not interview relatives, this being beyond our research budget. One issue is the reliability of self-report measures of well-being or client-dominated weightings of different dimensions. If we have to rely on vicarious views, whose do we adopt? For some outcome dimensions we do *not* require the client's own view. For example, if it is relevant, the appropriateness of personal presentation, with its implications for successful integration within communities, requires an observer's rating.

Value positions must be taken at each and every stage of an evaluation: what outcome dimensions to choose; how to measure positions and changes along them; how to deal with responses; how (implicitly) to weight different outcome dimensions into an overall effectiveness perspective; how to combine these effectiveness findings with costs; how to balance efficiency and distributional criteria; and so on. Our evaluation was not value-free. *No* evaluation is value-free. What we try to do in this book is lay bare our value positions so that any biases can be seen.

Evaluations in the human services inevitably have a *time* dimension. With the focus of this study on changes in well-being from hospital to community settings, we had to make the following decisions:

- *when to start* assessing client characteristics (ideally this would be before a client moved from their 'long-stay' ward to any hospital-based rehabilitation programme),
- *when to finish* (ideally we would go on assessing changes throughout clients' lives), and
- *how often* in between (ideally continuously or at least frequently).

The ideals are impossible to achieve. We often managed hospital-based assessments, but our community assessments had to be undertaken in sufficient time to complete our final report (before the research money ran out), but far enough into the period of community residence to pick up some of the longer-term client welfare and resource consequences. The assessment in the community nine months after clients left hospital may have been too soon for the full effects of institutionalisation to have been overcome or for the impact of relocation to the community to have been registered. Continuous assessment was out of the question. We had only two observation points and therefore we had to make straight-line interpolations between them. Two is undoubtedly the usual number of observations in evaluative studies of health and social care. We are currently looking again at people with learning difficulties who moved to the community within the demonstration programme to see how they have fared during the five years since leaving hospital.

In addition to our 'snapshot' pictures we gathered *significant events* information on the more obvious departures from straight-line changes in client welfare, identifying major changes in health, employment status, social contacts and so on as they occurred. We conducted some case studies of individual clients. Linked research projects in Calderdale and Maidstone (Leedham, 1989; Haycox and Brand, 1991) and in Darlington (Challis et al., 1989) were able to gather more case-level data. The continual monitoring and support through case management and other less formal activities by projects, and our links with them, provided a wealth of qualitative data. Indeed, the descriptive and qualitative material is fundamental to the interpretation of the evaluation findings drawn from quantitative evidence.

How broad should an evaluation be? Community services for people with mental health problems, learning difficulties, age-related physical frailty and other long-term needs come from a multiplicity of agencies. Community care is a system, and there is little sense in drawing boundaries around an evaluation to exclude large parts of it. In examining the macro-organisation of a project, we need to consider the roles of the voluntary sector even if the lead agency is statutory. In measuring costs, we should not exclude the normal daily living expenses of paying for accommodation, buying food and so on. In assessing outcomes, we must not forget the impact on the community at large.

A further evaluation issue is *instrumentation*, in this case for the assessment of outcomes, resource usage and costs, environments and staffing. By instrumentation we do not simply mean the scales used in quantitative methods, but the range of observation and interview checklists employed to provide both quantitative and qualitative material. A constraint on the research was the DHSS requirement to employ a common set of (quantitative) instruments across all the client groups, in our view an error which results in poorer measurement of some aspects of client well-being than might have been expected. (Some subsequent changes were possible for use with elderly people.) Decisions on choice of instruments are always compromises between the ideal and the practical. Although this study was able to cover a wide range of dimensions, and to make use of a number of previously developed instruments which were generally piloted in Care in the Community settings, the study did not, with hindsight, use the *best* instruments, nor was piloting of every one as thorough as we would have hoped. We describe the instruments themselves as we come to use them in subsequent chapters, at which point we will note difficulties with them. We make only very limited use of those instruments which caused most concern.

Few evaluations discuss the issue of *inter-personal comparisons*: the problem of deciding how to compare (and aggregate) information across individuals. Is a unit increase in welfare measured along some well-validated scale of equal value and equal importance for everyone? Does a 10 per cent increase in the 'skills score' for a client in the West Cumbria project equate (in terms of society's perspective on client welfare) with the same increase for a client in Hillingdon, or for one of the young people in Cambridge? Does a 10 per cent increase for someone with a very low 'skills score' in hospital equate with a similar proportional increase for someone with a much higher baseline score? A lot depends on the ordinal/cardinal properties of the scales employed – something we have not yet addressed, but to which we return in Chapter 5 – but generally less-than-cardinal outcome or other measures permit only less-than-full comparisons between individuals. But even fully cardinal measures (which are extremely rare) do not tell us *how* to aggregate the outcomes, say, for different clients; they just tell us that aggregations are possible without upsetting certain desirable properties of social choice. This is not the place to dwell on the theories of measurement and collective choice. The point is that assigning every individual an equal weight in the evaluation (what has been called the 'egalitarian-humanitarian' ethic), which is what we do here, and is what is done in virtually all evaluations, is no better *in principle* than any other weighting.

Comparison groups

The final design issue concerns the choice of *comparison groups*. The ideal evaluation of a community care policy would look something like this. After assessing the impact of the move from hospital to community for an individual long-stay resident, the clock would be turned back to assess the impact on the *same* person of the move to a *different* community setting or the consequences of not moving from hospital at all. Outcome, process and cost consequences could be studied in this way and the impact measures in the different circumstances would tell us all we needed to know. A real world evaluation has to make a number of compromises to get close to this ideal, bearing in mind both the research question to be addressed and the practical constraints. Thus, if we express the ideal evaluative design in algebraic terms, we can define outcome (say) as

$$(E2 - E1) - (C2 - C1),$$

where E denotes client welfare in the (new) service under examination (perhaps termed the 'experimental group') and C denotes client welfare in some alternative (the 'control group') and 1 and 2 denote time periods (2 following 1 – a 'before-after' approach). The task is to select *appropriate* and *feasible* definitions and measures for the various concepts.

There are basically three comparative designs open to the researcher: randomised controls, constructed controls, and statistical controls, the third being available for use in combination with the other two. The basic problem is that the different

> approaches to constructing or identifying comparable control and experimental groups ... vary in feasibility, cost, and resultant clarity and validity of findings. Unfortunately, those that are best from the point of view of scientific criteria can be the most difficult to implement in practice (Rossi and Freeman, 1982, p.200).

In the 1983 Circular, the DHSS indicated that the study was to look at the effectiveness and costs of different community settings. Although comparisons with hospital were of interest, and are obviously important for the wider community care debate, our task was to concentrate on community settings. Thus, the evaluation involved comparisons of groups of people living in different community settings – that is, different 'experimental' groups. The algebraic terms E and C both refer to community settings – in fact we will need to use all of the alphabet (and more) to cover all the varieties of community care to be found across the demonstration programme – and 1 and 2 refer to hospital and community circumstances. Our study is therefore concerned with the relative merits of alternative community care arrangements, but employing before-after (hospital-community) change measures. With professional, political and social preferences over at least a 40-year period emphasising the need to reduce reliance on long-stay hospital residence for people with long-term needs and to develop good quality community care in its place, and with little known about what kinds of community care work in what circumstances, it was anyway a rational response to concentrate on this latter question. This mirrors trends elsewhere, as noted in a recent review of psychiatric research:

> There appears to have been some movement away from the preoccupation with the decline of the mental hospitals towards more concentrated efforts to wrestle with the problems of community-based care (Shepherd, 1990, p.278).

This is by no means as restrictive as it may appear at first glance. If people moving to the community are long-stay hospital residents, it is possible that their welfare would have changed little had they remained in hospital. In the algebra used above, C1 and C2 could well be identical, or nearly so, if client welfare in hospital is fairly stable. There is an additional difficulty. The hospitals from which the clients moved were altered, perhaps in fundamental ways, by these departures. Many were scheduled to close. It would be extremely difficult to find a control group living in the same hospital settings remaining unaffected by these changes. Wards may close, staff may leave (and certainly not randomly), buildings may be allowed to deteriorate, costs may rise (or fall), resident and staff morale may fall (or rise), the remaining staff will spend more (or less) of their time than before on rehabilitative work, and so on. The hospital control group necessary for the experimental comparison of hospital and community services with random allocation of clients to hospital or community services quite possibly does not exist. In the Darlington project, patients in a neighbouring health authority were used in a quasi-experimental design to provide the best available comparison group (Challis et al., 1989). However, for reasons of both research commissioning and practicalities, our focus for all other projects had to be the comparison of different community care settings.

If we were laboratory scientists, we could define the target population of hospital residents who could move to the community and randomly allocate them to alternative settings. Each hospital resident within the target population would have the same chance of being selected for any of the community settings, and, provided enough people were studied, any differences between groups or settings would be due to the settings themselves, together with the usual random error. Randomised designs are common and effective where conditions or influence make randomisation easy, and when comparing relatively few explanatory variables. But they raise difficulties. They are unable to allow for structural factors within projects or organisations, and only with a number of large projects which could randomly assign *within* their areas would the design have been of assistance. A common qualm is that randomisation gives rise to the ethical (and political) problem of deliberately withholding care from half of the individuals being studied: 'arbitrarily and capriciously depriving control groups of positive benefits' (Rossi and Freeman, 1982, p.216), or 'fooling around with people' (Gilbert et al., 1975, p.148). Of course, we do not always *know* that positive benefits are associated with the care received by the experimental group (hence the evaluation in the first place), but the ethical issue may remain nonetheless.

With randomised designs it is necessary to obtain the voluntary cooperation of both clients and carers, and to maintain the distinction between the experimental and control interventions for the duration of the study. There was almost no chance of persuading health and local authorities to randomly allocate clients, even to different community settings within the same area, at the outset of the programme. Discharge decisions were taken by multidisciplinary combinations of hospital and community personnel, in consultation with clients and sometimes relatives. The researchers could have no influence, and randomisation was out of the question. Projects deliberately sought to match people and placements, including moving groups of friends together into community settings. Given the range of needs displayed in hospital, some clearly chose to first move the more independent or less expensive, either because their community budgets could only cope with such clients or to reduce local opposition from relatives, clinicians and politicians to *any* moves from hospital. Even if randomisation had been achieved in the first instance, maintaining the distinction between the different services would have been problematic. There could have been research contamination of the experimental and control groups because of the difficulties of keeping the two groups apart. Care programmes are unlikely to remain invariant over time, particularly if information leaks back to agencies or carers who, quite reasonably, wish to change to perceived best practice to improve client welfare.

In the circumstances surrounding the launch of the Care in the Community programme, in the deliberate glare of publicity, in the context of only a slow move to community care (at that time), and coupled with charges made in a number of well-publicised reports that joint finance programmes were insufficiently monitored, randomisation was not possible. The Care in the Community pilot programme was not, therefore, a classical experiment, nor was it exactly a natural experiment, but it still offers excellent evaluative potential.

The approach adopted is tantamount to a *quasi-experimental design* with statistical rather than constructed controls, although perhaps the more general *observational study* (Cochran, 1983) might be a more appropriate description. The approach also has some similarities to the *cross-institutional design* (Sinclair and Clarke, 1981). The aim to is to make the various groups of community care clients comparable through appropriate statistical analysis and standardisation. This is not only a more feasible and politically acceptable design than randomisation in the circumstances, it is also offers valuable additional insights often missed with randomisation (Goldberg, 1990). Although there will be some people looking for the community care equivalent of the elusive 'Brand X' which washes whiter than white, the great majority of people are rightly interested in what appears to work best *for whom* and *in what circumstances*. Adult fostering or supported lodgings placements may well turn out to be more appropriate than other settings for some people, but certainly not for all, and the quasi-experimental design with statistical controls forces us to ask these questions of the data. Every pilot project went to some lengths to tailor services to individual needs. Success may sometimes have been elusive, but it would have been absurd for the research design to ignore the individuality of care programmes and inter-client differences in outcomes, service packages, costs, and situational and confounding variables.

Statistical controls pose the considerable problem of obtaining data on every factor which might have an influence on the characteristic being studied (say, client welfare). This problem is no less severe with constructed controls (matching), but will not arise with perfect randomisation.

What, then, are the factors which need to be measured and subsequently employed in the standardisation of results? If we return to the production of welfare framework set out earlier we have suggestions for the kinds of factors which may be relevant, gathered there under the resource and non-resource input heads, though obviously in need of detailed specification. We draw on this framework later in the book.

The evaluation examines a number of overlapping samples of clients:

- *Baseline*: The baseline sample comprises all long-stay hospital residents identified as possible project clients and for whom some data were collected in hospital. Many baseline people did not move to the community during the study period; conversely some who did move were missed from the baseline. The baseline assessments and interviews give us the 'Time One' (T1) data.
- *Movers*: The sample of movers comprises all people assessed in hospital who later moved to the community under the auspices of the programme. By definition the movers are all members of the baseline.
- *Community*: The community sample comprises all clients for and from whom we obtained data about welfare and circumstances in the community. These data collections were intended to be conducted nine months after each client moved from hospital. The community assessments and interviews comprise the 'Time Two' (T2) data.
- *Follow-up*: The follow-up sample includes everyone for whom we have both T1 and T2 data.
- *Costed*: The costed sample comprises every client for whom we collected service utilisation data and calculated costs in the community. This sample need not necessarily be completely contained within any other sample although in practice we did not attempt to collect service utilisation information if other (prior) data had not been gathered.

It is impossible to summarise sample sizes succinctly because of variations in numbers by client group and by instrument. The basic scale of the evaluation is indicated by our working with more than 35 different district health authorities, 27 social services authorities, at least as many voluntary organisations, more than 50 hospitals (and over 300 wards within them), and more than 300 community living settings. All of these many sites combine to provide unique physical, political and professional combinations for the study of well over 1,000 hospital residents, most of whom moved into the community, and hundreds of staff members employed by projects or associated with them. Our monitoring role alone required that we included every facility and individual. Response rates were less than perfect for a number of reasons – clients unable or unwilling to communicate their views to us, people moving from hospital at very short notice ruling out baseline assessments, project delays in establishing community services making it too late for follow-up interviews to be conducted, or cases missed through clerical error, and occasionally non-cooperation of hospital and community managers and staff.

From demonstration to implementation

With demonstration programmes the links between evaluation results and their generalisation for wider implementation are not straightforward. This is, perhaps,

> because they employ special start-up funds, enjoy the non-specific 'Hawthorne effects' of being part of an experiment, and benefit from the contributions of charismatic individuals. They may treat only a sub-population of patients, and may not be able to sustain their initial enthusiastic momentum (Thornicroft and Bebbington, 1989, p.740).

For the Care in the Community programme, some of these potential complications were themselves demonstration tests. For example, the special funds received by projects offered an opportunity to test the effects on the initiation and continuation of support programmes of having financial resources at the right time in the right place. This, it will be recalled, is a familiar lament in the British community care debate. The special funds for this programme are included in the cost calculations later in the book, so that we have the opportunity to examine how far the programme's (comprehensive) costs are out of step with provision elsewhere. (The answer is 'not very much', and 'not at all' for some client groups.) Charismatic individuals *were* important in the programme, and their effects will need to be noted, but it is better to look for ways of recruiting more such people than simply to rule them out as confounding influences. Asking local managers to answer monitoring questions, particularly at meetings where several agencies sat at the same table, sometimes made them focus for the first time on key issues. This needs to be recognised as a Hawthorne effect of sorts, but it also points to a need for community care managers to be primed to think through the relevant issues, as in the community care planning requirements in the 1990 Act. We will come back to the generalisability of the demonstration programme experience later in the book, especially in the final chapter.

Rightly, the Care in the Community programme did not launch a 'sink or swim' experiment: it was a supported, monitored programme designed to explore successful avenues of care (and some cul-de-sacs) – to show what *could* be done, and to understand the circumstances in which this was achieved. The political and professional reservations about community care in the early 1980s, the difficulties of finding 'typical' long-stay settings in hospitals generally destined for closure, and – fundamentally – the strong preferences held by policy-makers, projects, and ourselves for concentrating research effort on the evaluation of different community care arrangements, combined to produce the design selected for this study. Our evaluation had to be broad, ranging from organisational process to individual client characteristics. Because strategic change in service systems and expectations of individual client changes were central interests, the evaluation demanded a longitudinal study. A key task was to try to identify transportable lessons from the pilot projects, whether they applied to strategic organisation and development, individual care plans, the style and technique of working, or the goals and assumptions which lay behind them. We sought to discover what processes of intervention at the service delivery level were associated with cost-effective outcomes for clients.

The commission from the DHSS included promotion and monitoring as well as evaluation, so our evaluative work has not been a hands-off exercise. It was built on six years of liaison with the DHSS and four or more years of collaborative working with the pilot projects. The findings reported in subsequent chapters were generated from structured and unstructured interviews with clients, care staff and managers, from observation, and from desk-based research and analysis, and were informed by our interpretation of research conducted elsewhere.

5 People and lives in hospital

Who were the people whose lives and welfare the programme aimed to improve? What lives were they leading before they moved to the community? Who was selected by projects to make the transition from hospital *patient* to community care *client*? Were the people who were selected different from those who were not? What do such differences imply for generalisations outside the demonstration programme?

These questions are addressed in this chapter. We describe the characteristics of people and lives before discharge into the community, providing a baseline from which to judge the relative successes and failures of the Care in the Community programme. The focus will be clients and their characteristics and their life-styles in hospital. In the nomenclature of the evaluation methodology, this chapter is concerned with the situation at 'Time 1', later to be compared with the situation at 'Time 2'.

The first section of the chapter presents basic demographic information on residents assessed as candidates for pilot projects. Clinical information and reason for admission to hospital are covered in the next section. The chapter then briefly describes residents' lives in hospital, built on data about length of stay, contacts with the outside world and satisfaction with services. We also look at measures of satisfaction with life in general. (Chapters 12 to 15 examine how client satisfaction changed between hospital and community.) The fourth section examines residents' skills, behaviour and personal presentation, factors associated with dependency and need for care, and factors which could affect the success and cost of integration into the community.

Two groups of residents are distinguished in the discussions which follow: the *movers*, who were assessed and selected for inclusion in pilot projects, and the *stayers*, who were assessed but remained in hospital. We naturally devote more attention to movers – there are implications for project organisation, resource allocation, outcomes and costs – although examination of stayers and comparisons across the two groups are also fruitful. We will begin an examination of selection criteria and methods, looking at these in more detail in Chapter 10. Did projects select clients so as to be representative of the hospital population, or were there systematic differences between movers and stayers? If differences are considerable it will be harder to generalise from the programme to the *long*-term pursuit of hospital rundown and community care. In the final section of the chapter we examine the combinations of factors associated with the selection of movers. At that stage we will concentrate on people with learning difficulties.

Background characteristics

The demonstration programme was to cover a number of adult groups: people with learning difficulties, people with mental health problems, elderly physically frail people, elderly people with mental health problems, young people with multiple disabilities, and people with physical disabilities. Much of what we describe in this section for the first four of these client groups is summarised in Tables 5.1 to 5.4. (These tables are largely self-explanatory, and we pull out only general findings.) The other two client groups were served by one project each within the programme. The three young clients of the Cambridge project are described in the text, but no background information was collected for the three physically disabled clients in Glossop. (In this section and elsewhere, we will not always report findings for these two small projects for reasons of confidentiality.)

We made no attempt to conduct full-hospital surveys; recent surveys by Levene et al. (1985), TAPS (1988), Clifford et al. (1991) and Lorna Wing (1989) can be used to compare our findings for smaller samples. Given the sheer scale (and geographical spread) of the programme, poor record-keeping in some hospitals, reluctance to make information available, and occasionally the speed with which some hospital residents became project clients, the sample sizes are sometimes small relative to the total number of movers, and certainly relative to the full hospital population. For instance, the sample of people with mental health problems for whom some of the information on resident background and life in hospital could be obtained is equivalent to 22 per cent of the full baseline sample. This is large enough to illustrate whom projects hoped to move to the community, and for exploratory testing of differences between movers and stayers, but this should be remembered when interpreting the results. Measurement of resident welfare yielded a larger sample, partly because staff did not need to search for resident records.

The stayers sample is smaller than the movers sample for all client groups. This is because a number of projects identified as potential movers only those hospital residents who eventually moved. It was never possible to gather data on full hospital populations. Another reason for limited data on the stayers is suggested by noticing that, for all client groups, the proportion of stayers among the baseline sample for whom we have full background information was smaller than the proportion of stayers among the full baseline. Thus one of the characteristics of the stayers seems to be their anonymity.

Gender

None of the Care in the Community projects displayed any preference for one gender over another in selecting clients *from the pool of residents assessed* as candidates for discharge. This is shown by the fact that there was no statistically

Table 5.1

Hospital resident background information: people with learning difficulties

	Stayers		*Movers*		Probability of no difference between stayers and movers	*Baseline*	
	Percentage 'Yes' responses	Sample size	Percentage 'Yes' responses	Sample size		Percentage 'Yes' responses	Sample size
Client is male	40	47	47	180	.548	45	227
Is borough of origin the same as borough of project?	70	27	83	123	.220	81	150
Level of handicap							
Profound or severe	33	33	50	104	.141	46	137
Moderate	30	33	31	104	1.000	31	137
Mild	36	33	19	104	.073*	23	137

	Stayers		*Movers*		Probability of no difference between stayers and movers	*Baseline*	
	Mean	Sample size	Mean	Sample size		Mean	Sample size
Age at beginning of funding round	48	46	40 [1]	177	.001**	41	223
Age at onset of learning difficulty	4	24	9 [2]	92	.287	3	116

Total number in baseline = 529

* Difference is significant at 10 per cent.

** Difference is significant at 1 per cent.

1 Minimum 16, median 38, maximum 75.

2 Minimum and median 0, maximum 51.

Table 5.2

Hospital resident background information: people with mental health problems

	Stayers		*Movers*		Probability of no difference between stayers and movers	*Baseline*	
	Percentage 'Yes' responses	Sample size	Percentage 'Yes' responses	Sample size		Percentage 'Yes' responses	Sample size
Client is male	63	16	63	72	1.000	63	88
Is borough of origin the same as borough of project?	70	10	79	65	.850	77	75
Diagnosis							
Schizophrenia	75	16	82	71	.794	81	87
Affective disorder	25	16	10	71	.219	13	87
Personality disorder (inc. alcoholic)	0	16	6	71	.756	5	87
Organic	0	16	1	71	1.000	1	87
Other diagnosis	0	16	1	71	1.000	1	87

	Stayers		*Movers*		Probability of no difference between stayers and movers	*Baseline*	
	Mean	Sample size	Mean	Sample size		Mean	Sample size
Age at beginning of funding round	50	16	48 [1]	72	.490	48	88
Age at onset of disorder	29	14	25 [2]	70	.116	25	84

Total number in baseline = 407

1 Minimum 22, median 50, maximum 69.

2 Minimum 8, median 22.5, maximum 55.

Table 5.3

Hospital resident background information: elderly people with physical frailty

	Stayers Percentage 'Yes' responses	*Stayers* Sample size	*Movers* Percentage 'Yes' responses	*Movers* Sample size	Probability of no difference between stayers and movers	*Baseline* Percentage 'Yes' responses	*Baseline* Sample size
Client is male	47	17	33	139	.253	35	156
Is borough of origin the same as borough of project?	–[1]	0	96	132	–[2]	96	132
Source of admission							
Residential home	0	15	5	108	.878	4	123
Private housing – living alone	47	15	32	108	.381	33	123
Private housing – living with spouse, family or friends	53	15	54	108	1.000	54	108
Sheltered housing	0	15	7	108	.674	6	123
Other source	0	15	4	108	1.000	3	123

	Stayers Mean	*Stayers* Sample size	*Movers* Mean	*Movers* Sample size	Probability of no difference between stayers and movers	*Baseline* Mean	*Baseline* Sample size
Age at beginning of funding round	76	17	78[3]	108	.488	78	125

Total number in baseline = 171

1 No data.

2 Insufficient data.

3 Minimum 63, median 77, maximum 100.

Table 5.4
Hospital resident background information: elderly people with mental health problems (movers sample only)

	Movers[1]	
	Percentage 'Yes' responses	Sample size
Client is male	27	77
Is borough of origin the same as borough of project?	97	29
Source of admission		
Residential home	18	74
Nursing home	18	74
Private housing – living alone	30	74
Private housing – living with spouse, family or friends	28	74
Sheltered housing	3	74
Hotel	1	74
Other source	3	74

	Movers	
	Mean	Sample size
Age at beginning of funding round	79[2]	60

Total number in baseline = 97
1 Results are reported for movers only because there was only one stayer with client background information in the baseline.
2 Minimum 66, median 79, maximum 90.

significant difference between the proportions of men in the stayers and movers cohorts. (The significance of the difference between movers and stayers indicates the probability that such a difference occurred by chance.) Significance at 10 per cent (or 1 per cent) indicates that there was less than a 1 in 10 (1 in 100) chance that the difference occurred by chance. There was a higher proportion of men (62.5 per cent of both movers and stayers) in the group of people with mental health problems than in any of the other client groups. There is generally a preponderance of men in the long-stay wards of psychiatric hospitals (for example, see TAPS, 1988). There were particularly high proportions of women in the elderly client groups, although these were not out of line with population demography.

Age

The youngest adult client group were people with learning difficulties. Half of the movers were aged under 39, with a range from 16 to 75. Movers were younger than stayers (a statistically significant difference). The age range for movers with mental health problems was narrower (22 to 69) around a higher average (mean 48, median 50). The three Cambridge project clients were aged 11, 12 and 15. As with other client groups, the ages reported here are those at the beginning of their project's funding round (April 1984 for first-round projects and April 1985 for others). At the other end of the age range, the elderly clients were generally well into their seventies (means of 78 and 79). For elderly physically frail people, age ranged from 63 to 100; for elderly people with mental health problems, the range was 66 to 90.

Projects for people with learning difficulties appeared to favour younger people in choosing from those assessed. Those who remained in hospital had an average age of 48 compared to 40 for those who left (significant at 0.1 per cent). This difference will be discussed later in the chapter. There were no significant age differences between movers and stayers in the other client groups.

Source of admission

For elderly residents and clients we used slightly different instrumentation. Because most had been resident in hospital for much shorter periods than people in other client groups (see below) we were able to gather information about the circumstances of admission. Most elderly people had moved to hospital from private housing where they had been living with spouse, family or friends (54 per cent of elderly physically frail residents; 28 per cent of elderly people with mental health problems). About a third had been living alone in their own homes immediately before admission to hospital, and comparatively few came from specialised sheltered housing schemes. Elderly people with mental health problems were the more likely to have been admitted from residential or nursing homes (18 per cent from each).

Reasons for admission to hospital

What was the 'nature of the problem' which caused the people in our study to enter hospital? We asked for information on the most recent admission (which started the episode which, for movers, ended when they became Care in the Community clients).

The overwhelming diagnostic category for people with mental health problems was schizophrenia (82 per cent of those who moved). Just under 10 per cent of the movers sample had affective disorders, 6 per cent a personality disorder, and 1 per cent 'another diagnosis'. On average, these residents had been in their mid-20s when their health problem first arose (mean age at onset of 25 for movers).

The schedule on which information on elderly people was collected asked for 'reason for admission to hospital'. Among movers to projects for elderly physically frail people, the most commonly *identified* reason was stroke (28 per cent), and others were senile dementia (2 per cent), heart disease (2 per cent), chest disease (4 per cent), cancer (6 per cent) and fractured femur (3 per cent). The majority of people in the other elderly client group had been admitted because of senile dementia (88 per cent).

For people with learning difficulties we asked ward staff to indicate 'level of handicap' (as phrased at the time), distinguishing just four categories (profound, severe, moderate, mild). Responses thus represent subjective ratings of a large number of staff, but nevertheless give a good general indication of severity of learning difficulty. Only two of the 137 people for whom we had data were rated as profoundly disabled, and both moved to the community. The movers had a larger proportion of people in the profound or severe categories compared to stayers (50 per cent to 33 per cent), and a significantly smaller proportion in the mild category. However, analyses of other data later in this chapter show that it tended to be the less dependent rather than more dependent clients who were selected to move to the community. Age at onset (or formal recognition) of disability was very low (mean of 2.4 years for movers, with just over three-quarters born with learning difficulty). Age at onset of learning difficulty bore no apparent relation to whether or not a client was discharged. All of the Cambridge clients had been disabled since birth.

Life on the inside and links with the outside

It is widely held that residents of long-stay hospitals frequently live in physical and social isolation from the outside community (Goffman, 1961; Blatt and Kaplan, 1966; Morris, 1969; Rivera, 1972; Jones et al., 1975; Ryan and Thomas, 1980). The long-stay hospital develops a social structure of its own, with the residents often becoming 'institutionalised'. This was a major concern for the Care in the Community projects because of the challenges it would pose for successful rehabilitation. They sought various solutions to help former residents adopt modes of behaviour appropriate to life outside hospital, and to discard behaviours peculiar to institutions. In the next section we look at residents' views on life in hospital, but first we show how long-stay hospital residents lived in relative isolation, with few and often weak links with the outside community. Tables 5.5 to 5.8 summarise the statistical evidence.

Life inside hospital

Length of stay. For residents with learning difficulties or mental health problems, basic data on length of current stay in hospital suggest considerable dislocation from the wider community. Half the sample with learning difficulties had been in hospital for at least 20 years, with mean (and median) duration of residence since the most recent admission of 21 years for movers (22 for stayers). One person had spent 58 years in hospital, continuously resident since early childhood. The shortest stay in hospital was one year.

The picture is scarcely less striking for people with mental health problems, although average length of stay was lower: mean of 16 years for movers, median 12 years. This average is lower than that found for the full hospital populations of people with similar characteristics – not short-stay and not with a diagnosis of senile dementia. For example, the average for two North London hospitals was found to be 21 years (TAPS, 1988), and in five other hospitals it was 25 years (Clifford et al., 1991). Information was not readily available on length of stay for stayers. Half the sample had spent 12 years or more in hospital since they were last admitted. The shortest duration of current admission was ten months, and the longest 45 years. For both client groups, these data refer only to the *most recent admission* to hospital. Many people had been admitted more than once.

Previous admissions. For all people with mental health problems in the baseline sample, the mean number of previous admissions to the hospital of residence was 3.3, while for those who moved out within the demonstration programme the mean was 3.4 (median 1.8). Forty-five per cent of all movers had experienced more than one admission to their last hospital, the highest being 15 admissions (43 per cent had been admitted to other hospitals). Many had spent a substantial proportion of their life in hospital.

People with learning difficulties are not so likely to have had repeated admissions to hospital. Once admitted to hospital they usually remain there, with fewer discharges and readmissions. Almost half had experienced no previous admissions, and only 5 per cent of movers had more than three previous admissions. The highest number recorded was 21. Forty-six per cent had spent time in other hospitals.

Most elderly clients of the programme, and also those stayers in the baseline sample, appeared to have 'presenting problems' or symptoms which arose in old age. Mean duration of current admissions for elderly physically frail people was only six months, and half of the sample had been in hospital for less than ten weeks. (This statistic is particularly influenced by the Darlington project, which worked with comparatively few people who could be called long-stay residents.) Longest duration of current admission was 4.5 years. Sixty per cent had not previously been admitted to their last hospital. For elderly people with mental health problems, average duration of current admission was longer (18 months), and half had spent six months or more in hospital. The longest continuous duration was 19 years. Almost half had never previously been admitted to hospital.

Table 5.5

Life in hospital: people with learning difficulties

	Stayers		*Movers*		Probability of	*Baseline*	
	Percentage 'Yes' responses	Sample size	Percentage 'Yes' responses	Sample size	no difference between stayers and movers	Percentage 'Yes' responses	Sample size
Has patient been admitted to other hospitals?	54	41	46	142	.527	48	183
Nature of contact with family or friends who live outside hospital							
Any contact with parent?	40	47	54	180	.121	52	227
Any contact with sibling?	38	47	31	180	.403	32	227
Any contact with other relative or friend?	15	47	14	180	1.000	15	227
Does anyone take the client home?	26	47	41	180	.084*	37	227
Does anyone visit the client in hospital?	55	47	58	180	.890	57	227
Does anyone telephone the client?	23	47	31	180	.435	29	227
Does anyone write to client?	21	47	26	180	.623	25	227
Any contact with parent in person at least weekly?	19	47	19	180	1.000	19	227
Any contact with parent not in person at least weekly?	6	47	7	180	1.000	7	227
Any contact with parent in person less than weekly?	15	47	26	180	.157	24	227
Any contact with parent not in person less than weekly	9	47	13	180	.581	12	227
Any contact with sibling in person at least weekly?	2	47	2	180	1.000	2	227
Any contact with sibling not in person at least weekly?	4	47	1	180	.403	2	227
Any contact with sibling in person less than weekly?	13	47	12	180	1.000	12	227
Any contact with sibling not in person less than weekly	9	47	10	180	.976	10	227

Any contact with other relative or friend in person at least weekly?	0	47	2	180	.862	1	227
Any contact with other relative or friend not in person at least weekly?	0	47	1	180	1.000	1	227
Any contact with other relative or friend in person less than weekly?	9	47	2	180	.052*	3	227
Any contact with other relative or friend not in person less than weekly	4	47	3	180	1.000	4	227

	Stayers		*Movers*		**Probability of no difference between stayers and movers**	*Baseline*	
	Mean	**Sample size**	**Mean**	**Sample size**		**Mean**	**Sample size**
Duration of current admission (years)	22	46	21[1]	180	.801	22	202
No. of previous admissions to this hospital	1	47	1[2]	180	.651	1	227
No. of contacts with friends or family per year	120	31	128[3]	80	.823	126	166

* Difference is significant at 10 per cent.
Total number in baseline = 529
1 Minimum 1, median 21, maximum 58.
2 Minimum 0, median 0, maximum 21.
3 Minimum 1, median 32, maximum 912.

Table 5.6

Life in hospital: people with mental health problems

	Stayers		*Movers*		Probability of	*Baseline*	
	Percentage 'Yes' responses	Sample size	Percentage 'Yes' responses	Sample size	no difference between stayers and movers	Percentage 'Yes' responses	Sample size
Is there any history of imprisonment?	13	16	11	71	1.000	12	87
Has patient been admitted to other hospitals?	31	16	43	68	.581	41	84
Nature of contact with family or friends who live outside hospital							
Any contact with parent?	19	16	29	72	.592	27	72
Any contact with sibling?	25	16	29	72	.592	27	88
Any contact with spouse?	6	16	1	72	.800	2	88
Any contact with other relative or friend?	44	16	22	72	.144	18	88
Does anyone take the client home?	25	16	31	72	.891	30	88
Does anyone visit the client in hospital?	31	16	46	72	.432	43	88
Does anyone telephone the client?	19	16	21	72	1.000	21	88
Does anyone write to client?	13	16	21	72	.679	19	88
Any contact with parent in person at least weekly?	6	16	15	72	.583	14	88
Any contact with parent not in person at least weekly?	0	16	6	72	.763	5	88
Any contact with parent in person less than weekly?	6	16	4	72	1.000	5	88
Any contact with parent not in person less than weekly	0	16	3	72	1.000	2	88
Any contact with sibling in person at least weekly?	0	16	3	72	1.000	2	88
Any contact with sibling not in person at least weekly?	0	16	3	72	1.000	2	88
Any contact with sibling in person less than weekly?	19	16	19	72	1.000	19	88

Any contact with sibling not in person less than weekly	13	16	8	72	.965	9	88
Any contact with parent in person at least weekly?	0	16	0	72	1.000	0	88
Any contact with parent not in person at least weekly?	0	16	0	72	1.000	0	88
Any contact with parent in person less than weekly?	0	16	1	72	1.000	1	88
Any contact with parent not in person less than weekly	6	16	0	72	1.000	1	88
Any contact with other relative or friend in person at least weekly?	6	16	1	72	.800	2	88
Any contact with other relative or friend not in person at least weekly?	0	16	1	72	1.000	1	88
Any contact with other relative or friend in person less than weekly?	13	16	11	72	1.000	11	88
Any contact with other relative or friend not in person less than weekly	13	16	8	72	.965	9	88

	Stayers		***Movers***		**Probability of no difference between stayers and movers**	***Baseline***	
	Mean	**Sample size**	**Mean**	**Sample size**		**Mean**	**Sample size**
Duration of current admission (years)	No data	0	16[1]	66	Insufficient data	16	66
No. of previous admissions to this hospital	3.1	16	3.2[2]	69	.793	3.3	85

Total number in baseline = 407

1 Minimum 1, median 12, maximum 45.

2 Minimum 0, median 1.8, maximum 15.

Table 5.7
Life in hospital: elderly people with physical frailty

	Stayers		*Movers*		Probability of no difference between stayers and movers	*Baseline*	
	Percentage 'Yes' responses	Sample size	Percentage 'Yes' responses	Sample size		Percentage 'Yes' responses	Sample size
Has patient been admitted to other hospitals?	No data	0	82	27	Insufficient data	82	27
Nature of contact with family or friends who live outside hospital							
Any contact with sibling?	0	17	7	139	.596	6	156
Any contact with spouse?	0	17	1	139	1.000	1	156
Any contact with child?	0	17	16	139	.161	14	156
Any contact with other relative or friend?	0	17	14	139	.217	12	156
Does anyone take the client home?	0	17	4	139	.948	3	156
Does anyone visit the client in hospital?	0	17	23	139	.057*	21	156
Does anyone telephone the client?	0	17	13	139	.240	12	156
Does anyone write to client?	0	17	8	139	.611	7	156
Any contact with sibling in person at least weekly?	0	17	2	139	1.000	2	156
Any contact with sibling not in person at least weekly?	0	17	1	139	1.000	1	156
Any contact with sibling in person less than weekly?	0	17	1	139	1.000	1	156
Any contact with sibling not in person less than weekly	0	17	1	139	1.000	1	156
Any contact with spouse in person at least weekly?	0	17	0	139	1.000	0	156
Any contact with spouse not in person at least weekly?	0	17	0	139	1.000	0	156
Any contact with spouse in person less than weekly?	0	17	1	139	1.000	1	156

Any contact with spouse not in person less than weekly	0	17	1	139	1.000	1	156
Any contact with child in person at least weekly?	0	17	14	139	.229	12	156
Any contact with child not in person at least weekly?	0	17	9	139	.364	8	156
Any contact with child in person less than weekly?	0	17	1	139	1.000	1	156
Any contact with child not in person less than weekly	0	17	1	139	1.000	1	156
Any contact with other relative or friend in person at least weekly?	0	17	17	139	.076*	15	156
Any contact with other relative or friend not in person at least weekly?	0	17	9	139	.363	8	156
Any contact with other relative or friend in person less than weekly?	0	17	4	139	1.000	3	156
Any contact with other relative or friend not in person less than weekly	0	17	2	139	1.000	2	156

	Stayers		*Movers*		**Probability of no difference between stayers and movers**	*Baseline*	
	Mean	**Sample size**	**Mean**	**Sample size**		**Mean**	**Sample size**
Duration of current admission (years)	No data	0	0.5[1]	134	Insufficient data	0.5	134
No. of previous admissions to this hospital	No data	0	0.8[2]	26	Insufficient data	0.8	26

Total number in baseline = 171
* Difference is significant at 10 per cent.
1 Minimum 0.1 years, median 0.2 years, maximum 4.5 years.
2 Minimum 0, median 0, maximum 5.

Table 5.8
Life in hospital: elderly people with mental health problems (movers sample only)

	Movers	
	Percentage 'Yes' responses	**Sample size**
Has patient been admitted to other hospitals?	28	47
Nature of contact with family or friends who live outside hospital		
Any contact with sibling?	14	77
Any contact with spouse?	18	77
Any contact with child	73	77
Any contact with other relative or friend?	35	77
Does anyone take the client home?	17	77
Does anyone visit the client in hospital?	83	77
Does anyone telephone the client?	20	77
Does anyone write to client?	5	77
Any contact with sibling in person at least weekly?	8	77
Any contact with sibling not in person at least weekly?	0	77
Any contact with sibling in person less than weekly?	1	77
Any contact with sibling not in person less than weekly	0	77
Any contact with spouse in person at least weekly?	10	77
Any contact with spouse not in person at least weekly?	1	77
Any contact with spouse in person less than weekly?	3	77
Any contact with spouse not in person less than weekly	1	77
Any contact with child in person at least weekly?	43	77
Any contact with child not in person at least weekly?	10	77
Any contact with child in person less than weekly?	13	77
Any contact with child not in person less than weekly	5	77
Any contact with other relative or friend in person at least weekly?	60	77
Any contact with other relative or friend not in person at least weekly?	12	77
Any contact with other relative or friend in person less than weekly?	16	77
Any contact with other relative or friend not in person less than weekly	7	77

	Movers	
	Mean	**Sample size**
Duration of current admission (years)	1.5[1]	70
No. of previous admissions to this hospital	0.9[2]	70

Total number in baseline = 97
1 Minimum 0.1, median 0.5, maximum 18.7.
3 Minimum 0, median 0, maximum 4.

Previous imprisonment. Eleven per cent of people with mental health problems who moved to pilot projects had been in prison at some stage in their lives. This proportion was not significantly different from those remaining in hospital.

Hospital environments. We developed and employed the Environment Checklist to rate hospital and community settings. Ratings were done by PSSRU interviewers. The instrument is fully described in Chapter 8, where we show how the surroundings in which people lived changed very considerably when they moved from hospital to community. The hospital characteristics revealed will surprise few people. In the majority of cases, hospitals stood in stark relief from surrounding buildings (85 per cent were readily identifiable from their surroundings), most were poorly located relative to ordinary community facilities, and almost all were rated as institutional and unpleasant. One of our researchers noted the following on a visit to a hospital from which some programme clients moved:

> The hospital has all the classic features of an institution. Everything is big. The grounds are vast, very attractive and beautifully maintained. The buildings are big, spartan and generally uninviting. There are wrought iron fire escapes, rows of massive dustbins, iron fences, trolleys of hospital laundry, a tall chimney and massive verandahs. The numerous signs stress that this is no ordinary residence and that the people who live here are 'different'. Next to the car park is the sign 'SLOW! MENTALLY HANDICAPPED PATIENTS CROSSING' (Leedham, 1989, appendix 7.2, p.4).

Most hospital rooms had an institutional appearance, bedrooms offered only limited privacy, and displays of individuality were comparatively few. Interviewers noted unacceptably high noise levels in a third of the mental handicap hospitals. More than a quarter of these hospitals also had age-inappropriate fittings and decor. Unacceptable smells were reported in a third, and in 43 per cent of hospitals for elderly people.

Links with the outside

To what extent and in what ways were hospital residents in contact with the outside world? What was their experience of the way of life of people on the other side of the hospital walls, the way of life many of them might hope for themselves? Did those who eventually moved out already have stronger links with the community than those left behind?

In most projects we carried out a fairly detailed analysis of contacts between residents and their relatives and friends outside hospital. Our data showed who had contact, what form it took, and frequency. For each group of relatives or friends, we examined whether they visited in person (defined as visiting the client in hospital or taking them home) or not in person (telephone calls or letters), and whether the contact took place more or less than weekly.

(Analysis of the data showed that proportions of contact weekly and less frequently were roughly equal.) With these data we can examine levels of contact for hospital residents, but we cannot comment on the willingness or ability of relatives or friends to make contact, for we do not know how many surviving relatives, for example, each resident had.

Clients with *learning difficulties* were more likely to have links with their parents than with anyone else. Over half the movers had contact with at least one parent, although parental contact was likely to be less than weekly. Face-to-face contact was the most common form of parental contact. Only 14 per cent of people who later moved to a project had any contact while in hospital with relatives or friends who were not parents or siblings. Contact with distant relatives was generally infrequent, usually taking the form of a letter or phone call. The movers sample enjoyed significantly more visits to the homes of relatives or friends while in hospital than the stayers (41 per cent compared to 26 per cent). More than half the clients with learning difficulties had no recent experience of a non-institutional, domestic environment. Overall, about four-fifths of people with learning difficulties lacked recent, regular or close contact with the outside world.

People with *mental health problems* were even *more* isolated. Less than half had any outside contact at all. For many of the indicators the proportions with outside contacts were not significantly different from zero. Where contact had been maintained with a parent, it was likely to be at least weekly, but 70 per cent had no parental contact at all. Siblings tended to make less frequent contact. For the two clients who had contact with their spouse, this was infrequent. All relatives and friends tended to visit clients or take them home rather than write or phone.

Elderly physically frail people were the most isolated. None of the 17 stayers and 77 per cent of the movers for whom we gathered data had any contact with family or friends. The movers with outside contacts received visits in the hospital, mainly from their children, and usually at least weekly. These findings are very different from those for *elderly people with mental health problems*, who had by far the most developed links with the wider society (save for the Cambridge clients). Eighty-three per cent of movers received visits in hospital. Seventy-three per cent had contact with their children, who, like other relatives and friends were in contact at least weekly.

All three Cambridge clients had links with their parents, although in all cases parental contact was less than weekly. One was taken home, all three were visited in hospital, and one received letters. Two of the three had contact with their siblings.

Looking across the samples of movers in the different client groups, the proportions receiving visits – the most common form of contact – were 83 per cent of elderly people with mental health problems, 58 per cent of people with learning difficulties, 46 per cent of movers with mental health problems, and 23 per cent of elderly physically frail people. For all clients, the tendency was for movers to have better developed social links with the community than stayers. (The differences were often not statistically significant, sometimes because of the small size of the stayers sample in most client groups.) Favouring the selection of people who already had better outside links has advantages for projects, and indeed for the community, but not for the people left behind. First, it eases the problem of community integration. Through people they already know, clients are able to build up wider social networks. The larger the number of outside contacts, the greater the likelihood that hospital residents will avoid institutionalisation, in the sense of displaying modes of behaviour and comportment peculiar to hospital. Acceptance by society is likely to be greater. Second, the possibility of drawing upon established community contacts for supplementing care and support for clients may be in planners' minds in choosing clients with higher contacts, for this could be expected to ease the cost and staffing burden for care agencies by shifting some of it onto relatives or friends. It may, of course, be preferred by clients.

This section has concentrated on the people who were later to become Care in the Community clients, as well as those who were identified as potential movers. We have seen that these people are quite isolated from the outside world. We should bear in mind that the typical hospital resident may be yet more isolated. Hospital rundown programmes of the future may not be able to rely on even the low levels of community contact reported here.

Hospital residents' views and feelings

How did hospital residents view their lives? The opinions of service users were the central concern of most projects, and nationally have grown in recognised importance (see Chapters 2 and 3). Where possible we wanted to interview each client before and after leaving hospital, and in the nature of things we therefore also interviewed a number of people who did not become clients. The information gained from our structured Interview for Morale and Life Satisfaction, enriched from case studies and anecdotes, can go some way to revealing the views and feelings of users. Despite the avowed necessity of providing information from across the range of hospitals, client groups and projects, the construction of quantitative measures of welfare, particularly when clients themselves are interviewed, suffers the usual difficulties inherent in the reduction of complex life-styles or views to limited categories and orderings. The structured interview may ask for reactions to issues which are irrelevant or unimportant to some, and may be unable to weight them appropriately. Inter-personal comparisons are similarly problematic. Responses depend in part on who is asking the questions, and the circumstances in which the interview takes place. When people have spent a considerable time in a rule-bound institutional setting, they may be reluctant to voice negative opinions. Thus, although it was PSSRU and not hospital staff who interviewed hospital residents, responses may not always have accurately reflected residents' opinions.

A different problem was that many residents, particularly those with learning difficulties or dementia, had difficulty understanding or communicating, thus affecting their ability to answer some of our questions. The responses elicited from clients inevitably came from those with relatively good cognitive and communication skills, and our results do not represent the views of people without such basic skills. What must be remembered is that quantitative measures rarely precisely mirror the social or personal reality they seek to describe, but are valuable in providing a broad consumer view and in offering points of comparison. They are crucial to our evaluation in enabling situations to be compared for their effects on clients.

Satisfaction with services

One part of the Interview for Morale and Life Satisfaction asked hospital residents to comment on their place of residence and the services received. Eighteen questions were taken from the Seltzer and Seltzer (1983) satisfaction questionnaire for people with learning difficulties and Wykes' (1982) assessment of satisfaction with services. The questions were designed in open-ended format (Sigelman et al., 1981), and asked so as to encourage narrative answers which were then interpreted by the interviewer as reflecting positive, negative or ambivalent (don't know) feelings. The items are listed in Table 5.9, together with the percentages of positive responses by client group. The response rate was highest among people with mental health problems (over 95 per cent of both movers and stayers). For the combined elderly client groups the response rate was over 80 per cent, and for people with learning difficulties 60 per cent, because of cognition and communication difficulties. (Note that there were subsidiary questions in this interview, including prompts on preferred place of residence and leisure activities. We report these findings later.)

For the majority of questions and all client groups, responses were interpreted as positive rather than negative. Rarely did the proportion of positive answers fall below 50 per cent, although we should not be surprised by this, and it is more interesting to look at *relative* proportions. Particularly high proportions of residents were satisfied with the level of comfort in hospital and with staff, and particularly low proportions were satisfied with the neighbourhood around the hospital and access to community facilities such as the shops and the town. Geographical isolation of the hospitals was especially frustrating for elderly clients who had been resident in hospital for comparatively short periods.

There were widespread positive opinions among residents with learning difficulties about how they spent their days (at work, occupational therapy, and so on), the people they worked with, and their personal effects (clothes

Table 5.9

Satisfaction with services in hospital

Items	*Percentage positive responses for clients within client groups*[1]					
	Learning difficulty		Mental health		Elderly[2]	
	Stayers %	Movers %	Stayers %	Movers %	Stayers %	Movers %
The place where you live	70	68	76	71	71	79
The neighbourhood	61	60	66	63	100	73
Comfort of place where you live	83	73	78	82	100	76
Your bedroom/dormitory	79	73	73	80	100	71
Space to keep possessions	74	78	75	79	57	82
Food	75	72	69	70	86	86
Access to shops, town, library, post office	52	59	65	65	17	44
Would you prefer to stay here? (% yes)	15	12	25	22	33	43
How do you spend your day (work, OT, ...)	80	80	75	79	60	58
Amount of free time	69	70	74	81	50	70
Do you have enough to do? (% yes)	73	72	74	77	40	72
Rules and regime of establishment	58	64	70	69	100	82
Opportunities to do what you want	66	66	70	76	60	72
The money you have to spend	64	77	61	66	75	72
Your clothes and possessions	82	83	68	80	80	82
The people you live with	64	68	69	73	60	81
The people you work with	85	80	73	86	Missing	47[3]
Staff of establishment	83	84	82	85	80	67
Sample size[4]	163	179	141	155	11	92

1 We do not report Glossop (2 responses) or Cambridge (0 responses).
2 Elderly physically frail and elderly people with mental health problems are grouped.
3 This is calculated from responses from only 15 movers.
4 Missing values reduced sample size on some items.

and other possessions). The importance of activities which offer a sense of identity and a valued status is emphasised. By contrast, elderly people were more dissatisfied with how they spent their day, an inter-client group difference in part explained by expectations formed from more recent experience in the community.

When we asked about the rules and regime of hospitals and opportunities to choose activities, a relatively high number of responses from people with learning difficulties and mental health problems were negative, possibly reflecting a perceived high degree of control over daily routines and limited ranges of options.

There were no statistically significant differences between movers and stayers in the proportions expressing satisfaction with services in the learning difficulty client group, except regarding the comfort of the establishment. For people with mental health problems, a far higher proportion of movers than stayers expressed satisfaction with life in hospital. Significantly higher proportions of positive responses were registered on attitude to other residents and to staff. It would seem from this that people who were generally better disposed to hospital were more likely to be selected by projects for the move to the community. This is good for community care programmes, but makes the job of caring for people in hospital yet more difficult. It is harder to distinguish differences between movers and stayers within the elderly client group because of the small sample size. All the same, movers appeared more likely than stayers to feel they had enough to do in hospital.

Perhaps the most telling result is that, despite generally high proportions of people expressing satisfaction with all aspects of hospital, few would prefer to remain in hospital when presented with the hypothetical alternatives of houses, group homes, own house or flat, living with family or other accommodation. Only 12 per cent of movers with learning difficulties and 22 per cent of movers with a mental health problem said they preferred to stay in hospital. In both client groups, people who stayed behind were more likely to prefer hospital than were people who eventually found a home in the community.

Other aspects of morale and life satisfaction

In addition to the checklist of items concerned with specific aspects of life in hospital, we also utilised three scales developed by other researchers: Cantril's ladder, the Psychosocial Functioning Inventory (PFI) and the Wakefield Depression Inventory. Cantril's ladder asks for a global rating of satisfaction with life; the other two consider how the respondent has been feeling in the past month. For elderly people, the PFI was replaced by the Philadelphia Geriatric Centre (PGC) Morale Scale, much of which compares current with previous morale.

Cantril's ladder is a simple measure. Respondents are asked to rate their satisfaction with life on a scale running from 0, representing the worst of all possible worlds, to 6, the best of all possible worlds (Cantril, 1965). Scores on this instrument ranged widely; in every client group but one the whole range from 0 to 6 was covered, and for elderly people with mental health problems scores ranged from 1 to 6 (see Table 5.10). This is a simple instrument, limited in scope but reasonably easy to comprehend and administer. Nevertheless, as with other morale and life satisfaction measures, response rates from clients were relatively low.

Looking across the client groups, people with learning difficulties tended to report being nearer to the 'best of all possible worlds' than people with mental health problems, with a significantly higher average score (3.9 as opposed to 3.3). Those people with learning difficulties who moved out of hospital were significantly happier with their lives in hospital than people who stayed behind, with a mean score of 4.1 as opposed to 3.3 for those who remained in hospital. There was no significant difference in the scores of movers and stayers for the mental health client group, but there were significant differences in project averages, ranging from 2.5 to 4.3. Within the elderly cohorts, those with mental health problems tended to register higher scores than the physically frail (respective means of 6.0 and 4.4), although response rates were low.

For those who were not in the elderly client groups we also used the morale sub-scale of the PFI (Feragne et al., 1983). Each question asks how often, in the past month, the respondent has felt certain emotions, such as boredom, restlessness, fear, relaxation, anger. Respondents choose between 'never', 'sometimes', and 'often'. Answers score 1 if the response indicates low morale, up to 3 for high morale. The possible range of scores runs from 17 to 51. (For missing single items, an average is taken from completed items.) This full range was covered by clients with learning difficulties. There were statistically significant differences between projects (means ranged from 34 to 45). For this client group and for people with mental health problems, scores on the PFI were not significantly different between movers and stayers, nor was there a difference between the two client groups.

The PGC Morale Scale was used to assess the morale of elderly hospital residents. This scale is widely used in gerontology, and in its anglicised form has been employed in the UK (Lawton, 1972, 1975; Challis and Knapp, 1980). It is manageable, with 17 yes/no questions. Three examples of questions are: 'As you get older do you feel less useful?' 'Do you feel lonely much?' 'Do little things bother you more this year?' Responses indicating positive attitudes score 1, negative attitudes score 0. As with the PFI, average scores elsewhere for the same respondent are substituted for single missing items. The mean scores for the three (project) hospitals accommodating elderly physically frail people were significantly different (5 per cent level). The mean score for elderly people with mental health problems was 11 (median 12), significantly higher

Table 5.10

Measures of morale and life satisfaction in hospital

	Stayers		*Movers*		Probability of no difference between stayers and movers	*Baseline*	
	Mean score	Sample size	Mean score	Sample size		Mean score	Sample size
People with learning difficulties[1]							
Cantril's ladder	3	30	4[2]	100	.081*	4	130
Psychological Functioning Inventory	39	50	38[3]	120	.600	38	170
Depression Inventory	10	52	12[4]	97	.160	11	149
People with mental health problems[5]							
Cantril's Ladder	3	103	3[6]	137	.617	3	240
Psychological Functioning Inventory	37	122	38[7]	148	.069*	38	270
Depression Inventory	12	120	10[8]	142	.081*	11	262
Elderly people with physical frailty[9]							
Cantril's Ladder	3	4	4[10]	30	.433	4	34
PGC Morale Scale	9	20	9[11]	93	.645	9	113
Depression Inventory	8	3	11[12]	40	.459	11	43

* Difference is significant at 10 per cent.
1 Total number in baseline = 529
2 Minimum 0, median 5, maximum 6.
3 Minimum 17, median 38, maximum 51.
4 Minimum 0, median 11, maximum 31.
5 Total number in baseline = 407
6 Minimum 0, median 3, maximum 6.
7 Minimum 20, median 39, maximum 50.
8 Minimum 0, median 8, maximum 36.
9 Total number in baseline = 171
10 Minimum 0, median 4, maximum 6.
11 Minimum 20, median 11, maximum 17.
12 Minimum 0, median 9, maximum 36.

than that for elderly physically frail people, although the latter sample comprised 23 people served by a single project.

The Depression Inventory (Snaith et al., 1971) is designed for use in detecting fairly short periods of depressive illness or prolonged periods of sadness. Among other questions, it asks people about their state of mind in the past month (they respond 'definitely', 'sometimes', 'not much', or 'not at all'), and to questions such as 'Have you felt tired for no reason?', and 'Have you been more irritable than usual?'. We followed the scoring pattern of the original authors, so that 36 indicates the *lowest* level of morale (high depression) and 0 the *highest*. The average score for movers with learning difficulties was 12, not significantly different from stayers. Project means varied significantly from 23 to 4. Scores for people with mental health problems ranged all the way from 36 to 0, although most people reported low levels of depression, with half the sample scoring 8 or less. Project means varied significantly (between 15 and 7), and movers exhibited lower levels of depression than stayers. There were no significant inter-project or inter-client group differences among elderly respondents, nor between movers and stayers. For elderly people with mental health problems the mean score was 12, and the median 7 (sample of 24 respondents).

The tendency over all client groups, therefore, was for those selected to move to register greater happiness with their lives than those not selected, consistent with the finding for levels of satisfaction with services. Project managers preferred to choose people who were better disposed towards life, leaving the less satisfied to remain in hospital.

Skills, behaviour and presentation

Assessment of need is fundamental to the planning of community care placements and support, and within the demonstration programme was a key criterion for selecting residents for discharge. Projects used a range of assessment techniques for a variety of need dimensions, as we will describe in Part II of this book. For our part, we assessed resident characteristics in three areas – skills (in the activities of daily living, including the ability to act independently), behaviour (adaptive and maladaptive, covering symptoms to some degree), and personal presentation. All three indicate the work needed to prepare residents for the move to the community and to support them once there. They may also be linked to the success or otherwise of attempted resettlement and integration into the community.

Skills and behaviour

In order to assess each hospital resident's skills level and behavioural characteristics, interviews were conducted with hospital staff who knew the resident well. (We later used the schedules in interviews with community staff, as we report in Part III.) Schedules for measuring skills and behaviour available in 1984 for people with learning difficulties and mental health problems were believed by the research team at that time either to be too detailed and specific for the Care in the Community evaluation, or to lack the sensitivity necessary to monitor change over time. Most such scales had been developed with a particular client group in mind, whereas the team needed measures suitable for a variety of client groups (a specific request of the DHSS). It was decided to take a well-formed existing instrument as the core – the Social Behaviour Scale (SBS) was chosen – to which extra items were added from other schedules.

The SBS has gone through many variants since Wing's prototype Ward Behaviour Scale (Wing, 1960, 1961). This first scale was developed for use with people with long-term schizophrenia, but was later altered to accommodate other mental health conditions. It begat many other instruments, including the Hall and Baker (1983) Rehabilitation Evaluation or REHAB scale. As Wing himself reports, the SBS is typical of other behaviour schedules used 'simply as crude and contaminated, but convenient, methods of measuring the intrinsic component of social disablement in order to test hypotheses' (Wing, J., 1989, p.175). The version used here is what Wing calls SBS4, although it was originally published as the Social Performance Scale (Wykes, 1982; Wykes et al., 1982; Wykes and Sturt, 1986). Alone, the SBS is insufficient as a measure of skills and behavioural problems, and we added from instruments developed for use with people with learning difficulties – the Disability Assessment Schedule (Holmes et al., 1982) and the AAMD Adaptive Behaviour Scale (Nihira et al., 1974) – as well as from REHAB. With the exception of three dichotomous items, scores run from 1 (low skills or poor behaviour) to 3 (high skills or no behaviour problem). (Although this scoring differs from SBS4, it is possible to reproduce summary statistics for comparison with other studies using it.) Total scores on the 'skills and abilities' section of the schedule run from 31 to 90; total scores on the 'symptoms and behavioural problems' section run from 26 to 78. The mixing of schedules and standardisation of scoring templates were necessary consequences of the need to use the same instrumentation for all client groups (although we were able to relax this in the second round of programme funding, when all but one of the elderly projects started). As previously noted, this has generated both benefits and difficulties.

It is instructive to use the skills and behaviour instruments in both summary form and disaggregated to individual items. Total scores were significantly different between the client groups. The young people in the Cambridge project had the lowest skills scores (mean 35, close to the minimum of 31), partly a reflection of age but mainly of disability. They also registered the most severe behavioural problems (mean 61). In Glossop, the three adults with physical disabilities had few skill deficiencies (mean 77) or behavioural problems (mean 74). Our findings for the other client groups are summarised in Table 5.11, with individual item details in Tables 5.12 and 5.13. Hospital residents in the learning difficulty movers sample were much less skilled, less able to function independently, than movers with mental health problems (means of 62 and 74), but there was no difference in reported behavioural problems (means of 68 and 70). Projects also showed a very significant tendency to select people with higher levels of independent functioning and fewer behavioural difficulties from the group of all hospital residents assessed. As we have already found in relation to other characteristics, there were significant inter-project variations. For example, looking at the sample of movers, the ability of people with learning difficulties to function independently varied from a mean of 52 in one project to 65 in another. For people with mental health problems, project means on this skills measure varied between 68 and 76. Both differences are statistically significant, and both had implications for the community support programmes needed, and for the costs.

Turning to the skills and behavioural problems covered by the questionnaire tells us more about the tasks facing projects as they sought to assist hospital residents to integrate into the community and live more independently (Tables 5.12 and 5.13). Noteworthy characteristics of the people with learning difficulties who moved to the community were:

- Less than half could wash or bathe without assistance.
- Two-thirds could dress adequately without help.
- Less than one-third were literate and less than one-half numerate.
- Communication and other interactions with fellow residents were rated as 'below normal' (compared to a general population) for nearly half of the sample.
- A third rarely or never participated in decisions about the roles they performed in hospital and another third only occasionally played an active part.
- Only 20 per cent could shop alone with supervision, only 13 per cent could manage their own financial affairs, and the same percentage could find their own way or use public transport.
- One-half were said to be unable to organise or plan their own activities.
- Attention-seeking behaviour was a frequent or occasional problem for a third of clients.
- Physical aggression or verbal abuse was reported for almost the same proportion.
- For one in ten clients regular or occasional sexually offensive behaviour was noted.

These hospital-assessed characteristics were generally rather more problematic or challenging than among people with mental health problems. For the latter

Table 5.11

Measures of skills, behaviour and presentation in hospital

	Stayers		*Movers*		Probability of no difference between stayers and movers	*Baseline*	
	Mean score	Sample size	Mean score	Sample size		Mean score	Sample size
People with learning difficulties[1]							
Skills	55	144	62 [2]	225	.000**	59	369
Behaviour	65	144	68 [3]	225	.000**	67	369
Personal Presentation Checklist total	18	119	19 [4]	201	.005**	18	320
Clothes	4.6	126	4.5	209	.372	4.5	335
General	4.4	126	4.6	207	.261	4.5	333
Posture	4.5	119	5.0	201	.001**	4.8	321
Traits	4.1	126	4.3	205	.019*	4.2	331
People with mental health problems[5]							
Skills	70	161	74 [6]	153	.000**	72	314
Behaviour	68	161	70 [7]	153	.005**	69	314
Personal Presentation Checklist total	19	157	0.8	151	.002**	20	308
Clothes	4.2	158	4.5	152	.010**	4.4	310
General	4.9	158	5.4	152	.001**	5.2	310
Posture	5.6	157	5.7	151	.413	5.6	308
Traits	4.5	158	4.6	152	.111	4.6	310

* Difference is significant at 10 per cent.
** Difference is significant at 1 per cent.
1 Total number in baseline = 529
2 Minimum 36, median 62, maximum 83.
3 Minimum 48, median 68, maximum 75.
4 Minimum 6, median 19, maximum 22.
5 Total number in baseline = 407
6 Minimum 53, median 75, maximum 84.
7 Minimum 50, median 71, maximum 75.
8 Minimum 0, median 21, maximum 22.

cohort of movers, however, there was still some way to go before they could reasonably be expected to manage independently in the community.

- Only half participated more than occasionally in decisions about their own activities and roles.
- Only half could prepare meals without supervision.
- Less than half could independently manage their own financial affairs.
- Approximately one in eight could barely read or write.
- Four in every ten were said to have never or only occasionally initiated conversation or interaction with other residents.
- A third acted out delusions occasionally or frequently, and almost as many had intense or moderate symptoms of anxiety.
- One in five was rated as deeply or moderately depressed.

Anyone familiar with England's psychiatric hospitals will recognise these descriptions of people with mental health problems as characteristic of the less dependent and probably 'easier-to-rehabilitate' long-stay population (compare Levene et al., 1985; Ford et al., 1987; TAPS, 1988; Clifford et al., 1991). Although 'less dependent' with less severe mental health problems and more self-care skills, project clients required a great deal of preparation for community living, and a lot of support once they had moved.

Skill deficiencies and behavioural problems among both client groups were a feature of the initial presenting or underlying characteristics of individuals and partly a result of the institutional environment – the classic interaction between personal competence and environmental press (Murray, 1938), the latter in its many manifestations stimulating and constraining personal preferences, abilities and needs. With the learning difficulty group particularly, some deficiencies in hospital undoubtedly resulted from the 'infantilisation' of residents and few opportunities for skills development. This was illustrated graphically when one researcher was told by a staff nurse, 'I treat them just like my own children when they were young – you can't go wrong like that'. Another hospital for people with learning difficulties provided residents with different coloured clothes according to whether they were well or badly behaved. In this particular study we are not able to examine the statistical associations between social environmental press and individual competence in the hospital setting, although cognisance should be taken of them in evaluating the efficacy and efficiency of community care.

In projects for *elderly people* we used a different scale for assessing skills and behaviour – the Behaviour Rating Scale of the Clifton Assessment Procedures for the Elderly (CAPE) developed by Pattie and Gilleard (1979). Total scores on CAPE can range from 36, which indicates *low* levels of skills or severe behaviour problems, to 0, indicating *high* skills or no behaviour problems. There are four sub-scales: physical disability (scores ranging from 12 for 'poor' to 0 for 'good'), apathy (10 to 0), communication difficulties (4 to 0) and social disturbance (10 to 0).

Table 5.12
Skill levels in hospital for people with learning difficulties and mental health problems (movers sample only)

Skill characteristic	MH (%)[1]	LD (%)[1]
1. Vision[1]		
– blind or almost blind	2.0	3.1
– poor vision	10.5	7.8
2. Hearing[1]		
– deaf or almost deaf	3.3	1.6
– poor hearing	5.2	7.8
3. Mobility		
– non-mobile, needs help on level ground	0.7	2.6
– needs help upstairs or some guidance, e.g. if blind	3.9	9.8
4. Conversation, social mixing with patients		
– rarely or never	5.9	16.8
– only with prompting or some impairment	29.4	39.4
5. Initiation of conversation/interaction with patients		
– rarely or never	9.2	23.0
– occasionally but mostly passive	30.7	27.2
6. Non-verbal communication		
– lacks interest, expressionless, inert, ...	3.3	6.8
– some non-verbal communication but limited	26.8	32.8
7. Length of conversations		
– mute or occasional sounds	0	14.7
– spoke in short sentences only	28.1	42.1
8. Clarity of speech		
– unclear, impossible to comprehend, bizarre	0	11.2
– partly unclear or nonsense	17.0	39.4
9. Eating habits at mealtime		
– chronically disruptive, unacceptable	2.6	5.2
– needs some supervision	15.0	24.4
10. Done fair share of collective ward tasks		
– has not	7.1	11.8
– some collaboration only	23.6	21.6
11. Task sharing with other patients		
– major or constant disagreements	6.5	10.4
– one or two minor disagreements re. task sharing	11.6	24.7
12. Rows with other patients		
– major rows or constant minor rows	9.3	18.8
– one or two minor rows in last month	23.8	31.8
13. Participation in decisions re. roles		
– rarely	18.9	33.7
– occasionally takes active part	31.1	34.7
14. Wash and bath self		
– rarely adequately even with supervision	0.7	13.5
– adequately only with supervision, help	25.7	41.1
15. Dress		
– rarely adequately even with supervision	1.3	8.9
– adequately only with supervision or help	18.4	29.2
16. Cooks and get meals alone		
– rarely adequately even with supervision	13.5	46.0
– adequately only with supervision	36.1	42.9

Table 5.12 (continued)

Skill characteristic	MH (%)[1]	LD (%)[1]
17. Basic housework and care of clothes		
– rarely adequately even with supervision	5.9	17.7
– adequately only with supervision	30.9	42.5
18. Shop alone		
– rarely performs adequately even with supervision	2.7	35.3
– adequately only with supervision or some help	24.3	43.9
19. Manage own financial affairs		
– rarely adequately even with supervision	14.4	58.5
– adequately only with supervision	37.0	28.4
20. Find way around		
– rarely adequately even with supervision	7.6	50.0
– adequately only with supervision	20.0	37.4
21. Uses amenities in community (church, pub, ...)		
– not in last month	19.2	25.7
– at least once but less often than weekly	23.2	30.9
22. Has missed opportunities in last month to use these facilities – % yes[2]	36.4	29.6
23. Do staff encourage resident to do these activities – % yes[2]	62.8	68.1
24. Do staff stop resident doing things, reducing independence – % yes[2]	36.9	45.8
25. Independently plans/organises weekly activities		
– not at all	19.7	47.1
– organises and plans some but not all	42.1	39.2
26. Understanding communication		
– almost nothing	0	1.6
– some, e.g. simple commands	2.6	14.5
27. Reading		
– none	3.4	64.9
– few words only	7.6	14.6
28. Writing		
– none	4.2	69.1
– few words only	10.4	13.8
29. Counting and money		
– none, or can say a few numbers	1.3	50.0
– can sort out a number of items	6.6	19.1
30. Looking after own clothes and possessions		
– little or no attempt	3.9	27.9
– attempts but untidy	32.0	20.5
31. Appearance if left to own devices		
– always disorderly	11.1	24.9
– sometimes disorderly	30.1	36.3
Sample size[3]	153	193

1 All but items 22, 23 and 24 have three categories of response. Percentages are reported for only two categories (the third completes the 100%). The category excluded in every case is the skill level expected in a general population: for example, normal vision (item 1), normal hearing (item 2) or full ability to manage one's own affairs (item 19).
2 Items 22, 23 and 24 required Yes/No responses.
3 Missing values varied from item to item, ranging from 0 (items 1 to 9, and 30) to 20 (item 16) for the mental health sample, and from 0 (items 1 to 3, 9, 26, 31) to 40 (item 10) for the learning difficulty sample. In most cases missing assessments arose because hospital residents had not had opportunities to test these particular skills.

Table 5.13

Behavioural problems in hospital for people with learning difficulties and mental health problems (movers sample only)

Behavioural characteristic	MH (%)[1]	LD (%)[1]
1. Depression or weeping		
– deeply depressed at least half of the time	1.3	1.0
– moderate or severe depression, but less than half of the time	19.0	21.9
2. Suicidal preoccupations		
– has made suicide attempt	0.7	0
– talked about suicide or non-serious gesture	8.6	0.5
3. Anxiety, panic, phobias		
– intense form of symptoms present at least half of the time	5.2	2.1
– moderate or intense symptoms, but less than half of the time	24.8	17.1
4. Slowness of movement		
– usually extremely slow (eat, walk, ...)	7.2	14.1
– occasional periods of extreme slowness	15.0	15.7
5. Underactivity		
– stood/sat in one place all/most of the time, no spontaneous movement	7.8	13.1
– some periods of extreme underactivity but mostly not 23.5	23.0	
6. Overactivity		
– usually extremely overactive (restless, pacing a lot, ...)	3.3	1.0
– some period of extreme restlessness but most not	17.0	18.7
7. Elated or euphoric behaviour		
– elated or intense euphoria for days	3.3	0.5
– elated or intense euphoria for hours	9.8	10.9
8. Odd gestures, mannerisms		
– frequent, not every day	13.7	16.6
– occasional, not every day	23.5	20.2
9. Acting out delusions, hallucinations		
– frequently, happens most days	9.8	3.1
– occasional, not every day	22.9	2.6
10. Attention-seeking behaviour		
– serious or frequent problem	5.2	7.3
– moderate or occasional problem	17.6	26.4
11. Aggressive or violent behaviour		
– struck person or persistent damaging	5.2	10.9
– threatening, verbally abusive, but did not strike anyone	14.4	19.8
12. Obsessional behaviour		
– intense symptoms at least half of the time	3.3	7.3
– moderate or intense, but less than half of the time	5.9	6.2
13. Self-injury		
– more than twice in month or requires constant supervision	0.7	3.6
– one or two occasions in past month	1.3	5.2

Table 5.13 (continued)

Behavioural characteristic	MH (%)[1]	LD (%)[1]
14. Stealing (e.g. food, cigarettes)		
– more than twice in past month	1.3	9.8
– once or twice a month	3.9	5.2
15. Collecting, hoarding meaningless items		
– every day or management problem	2.0	7.3
– hoards occasionally but not serious management problem	13.2	13.5
16. Shouting, swearing, offensive, screaming		
– daily or frequent	5.2	9.8
– occasional but not serious	19.6	30.6
17. Incontinence during the day		
– urine or faeces more than twice a month	2.0	7.3
– once or twice a month	0.7	6.2
18. Incontinence at night		
– urine or faeces more than twice a month	2.6	7.8
– once or twice a month	3.3	8.3
19. Confused		
– almost always	1.3	2.6
– sometimes	17.0	20.7
20. Objectionable at night		
– more than once a week	1.3	2.1
– sometimes	5.9	6.8
21. Awake at night		
– more than once a week	6.6	5.4
– sometimes	15.9	14.1
22. Accuses others of doing harm, stealing, etc.		
– more than once a week	4.6	7.3
– sometimes	9.8	17.2
23. Wanders or runs away (if not supervised)		
– more than once a week	0.7	2.1
– sometimes	5.2	6.8
24. Stereotyped repetitive activities, echolalia		
– every day	6.5	6.8
– sometimes	5.2	11.5
25. Sexually offensive behaviour		
– more than once a week	0.7	2.6
– occasional	4.6	7.3
26. Any other problems		
– serious or frequent problem	17.6	10.8
– moderate or unusual problem	16.2	13.5
Sample size[2]	153	193

1 All items have three categories of response. Only the first two are listed here. The third indicates, in each case, no (or very rare) behavioural problems.
2 Missing values vary from item to item.

Overall scores on the CAPE were not significantly different between the two elderly client groups, although scores on the communication difficulties and social disturbance sub-scales were significantly higher (more severe behavioural problems) among elderly people with mental health problems (Table 5.14). There were no significant differences between projects in overall or sub-scale CAPE scores, or between movers and stayers. Comparing these scores with Pattie and Gilleard's (1979) normative scores for different groups of elderly people (Table 5.15) suggests that clients with physical frailty were less dependent and behaviourally disturbed than a chronic geriatric group, but similar to an acute geriatric population. Elderly clients with mental health problems had marginally lower dependency and behaviour ratings than the normative judgement for a chronic psychogeriatric group (and marginally higher ratings than an acute psychogeriatric population), again suggesting that programme clients were less dependent than the general long-stay hospital population (compare Anderson, 1990).

Personal presentation

Each client's personal presentation was assessed by the interviewer on a standard checklist. The evaluative question was whether clients took care over their appearance and dress, at least to a standard which would not encourage others to label them as 'unusual'. Value assumptions are a problem here, more so than for most instruments, for concepts of what passes as unusual vary so much. Moreover, the cultural and social context in which individuals present themselves is relevant; what is unusual in hospital is different from what is unusual in the community. Some people may wish to assert their individuality by refusing to conform to conventional standards of appearance, making for a further confounding influence. But in the community, people can stand out as different by virtue of their ill-fitting or inappropriate clothing, or their odd or unkempt appearance, and this may influence the reaction and interaction of other people to them. For example, rightly or wrongly, neighbours may be more willing to accept a group of clients if they look neat and cared for than if they look dirty, untidy and 'peculiar' in some way, with implications for the success of social integration. Different facilities place different emphases on self-care and go to greater lengths to make available personalised clothing and mirrors. Thus it is difficult to be utterly objective about any research assessment of personal presentation, and it is important to avoid patronising judgements, but inappropriate or unusual presentation is clearly relevant for community integration.

The Personal Presentation Checklist was developed in the PSSRU to cover important aspects of personal presentation which would be obvious to anyone meeting a client for the first time. It was divided into four sections: clothes, posture (both sections scoring from 0 to 5), general appearance and unusual

Table 5.14

Measures of skills, behaviour and presentation in hospital

	Stayers		*Movers*		Probability of	*Baseline*	
	Mean score	Sample size	Mean score	Sample size	no difference between stayers and movers	Mean score	Sample size
Elderly people with mental health problems[1]							
CAPE Behaviour Rating Scale total	15.0	3	15.6[2]	17	.868	15.5	20
Physical disability	4.7	3	6.0	25	.384	5.8	28
Apathy	8.0	5	6.6	23	.087*	6.9	28
Communication difficulties	1.2	5	0.9	32	.457	0.9	37
Social disturbance	1.7	3	1.5	37	.948	1.6	40
Personal Presentation Checklist total	19.4	5	19.4[3]	42	.977	19.4	47
Clothes	4.0	5	4.5	43	.381	4.4	48
General	5.6	5	4.9	43	.085*	4.9	48
Posture	5.4	5	5.5	43	.861	5.5	48
Traits	4.4	5	4.5	42	.851	4.5	47
Elderly physically frail people[4]							
CAPE Behaviour Rating Scale total	14.2	19	13.8[5]	111	.696	13.8	130
Physical disability	6.2	19	6.0	124	.716	6.0	143
Apathy	7.2	19	6.3	115	.116	6.4	134
Communication difficulties	0.4	19	0.4	126	.725	0.4	146
Social disturbance	0.5	23	0.9	132	.198	0.9	155
Personal Presentation Checklist total	19.0	4	20.2[6]	37	.335	20.1	41
Clothes	3.8	6	4.7	45	.013*	4.6	51
General	5.0	6	5.6	46	.062*	5.5	52
Posture	6.0	4	5.0	37	.273	5.1	41
Traits	4.8	6	4.9	46	.836	4.9	52

* Difference is significant at 10 per cent.
1 Total number in baseline = 97
2 Minimum 5, median 16, maximum 24.
3 Minimum 12, median 20, maximum 22.
4 Total number in baseline = 171
5 Minimum 6, median 13, maximum 26.
6 Minimum 13, median 21, maximum 22.

Table 5.15
The CAPE scale and sub-scales: normative scores and scores for clients in the projects for elderly people

Data and samples	Physical disability	Apathy	Communication difficulties	Social disturbance	CAPE total
Normative data[1]					
Community, 'well' group	1	1	0	1	3
Community, 'care' group	2	3	0	1	6
Acute psychiatric group	2	4	0	1	7
Acute medical group	6	6	0	1	13
Old people's home (LA)	4	5	0	1	10
Old people's home (elderly mentally ill)	5	5	1	2	13
Acute psychogeriatric group	5	6	1	2	14
Chronic geriatric group	8	7	1	2	18
Chronic psychogeriatric group	7	8	1	2	18
Actual scores, Care in the Community					
Elderly physically frail	6	6	0	1	14
Elderly mentally ill	6	7	1	2	16

1 As suggested by Pattie and Gilleard (1979).

traits (both scoring from 0 to 6). Higher scores indicated a less unusual appearance. The interviewer noted whether there was anything unusual about specified aspects of appearance. (Attempts were made to minimise value assumptions and rater biases by frequently cross-checking ratings.) In Table 5.16 we list the items on the checklist together with percentages of movers in each client group who were rated as displaying inappropriate or unusual presentation, relative to the hospital context. Average scores for the various samples are given in Tables 5.11 and 5.14. There was a significant difference between movers and stayers in both the learning difficulty and mental health client groups, the former exhibiting fewer unusual traits.

Explaining client selection for projects

We have seen in this chapter how the people who moved from hospital to a new life in the community were different in many respects from those who

Table 5.16
Personal presentation, hospital rating, movers sample

Dimension and item	Percentage of clients for whom presentation was NOT appropriate						
	All MH	All LD	All EPF	All EMI	Cambs	Glossop	All projects
Clothes							
Cleanliness	14	13	4	9	0	0	12
Suitability (for time or place)	5	6	11	5	0	0	6
Maintenance (torn?)	11	11	4	12	0	0	10
Worn properly	5	7	2	5	0	0	6
Fit (too large? too loose?)	11	16	7	16	0	0	13
General							
Face	11	20	7	26	100	0	16
Hair	8	11	2	5	33	0	8
Hands	7	13	2	9	67	0	9
Glasses or teeth	21	32	15	37	33	50	27
Smell	3	5	4	7	33	0	4
Eyes	6	26	9	30	67	0	17
Posture							
Head hangs down	8	12	16	9	33	0	11
Stomach sticks out (posture)	6	9	14	2	0	0	7
Shoulders slumped/back bent	8	18	25	20	33	0	15
Walks with toes in or out	5	15	27	5	33	0	10
Walks with feet apart	4	10	13	5	0	0	7
Walks on tiptoes	1	3	20	0	0	0	3
Unusual traits							
Dribbling	1	5	0	2	0	0	3
Very loud talking	3	6	2	10	0	0	5
Sticking tongue out	1	7	0	0	67	0	3
Rocking	1	7	2	2	0	0	4
Other (specified by rater)	27	29	9	38	100	0	27

stayed in hospital. They were less dependent and more highly skilled; their personal presentation was rated as less unusual; they had more experience and contact with the community; they were more satisfied with their lives; they displayed fewer behavioural problems. These are all bivariate comparisons or associations, but it is more instructive to examine *combination* of client characteristics, for it is the interaction of characteristics which influences actual decisions. Our interest in this issue stems directly from what we and others have observed about the organisation of hospital closure programmes: the people who leave hospital first are not typical of the full long-stay population, and those who remain or move last have more demanding symptoms or challenging behaviours (for example, Falloon and Marshall, 1983; Curson et al., 1988; Jones, 1989; Wing, L., 1989; Korman and Glennerster, 1990). We have carried out this examination for just one client group for illustrative purposes, concentrating on people with learning difficulties because of comparative sample size and because we are aware of similar work for other client groups.

The method chosen for analysing client selection was logistic regression or logit analysis: the independent variables (client characteristics) are used to predict the probability of moving from hospital. A multivariate statistical method is needed to allow examination of combinations of hypothesised determinants of discharge, and logit is superior to multiple regression when the dependent variable is dichotomous. All available client information was used in an attempt to explain statistically the likelihood of selection for a pilot project. The results are given in Table 5.17, where a positive coefficient indicates that a variable *increased* the probability of moving, the larger the coefficient the more it pushed up this probability. Independent or explanatory variables were introduced into the logit analysis with one eye on the numbers of missing observations (which is the reason for our estimation of more than one series of analyses), and retained if they were statistically significant. These exploratory analyses reveal some interesting tendencies in the selection of clients with learning difficulties across the demonstration programme.

Age was associated with movement from hospital. Younger residents were more likely to leave under the auspices of the demonstration programme. Many older residents who remained in hospital doubtless chose to do so because they had no desire to have their comfortable, familiar life-styles disrupted. Those older hospital residents who did move tended to go to old people's homes or sheltered housing (see Chapter 8).

Social contacts with parent(s), or via visits and more frequent contacts by friends and family were associated with a higher probability of leaving hospital. *Experience of the community* also had an effect, with use of community facilities within the past month increasing the likelihood of leaving hospital. Those who moved out tended to have relatively highly-developed (though weak) links with the community than those who remained in hospital. Projects could thus hope to draw upon a ready-made reservoir of community support which, although limited, looked somewhat better than the situation facing health and social care workers seeking to move later cohorts of people. Movers were also more likely to have had some previous experience of hostel residence since their first admission to hospital.

Skills and *behaviour* are both relevant to predicting the discharge probability. Residents with higher skills and fewer behavioural difficulties were more likely to leave hospital, and those who displayed few or no odd gestures and mannerisms and/or displayed no or only mild obsessive behaviour were also more likely to move. Physical characteristics such as hearing and mobility difficulties, 'psychiatric' symptoms such as confusion, disturbed sleep patterns, and attempted or demonstrated intent of suicide were other significant influences,

Table 5.17
Logit equation estimates for predicting movers (people with learning difficulties)

Independent variables[1]	***Logit equation coefficients***[2]			
	Eq'n 1	**Eq'n 2**	**Eq'n 3**	**Eq'n 4**
Constant term	-1.34	11.49	-4.86	2.90
Person is *deaf or hard of hearing* (DV)	-1.04			
Person has *not used community facilities in the past month* (DV)	-0.81			
Person is *not able to make plans* (DV)	-1.19			
Person has made an attempt or displayed the intention of *suicide* (DV)	-3.18			
Person is almost always *confused* (DV)	-1.84			
Person has a *disturbed sleep pattern* over once a week (DV)	-1.77			
Person is *mobile* everywhere (DV)	1.30			
Person rarely *takes decisions* (DV)	1.04			
Person displays few or no *odd gestures and mannerisms* (DV)	0.91			
Person displays no or mild *obsessive behaviour* (DV)	1.09			
Age at beginning of funding round		-0.03		-0.04
Reciprocal of *'Behaviour'* score		-6.09		
Contact of person with family or friends takes place quarterly or more frequently (DV)		1.14		
Client is *visited* in hospital (DV)		10.54		
'Behaviour' score multiplied by dummy variable *'client is visited in hospital'*		-0.17		
'Skills' score			0.02	
'Behaviour' score			0.05	
Score on *'Posture'* Section of Personal Presentation Checklist		0.19		
Person has had a *hostel placement* since first admission to hospital (DV)				0.19
Sample size	240	187	305	192
Percentage of correct predictions	75.41	81.28	64.26	75.52
Lave's R^2 statistic	.33	.15	.09	0.12

1 DV indicates dummy variable, taking value 1 if characteristic is present, 0 if not.
2 All coefficients are significant at the 0.05 level.

each pushing down the probability of selection. Later leavers will need more rehabilitative training in both hospital and community. The 'posture' rating on the *personal presentation* checklist was a significant predictor. By today's standards, perhaps, projects were not (as a group) particularly ambitious in challenging societal norms by seeking to integrate people with relatively few skills, difficult behaviours and unusual appearance into the community, although between them they certainly helped a large cohort of quite dependent people make the difficult transition from hospital. Given the opposition to hospital closure in some quarters, this selection pattern made some sense, although it makes it harder still to run a hospital and may not have assisted those left behind. It is known that hospital costs are higher for more dependent residents (Johnes and Haycox, 1986; Haycox and Brand, 1991), and we show in Chapter 13 how community costs are similarly positively correlated with client dependency (broadly defined). The observed selection pattern will have helped keep average community costs down but pushed average hospital costs up, and we will therefore also be examining the longer-term costs of hospital rundown and community programme development.

The analyses in this section confirm in the multivariate domain what we were already finding in our two-way tabulations, and also what others have found from single hospital studies for a variety of client groups: community care projects, given the opportunity, tend to select the more skilled, the more independent, the better (socially) connected, younger residents. Level of handicap was *not* a statistically significant factor in the presence of other explanatory effects (contrary to the impression gained from the bivariate association discussed earlier). We found, in fact, that the factors which together help explain selection for discharge are not always the same as those which correlated in two-way analyses. It is the interaction and combination of factors which is more appropriate as the basis for explanation. In these analyses of the demonstration programme, the movers have been compared with stayers in the pool of people assessed as potential clients, and this pool, in its turn, was probably an atypical, less dependent group of the hospital population. We have little doubt that projects were, to use parlance now common in such circumstances, 'skimming the cream' of the hospital population. But although the movers were less dependent than the stayers, in terms of some measures of skills and behaviour, we should be cautious in making assumptions as to how independent they really were. Most needed a great deal of support and assistance in the community. These points need to be remembered as we proceed through other evaluation questions, although we repeat that the demonstration programme's importance in offering the opportunity to examine the comparative effectiveness, processes and costs of different community care arrangements should not be under-estimated.

People and lives in hospital

The Care in the Community demonstration programme was the first nationwide programme to be funded by central government to examine and encourage the policy of replacing long-stay hospital accommodation with supported and managed places in the community. In this chapter we have reported the key characteristics, circumstances and needs of groups of people living in more than 50 of England's hospitals who were seen by pilot projects as candidates for rehabilitation. We have compared the movers with the stayers. Among our findings are the following.

- Most clients with a learning difficulty or a mental health problem were likely to exhibit symptoms of institutionalisation, having spent many years in hospital and having only limited contact with the outside. Despite this, most expressed a preference to leave when offered the opportunity.
- The majority of the elderly physically frail clients had lost contact with family and friends, so that services for these clients would have an especially important role in building social networks.
- Elderly clients were particularly likely to express dissatisfaction with access to community facilities such as shops, and with the way they spent their day: they clearly missed the experiences of community living.
- Relatively high proportions of people with learning difficulties and mental health problems valued their activities during the day (occupational and industrial therapy, and so on), and liked the people they lived and worked with, but they were dissatisfied with the rules and regime of the institution.
- People with mental health problems were more likely to be selected for projects if they had expressed a positive attitude to life in general and to aspects of institutional life in particular; thus it appears that projects preferred people who had more conciliatory attitudes.
- Almost all clients had some missing or under-developed skills, as well as some behavioural problems, presenting challenges for clients and community staff alike, despite the tendency for projects to pick more independent people as movers.
- Detailed multivariate analyses of data on people with learning difficulties revealed that, on numerous criteria, less dependent people were more likely to leave hospital. Future hospital closure policies will need to take account of the probable higher cost of discharging those left behind.

Part II: Resources and processes

6 Resources and processes of community care

The national and local objectives for the Care in the Community demonstration programme were made manifest in many ways. Our foci in this second part of the book are the *resources* and the *processes* of community care, the inputs and services which were combined by pilot projects for the former hospital residents. We are interested in the resources and their origins, the staffing and other service organisation and delivery experiences. We also need to explore how the behaviour of agencies and key personnel was directed (or diverted) under the various organisational arrangements adopted and developed by projects. A research goal was to identify those processes of community care that appeared to 'work', bearing in mind the need to explore client outcome and cost results in a complete evaluation, and to tease out the incentives that enabled them. The hope is that similar forces can be transported beyond the demonstration programme.

In the terms of our production of welfare framework (Chapter 4), we are saving our evaluation of the final outcomes for Part III, and we are now principally concerned with inputs and the processes linking them to outcomes, although the division of topics is obviously not quite as neat and tidy as this might imply.

We first describe the financing of projects and services, with a particular look at project grants, social security payments and dowries (Chapter 7). We then consider the community services which these funds helped to develop, including an account of the difficulties that emerged (Chapter 8). Chapter 9 discusses staffing, and Chapter 10 the related issue of case management, central to the Care in the Community programme as well as to the legislative changes introduced in April 1991. The final process chapter addresses the service management and joint working arrangements which the programme generated.

Client numbers and accommodation

The remainder of this book is concerned almost exclusively with community care, its clients and staff. Table 6.1 sets the scene by summarising some of the basic quantitative achievements of the 28 pilot projects, giving client group, lead agency, target and actual numbers of clients, and accommodation outcomes.

Table 6.1
Basic achievements by projects

Project	Client group[1]	Agency lead	Client Numbers Target	Actual 3 yrs[2]	Total[2]	Residential accommodation types used[3]
Bolton	LD	LA/DHA	80	47	68	RESID SGH FOST IND
Calderdale	LD	LA	32	24	25	SGH
Camden	LD	LA/VOL	17	7	14	SGH USGH
Derby	LD	DHA/VOL	40	27	46	RESID HOST SHELT SGH USGH FOST IND
Islington	LD	LA	8	0	5	IND
Kidderminster	LD	LA	33	24	25	RESID HOST SGH FOST
Liverpool	LD	VOL/DHA	12	14	14	SGH
Maidstone	LD	LA	50	36	52	RESID HOST SHELT SGH USGH FOST
Somerset	LD	LA	45	48	64	RESID HOST SGH USGH
Torbay	LD	DHA/VOL	10	10	10	RESID
Warwick	LD	LA/VOL	40	12	30	RESID HOST USGH
Cambridge	AM	DHA	3	3	3	SGH
Glossop	PD	LA	3	3	3	SGH
Brent	MH	DHA/LA	60	42	52	RESID HOST USGH FOST IND
Bucks	MH	DHA	100	92	99	RESID HOST SGH USGH LODG IND
Chichester	MH	DHA	30	11	22	RESID USGH
Greenwich	MH	LA	16	10	16	SGH IND
Waltham F.	MH	VOL	18	12	14	USGH
Warrington	MH	VOL	16	17	18	HOST
West Berks	MH	LA	50	5	5	SGH USGH IND
West Lancs	MH	LA	40	6	0	Not applicable
Coventry	EPH	LA	17	22	23	SHELT
Darlington	EPH	DHA/LA	54	100	101	SHELT USGH FOST IND
Winchester	EPH	DHA	10	18	23	SHELT
Camberwell	EMH	VOL	30	0	0	RESID
Hillingdon	EMH	LA	40	45	45	RESID
St Helens	EMH	DHA	20	0	20	RESID
W. Cumbria	EMH	LA	18	23	26	RESID
Total			900	658	823	

1 Abbreviations: LD = people with learning difficulties; MH = people with mental health problems; AM = adolescents with multiple disabilities; PD = people with physical disabilities; EPF = elderly people who are physically frail; EMH = elderly people with mental health problems.

2 Over the three years of central funding, and over the period of the PSSRU research (different for first and second round projects), respectively.

3 Accommodation occupied by clients nine months after leaving hospital. This includes accommodation for clients who moved after the central funding period. Definitions are given in Table 6.2. Abbreviations are: RESID = residential home; HOST = hostel; SHELT = sheltered or very sheltered housing; SGH = staffed group home; USGH = unstaffed group home; FOST = foster placement; LODG = supported lodgings; IND = independent living.

Client numbers

In the columns reporting client numbers we focus on target and actual numbers of movers. Target numbers were specified at the outset in the formal agreements between local agencies and the DHSS, often following discussion and revision. The first column of numbers gives the targets which projects took with them into the first year of DHSS funding, although, as we discuss in Chapter 8, even these targets had to be altered in one or two cases as initial intentions proved unworkable. A variety of factors prompted revisions, some beyond the control of the projects themselves.

The numbers of people moving from hospital over the three-year period of central government funding, recorded in the next column, are instructive, and are certainly not unrelated to 'project performance' in a very general sense. Projects were trying to establish long-term residents of hospitals in well-supported community placements on the assumption that this was beneficial. Thus, other things being equal – a most important qualifying clause – the earlier this successful rehabilitation was achieved the better. While speed of rehabilitation is a dangerous goal on its own (many commentators have laid much of the blame for the abject failings of the hospital closure policies in parts of Italy and the US on the over-emphasis on this particular objective), throughput remains a widely-used measure of service effectiveness. None of the pilot projects saw speed of resettlement as the sole or dominant aim, but it nevertheless requires examination. (Client turnover in the community, as a result of deaths or returns to hospital, was quite high among the elderly client groups, but not built into many project plans.)

The next column of Table 6.1 notes the number of people who moved from hospital to the community during the period in which the PSSRU research team was able to work with projects. As far as these client moves are concerned, this period commenced from the first day of DHSS funding and generally ran until late autumn 1988. This meant that first-round projects (funded from April 1984 until March 1987) had one year more than second-round projects (April 1985 to March 1988) in which to move people to the community. It is therefore not at all sensible to use this third column of client numbers as some kind of virility or efficiency indicator for projects. It simply records the number of people moving up to the date we stopped counting. Given the process of counting, and particularly the blurred or contested definitions of who was and who was not 'a client', illustrated in the next paragraph, we did not stop counting on the same day in every area. It was also our intention to continue to follow-up clients for as long as possible to maximise the sample sizes for the analyses of outcomes and costs. A final consideration in relation to two projects was our decision to delay the cut-off date for data gathering to include in our sample the first few clients to be resettled in those areas. Each and every project continued in some shape or form to move people from hospital to the community, either to replace original clients who had moved on, returned to hospital or died, or as part of a wider scheme to develop community care in the locality. The 'total' number of clients is therefore arbitrarily truncated by the research process.

One project disagreed with our statement of their target number of movers and with the number moved to date. Some of their clients moved great distances away from the area immediately upon leaving hospital. (One moved over 100 miles away and another to the United States.) The project insisted that these were 'project clients', although it was not clear how they were benefiting from services established with DHSS funding under the Care in the Community programme. We could not reach agreement with another project about some of the facilities to which people moved. These were in the hospital grounds, and we interpreted them to be hospital facilities; the project claimed they were community facilities. One project helped people move to community settings, often many miles from the former hospital of residence, but they were not formally discharged from hospital for anything up to 12 months. We found ourselves in the odd position of conducting community interviews and costing community care packages for people who were still defined as 'in-patients'. Some of these people later went back into a hospital ward without *ever* having been formally discharged. We have counted these people as movers.

Destinational outcomes

The accommodation destinations for client movers are also included in Table 6.1. At this juncture we simply list the types of accommodation being used by clients at the time of the follow-up (Time 2) community assessments. We shall give more details in Chapter 8. The types of community accommodation are defined in Table 6.2. These accommodation labels are used to organise some of our analyses, and are preferred to the labels attached to facilities by individual projects because of inter-project differences in definition and inconsistency in use.

In Chapters 8 and Part III below we will not confine our evaluation to the cohort of people who moved from hospital during the three-year period, but look at any client discharged with the assistance of a project during the period in which we were able to gather research data. This has the virtue of maximising our sample sizes with knock-on benefits for analytical robustness. We shall also say more about readmissions to hospital and deaths.

Table 6.2
Definitions of accommodation types

A *residential home* (abbreviation RESID) has:
- continuous staff cover by day
- waking staff cover by night
- six or more client places

A *hostel* (HOST) has:
- continuous or intermediate (regular but not continuous) staff cover by day
- sleeping in or on-call or no cover by night
- six or more client places

Sheltered housing (SHELT) has
- continuous or intermediate or ad hoc staff cover by day
- waking or sleeping or on-call staff cover by night
- the number of client places in the whole facility is greater than the number of places in the individual living unit

A *staffed group home* (SGH) has
- continuous or intermediate staff cover by day
- waking or sleeping in or on-call or no cover by night
- more than one but less than six client places

An *unstaffed group home* (USGH) has
- ad hoc or no staff cover by day
- on-call or no staff cover by night
- more than one but less than six client places

Foster care (FOST) has
- intermediate foster family support by day
- on-call foster family support by night
- client(s) move into established household

Supported lodgings (LODG) have
- ad hoc or no staff cover by day
- on-call staff cover by night
- clients usually move into pre-existing household (that is, do not establish it themselves)

Independent living (IND) has
- ad hoc or no staff cover by day
- on-call or no staff cover by night

7 Financing community care

At the core of almost every attack on community care policies over the last two decades are claims that resources are too few, too late or tumultuous. Either the money is unavailable, or it is available only after the event, or its availability creates such turbulence and confusion as to misdirect or distort key decisions. The House of Commons Social Services Committee (1985, para. 21) opined that the country 'was providing a mental disability service which is under-financed and under-staffed both in its health and social care aspects', a view repeated in the Committee's 1990 report. Savings from running down hospitals have been argued to be insufficient to fund the community services needed by former residents, with most savings not realised until hospitals actually close. The Audit Commission (1986) vividly illustrated the perverse incentives within organisational and financial arrangements, and like Sir Roy Griffiths (1988), pointed to the resource confusion stemming from the fragmentation of responsibilities. To the disappointment of some people, the debate stimulated by the 1990 *National Health Service and Community Care Act* did not persuade the Government to introduce ring-fenced community care grants. The new Mental Illness Specific Grant has been criticised for being too small. Social security support for people in the community is criticised for its inadequacy and disincentives.

These are familiar laments. When the demonstration programme was launched these difficulties might not have been expressed with the same forcefulness or illustrated with such didactic skill as achieved by more recent commentaries, but the funding and organisation of the programme responded to them. Unlike previous attempts to alter the balance between hospital and community care, the DHSS's programme brought substantial additional finance and concentrated on a sufficiently small number of areas to have an impact.

In this chapter we look at the financing of community care. We take three perspectives. We first examine the level of grant aid offered to projects, although it would be premature to attempt a full answer to the general question concerning the impact of the grants as the remainder of the book is devoted to this issue. The chapter then turns to the financing of projects through the social security system. Many clients and projects relied heavily on these benefits to enable them to purchase the residential and other services necessary for an acceptable standard of community living and support. We will explore the issues raised by the Audit Commission, Griffiths and others, pulling out conclusions for community care outside the demonstration programme. Finally, we consider joint finance and dowry payments. Comparatively few projects were dependent on (local) joint finance or 'dowry' transfers during the three years of central government funding, but in association with social security payments, these monies were expected to be the mainstay of support in the longer term.

Pump-priming programme grants

Although £17 million (£25 million at 1991 prices) was pumped into the projects by the DHSS, this large sum was never intended to be enough to resettle and continue to support all of the hospital residents whom projects targeted in their initial plans. It was always intended that central government grants would be supplemented by local health and social care resources (statutory and nonstatutory) or social security payments. A requirement of central funding was that local budgets would bear the cost of continued provision of care and support once DHSS grant aid ceased. The central grant was therefore a fine example of pump-priming funding, aiming to promote continued activity within and after the demonstration programme.

The grant allocations at the outset are given in Table 7.1. For two projects the distribution of grant aid between revenue and capital spending was not laid out in the contract between local agencies and the DHSS because of initial uncertainties about the cost of planned capital investments, and in quite a few other projects either the total amount of grant aid received or the capital percentage altered over the programme period. (Table 7.1 does not list the amounts actually paid out.) The final column in the table reports the amount of grant aid per targeted client. This is an indicator of limited value since both numerator and denominator altered, but as an indication of funding *intent* it is interesting to note the spread from £4,800 to £46,875 per client (over three years), around a median of £18,600. Given what was already known at that time about the costs of community care, and that quite a high proportion of grant aid was to be spent on capital, and even allowing for the inevitable time lag between the start of a project and work with the first client, these per client grant payments fall some way short of the full cost of community care. Projects needed to supplement these funds from other sources.

A variety of local deals between and within statutory and voluntary agencies were planned at the launch of each project. For example, several used district or regional sources – such as North West RHA's bridging fund for people with learning difficulties – and dowry transfers. These deals did not always work out as intended, and there were one or two acrimonious disputes between agencies in the period after DHSS grant aid ceased (see below). Every project drew on 'ordinary' services offered by health and local authorities and other agencies. There were some clients who did not see a GP in the first nine months after leaving hospital (the period over which we gathered data), and quite a few did not use adult education facilities, job centres, libraries or parks, but the majority made use of ordinary community resources and facilities. The costs of these, particularly when clients were fully integrated with other

Table 7.1
Care in the Community demonstration programme grants

Project	Client group[1]	Total grant at outset[2] (£000)	Percentage capital[3] (%)	Grant cost per client (target)[4] (£)
Bolton	LD	1700	8	21250
Calderdale	LD	1028	20	32125
Camden	LD	546	7	32118
Derby	LD	796	7	19900
Islington	LD	375	36	46875
Kidderminster	LD	471	0	14273
Liverpool	LD	298	2	24833
Maidstone	LD	751	0	15020
Somerset	LD	806	45	17911
Torbay	LD	100	100	10000
Warwick	LD	460	-[3]	11500
Cambridge	AM	36	28	12000
Glossop	PD	135	85	45000
Brent	MH	1029	9	17150
Bucks	MH	994	65	9940
Chichester	MH	627	72	20900
Greenwich	MH	511	45	31938
Waltham F.	MH	365	30	20278
Warrington	MH	328	-[3]	20500
West Berks	MH	538	57	10760
West Lancs	MH	192	12	4800
Coventry	EPH	303	0	17824
Darlington	EPH	930	3	15000
Winchester	EPH	135	4	13500
Camberwell	EMH	1206	59	40200
Hillingdon	EMH	753	0	18825
St Helens	EMH	764	73	38200
W. Cumbria	EMH	332	25	18444

1 Abbreviations: LD = people with learning difficulties; MH = people with mental health problems; AM = adolescents with multiple disabilities; PD = people with physical disabilities; EPF = elderly people with physical frailty; EMH = elderly people with mental health problems.
2 Some grant allocations changed later on.
3 Some capital proportions changed later on. The grant allocations to Warwick and Warrington did not specify the capital percentage.
4 These are *not* performance indicators in any shape or form!

members of the community, are hard to identify, although the research design allowed us to measure costs comprehensively, no matter from which budget or pocket they were funded. Revenue under-estimates were common across the programme, mostly due to higher than anticipated staffing requirements resulting from under-estimates of clients' support needs. Securing additional revenue funds proved difficult – as it would in the normal cut and thrust of community care development outside a pilot programme – emphasising the need for realistic plans and timetables. Revenue under-spend arose usually when it proved difficult to appoint full staff teams for resettlement work, or when suitable buildings were not secured.

One of the most important practical barriers to hospital closure policies is the absence of adequate double or parallel funding of hospital and community facilities as one runs down and the other builds up. *Capital funding* presents special difficulties. In the very short run, the marginal cost of providing community care for a few extra people is small, not least because little new capital investment is required and the marginal saving to a hospital of closing a few beds is also small. But many projects resettled people in groups, so the assumption of small costs or savings at the margin is misplaced, and the margin is fairly thick. What is more, short-run marginal cost is not the relevant datum here: a national policy of hospital rundown and community care development needs *long-term* cost projections. These capital needs were recognised in the demonstration programme, with about 30 per cent of central funding targeted for capital spending.

Some projects, such as Torbay, requested (and received) only capital funding. In Torbay revenue funding came from social security benefits and DHA resources, and the hostel quickly became self-financing from social security receipts. Some other projects, such as Kidderminster, Coventry and Hillingdon, sought *no* capital funding from Care in the Community coffers but built up their services from local resources: Housing Corporation grants, voluntary organisation endowments or other income, local authority housing and social services expenditures, 'free' NHS facilities converted from other uses, private loans and mortgages repaid from resident charges, and local joint finance monies. There were unexpectedly high capital costs in some projects, especially those located in London and the South East when the property price boom took off and when there were delays in acquiring buildings or completing conversion work. The Chichester project faced high capital costs when it had to renovate a listed building, and the Greenwich project found housing prohibitively expensive. The Camberwell project was unable to find a building suitable for conversion to a specialist residential home and had to build its own, turning revenue funding into capital for this purpose. In Maidstone part of the revenue grant was converted into capital. Some projects forgot to make allowances for furniture, carpets or adaptations, which required minor virement.

It is interesting to compare the Care in the Community capital grants with the recently initiated DH Capital Loans Fund of £50 million. First and obviously, the demonstration programme capital grants were gifts not loans. Second, they were rather more substantial. The pilot projects benefited to the tune of more than £4,285 per targeted client at 1984 prices (it was actually more because of the shifts from revenue to capital in at least four projects), compared to roughly £2,500 per client (revalued to 1984 prices) if the new DH fund is allocated to the 15,232 people scheduled for discharge from hospital over a five-year period (House of Commons Social Services Committee, 1990).

Social security financing

It hardly needs saying that social security plays a critical role in the lives of people moving into the community from long-stay hospital placements. Resourcing the move to the community has always proved difficult because the packages of care needed by clients are funded from many sources. Many projects made creative use of the social security system, and state benefits represented a major source of continuing funds (see Table 7.2):

- Although projects delivered different types of service (Chapter 8), they all depended for some of their revenue on clients' statutory benefit entitlements.

Table 7.2
Benefits and other income received by clients

Benefit type	Numbers of clients by client group				
	Learning diffs.	Mental health	Disabilities[1]	Elderly	All (%)
Supplementary benefit	189	90	0	0	279 (66%)
Additional requirements	9	3	0	1	13 (3%)
Housing benefit	105	17	0	14	136 (32%)
Severe disablement allowance, incl. invalidity benefit	173	58	3	1	235 (56%)
Retirement pension, incl. supplementary pension	17	19	0	57	93 (22%)
Attendance allowance	47	2	0	9	58 (14%)
Mobility allowance	31	1	2	4	38 (9%)
War/widow's pension, incl. industrial injuries benefit	0	3	0	3	6 (1%)
Single payments	42	9	0	0	51 (12%)
Personal resources	32	10	0	30	72 (17%)
Wages	91	19	2	2	114 (27%)
Total no. of respondents	230	126	5	59	420 (100%)

1 People with physical disabilities (Glossop) and young people with multiple disabilities (Cambridge).

- Most clients moving into voluntary and private registered residential and nursing homes qualified for residential care allowances.
- Some congregate living settings were funded entirely from clients' supplementary benefit allowances (after the initial capital outlay).
- In one project these revenue funds were supplemented by annual *ad hoc* payments from the health authority. Where clients held tenancy rights, ordinary housing costs were paid from supplementary or housing benefit entitlements.
- Lump sum payments and resettlement grants covered some of the expenses of furnishing and decorating new homes and providing clothes. Many projects recounted tales of people arriving from hospital without a change of clothes, or without the aids needed for daily living, such as incontinence pads and wheelchairs, even without glasses or teeth.
- In some projects mobility allowances funded private transport for groups of people.

Clearly the benefits system not only contributed to the successful operation of pilot projects but also played a part in determining service design.

At a time of tight budgets the advantages of external funding are apparent. Entitlements as of right bring flexibility to shape and develop services without the need to secure advance agreements on finance. Yet over-reliance on such lateral sources of funding can create instability. Moreover, many people mistakenly believe that the social security system is comprehensive and upholds the principles of normalisation and integration. This misapprehension endures despite widespread evidence of the inability of benefits to provide a reasonable standard of living. Thus the problem of inadequacy is added to the danger of instability. A third difficulty is that the social security system has developed in piecemeal fashion in response to varying pressures, particularly the sometimes conflicting objectives of meeting need and maintaining work incentives, overlaid with political decisions about what share of national resources should be devoted to this area of public expenditure. These pressures from within or outwith the benefit system can create incentives for particular provisions or activities which may not be the most appropriate or in the best interests of clients.

The incidence of these three potential difficulties with benefits – instability, inadequacy, and perverse incentives – and their impact upon the quality of community care and clients' lives are considered below. First, we describe clients' financial resources and receipts.

Wages and personal resources

The information gathered during our evaluation reflects the system as it was prior to the system changes introduced in April 1988. Most clients in our sample moved from hospital before this date, and more than three-quarters of the follow-up community interviews were completed by then. In fact, the general principles of the social security system prior to the 1988 reforms are not greatly different from those now applicable, and we note some of the changes as we proceed. Information was collected for over 400 community care clients in interviews with them and with staff. Interviews, using the Client Service Receipt Interview, were conducted between January 1987 and August 1988. We asked about income from employment, social security benefits and other sources such as private pensions or savings. This is a sensitive area for many people and data collection was not always straightforward. Some staff and projects did not know or considered the information confidential; some sought special agreement from clients or, in one project, clients' relatives.

A quarter of the 420 people for whom we had income information earned a wage from employment, but the disincentive to work, created in part by the benefit system, was enormous (see below). Of those in paid employment, only three people earned more than £4 per week. (Their wages were £40, £15 and £7.80 per week.) Some earned as little as 50 pence per week from sheltered employment, day centres or industrial therapy units. One client in six had some personal resources, sometimes savings built up while resident in hospital, but certainly less than the £6,000 limit allowable for claiming supplementary benefit. Half the group of clients with personal financial resources were aged over 65 and many had spent comparatively short periods in hospital. These people often had to contribute to the costs of services as their resources or capital exceeded the limit of £3,000 allowed for full entitlement. Only two clients had personal resources which precluded benefit receipt.

Benefits claimed by projects and clients

The first point to note in relation to benefits received (Table 7.2) is that most clients were not entitled to national insurance benefits, since entitlement to this side of the social security system is dependent on contributions paid. It is most unlikely that long-stay hospital residents will build up sufficient contributions to qualify. When discussing social security, therefore, we are mainly restricted to income maintenance or needs-related benefits, with the exception of the state retirement pension.

Two-thirds of clients received *supplementary benefit*, the amount depending on the basic scale rates and individual resources compared to 'requirements'. (Income support replaced supplementary benefit after April 1988.) Because the community interview came about nine months after the move from hospital, few clients received the long-term supplementary benefit rate, although receipt of severe disablement allowance for 52 weeks ensured entitlement to the long-term rate. *Additional requirements* were available for people claiming supplementary benefit. These were intended to cover special expenses, and those claimed by the sample group were for heating, special diets, laundry and clothing. *Single payments* were also available during this period; they were claimed for house set-up costs (although these were also sometimes funded from project grants), clothing, footwear and cold weather payments.

The situation regarding supplementary benefit claims for people classified as *boarders* was fairly stable prior to the April 1988 changes, with the level of benefit related to the services provided in an establishment. A boarder was someone who paid a charge which included the cost of accommodation and at least some cooked or prepared meals which were both prepared and consumed in the accommodation or in associated premises. There were two main categories of boarder: people in *residential care or nursing home* establishments and those living in *board and lodging* establishments.

The supplementary benefit regulations and entitlements for people in residential care and nursing homes depended on who provided or sponsored the placement, and the registration category. (These regulations remained until the 1990 legislation came into effect.) In private or voluntary establishments the level of payment was related to the number and type of staff and therefore the type of care provided. Supplementary benefit covered the costs of accommodation and meals up to the limit for the accommodation type. There have been nationally set limits since April 1985. In one of the pilot projects in which clients claimed supplementary benefit as boarders in a registered residential care home, for example, each resident paid £150 per week (in 1986-87) to the voluntary organisation for accommodation and care, and retained £9.25 for their personal allowance. Some were additionally entitled to attendance allowance, which was counted as income for supplementary benefit calculations, so that the total amount received was unchanged. Some people had personal resources over and above the capital limits and so funded part or all of the placement costs. In local authority homes, by contrast, a minimum charge was levied on the resident equivalent to a single person's retirement pension, less the personal allowance of what was then £7.90 per week. If the resident's income was below this amount (and capital holdings below £3,000) there could be a top-up from supplementary benefit. If personal income was above this level, charges were made to the resident on a sliding scale up to the full charge as calculated by the local authority, with the remainder funded by the providing authority.

The second category of boarders for supplementary benefit regulations were people living in *board and lodging* accommodation. These also fell into two categories, people in ordinary board and lodging and people living in (registered) hostels. Supplementary benefit was paid up to the local or national limit for the type of accommodation provided for the claimant and a meals allowance paid to the claimant where meals were not included in the accommodation charge. Some projects registered some of their accommodation as hostels for DHSS purposes in order to maximise benefit entitlement while retaining some client choice and control over resources. Provision of ordinary board and lodging accommodation meant that charges were subject to preset local limits for full board and lodging.

One third of clients for whom we collected information on income sources claimed *housing benefit*, available to those who were paying rent or general property rates (water rates were paid through supplementary benefit), but excluding those who, for DHSS purposes, were classified as boarders and claimed these supplementary benefit allowances.

Severe disablement allowance was one of the benefits specifically for people with disabilities, and over half the demonstration programme clients claimed it. Although not means-tested, eligibility for severe disablement allowance was subject to assessment as 'at least 80 per cent disabled', or incapacity for work for 28 weeks. For those relying on benefits as their main source of income, it was often necessary to claim a top-up from supplementary benefit, as severe disablement allowance was paid at 60 per cent of its contributory benefit equivalent (which was invalidity benefit) and below supplementary benefit scale rates. Clients claiming the usual top-up from supplementary benefit to supplement severe disablement allowance had their earning power limited to £4 a week before the amount of benefit was cut. (This compared to possible earnings of up to £15 before benefit deductions for those claiming invalidity benefit.) Receipt of *attendance allowance* qualified the client for severe disablement allowance entitlement, but qualification required demonstration of need for attention or supervision which had existed for six months, which meant a considerable delay for someone leaving hospital, to which was added a further delay of over six weeks, this being the average time taken to process a claim for attendance allowance (*Disability Rights Bulletin*, Spring 1988). On the other hand, attendance allowance had the advantage of not being taken into account in calculating income for supplementary benefit (other than residential or nursing home allowances), thus raising a recipient's income. At least 14 per cent of the population sample received this benefit. (There were some outstanding claims.)

Mobility allowance was received by one client in eleven. This was another non-contributory and non-means-tested cash benefit, payable to people who had difficulty in walking caused (mainly) by a physical condition. Unlike attendance allowance, it was not available to people whose onset of condition was after their 65th birthday. Although there were some claims undergoing appeal for people with mental health problems, this benefit made a larger contribution to the personal resources of people with learning difficulties. It represented not only extra income of approximately £22 per week (and, like attendance allowance, was ignored as income for supplementary benefit entitlement), but also widened a claimant's range of opportunities in the community by increasing their travel options. The method of assessment for both mobility and attendance allowance did not easily enable people with mental health problems to be included, and the proportion of the cohort covered was small given their disabilities. Moreover, entitlement required 'proof' of disability by professional validation, which some groups working on behalf of people with disabilities argued to be contrary to principles which they and many other people were trying to establish.

The threat to stability and quality

To what extent does reliance on the social security budget for long-term funding of community care threaten the stability and quality of service provision?

The 1985 report from the House of Commons Social Services Committee provided one of a number of criticisms during the 1980s of the instability of community care systems stemming from over-reliance on state benefits. In the early 1980s, social security was just about the only mechanism by which substantial extra funding could be focused on dehospitalisation programmes. Pilot projects were obviously less reliant on this financial base, but still faced uncertainties and difficulties during the grant period. (Shortly after grant funding ceased, the instability of social security funding was amply illustrated. Health authorities, committed to hospital closures and wanting to put their reprovision plans on a sound financial footing, aimed to maximise client entitlement through the use of residential care homes (registered under the *Registered Homes Act 1984*) owned by housing associations or trusts set up for the purpose. The DHSS questioned the payment of benefits to residents supported by health authority staff, likening their situation to hospital care. In 1988 the decision was made that residents in such situations were to be treated as if they were patients in hospital, thus reducing their entitlement to some social security benefits. Subsequent secondments of staff from the health service to non-statutory agencies further muddied the waters. In February 1991, a Social Security Commissioner decided that hostels were not to be treated as hospitals even if owned by a health authority.)

A common problem within the programme was the threat to revenue funding when residential facility occupancy rates fell. A facility's revenue from benefits would almost inevitably decrease at a faster rate than staff and other costs. When a resident had to return to hospital for a period of more than six weeks (thereby losing part of their income maintenance entitlement), projects had the dilemma of choosing between financial prudence and offering the client a permanent home. A second problem was the failure of board and lodging rates to keep up with cost inflation, threatening jobs or quality of care or both. The fundamental changes to the social security system of April 1988 came too late for our evaluation of the demonstration programme, although these instability problems appear still to dog community care.

The adequacy of social security funding

Were benefit levels adequate to fund comprehensive, high-quality community services, which offered choice to people with disabilities?

Since 1970 several new benefits have been introduced (attendance allowance, the Family Fund, mobility allowance, invalid care allowance), each intended to improve access to community services for people with disabilities. By recognising needs and the burden on carers, it was hoped that expensive and often inappropriate institutional care could be avoided. However, these benefits failed to overcome a number of major problems, each of which arose in the demonstration programme. First, the benefit entitlement for people with disabilities still relied more on the type or cause of disability than its severity. For example, the eligibility criteria for mobility allowance were biased towards people with difficulties in walking, with a physical cause, and *not* whether there were extra costs associated with mobility, and this despite the well-established relationship between poverty and disability. In 1983, 60 per cent of disabled people were living in or on the margins of poverty compared with 28 per cent of those without disability (House of Commons Social Services Committee, 1985). Second, there was the problem already noted that annual benefit increases were not uprated to match costs of living, and rarely do benefit levels provide a disposable income above subsistence level. Third, changes to regulations can affect claimants' standards of living. Special payments made for particular needs also contrive to reinforce dependence and classification associated with institutional living, but rarely cover the full cost of the extra requirements.

From the sample of 420 people for whom we collected income and social security receipt data, we selected 258 people for whom we could separate housing benefit from social security benefits and for whom we had information on the total costs of community care. We were interested in the relationship between (care) costs and (social security) receipts. Community care needs not only to replace the 'free' hotel services of hospitals with residential accommodation, but also a range of specialist services previously provided in hospital which might now come from a mix of agencies in the community, including day care, peripatetic specialist inputs, employment placement and leisure activities. Average total benefit receipt by client group is reported in Table 7.3. Elderly people with mental health problems received much lower amounts than others, largely because of their accommodation placements in local authority Part III homes, which entitled them only to retirement pensions. Table 7.4 shows that social security receipts amounted to at most about one-third of the comprehensive cost of community care.

Table 7.5 expresses these receipts as a proportion of accommodation costs, a more appropriate set of statistics given that social security is generally not expected to fund many non-residential services. Clearly, social security alone cannot provide funding for a comprehensive community service. The third

Table 7.3
Average total social security received per week (1986-87 prices) by client group

Client group	Mean £	Standard deviation £	Cases N
Learning difficulties	116.60	45.37	113
Mental health problems	82.79	36.60	111
Elderly, physical frailty	93.40	21.32	20
Elderly, mental health probs	40.07	5.42	39
All clients	91.15	44.98	283

Table 7.4
Social security received as a proportion of total cost of care package

Client group	Mean £	Standard deviation £	Cases N
Learning difficulties	35.35	22.92	88
Mental health problems	34.17	17.81	111
Elderly, physical frailty	31.18	7.06	20
Elderly, mental health probs	20.47	4.67	39
All clients	32.27	18.61	258

Table 7.5
Social security received as a proportion of cost of accommodation and living expenses and staff support

	Percentage accommodation and living expenses		Percentage staff support	
Client group	Mean %	Standard deviation %	Mean %	Cases N
Learning difficulties	91.44	27.8	55.2	75
Mental health problems	62.94	29.7	48.9	111
Elderly, physical frailty	66.38	25.9	50.8	20
Elderly, mental health probs	21.71	5.2	21.7	39
All clients	65.38	34.7	-	245

column of Table 7.5 shows social security received as a proportion of accommodation and living expenses *and* self-support where this is provided out of the accommodation budget. With the exception of elderly people with mental health problems, the percentage is similar across client groups.

Using our consistently defined accommodation types (see Table 6.2 for definitions), which might not coincide with those used for some benefit purposes, we have arranged average benefit levels by accommodation type in Table 7.6 for each of 15 projects. Differences between projects for the same type of accommodation were due to a number of factors: different philosophies of care, and particularly the emphasis given to client choice and autonomy (which then influenced how they used the benefit system); different interpretations of regulations and entitlements by local offices (for example, in relation to attendance allowance); registration category; managing agency (for example, the residential homes in projects X and Z were managed by the local authority, whereas in project F a voluntary organisation had management responsibility); and receipt of particular types of benefit (one client in project Z received industrial injuries benefit, slightly raising the average for the whole group).

It is unrealistic to move people from long-stay hospitals to the community in pursuit of improvements in quality of life if they do not have enough money to enjoy wider and richer opportunities. Buying a cup of coffee in a local cafe becomes a major financial decision for clients with small personal allowances, and holidays, outings and large items of clothing are often out of the question. Stewart (1988) drew on five studies of mental health social work agencies to estimate that two-thirds of service users are also benefit claimants relying mainly on means-tested benefits, and about half said they had financial problems. (Money problems, such as debt or delay in benefit payment, can exacerbate anxiety and depression, and so the adequacy problem of social security funding can be yet more serious for some people.) Kay and Legg interviewed 100 people who had left psychiatric hospital care in London. They found that 91 were unemployed and relied on social security benefits, but 'nearly two-thirds said that no-one had checked their benefit entitlement or whether they were clear about how to claim, prior to their discharge' (1986, p.17).

In each of the pilot projects, staff spent considerable time and resources assisting clients to claim benefits, for very few had any other advocates, and problems with social security benefits can be acute for people moving out of hospital with limited experience of dealing with bureaucracies. The path was often smoothed by investment in good working relationships with the local social security office, and this proved to be especially important when a large number of people moved from hospital at one time. When local offices were informed of project intentions well in advance, delays were sometimes reduced.

Table 7.6

Average benefit receipt by client group and residential type (1986-87 prices)

Client group		*Type of residential accommodation in community*[1]								
	No. of clients	RESID £	HOST £	SHELT £	SGH £	USGH £	FOST £	LODG £	INDEP £	Average £
Project A	12				120.40					120.40
Project B	34	102.63	131.18	92.77	90.14	113.74	80.76		53.93	94.01
Project C	10		156.07							156.07
Project D	25		155.73		152.24	156.07				155.46
Project E	16		45.45							45.45
Project F	16	156.07	148.85		154.70		84.60			147.48
All people with learning difficulties	**113**	**111.54**	**123.57**	**92.77**	**114.44**	**134.90**	**82.04**		**53.93**	**116.60**
Project G	40	39.20	76.27		88.55	79.11	91.85		52.63	77.42
Project H	26		45.50			38.64		82.02		48.39
Project I	18	124.88	58.58			63.55				93.11
Project J	15		136.56							136.56
Project K	12					92.52				92.52
All people with mental health problems	**111**	**116.31**	**81.86**		**88.55**	**75.89**	**91.85**	**82.02**	**52.63**	**82.79**
Project L	11	40.50								40.50
Project M	28	39.90								39.90
All elderly people with ment. hlth probs	**39**	**40.07**								**40.07**
Project N	8			79.00						79.00
Project O	12			102.99						102.99
All elderly people with physical frailty	**20**			**93.40**						**93.40**
All clients	**283**	**61.73**	**104.26**	**93.23**	**111.85**	**78.91**	**87.64**	**82.02**	**52.95**	**91.15**

1 Abbreviations are: RESID = residential home, including old people's home; HOST = hostel; SHELT = sheltered or very sheltered housing; SGH = staffed group home; USGH = unstaffed group home; FOST = adult fostering; LODG = supported lodgings; INDEP = independent house or flat.

Perverse incentives

Did the regulations and conventions governing social security benefits create the wrong or 'perverse' incentives within the community care system?

The Audit Commission's (1986) report argued that one important reason why progress towards community care had been slow and uneven was because non cash-limited social security payments made it more attractive to statutory agencies to encourage or allow the development of residential rather than domiciliary care, and (passively or actively) to shift the balance of residential provision towards the private and voluntary sectors. Quite a few local authorities resisted these pressures, but many were soon to be rate-capped (and, more recently, charge-capped), and it was possible to hold out only for so long. The Audit Commission usefully tabulated the component costs of different care packages, including hospital in-patient care and independent living. For a number of client groups, and for people with a variety of financial and familial circumstances, the low- (and sometimes lowest-) cost option for the public authority which had the power to choose or influence the local balance of provision was actually a high- (sometimes the highest-) cost care package for all provider agencies taken together, and care arrangements which imposed the lowest social costs were often comparatively expensive to the authority with direct responsibility. It was hardly surprising that the balance of provision was askew. It may have been less costly to society to move someone from hospital to the community, but there was no incentive for local authorities to do so, for the cost saving from closing a hospital bed nearly all fell to health authorities. Joint finance is supposed to help sort out this disincentive but, as we saw in Chapter 2, this was not widely the case. These problems generated concerns about the wide regional variations in care arrangements, the lack of any need assessment requirement for non-statutory residential care, worries that the profit motive might sometimes be stronger than the motive to provide high-quality care, and difficulties in ensuring access to day support when people are in dispersed private facilities.

By subsidising costs, the Care in the Community programme helped to reduce the financial incentives to provide inappropriate or socially costly care. Unless constrained by their contract with the DHSS and, of course, by their commitment to a particular style of community care (which was very strong in many cases), participating health and local authorities still had little incentive to offer care in domiciliary settings and every incentive to use those types of residential establishment that maximised benefit receipt. What emerged from the programme, therefore, was a greater mix of community provision than was generally to be seen in England at the time, although the mix represented the resolution of the same competing tendencies – the quest for quality and normalisation on the one hand, versus the pursuit of local or self-interested financial prudence on the other. (However, one or two projects in the pilot programme gave every evidence of being impervious to financial considerations, and difficulties emerged for them as they moved towards mainstream funding arrangements.) Decisions to register facilities as hostels rather than residential homes to retain flexibility and greater client control lost some projects revenue.

A further perverse incentive within the benefit system discourages community clients from seeking paid employment. The care philosophy of many projects was built around a commitment to a full and 'ordinary' life-style for clients, including work opportunities. However, the difference between payment for work and benefits when not working, the so-called replacement ratio, was very low for most clients, and for some was negative: they lost more in benefits when they moved into paid employment than they earned in wages. It was not hard to identify the causes of this. Because of their disabilities, or because they lack work experience or qualifications, most clients were only offered sheltered, unskilled or part-time employment, paying low wages. Working also often involved travelling expenses, clothing, lunch and other hidden costs which had not been incurred before. Not one of the programme clients earned anything like the lowest amount payable through supplementary benefit for a place in a residential care home. Earnings from employment over £4 were removed pound for pound from supplementary benefit, and because severe disablement allowance was seen as a replacement for earnings, holding a job over a period of time threatened the validity of claims. Thus while many clients needed staff support, without social security benefits it was impossible to provide it. Some schemes around the country have found ways of providing 'gifts' instead of money as recompense for work done, but this is an unsatisfactory solution because it is unstable and because it encourages dependency on statutory and voluntary agencies which can inhibit development and personal autonomy and could be demeaning. If a project depended on maximum benefit for its very existence, it was difficult to encourage clients to seek paid employment. In a society which values paid employment, this is a very limiting constraint on integration and rehabilitation.

Case management

Our examination of the benefits received by Care in the Community clients, therefore, leads us to draw similar conclusions to those which have been reached by others. Reliance on the social security budget to fund service provision was considerable, but dogged by three problems. Means-testing and other characteristics of the system created instability, for changes in levels of payment, regulations and eligibility criteria directly affected the incomes of clients and agencies, in turn making it harder for service delivery or coordinating agencies to plan and maintain high-quality care. Second, the benefits received were not adequate to fund community care at even 'average levels' of quality and comprehensiveness. This left many people without the usual opportunities for employment, leisure, holidays and so on. In no single case did a client's entitlements fund the kind of life-style that would be tolerated as minimally acceptable for the vast majority of the UK population. Third, there were too many 'perverse incentives' within the benefit system working against the provision of the most appropriate, most valued and even the most inexpensive community care.

These problems did not arise within the demonstration programme with quite the same frequency or intensity as was often to be found elsewhere, partly because almost every client was supported by a case manager or keyworker. We will see in Chapter 10 that case management meant very different things and was sometimes minimal, but the fact that most clients had some kind of professional case support resulted in their missing fewer benefits than if they had been left to their own devices. For example, there is evidence that people with mental health problems living in the community who do not have the benefit of such staff support or other advocates tend to claim and receive fewer benefits than programme clients (see, for example, Allen et al., 1991).

Joint finance and dowry transfers

The Audit Commission (1987) estimated that hospitals accommodated 27 per cent of all adults with learning difficulties in England and Wales but accounted for about 49 per cent of the total spending. This latter percentage may be an over-estimate, for it is not obvious that all of the indirect costs of community care have been included in the calculations, but the broad implication is not in doubt: hospitals spend large sums of money on a small proportion of the client group. The same would be true for other adult client groups served by community care (Audit Commission, 1986). The task of shifting some of these hospital resources to the community to fund capital developments and revenue costs is one of the most problematic policy challenges, for hospitals cannot release resources until *after* people leave, while community facilities need them *before* they leave. A number of questions are raised by this transfer of funding, in particular whether the hospital savings are sufficient to cover the costs of community care, and whether they are realised quickly enough. We will not address these two questions until Part III of this book, but to conclude this account of the financing of the Care in the Community pilot projects we describe the dowry arrangements both within and after the demonstration programme.

Joint financing arrangements were introduced in 1976. It was hoped that by making NHS funds available to social services departments, and occasionally to voluntary organisations or education authorities, the provision of a better and more cost-effective balance of care would be encouraged. In the early years, joint finance enjoyed only limited success. (Nationally only about 5 per cent of joint finance money was spent on mental health services, and about 33 per cent on services for people with learning difficulties.) In particular, the financial benefits to local authorities were of limited duration (Wistow, 1983, and Wistow and Hardy, 1986, offer useful reviews). The 1983 Care in the Community Circular sought to overcome some of the disincentives, and introduced a system by which NHS funds could be transferred with identified individuals. Some of the pilot projects planned to make use of this 'dowry' funding.

Variations in dowry policies

Dowries are either lump sum payments or, more commonly, continuing grants made by health authorities to local authorities or voluntary organisations in respect of people to be cared for in the community instead of in hospital. They are usually paid only when people move from hospital to the community: they are initiated by the decanting rather than diversion of clients, and are usually only paid when a hospital bed is permanently closed as a result. Dowries are usually tied to long-stay hospital residents. The term dowry is also sometimes used to refer to transfers between health authorities in respect of patients currently living in one district's hospital 'repatriated' to another, and certainly these intra-NHS transfers were encouraged by some regional health authorities to assist the development of community care. Generally, dowries are seen as revenue transfers, hopefully working in parallel with separate capital funding arrangements. Examinations of dowry policies have uncovered marked inter-regional differences in policies and practical arrangements (Normand, 1986; Wistow and Hardy, 1986; Audit Commission, 1989; Beecham and Knapp, 1990; House of Commons Social Services Committee, 1990). There are perhaps five basic elements to these national variations, which can be illustrated with examples from different regions and from the demonstration programme.

First, there were differences in *regional control*. Regional health authorities intervened to a greater or lesser extent in setting and implementing dowry policies. For example, North Western RHA developed a strong philosophical statement for services for people with learning difficulties to which service provision had to adhere to qualify for dowry transfers, reducing variation in service models. In contrast, North East Thames RHA had a deliberate 'hands-off' policy for mental health service models, resulting in a wide variety of arrangements across districts. Quality assurance responsibilities lie with districts, with regional personnel coming in as arbiters when necessary. Even so, the financial basis on which dowries are calculated and subsequently adjusted is a regional policy. In Northern RHA dowries appeared more likely to be agreements between districts.

Second, dowries are related in some way, sometimes loosely, to *hospital costs*. The most disaggregated dowry formula will base the financial transfer accompanying a client on the actual costs of the hospital for the year when they left. In North East Thames, dowries were calculated as a percentage uprating of the figure set when closure programmes commenced. This applied, for example, to the Waltham Forest project's clients moving from Claybury Hospital. Maidstone also received dowry support on this basis. Less disaggregated dowry baselines pool average costs across a number of hospitals. One RHA set the dowry equal to the average revenue cost in all its psychiatric hospitals except one very low-cost hospital. Despite this omission, the low-cost hospital had to transfer funds at the rate based on its higher-cost neighbours, finding itself in danger of being seriously denuded of funds. This helped at least one of the Care in the Community projects, but embittered the hospital manager who was finding it increasingly difficult to maintain standards of care. South East Thames operated a brokerage system for the replacement of its mental handicap hospitals through its regional mental handicap funding policy. Although average hospital revenue cost will usually be the upper limit on dowries, often only a proportion of this amount is transferred to a new service, perhaps the actual amount saved (as with the Derby and Brent projects in their early years). Obviously, this is partly because fixed cost elements cannot be saved until whole wards or whole hospitals actually close, and partly because of different community arrangements (see below).

Third, it was obviously intended by central government that the transfer of care through dowries should be as near to self-financing as possible in the long run. However, provision is made in all regions for bridging finance, in the form of both 'start-up' capital funds – because services need to be in place before people can move out of hospital, and hospital sites cannot be sold until vacated – and 'double-running' revenue costs – because of the necessary delays in adjusting hospital staffing and other resources to falling bed numbers and in bringing community facility numbers up to full occupancy without jeopardising standards of care. Different *add-on* practices are utilised across the country.

In North East Thames, where dowry transfers were tied to the creation of a *new* place in the community (new-build or conversion), the need for a parallel capital programme was met in part from cross-site funding (at least until the late 1980s' property price boom ended). North West Thames considered the use of mortgages, transferring capital costs onto a revenue budget which might be under less pressure. In the region capital funds were available from mainstream allocations and land sales, but DHAs were expected to explore other sources such as the Housing Corporation or local housing. In the West Midlands region capital was available through the RHA, but the joint strategy required investment contributions from all parties – local authorities through their main capital allocation programme, and voluntary agencies through the Housing Corporation or private sources. As well as capital financing, double revenue finance was also needed, although finely-tuned tapers and imaginative use of DSS benefits helped to overcome the timing problem. The more gradual the decline in long-stay in-patient numbers and the slower the adjustment of staffed beds to the decline in patients, the greater the need for bridging funds, both capital and revenue. For individual people, sliding-scale double funding is needed for a time; regional practices varied from nine months to up to four years.

A hospital rundown programme which is clearly tied to the revenue transfer programme helps to ensure the planned and perhaps rational release of funds, in turn requiring rational and acceptable patient relocation within the hospital and ward closure programmes. Phased hospital closures within a region help to spread the bridging (capital and double revenue) costs. Closing smaller hospitals first produces a better ratio of realised site values to continuing revenue costs, since smaller hospitals usually have higher capital-to-revenue ratios, and a better ratio of overhead savings to direct care costs, since smaller hospitals have higher fixed to variable revenue cost ratios. But it may well be in the smaller long-stay hospitals that the quality of care is best, and the interests of a region's long-stay population may be better served by working to close the larger institutions first. Selective hospital closures may also leave some districts with virtually no rehabilitated clients for the first few years of a region's programme. This is just another example of the tension between good care practice and good financial practice.

The fourth source of inter-region differences in dowry policies and practices is variation in the *community-end adjustments* to the hospital baseline calculation. The dowry may vary in response to:

- the passage of *time*, with dowries tapered in recognition of both the difficulties of saving fixed hospital costs and the special circumstances that apply to early leavers from hospital (an explicit retraction programme allows a planned reduction in hospital budgets and services, releasing resources for community development with fewer unexpected fluctuations; see, for example, Normand and Taylor, 1986);
- *patient characteristics*, especially the perceived dependency of patients, as predicted for the community from a hospital assessment (a notoriously poor prediction);
- *recipient agencies*, with local authorities or voluntary organisations receiving lower dowry transfers than DHAs (in Trent Region non-NHS recipients were getting half the amount transferred to NHS recipients, a policy which had implications for the Derby project, for example);
- *service plans* and particularly expected service costs, for example a small group home may attract a different dowry from independent living accommodation;
- *social security* benefits or a client's private income, with the higher-rate board and lodging allowance often seen as a crucial source of additional revenue for dehospitalisation policies (usually, dowries are adjusted down if social security benefits can be obtained, although in North Western RHA dowries are unaffected); and

- whether or not patients are staying *in the region*, the general practice being not to transfer money in perpetuity outside the region, with dowries being withdrawn on a client's death (North West Thames will only accept people back from other regions if dowries are available).

Typically, with less dependent people moving out of hospital first, often into independent living settings or into established local authority or voluntary facilities, hospitals in some regions have been able to avoid transferring large sums in the very early years of a rundown programme. If the sums to be released in the early years are small, there is little incentive for hospitals to adjust staffing levels and other resources to falling patient numbers, perhaps pushing in-patient costs beyond the level actually necessary to maintain standards of care (even after taking into account the higher average dependency level among stayers), and making the final stages of closure all the more painful. This in turn can force a health authority to call a temporary halt to its rundown programme. However, many hospital managers would argue that those resources are needed to fund improvements in the quality of the care they are offering.

Fifth, dowries can be *protected* over time – most intra-regional transfers are made in perpetuity – and within the client group or other context. Ring-fencing of resources has been essential to prevent poaching by acute services in some areas, and to ensure that dowries are seen as additional service development money and not as replacements for previous expenditure commitments. Policy in North West Thames was for money released from hospital to stay in client group budgets, and money released from the natural decline in the hospital populations to form a development pool. This ring-fencing arguably speeds up the hospital rundown programme and therefore more quickly reduces the need for double revenue funding. On the other hand, if the sum of dowries plus other income (especially social security) is greater in value than the cost of providing community care, ring-fencing will prevent the funds reaching other clients.

The contributions of dowry funding

Dowries have their faults, and experience within the demonstration programme revealed some of the difficulties, but they contributed enormously to the establishment of community care services.

Some of the criticisms of dowries are in fact referring to problems with bridging support in the form of capital and double revenue funding. For dowries themselves, one of the most common problems has been their magnitude. They are often pitched too low for the development of good community care, or too high for the comfort of hospitals which are being stripped of resources. In some cases, they are too low and too high at one and the same time. They may cover only accommodation and residence-based care in the community, without financial provision for day and support services, or they may be reduced in value when paid to non-health authority agencies under the assumption (which is not necessarily tested) that these agencies receive less dependent clients and/or that the deficit can be made up from social security benefits. Some health authorities are not paying dowries in perpetuity despite earlier indications that this was their policy. Inadequate provision for inflation can cause huge problems when costs in the community are running ahead of the allowable NHS inflation adjustment to dowries. Another reason for inadequate revenue funding in the community may be inadequate *capital* provision, for then dowries may get partly capitalised. For voluntary organisations, retrospective dowry payments create a further difficulty since they may not have a cushion of finances to carry them through until funding is received. The basic problem here is one of unreasonable or unfulfilled expectations: either savings from hospital contraction are smaller than health authorities were expecting, or they are expecting too much by way of care from the comparatively low dowry transfers that are made, or community care agencies are not receiving the continued funding they were led to expect when they started out.

If too much money leaves hospital with the residents, hospital services suffer. Dowries paid on the basis of regional averages rather than hospital-specific costs penalise low-cost hospitals, which is both iniquitous in its differential denuding and in its perpetuation of what may have been long-term underfunding, and also inefficient in that it may penalise those hospitals which have done most to achieve efficiency improvements. A rather different problem for hospitals has been a difficulty in actually closing long-stay beds, for it is not difficult for 'new long-stay' residents to accumulate in hospitals, particularly if there are no community support facilities to which these people can be discharged, even if the dowry money associated with the 'bed' has already been transferred out of the hospital. Extended periods of bridging finance and/or increases in revenue allocations are needed. A greater problem then arises when the 'new long-stay' move back to the community with dowries. These problems occur because the number of long-stay beds in a hospital is not necessarily unambiguously measured, and the number of long-stay residents upon whom dowries are to be targeted does not necessarily remain fixed.

Despite these difficulties, without dowry transfers between agencies, the movement of people from hospital to community would have progressed no faster during the 1980s than it had in earlier years. One of the lessons of the 1970s is that joint planning is toothless without joint finance. Even in the demonstration programme, with its external grant aid, dowries helped community care happen. They often provide the trigger for action following years of delay and frustration (Korman and Glennerster, 1990). Having precipitated action, dowries help to promote good quality community care. We shall see later that demonstration programme clients were enjoying a quality of life in the community which was generally no worse than hospital and possibly better, a finding which has also emerged from studies of other dowry-funded hospital closure programmes (Leedham, 1989; TAPS, 1990; Wing, L., 1989). In contrast, people with mental health problems or learning difficulties living in the community but *not* covered by dowry transfers very often live in dire circumstances, with homelessness, poverty, unemployment and criminality not uncommon (for example, see Appleby and Desai, 1985; Brimacombe, 1986; Timms and Fry, 1989; Shanks, 1989; Wallace, 1987; Allen et al., 1991). These problems tend to be avoided by those people with dowries for a number of reasons. They are clearly identified as potential clients, and so are unlikely to drift without support or supervision. Second, some dowry payments are contingent on care plans being drawn up and agreed. Third, some hospitals are given responsibility for overseeing the early period of community living for former in-patients. Finally, dowries are tantamount to case-specific budgets which often are (at least, comparatively) predictable and generously funded. They can therefore encourage longer-term community care planning.

Overall, while dowries have their drawbacks, none of them suggests that the cause of community care would be better served by getting rid of them. Many of the difficulties arise with particular variants on the standard dowry theme, as we observed them operating across the programme of pilot projects for example, and lessons transferred across regions and districts would improve practice. Dependency-sensitive dowries, while more complex and costly to administer, would appear to produce benefits for both hospitals and community services. They can be tapered via a bridging fund, although there is no obvious justification for discrimination against local authorities and voluntary agencies by offering lower dowries. It is also unhelpful to reduce the value of a dowry by the amount of social security benefit received, for this, as we have seen earlier in the chapter, creates or perpetuates disincentives to good practice and generates greater uncertainty. Long-term security of transferred funding is essential, and community care agencies need compensation for cost inflation.

Our main conclusion, however, grows directly out of the demonstration programme's special status. *Outside* the programme, inadequate capital and double revenue funds have limited the changes which dowries were intended to bring about. *Within* the programme, the grants provided by the DHSS over a three-year period operated in many respects precisely as a source of capital and double-running funds. Similar funds are needed elsewhere if community care is to replace hospital provision. Capital and additional revenue funds as they are currently provided in some regions are too insecure, fluctuating from year to year with property prices and hospital sale revenues. A more radical reform which has been suggested would be the wholesale replacement of dowries with a system of targeted grants (Griffiths, 1988; House of Commons Social Services Committee, 1990). This would take national policy closer still to the practice within the demonstration programme.

8 Community accommodation and service utilisation

Funded from central government grants, local joint finance, clients' social security benefits and other sources, the 28 pilot projects developed, bought into and linked with a wide range of accommodation placements and other services. In this chapter we describe the community services used by clients.

A single chapter cannot contain all service-related aspects of the programme. Services were combined, with greater or lesser forethought, into individually-tailored 'packages' or combinations, upon the decisions of case managers, keyworkers, other staff, carers and clients, in response to assessed needs and expressed preferences (although the relative weighting of needs and preferences was very variable, as was the sophistication of assessment). We consider case management variants and attendant activities in Chapter 10. The staffing implications of clients' service plans, preferences and needs are the subject of Chapter 9. In the vernacular of our production of welfare conceptual framework, service attainments (gauged in terms of both quantity and quality) are intermediate outcomes on the road to the achievement of those (final) outcome goals which are valued in their own right, such as improvements in health and welfare. In Chapters 12 to 15 we present the outcome and cost evaluations, and we return to the outcome interpretations of the service achievements described here.

Decisions about the services needed and used by Care in the Community clients were taken by at least four groups of people. What was observed as utilisation (and recorded during our data collections) was the resolution of the different forces, preferences and opportunities held by these groups. First and foremost, in many instances, were the demands of clients. Almost every client had a case manager, keyworker or equivalent, one of whose tasks was to interpret the client's needs, to act as a support, advocate or conduit for the client's wants, and to coordinate and galvanise available provision. On this 'demand side' of the community care system, therefore, there were at least two different groups of actors and potential decision-makers (clients and their case managers), with potentially different views as to what was appropriate or desirable given the client's circumstances. The third and fourth sets of influences on service utilisation were on the 'supply side' – the managers and staff of community care services within the locale. The staff of accommodation facilities (other than those facility-based case managers) were involved as providers of the key community support service. These decision-makers not only helped determine the supply of services (where supply is to be interpreted at least in terms of existence, availability, quantity, quality and cost), but also exerted influences on demand by the breadth of their interpretations of the residential task and the service deficits needing to be filled from elsewhere. The other decision-makers were the managers and staff of day facilities, educational resources, peripatetic and other specialist provision such as community psychiatric nursing and general practice, each with their own priorities, targets and constraints.

The pilot projects were clearly able to bring their philosophies and objectives for community care to bear on only some of these actors and decision-makers. They certainly sought to recruit or train staff who shared their broad aims, and they endeavoured to establish case management mechanisms which were most likely, for example, to encourage the style and extent of client involvement which projects favoured. They could try to influence but they could not determine the attitudes and availability of GPs or job centres or local housing resources. Indeed, as we describe later in this chapter, some of the projects were remiss in not involving some of these other services or agencies in the early stages of application, planning and (in some cases) rehabilitation.

Notwithstanding these local constraints and planning lacunae, projects' broad philosophies and value positions were of some influence. Before describing accommodation and the utilisation of other services, we therefore consider the most commonly discussed aspects of service philosophy: normalisation, community integration, client choice and empowerment, and risk-taking. (The four are inter-linked. The last three are either corollaries or components of normalisation, depending on your interpretation.) The chapter then turns to service needs and utilisation, showing how principles helped to shape the provision of residential accommodation and other service packages.

Service principles in practice

Many of the projects elected to deliver services in what were innovative ways for their local context, as one might hope of a demonstration programme. The inspiration for innovation often came from comparatively new and controversial philosophies of care such as normalisation. Translating any philosophy into practice is not straightforward, and may demand compromise. The service objectives set by projects in their initial plans therefore underwent some revision. We described in Chapter 3 how many projects adopted some form of normalisation aim, but sometimes found it necessary to lower or reinterpret their aspirations. Consumerism was specified only rarely as a separate objective but grew in stature and influence. It can be painful to abandon carefully chosen and laudable aims, but projects accepted, sometimes reluctantly, that pragmatism was better than dogmatism. We will later illustrate some of the difficulties which followed from too rigid or unimaginative adherence to broad values such as normalisation, although we hasten to add that many of the problems that have beset long-term care services for decades are the result of rigid and unimaginative commitment to Victorian principles of isolation, segregation, discrimination and paternalism. The vast majority of projects knew full well, or very quickly discovered, that a blending of approaches was the key to successful community provision within the complex mixed economy of English health and social care. The philosophies, values and care packages which emerged were therefore as much a result of choice and availability as an attempt to adhere to ideals.

Normalisation

The normalisation principle is most closely associated with the work of Wolfensberger (1970, 1972), who used the term to describe a situation where someone lives in a culturally normative community setting in ordinary community housing, can move and communicate in ways typical for his or her age and is able to utilise, in typical ways, typical community resources: developmental, social, recreational and religious facilities; hospitals and clinics; post office; stores and restaurants; job placements.

Normalisation concerns the value that society places on stigmatised groups of people, such as those with mental health problems or learning difficulties, and urges that they no longer be treated as less worthy than other ('ordinary') citizens. Some interpretations of the normalisation perspective tend towards positive discrimination in favour of people with disabilities, in the form of provision of more and better services to help compensate for disadvantage. Normalisation places particular emphasis on the need for opportunities to develop and maintain skills in one's personal life, favouring the development of service packages which are individually tailored to needs. Well-known variants of normalisation promote 'ordinary' environments and settings; 'valued' means to enhance one's status (the so-called 'valuisation' approach); and the pursuit of key accomplishments such as community presence, choice, competence, respect and community participation (King's Fund Centre, 1982, 1988; O'Brien, 1987; O'Brien and Tyne, 1981). The influence of the normalisation approach can be seen in the recommendations of the Jay Committee (1979), the Care in the Community Circular (DHSS, 1983), the 1989 Community Care White Paper (Cm 849), and in the service guidelines of such organisations as the National Federation of Housing Associations (NFHA), Good Practices in Mental Health (GPMH), Campaign for Mental Handicap (CMH) and the National Association for Mental Health (Mind). As the NFHA and Mind comment,

> the major contribution of normalisation has been in making explicit the objectives which a service should be striving to fulfil. Too often services are set up with only the most rudimentary ideas of what they are setting out to achieve (1989, p.20).

Normalisation has been frequently misunderstood. It implies that the ties and controls long exercised by statutory agencies over individual lives should be loosened, but it is not enough to assume that something better will emerge of its own volition. Some people believed that normalisation was just common sense, treating people as if they had no disabilities or making people 'normal', when in fact the principle is about good quality care in valued settings.

> When we use the word 'ordinary', we do not mean dull, or exactly like everyone else, or standard, or even average. 'Ordinary' simply means having the opportunities and options which most people have. We live in a world where it is ordinary to have variety and opportunity and choice. It is ordinary to be special, at least to someone. It is ordinary to have opportunities for parts of our lives to be special and also to be different in ways which other people value very highly (King's Fund Centre, 1988, p.2).

Some projects found themselves arguing over assumptions which were misconceived in the first place. One project leader was firmly of the view that 'more than three people in a living unit isn't normalisation' and was critical of provision in larger units elsewhere, even when the clients there were progressing well and liked living there. One staff member told us that a client did not need to wash unless he chose to, because self-determination was sacrosanct. This appears to be an inappropriate interpretation of normalisation.

Community integration

The 1971 White Paper, *Better Services for the Mentally Handicapped*, emphasised integration as one of the key objectives of national policy:

> Mentally handicapped children and adults should not be segregated unnecessarily from other people of a similar age, nor from the general life of the local community (Cmnd 4683, 1971).

Integration in practice could therefore mean clients utilising, preferably as individuals rather than in groups, such ordinary services and facilities as GPs, dentists, opticians, colleges, clubs, shops, cafes and churches, as well as competing for jobs available to anyone in the population ('open employment'). Integration can encourage the development of a positive self-image, and personal competence generally. In the Brent project, adult homefinding or fostering programmes gave the flexibility for better integration of clients in ethnic groups. At the same time integration has been argued to help the process of attitudinal change in the wider community, encouraging greater respect for people with, say, mental health problems, and breaking down stereotypes. Integration therefore means that clients need to join in ordinary activities and use mainstream services, and that the general public, neighbours and members of local communities need to stop the occasional incidents of hounding and victimisation. Integration is not unequivocally desirable, as recent discussions of 'asylum' rightly emphasise. Competitive employment, high levels of social functioning and a return to ordinary life-styles may cause great anxiety, precipitate clients back into long-term hospitalisation or encourage them to withdraw (Talbott, 1984; Harris et al., 1986; Cournos, 1987). A balance needs to be struck between the demands (or 'environmental press') of a care or life setting and the abilities (or 'competence') of an individual. That there is a continuing need for some form of asylum or haven for some people with long-term needs now seems beyond argument. The 1990 report on community care from the House of Commons Social Services Committee suggested that asylum performed the twin functions of refuge (from cruelty, exploitation, stress and so on) and reparation (including the identification of needs and causes of disablement), neither of which functions necessarily requires separation and segregation.

Community opposition. Successful social or community integration depends on a host of factors. Some of them relate to the community itself. Segal's informative research study in California looked at the 'external social integration' of former mental hospital residents now living in sheltered-care facilities (Segal et al., 1989). He and his colleagues found that the degree of external social integration (defined as extent of self-initiated participation in and use made of the community) depended

> a great deal on the extent to which community care residents have key characteristics of the dominant social group in the environment [locale], and the willingness of that group to tolerate differences in its midst (p.61).

Particularly interesting in view of the growing attention given to Britain's 'NIMBY (not in my back yard) syndrome', particularly prevalent in some middle-class areas, is their comment that their results 'suggest precautions about placement in conservative middle-class communities. These neighbourhoods seem better able to tolerate the more competent and least threatening community care residents' (p.62).

Local opposition to Care in the Community took many forms:

- attempts to prevent care agencies purchasing houses or converting other buildings for residential or day facilities,
- questions and unsubstantiated claims about how 'dangerous' clients would be,
- criticisms of queue-jumping for public housing ('You have to be mentally ill to get a good house round here', quoted by Leibrich, 1988, p.44),
- and the prejudice and personal abuse that faces some clients because of their 'odd' appearance.

None of this is peculiar to the demonstration programme. O'Grady (1988) opines that community psychiatry has simply shifted the 'locus of rejection' from the isolated hospital, with a majority of the general public viewing people with serious mental health problems as 'dangerous, dirty, unpredictable and worthless'. A DHSS-sponsored survey reported that *half* the general population were either 'opposed' or 'strongly opposed' to integrating people with learning difficulties into the community, for fear this would affect their families or neighbourhoods, push property values down, increase the probability of criminal acts, and generate traffic and noise (Leighton, 1988). In Cuckmans

Drive, St Albans (not in the pilot programme), four families pooled their resources, some taking out a second mortgage, to purchase a house (at £160,000, this was no mean feat) to prevent the health authority buying it to accommodate six elderly people with learning difficulties (Hurst, 1990). This is not an isolated incident of concerted community opposition (Mills, 1988), a lot of which appears to stem from ignorance and alarmist media reporting (see, for example, 'Menace of freed mental patients who refuse pills', *Today Newspaper*, 29 September 1986). It is interesting to record that Boydell et al. (1989) could find no effect of group homes on local residential property prices in Toronto, and cite similar findings in the US.

In the demonstration programme, projects took different public relations routes. Most preferred to adopt a low profile, based on the premise that most people do not have to seek permission from neighbours in order to move into a house or street. However, projects varied in size and nature, and one client moving into an independent flat is different from eight clients moving into a fully-staffed group home or 16 people moving into a hostel. (The irony of more recent events, and the cause for such concern, is that the most vociferous opposition has been levelled at 'ordinary', small-scale housing plans.) Generally, although there was community opposition to the *opening* of facilities, there was greater acceptance after people had moved in, a finding which accords with earlier research (O'Connor, 1976; Locker et al., 1981; Seltzer, 1985).

Projects were quite inventive in their public relations strategies – a barbecue for neighbours in Liverpool, a letter outlining plans to a local councillor in Bolton, an invitation to local children to plant flowers in the garden of a residential home for elderly people in Cumbria – yet such strategies can still be ineffective. In the Chichester project, the plans for and establishment of a cluster home elicited a string of unfounded complaints from an immediate neighbour, who eventually moved house. The low profile approach is not an option if the local media decide to present negative accounts of community care, or if public meetings are called by neighbours. (In at least two areas, however, public meetings called against the wishes of the projects in fact resulted in longer-term practical and moral support for new facilities and their residents. Sometimes the staunchest adversaries became champions of the community care cause.) The Bucks project held an information day, inviting people from local churches, GPs, shopkeepers, pub landlords and the police, as well as community residents. Similar events were held in Somerset and elsewhere. Public attitudes can, it seems, be shaped through education as well as through experience of living near clients (Trute and Loewen, 1978; Peterson, 1986).

Ordinary community services. Living in an ordinary house in an ordinary street, and accepted by neighbours, is not the same as community integration and participation. All but a very few clients had continuing needs for service inputs from care agencies, even many months after leaving hospital. Were these needs met without 'undue' segregation?

The nature of the demonstration programme itself made integration more difficult, partly because of the separate funding and partly because the availability of capital grants tended to encourage 'special' and perhaps segregated facilities. Lack of appropriate facilities or opportunities was also a major factor. There were certainly exceptions. The Brent resource centre and the Chichester activity centre helped build bridges between residential settings and communities. Moreover, many of the services used in all projects were available to the whole population – dentists, opticians, visits to the GP surgery, domiciliary visits from a home help, and so on. (We will detail the actual utilisation later in the chapter.) Integration was least successful in the areas of education and employment. It proved difficult to persuade some education departments to include clients in mainstream services, although providing separate (segregated) classes within a non-segregated *setting* such as a school or college may have been the better short-term arrangement for some people. This does at least make possible informal contacts with other 'non-client' students.

Very few clients secured *open employment* in the first year in the community, the inevitable but regrettable consequence of limited experience, very little training, a punitive poverty trap and the general state of the labour market.

Community leisure facilities. Integration should also mean using ordinary leisure facilities. During the research interviews with community staff we asked about utilisation by clients over a one-month period (response categories were: not in past month, less often than once a week, or at least once a week). We also asked about missed opportunities to participate. The findings can be seen in Table 8.1. By no means every client was using community facilities outside the residential setting. Of the 122 people with mental health problems for whom we had this information, 16 per cent had not used community facilities in the past month, and another 16 per cent did so but less frequently than weekly. For people with learning difficulties the corresponding proportions were considerably lower at 4 and 13 per cent. Community integration as measured by this crude utilisation rate was generally greater for people living in more independent settings (foster placements, supported lodgings, independent housing and group homes), and least for hostel and residential home residents. This is partly a consequence of age and preferences. Further analyses showed that, as one would expect, and as observed for former Darenth Park Hospital residents, it tended to be the least disabled and more independent clients who achieved better integration (Korman and Glennerster, 1990; Wing, L., 1989).

It is important not to exaggerate the influence of community opposition upon the degree of integration by clients, for greater constraints were imposed by inadequate staffing levels – residents of a group home, for instance, who

Table 8.1

Utilisation of community facilities, and missed opportunities to participate in the community

Frequency or missed opportunities and client group	Type of residential accommodation in community[1]:								
	RESID	HOST	SHELT	SGH	USGH	FOST	LODG	INDEP	All
Frequency of utilisation of facilities									
People with mental health problems (N)	12	46	0	12	37	5	3	7	122
- not used in past month (%)	8	20	–	8	22	0	0	0	16
- less often than once a week (%)	25	24	–	8	5	20	0	14	16
- at least once a week (%)	67	56	–	83	73	80	100	86	69
People with learning difficulties (N)	7	112	15	92	7	9	0	6	248
- not used in past month (%)	14	4	13	1	14	0	–	0	4
- less often than once a week (%)	29	17	13	8	0	11	–	0	13
- at least once a week (%)	57	79	73	91	86	89	–	100	84
Missed opportunities									
People with mental health problems (N)	12	46	0	11	37	5	3	7	121
- yes, has missed opportunities (%)	58	72	–	64	35	40	33	29	54
People with learning difficulties (N)	7	110	11	91	6	9	0	5	239
- yes, has missed opportunities (%)	57	38	45	34	50	11	–	20	36

1 Abbreviations are: RESID = residential home, including old people's home; HOST = hostel; SHELT = sheltered or very sheltered housing; SGH = staffed group home; USGH = unstaffed group home; FOST = adult fostering; LODG = supported lodgings; INDEP = independent house or flat.

need to be accompanied outside the facility cannot all choose to do different things at the same time unless there is one-to-one staffing, which is most unusual. In the early weeks of a new facility, with new residents and staff, ignorance of what was available locally was also a factor. Of more influence in the longer term were the financial constraints that accompany reliance on social security benefits.

Comparisons with hospital. Equivalent interviews were conducted with hospital staff about hospital residents. (Their responses regarding utilisation of community facilities were recorded in Table 5.15, item 21.) Comparing responses for clients for whom we have both sets of data reveals that:

- 19 per cent of people with mental health problems used community facilities *less* often in the community than they did when living in hospital,
- 54 per cent used community facilities with the *same* frequency, and
- 27 per cent used community facilities *more* often.

For people with a learning difficulty the corresponding changes were

- 7 per cent used community facilities *less* often in the community hospital,
- 43 per cent used community facilities with the *same* frequency, and
- 49 per cent used community facilities *more* often.

For both client groups integration rates appear to increase, although we do not know from this particular set of statistics whether the facilities were fully integrated or whether they segregated people with 'special needs' from other users. By contrast, although using different methodologies and instruments, neither Gibbons and Butler (1987) nor Wykes (1982) found a difference in the utilisation of leisure facilities between hospital and hostel residents described as 'new long-stay psychiatric patients'. (For comparison, Shadish and Bootzin, 1984, in the US found no difference in social integration between hospital and nursing home settings for a similar group of people.)

Our finding that community integration improved came from the information gathered on the Social Contacts Record completed by staff for some hospital residents and community clients. For a variety of reasons response rates were low (143 people in hospital and 145 in the community), and there was little sample overlap, so we should not make too much of the results. Basically, the average number of 'outings' from the place of residence over a two-week period was twice as high in the community as in hospital. The destinations were also different – people with a mental health problem were, for example, more likely to be going shopping than was the case for hospital residents, but day trips and excursions – almost always group activities – had almost completely ceased.

Some idea of clients' views on their links with the community was obtained during our conversations with those people willing and able to answer the questions in the Morale and Life Satisfaction Interview. The full list of questions was described in Chapter 5 (and the responses for the full hospital sample in Table 5.9), one of them asking about the ease with which clients could get to the shops, town, post office, library and so on. Focusing on those clients interviewed in both settings – so that we take a sub-sample of those people covered by the results in Chapter 5 – the levels of satisfaction in the community were high, and a significant improvement on hospital.

- 91 per cent of people with mental health problems expressed satisfaction about ease of access in the community, compared with 66 per cent in hospital (sample of 120 respondents);
- 85 per cent of people with learning difficulties were satisfied with access from their community bases, compared to only 54 per cent in hospital (sample of 162); and
- 63 per cent of elderly physically frail people and 99 of elderly people with mental health problems expressed satisfaction in the community, compared with 50 and 60 per cent, respectively, in hospital (samples of 25 and 34 people).

Choice and empowerment

Each person moving to the community was given the choice of staying in hospital, although in some cases the alternative was to move *later* if hospital closure was planned. Although it was not always possible to provide complete information, those processes of preparation and rehabilitation which involved community-based staff (including case managers) helped to counter the widespread ignorance usually reported among long-stay hospital residents. This tallies with previous work showing that hospital residents make constructive choices if offered appropriate information (Abrahamson and Brenner, 1982; Antebi and Torpy, 1987). Some people chose to stay in hospital even after proceeding some distance down the rehabilitation path.

Hospital residence may not, and 'institutionalism' does not, encourage individuality. Community staff thus took pains to facilitate and support client choice, and it was widely reported that choice had successfully expanded the range of activities and experiences, and enhanced client autonomy (see, for example, Bolton Community Health Council, 1987). Our assessments of living environments confirmed that clients were more willing and able to make choices unaided and unprompted, encouraging individuality, empowerment and identity (compare Gibbons and Butler, 1987; Hargreaves et al., 1984; Gudeman et al., 1985; Jones et al., 1986; Davies, 1987). The results of our assessments of community and hospital environments are discussed in the section on accommodation later in this chapter.

Clients expressed opinions about their lives in the community which confirmed that they appreciated the wider range of choice. Three questions focused on choice: the amount of free time clients felt they had, the opportunities to do what they wanted, and choices over clothes and possessions. Responses were coded as positive (expressing satisfaction) or negative (dissatisfaction),

Table 8.2
Clients' views about choices available to them

	Percentage of clients expressing satisfaction							
	Mental health		*Learning difficulties*		*Elderly phys. dis.*		*Elderly ment. health*	
Client group	**Comm.** %	**Hosp.** %	**Comm.** %	**Hosp.** %	**Comm.** %	**Hosp.** %	**Comm.** %	**Hosp.** %
Amount of free time available	93	82	85	73	96	94	82	71
Opportunities to do what you want	88	78	82	66	84	91	91	74
Money to spend	66	64	82	80	96	91	62	63
Own clothes and possessions	86	80	97	84	92	84	96	83
Sample size	120	120	162	162	25	25	34	34

and compared with the responses given by the same people when they were interviewed in hospital (Table 8.2). Compared to many other dimensions covered by interviews with clients, responses to these three items reveal more satisfaction, with some expressed improvements over hospital. By no means every client was satisfied with their life-style in the community, and it can be seen from the table that low incomes were a problem, and certainly limited effective choice. Levels of satisfaction with personal finances were no better in the community than in hospital, and disposable income in the community was often lower.

Projects had to overcome a number of barriers in order to extend choice, encourage autonomy and promote consumerism more generally. Staff new to community support work had to learn to let clients make their own decisions and face the consequences. Choice means taking risks – freedom to choose 'often becomes subverted to the freedom to be crazy, exploited, hungry, and homeless' (Freedman and Moran, 1984, p.17) – and it is fear of the consequences of taking risks that generates concern and controversy, and obviously stimulates criticism. Some professional and financial constraints stemmed from the temporarily artificial boundaries drawn around projects, which left little opportunity for meaningful choice. Projects which comprised a single or limited range of accommodation facilities, located within areas where few other community care developments were available, particularly faced this problem. Social prejudices and worries about client stress were other limiting factors. The reluctance to consult clients was sometimes rationalised in terms of avoiding the unnecessary stress of building up clients' hopes or asking them to make difficult choices from unfamiliar options. Some of the projects for people with mental health problems later felt they had involved users too early. (In one case, clients were involved long before suitable housing had been secured, and many changed their minds about moving by the time the housing was ready. Another project faced a revolt when, fed up with waiting around for facilities which never materialised, residents demanded to leave the rehabilitation ward and return to their previous wards where there was no pressure to achieve, and where meals arrived ready prepared.) There is no simple way to involve vulnerable people in a process that may completely change their lives, but which subjects them to more uncertainty than they have grown accustomed to during their years in hospital.

Although few projects expressly pursued consumerism as an objective from the outset (Chapter 2), many had planned to involve service users in key decisions, and by the time we completed our evaluation in 1989 almost all had developed mechanisms for making their services not only needs-led, as perceived by staff or relatives, but wants-led, as expressed by clients themselves. Formal mechanisms such as tenants' groups, residents' committees, and representation on steering, advisory, management or planning groups helped empower clients as decision-makers. Some projects made clients licensees of housing associations. Case management offered a formal but less threatening way to recognise clients' views (although we are not aware of any client initially choosing their case manager), and other forms of 'participative consumerism' were able to emerge (Jowell, 1988). Influenced by the growth of an articulate consumer movement and the success of self-advocacy in some other areas, several projects (including Kidderminster, Maidstone and Somerset) encouraged independent citizens' advocacy schemes. At the time, there were few such groups in Britain.

Case management can involve clients directly in assessment and review meetings, or at least afford the opportunity for views to be fed into the discussion, and some projects went further, encouraging clients to prepare their own programme plans. Advocacy and empowerment do not flow automatically from case management or individual programme planning. Most professional staff were trained to speak on behalf of others, and it proved difficult for some to give up this authority, particularly when new review and resource allocation procedures were introduced which brought together a new mix of professions and personalities. Large multidisciplinary groups embodying a host of different (and perhaps competing) professional cultures sometimes left little room for the client. We will return to these issues in Chapter 10, but it is worth repeating that economic status is crucial, and the budgetary devolution within case management as practised in Maidstone and Darlington proved particularly effective. In Maidstone, for example, a weekly contract was agreed between user and providers. Although not giving the user control over the budget itself, this ensured some influence over how the money was spent, and enabled support to be channelled to the activities they preferred. The short-term nature of the contract allowed mistakes to be made with relative impunity, preserving flexibility.

Risk

Responsibility at the case, facility or agency level for community care of former hospital residents with long-term mental health problems or learning difficulties was a relatively new experience for many social services departments in the programme. Society's expectations of dependency, disability and unusual behaviour create prejudice and stereotyped images and encourage risk-aversion, particularly when coupled with media or other pressures to practise 'defensive' social work. Risk management was also made difficult by inter-agency liaison requirements. There were many instances where health and social care agencies attached utterly different risks to a particular practice, even one which both groups had been undertaking for some time. Other contributing factors were an emphasis on innovation and demonstration and occasional strained relationships between projects and host agencies.

Every practice decision involves risk – even encouraging independence in ordinary daily activities risks injury if staff oversight is reduced – but some areas are more sensitive than others. The *administration of drugs* and medicine is one such. Self-administration was an early aim in some projects, and an ultimate aim in a few others. One hostel used by people in the Bucks project developed a quasi-self administration model with the input of an NHS adviser. *Money management* is a key facet of personal independence, and the practice dilemma was how to encourage autonomy without generating disproportionate vulnerability or the risk of exploitation. Compromises between individual rights and safety were often necessary, such as with *smoking*. Facilities which operated very liberal regimes in most respects nevertheless felt it prudent to try to stop smoking in bedrooms and to fit smoke detectors. Personal *relationships* and friendships between clients and others in the community caused anxieties, and balancing the gains from socialisation against the risks of exploitation was not easy. The management and support of sexual behaviour, so as to reduce the risks of HIV infection or unwanted pregnancy while encouraging freedom of choice and action, posed particular challenges.

The trade-off between protection and autonomy must be made for individual clients, taking into account levels of ability, types of behaviour, needs and preferences. In the projects for people with learning difficulties, staff were not always clear that clients understood the risks and possibilities, and anyone moving to the community after many years in hospital (commonly preceded by the protective care of the family) would necessarily have had only limited experience of the choices, delights and problems that awaited them. In fact, our judgement would be that most clients erred on the side of caution, fearing the break with a structured life-style, for it must obviously be difficult for some people to imagine life outside the protective routine of the hospital ward and the friendly familiarity of sheltered employment, particularly when the alternative is a half-built residence near a busy and noisy town centre. Familiarisation programmes for hospital residents, such as those in Greenwich, Islington, Somerset and Warrington, generally appeared to help orientation and learning, but were demanding on staff time, and required solid line management support (not just supervision) in risk management. Formal codes of practice relating to risk-taking were noticeable by their absence.

We would not want to imply that risks only appear once people leave the protective environment of the hospital. It is too commonly assumed that the problems of exploitation, destitution, injury or mortality are somehow peculiar to life in the community. One client moved from hospital only on condition (imposed by hospital consultants) that she have 24-hour staff supervision. This proved impossible to manage within group living and she returned to hospital after two weeks. Shortly afterwards she was allowed out of the hospital without supervision to visit her parents. She got off her bus and was killed as she crossed the road. Client death is a particular case in point, for when this occurs in the community, projects often experienced exaggerated complications, and they sometimes initiated what may have been over-cautious reactive policy change. The coroner's open verdict following the death of one of the first movers in one project was traumatic for all concerned, but whether it should have brought other moves to a halt is debatable.

Accommodation in the community

The most basic outcome of the pilot programme was the successful resettlement of a large number of long-stay hospital residents in supported community placements. This considerable achievement should not overlooked. By 'community' we mean anything outside hospital. One of the questions raised by the provision of residential home and hostel places was the danger of 'trans-institutionalisation', the replacement of one institutional living environment with another. The general point is that community destinations do not necessarily mean positive outcomes. It is one thing to detail the failings of hospitals, the constraints they impose on life-styles, the basic rights and opportunities they deny residents, but it is a *non sequitur* to assume that community care must therefore be better. Simply moving people from large hospitals to smaller community settings is no guarantee of improvement. We should not only examine whether community placements offer pleasant and valued living environments – perhaps in accordance with certain principles of normalisation or ordinary living (Would this accommodation be acceptable to me?) – but also consider their effects on clients' lives.

The 28 projects set out to meet accommodation needs in different ways. Some projects, particularly the smaller ones, offered a single accommodation

Table 8.3
Usual community residence nine months after leaving hospital

	Client group[1]				
Location[2]	**Learning diffs.**	**Mental health**	**Elderly phys.frail**	**Elderly ment.health**	**All clients**[3]
Residential home	13	25	0	91	129
Hostel	126	66	0	0	192
Sheltered housing	25	0	48	0	76
Staffed group home	126	33	0	0	162
Unstaffed group home	20	56	2	0	78
Foster placement	20	7	3	0	30
Supported lodgings	0	5	0	0	5
Independent	13	27	89	0	129
Accommodation not classified[4]	13	7	5	0	25
Total	356	226	147	91	826
In hospital[5]	1	23	7	0	31
Died[5]	0	2	41	10	53

1 The three Cambridge adolescent clients with multiple disabilities were all resident in a staffed group home. The three Glossop clients with physical disabilities were all living in sheltered accommodation.
2 Using the definitions giving in Table 6.2. For clients who were in hospital after nine months or who had died, the *most recent* community accommodation is recorded.
3 Totals include the Cambridge and Glossop clients.
4 These people were living at known addresses in the community, but we did not have sufficient information to classify the accommodation type.
5 Clients who have died or who were in hospital nine months after discharge. Their former place of community residence has been recorded above.

type, from which some clients might later graduate outside the project, and other projects offered a range from closely supported congregate living to almost complete independence. The range of service models reflected different philosophies of care, local housing circumstances, budget limitations and associated aspects of scale. It also reflected the local response to client needs. Accommodation locations after nine months for the people who moved from hospital during the course of our research are given in Table 8.3. By the time we conducted the nine-month follow-up, some clients had died or returned permanently to hospital. For the relatively few clients who moved from one placement to another, the location at follow-up is recorded. For clients who were *temporarily* in hospital, and who were known to have returned to the community shortly after, the usual community placement is given.

We will have more to say about these accommodation destinations in the later chapters concerned with costs and outcomes, and the physical and social environmental correlates are described below, but five key findings should be noted here:

- Not one of the clients was *homeless*, nor had they been since leaving hospital.
- Very few clients were living with their families, and only in the Darlington project was family placement an explicit policy (made possible in part because the clients had only been hospital residents for short periods; see Challis et al., 1989).
- No one had spent any time in prison, either on remand or under sentence.
- There were few accommodation changes in the first nine months. This was a failing in some cases, where clients or projects wanted to move on (a particular difficulty arose with the silting up of some core houses), but also signified that there was no drifting from one temporary residence to another.
- Clients were not despatched to boarding houses in rundown seaside resorts. Hardly anyone moved away from a project's 'area' (usually the town or local authority), and those that did went to planned placements, either to live with relatives or to specialised voluntary sector facilities.

Assessing accommodation needs. Projects used a variety of methods to assess clients' community needs and preferences (see Chapter 10 for details). These assessments were either carried out in hospital or in some 'halfway' facility, but it was never easy to predict a client's needs or preferences once in the community. Comparing client characteristics in hospital as assessed by the research instrumentation with community accommodation at nine months (or, for those people who had died or returned to hospital, the last place of residence in the community) reveals no marked pattern (Tables 8.4 to 8.6). The hospital-assessed skills, behaviour, morale and other characteristics appeared to vary only slightly by subsequent community accommodation destinations, although in fact many differences attained statistical significance (see the penultimate columns of the tables). There were significant skills differences but not behaviour differences for both the mental health and learning difficulty client groups. Some of the morale indicators showed marked differences between accommodation types.

Different philosophies of care emphasise different housing provision. There may be a tendency for planners to decide how other people should live on the basis of how they prefer to live themselves, but this may not suit clients' needs and wants. Desirable semis in leafy suburbs may be less suitable than local authority flats near the town centre. Domestic privacy is prized in our society, but could spell isolation and loneliness for someone with long-term support needs or housebound with a physical disability. Ordinary living might thus mean neglect and low quality of life. Selecting groups of clients to share accommodation was not straightforward. Professional perceptions of friendship patterns may be at variance with clients' perceptions or preferences, and friendships developed in the special environment of the hospital may not survive a move to the community. Staff who knew clients for years in hospital were not necessarily the best judges of compatibility. There is a need for the clear statement of residents' rights, as some projects used or developed (and

Table 8.4

Clients' hospital characteristics by community accommodation, for people with mental health problems

Client characteristics	*Mean score for clients within each accommodation type[1]:*									
	RESID	HOST	SGH	USGH	FOST	LODG	INDEP	All	Sig[2]	N
Aggregate skills score	74	73	75	76	70	76	77	74	.169	146
Aggregate behaviour score	68	69	70	71	72	69	70	70	.419	146
Schedule of Social Interaction	5	4	5	5	5	6	5	5	.089	143
Psychosocial Functioning Inventory	39	37	41	39	44	38	36	38	.003	141
Depression Inventory	9	12	8	9	7	7	11	10	.001	137
Personal Presentation	22	20	19	20	21	22	21	20	.177	145
Duration of most recent period in hospital[3]	28	157	44	181	276	–	33	147	.230	65
Age at move to community	65	50	53	47	51	–	55	53	.853	70
Age at last admission to hospital	63	32	31	34	20	–	46	32	.076	66
No. of previous admissions to this hospital	2	3	1	2	2	–	7	3	.194	45
Diagnosis										
Schizophrenia (%)	0	86	73	82	83	–	83	82	.668	70
Affective disorder (%)	0	7	18	6	17	–	17	10	.668	70
Other (%)	100	7	9	12	0	–	0	8	.668	70

1 Abbreviations are: RESID = residential home, including old people's home; HOST = hostel; SGH = staffed group home; USGH = unstaffed group home; FOST = adult fostering; LODG = supported lodgings; INDEP = independent house or flat.

2 Significance of F test for differences between accommodation types, except for differences in diagnosis which are tested using the likelihood ratio.

3 In months.

Table 8.5

Clients' hospital characteristics by community accommodation, for people with learning difficulties

Client characteristics	*Mean score for clients within each accommodation type[1]:*									
	RESID	HOST	SHELT	SGH	USGH	FOST	INDEP	All	Sig[2]	N
Aggregate skills score	67	60	65	60	68	54	74	61	.000	217
Aggregate behaviour score	70	68	69	68	70	69	69	68	.742	217
Schedule of Social Interaction	1	4	4	4	4	5	4	4	.043	139
Psychosocial Functioning Inventory	47	39	38	37	39	36	40	38	.001	112
Depression Inventory	5	11	10	14	9	16	8	12	.003	89
Personal Presentation	20	17	19	19	20	19	21	18	.000	192
Duration of most recent period in hospital[3]	304	210	395	310	321	–	217	249	.101	153
Age at move to community	51	37	48	41	42	–	49	39	.104	168
Age at last admission to hospital	26	18	19	14	20	–	17	17	.611	160
No. of previous admissions to this hospital	2	1	–	1	–	–	1	1	.871	39
Level of handicap										
Profound (%)	0	3	–	0	0	–	–	2	.423	101
Severe (%)	100	49	–	48	50	–	–	49	.423	101
Moderate (%)	0	34	–	24	0	–	–	30	.423	101
Mild (%)	0	14	–	28	50	–	–	19	.423	101

1 Abbreviations are: RESID = residential home, including old people's home; HOST = hostel; SHELT = sheltered or very sheltered housing; SGH = staffed group home; USGH = unstaffed group home; FOST = adult fostering; INDEP = independent house or flat.

2 Significance of F test for differences between accommodation types, except for differences in diagnosis which are tested using the likelihood ratio.

3 In months.

Table 8.6
Clients' hospital characteristics by community accommodation, for elderly people

	Mean score for clients within each accommodation type[1]			
	RESID	**SHELT**	**ALL**[2]	**N**
Aggregate CAPE score	16	12	14	33
CAPE subscores:				
Physical disability	6	5	6	51
Apathy	7	5	6	40
Communication difficulties	1	0	1	59
Social disturbance	2	1	1	71
Schedule for Social Interaction	5	6	5	62
PGC Morale Scale	12	9	10	169
Depression Inventory	12	12	12	55
Personal presentation	19	20	20	69
Duration of most recent period in hospital[3]	6	8	7	105
Age at move to community	81	82	81	66
Age at last admission to hospital	79	81	79	61
No. of previous admissions to hospital	1	1	1	44

1 Abbreviations are: RESID = residential home; HOST = hostel; SHELT = sheltered or very sheltered housing; SGH = staffed group home; USGH = unstaffed group home; FOST = foster placement; LODG = supported lodgings; IND = independent living.
2 We did not conduct tests of significance for this client group because of the small sample sizes and limited accommodation options.
3 In months.

see, for example, the recommendations drawn up by organisations such as Mind and the National Federation of Housing Associations), but there is also the need for imaginative and flexible accommodation policies. There will be circumstances, for example, in which hostels or residential homes offer *greater* independence and privacy than the sometimes rather forced style of small group living settings (Ritchie et al., 1983). The goal of many plans for residential facilities was to achieve a degree of domesticity which maximised clients' abilities, autonomy and independence, but this was constrained by the inappropriateness of the local housing stock and the inadequacy of budgets. This did not equate with a policy of 'ordinary' housing at all costs.

Development issues

It would be naive to assume that a project could start from scratch and mould services to client needs in a vacuum. Some of the problems encountered by projects were simply the result of inexperience and haste. Many projects learned by experience (sometimes reacting 'on the hoof' to opportunities and constraints) as they sought to develop new areas of work within the comparatively short time-scales of central funding. Plans pulled together quickly to meet the deadline for applications (with a very short lead time for the first round) often required revision in the light of experience.

The availability of housing of the right kind proved a major constraint, and the local political and economic environments influenced whether a project used non-statutory or public housing. In Maidstone the private sector was used because of a dearth of both public sector facilities and housing associations in the area. The West Lancashire project's plans to use Housing Corporation funding were frustrated because the Corporation did not see their locality as a priority area. The housing plans of the Bolton project also foundered for a while. After initially being assured of spare capacity by the local authority housing department, the stock was discovered to be mainly inappropriate family-type accommodation with insufficient ground-floor space to meet the needs of disabled people. This same problem beset other projects, although inter-project comparisons show that confining housing to the public sector did not delay the development of community care any more than when housing from other sectors was used. If it is possible to generalise, hostels and other congregate care settings posed fewer difficulties than ordinary housing, and the dilemma facing one or two projects was the choice between an early move from hospital to a hostel and a delayed move to the ordinary housing which was more congruent with the care principles of the scheme.

As a consequence, the development of buildings was frequently out of sequence with other activities. Clients in some projects were identified and assessed before community resources were available, and housing was acquired and clients discharged before day resources came on stream. The Chichester project was only able to open its activity centre after most clients had moved out of hospital. The Waltham Forest community centre met with building problems which put back its completion for nine months. In contrast, housing occasionally came on stream only to remain unused for an embarrassingly long time, as in Islington, with credibility difficulties and political repercussions for managers and staff. There was mixed success in gaining access to public and voluntary sector housing. While some projects – including Winchester, Bucks, Somerset and Islington – worked successfully with local authority housing departments, others found local departments would not compromise their own priorities despite repeated lobbying. Liaison with architects and surveyors, even in-house, was not all plain sailing. It was especially frustrating for those projects which were unable to obtain planning consent or permission from council committees in time for people to move from hospital after preparatory work. Building delays, conversion slippages and rising costs were perhaps inevitable, with the St Helens and Camberwell projects suffering more than others.

Regulations also limited the options. 'Institution' was stamped on otherwise pleasant residences. The *Registered Homes Act 1984* required the monitoring and regulation of standards of residential provision, but also worked against the aims of projects built around normalisation by imposing institutional standards on domestic properties. Safety notices, necessary under the Act, do not encourage a homely atmosphere. Fire regulations worked against some plans. Fire extinguishers, alarms, smoke detectors, fire doors and exit signs tend to be obtrusive, and many facilities would have preferred to manage without them. Local negotiations with fire officers led to the relaxation of some regulations. An informal agreement was reached between staff and the local fire officer about the use of chip-pans in Cambridge. One of the core houses in Warwickshire successfully 'disguised' an internal fire escape as a spiral staircase which added character to the building. In West Cumbria, however, an attempt at creating a homely atmosphere was thwarted when the fire officer insisted that reinforced glass be used in the windows. Strict fire regulations in hospital about the use of frying pans and the need for flame retardant clothing similarly impeded rehabilitation work. We have previously mentioned the ban on smoking in bedrooms, which sacrificed individual freedom for collective safety. A range of practical decisions taken in the best interests of clients impose bounds on normalisation and 'ordinary living'.

A growing problem in some parts of the country, though not one which confronted pilot projects in their early development activities, is the concentration of community facilities for former hospital residents in particular areas. Some streets or districts which have houses of the right size and price for conversion into home for group living may become 'care ghettoes'. The three Liverpool staffed group houses were in adjacent streets, and one of the streets now has more than half-a-dozen similar facilities. In Chichester, a new group home run by Mencap was opened next to one of the project's cluster homes, and a day hospital opened opposite.

Environmental characteristics

The physical and social environments of hospital wards and community residential facilities were rated using an instrument, the Environment Checklist, developed specifically for this study from the work of Raynes et al. (1979), the PASS instrumentation, and Apte's Hospital and Hostel Practices Profile (Apte, 1968; Wykes, 1982). Sixty-nine per cent of the 221 community settings were rated during the study. Interviewers rated facilities on almost 50 checklist items during visits to interview clients or staff. The ratings ranged over the following areas:

- Ease of identification of the establishment from surrounding buildings.
- Location relative to other houses, public amenities and undesirable sites.
- General impression of outside – attractiveness and institutional character.

- Pleasantness and institutional aspects of living rooms (furniture, carpets, curtains, decoration, pictures, ornaments, plants, etc.).
- Pleasantness and institutional aspects of dining rooms (furniture, carpets and curtains, decoration, etc.).
- Pleasantness and institutional aspects of bedrooms (furniture, carpets and curtains, decoration, mirrors, residents' possessions).
- Pleasantness and institutional aspects of other rooms – kitchens, bathrooms, toilets, utility rooms.
- Acceptability of temperature, noise level, smell, general cleanliness, obtrusiveness of fire precautions or other safety precautions, adaptations for disability.
- General impression of institutional aspect of building (physical environment).
- Age-appropriateness of fittings and decorations.
- Encouragement of age-inappropriate possessions.
- Use of first names of staff by clients.
- Encouragement of residents to join in activities if left out.
- Institutional appearance of food and other household supplies.

The numbers of environments rated using the checklist are given in Table 8.7. Some of the environmental aspects were rated in terms of both 'pleasantness' and 'institutional/domestic nature' using two four-point scales, although in the tables which follow we shall collapse them into two:

- very unpleasant *or* fairly unpleasant, *as against* satisfactory or pleasant, attractive; and
- very institutional *or* fairly institutional, *as against* satisfactory *or* homely.

Pleasantness and institutional ratings tended to be highly correlated. Summary findings are given in Table 8.8. Other aspects were rated in terms of acceptability or appropriateness (see Table 8.9).

Table 8.7
Numbers of completed environment checklists

Client group	*No. of completed checklists* Hospital	Community	Total no. of community facilities used
Learning difficulties	135	100	132
Young people (mult.dis.)	0	1	1
Physical disabilities	2	3	3
Mental health problems	47	39	75
Elderly, physical frailty	16	3	3
Elderly, mental hlth probs	17	6	7
All client groups	217	152	221

Hospital-community differences. There were big differences between hospital wards and community settings on most environmental features and across client groups. If pleasant and domestic settings are better than unpleasant and institutional ones, community accommodation was vastly superior to hospital. Community accommodation was less likely to stand out from surrounding buildings; it was better located in relation to other houses, public amenities and away from undesirable sites; it was more attractive both inside and out; it was more likely to be homely or domestic in scale; it incorporated more attractive and less institutional living rooms, dining rooms, bedrooms and other rooms (kitchen, bathroom, toilet, utility room); and it offered food which appeared, and was served, in more attractive and less institutional ways. Most of these differences between hospital wards and community settings were statistically significant. For the full sample, there were *no* differences between hospital and community in relation to the acceptability of temperature and cleanliness, and only marginal differences in the age-inappropriateness of fittings and decor, acceptability of noise level and smell. Hospitals were much more likely to have obtrusive fire precautions. Age-inappropriate possessions were encouraged more often in hospital, although the difference is not significant for all client groups. In hospital, first names of staff were less frequently used by clients, and residents were given less active encouragement to join in activities.

By the criteria of normalisation, or by the standards of those who seek to avoid aspects of institutionalism, on *none* of the indicators did hospitals offer a better living environment than the community facilities to which people moved.

Community accommodation differences. There were surprisingly few differences between community accommodation types, as Table 8.10 illustrates. Only statistically significant differences are listed ($p \leq 0.05$), although note that some cells contain very small numbers of facilities. Larger congregate living settings such as residential homes, hostels and sheltered housing complexes were rated as less pleasant and more institutional than other settings, but preferable to hospital. (Wing, L., 1989, Chapters 7 to 9, reported a similar pattern for the community facilities used by former Darenth Park residents. Also see Kunze, 1985, and the review by Atkinson, 1988.) It was the case, therefore, that smaller and more independent community accommodation settings came closer to achieving the objectives of the normalisation principles of care espoused by many projects, again consistent with results elsewhere (for example, Korman and Glennerster, 1990, and see Chapters 14 and 15 below).

These features of accommodation settings may be ends in themselves, in so far as they indicate that people with long-term needs are valued by society at least to the extent that they live in generally pleasing and acceptable environments. They also suggest the attainment of certain basic rights. But they are also means to other ends. In Warrington, for example, hostel residents initially

Table 8.8
Physical environmental characteristics of hospital wards and community settings

Environmental characteristics and hospital/community setting	Mental health	Learning difficulties	Elderly	All clients[1]
Exterior of building is very or fairly unpleasant (%)				
- hospital	83	73	79	76
- community	8	7	11	7
Exterior of building is very or fairly institutional (%)				
- hospital	98	94	97	96
- community	8	7	38	9
Living rooms are very or fairly unpleasant (%)				
- hospital	79	54	70	62
- community	5	3	11	4
Living rooms are very or fairly institutional (%)				
- hospital	96	83	91	86
- community	0	8	0	7
Dining rooms are very or fairly unpleasant (%)				
- hospital	84	83	92	78
- community	6	6	14	6
Dining rooms are very or fairly institutional (%)				
- hospital	93	85	96	89
- community	6	11	57	12
Bedrooms are very or fairly unpleasant (%)				
- hospital	92	73	94	80
- community	8	5	13	6

preferred the blankets they were used to in hospital to the attractive duvets provided, they preferred the single large communal living room to the smaller, dispersed living rooms, and they disliked single bedrooms. These were mainly transitional problems for the hostel staff, but remind us that we must not fall into the trap of ignoring clients' views and preferences. In Chapters 13 and 14 we report how some environmental features and accommodation types were linked to the costs of community care and to client outcomes, the latter measured as changes in welfare between the hospital and community assessments.

The small number of private sector facilities used by a few projects did not measure up to the standards found in most statutory and voluntary sector facilities, although the numbers were too small for meaningful analysis.

Table 8.8 (continued)

Environmental characteristics and hospital/community setting	Mental health	Learning difficulties	Elderly	All clients[1]
Bedrooms are very or fairly institutional (%)				
- hospital	93	82	97	87
- community	0	5	37	6
Other rooms are very or fairly unpleasant (%)				
- hospital	95	89	94	91
- community	32	35	44	34
Other rooms are very or fairly institutional (%)				
- hospital	98	92	97	94
- community	10	30	78	27
Appearance of food is very or fairly institutional (%)				
- hospital	88	83	100	86
- community	0	2	17	3
Appearance of other supplies is very or fairly institutional (%)				
- hospital	91	87	96	89
- community	3	5	0	4
Interior of building is very or fairly unpleasant (%)				
- hospital	92	68	84	75
- community	5	6	11	6
Interior of building is very or fairly institutional (%)				
- hospital	93	86	97	89
- community	8	8	45	10
Total number of facilities[2]				
- hospital	47	135	32	216
- community	38	98	9	151

1 Includes Cambridge and Glossop projects not included in other columns.
2 Numbers of missing values are different for different items.

Concerns about institutional modes of community care in this sector have been voiced by many people (see, for example, Audit Commission, 1989; House of Commons Social Services Committee, 1990; Pilkington, 1990).

Client satisfaction with accommodation. Researchers' perceptions may not match with residents', so we also asked residents about their satisfaction with accommodation and their daily lives. The percentages of satisfied responses in the community and in hospital are summarised in Table 8.11. (Recall that while response rates were high for people with mental health problems and elderly people, some questions could not be answered by some people with

Table 8.9
Social environmental characteristics of hospital wards and community settings

Setting and social/physical environment characteristics	Mental health	Learning difficulties	Elderly	All clients[1]
Establishment is identifiable from surroundings (%)				
- hospital	98	78	91	85
- community	21	15	88	20
Establishment is poorly located (%)				
- hospital	51	42	6	38
- community	3	7	11	7
Temperature is acceptable (%)				
- hospital	94	93	84	92
- community	95	94	100	95
Noise level is acceptable (%)				
- hospital	83	67	72	71
- community	90	99	100	97
Smell is acceptable (%)				
- hospital	84	65	57	68
- community	90	94	100	93
Cleanliness is acceptable (%)				
- hospital	83	92	81	88
- community	87	94	100	93
Fire precautions are obtrusive (%)				
- hospital	20	42	21	34
- community	76	72	38	72
Age-inappropriate fittings and decor are used (%)				
- hospital	6	8	0	9
- community	0	1	0	1
Age-inappropriate possessions are encouraged (%)				
- hospital	37	52	11	43
- community	61	57	17	55
First names of staff are *not* used by clients (%)				
- hospital	33	16	55	26
- community	0	0	0	0
Clients are not encouraged to join in activities (%)				
- hospital	45	42	21	40
- community	50	19	25	26
Total number of facilities[2]				
- hospital	47	135	32	216
- community	38	98	9	151

1 Includes Cambridge and Glossop projects not included in other columns.
2 Numbers of missing values are different for different items.

Table 8.10

Environmental differences between accommodation types (significant differences only)

Environmental characteristics	Percentage of accommodations by types[1]								
	RESID	HOST	SHELT	SGH	USGH	FOST	LODG	INDEP	Sig.[2]
People with mental health problems									
Building identifiable from surroundings (% no)	0	38	–	100	90	100	100	100	.011
Supplies are domestic, not institutional (% yes)	50	100	–	100	100	100	100	100	.025
No. of facilities (MH)	2	8	–	3	10	1	1	6	
People with learning difficulties									
Building identifiable from surroundings (% no)	40	76	71	94	100	100	–	50	.021
Living rooms are pleasant, attractive (% yes)	0	64	29	61	0	89	–	50	.009
Living rooms are domestic, not institutional (% yes)	0	46	29	61	0	89	–	50	.012
Dining rooms are domestic, not institutional (% yes)	0	64	33	56	0	83	–	0	.046
Bedrooms are pleasant, attractive (% yes)	17	67	0	76	0	63	–	100	.001
Bedrooms are domestic, not institutional (% yes)	17	62	0	76	0	63	–	100	.002
Fire precautions are obtrusive (% no)	20	55	100	82	100	100	–	50	.003
Supplies are domestic, not institutional (% yes)	60	96	100	97	100	100	–	100	.032
No. of facilities (LD)	6	22	7	33	2	8	0	2	

1 Abbreviations are: RESID = residential home, including old people's home; HOST = hostel; SHELT = sheltered or very sheltered housing; SGH = staffed group home; USGH = unstaffed group home; FOST = adult fostering; LODG = supported lodgings; INDEP = independent house or flat.

2 p value of Chi-square test of inter-accommodation type differences. Only characteristics with $p < 0.05$ are listed.

Table 8.11
Residents' views about accommodation

	Percentage of clients expressing satisfaction							
	Mental health		*Learning difficulties*		*Elderly phys. dis.*		*Elderly ment. health*	
Aspect of accommodation	**Comm.** %	**Hosp.** %	**Comm.** %	**Hosp.** %	**Comm.** %	**Hosp.** %	**Comm.** %	**Hosp.** %
Place of residence	91	71	93	71	96	80	92	87
Neighbourhood	86	64	88	75	72	75	96	87
Comfort of accommodation	92	82	97	72	100	100	100	100
Bedroom	93	78	94	74	100	96	96	90
Space for own possessions	90	79	92	79	96	87	71	76
Quality of food	89	72	94	74	100	84	96	83
Preference to stay here	63	21	70	13	96	58	63	30
Rules in house/ward	90	69	82	60	92	91	78	71
People you live with	84	78	91	64	84	83	83	84
Staff in house/ward	94	86	94	84	100	100	81	94
Sample size	120	120	162	162	25	25	34	34

learning difficulties. Nevertheless, we were able to successfully interview 341 people twice, and a number of others once. Responses from the latter are excluded from this table. Note also that some clients may have been reluctant to voice criticisms. Their willingness would depend in part on the circumstances in which they were interviewed and whether they had been encouraged to voice negative opinions in the past. See Deutscher, 1973.) Satisfaction levels in the community are consistently high, with few items being positively rated by less than 80 per cent of respondents. The aspect about which most dissatisfaction was expressed concerned preferred place of residence. Having moved from hospital, more than a third of the respondents with mental health problems (elderly and others) and 30 per cent of those with learning difficulties wanted to live somewhere other than their current residence. Their preferred places of residence are given in Table 8.12. Of those expressing a desire to move, few wanted to return to hospital or to live with their families.

Rarely did respondents express greater satisfaction with hospital than community settings: the overwhelming majority preferred living in the community, a result also found by, among others, Gollay et al. (1978), Birenbaum and Re (1979), Passfield (1983) and Cattermole (1987).

Table 8.12

Preferences for moving from community accommodation

	Percentages of clients in each community setting preferring (or not) to move, and place to move to[1]:								
	RESID	HOST	SHELT	SGH	USGH	FOST	LODG	INDEP	All
People with mental health problems (N)	10	45	0	12	33	5	3	6	114
Preference for other location (% yes)	30	33	–	25	24	40	0	50	
Other location preferred[2]									
new house or group home	33	20	–	33	25	0	–	25	
own flat or house	0	40	–	33	50	0	–	50	
with family	67	20	–	33	13	0	–	0	
hospital	0	13	–	0	13	0	–	0	
other	0	7	–	0	0	100	–	25	
People with learning difficulties (N)	5	70	12	55	7	6	0	6	161
Preference for other location (% yes)	20	30	17	26	29	33	–	17	
Other location preferred[2]									
new house or group home	0	28	67	25	50	0	–	0	
own flat or house	0	28	33	33	50	100	–	100	
with family	0	28	0	8	0	0	–	0	
hospital	0	6	0	0	0	0	–	0	
other	100	11	0	33	0	0	–	0	
Elderly people (N)	29	0	27	0	0	0	0	0	56
Preference for other location (% yes)	10	–	4	–	–		–	–	
Other location preferred[2]									
new house or group home	0	–	0	–	–	–	–	–	
own flat or house	0	–	0	–	–	–	–	–	
with family	33	–	0	–	–	–	–	–	
hospital	0	–	0	–	–	–	–	–	
other	67	–	100	–	–	–	–	–	

1 Abbreviations are: RESID = residential home, including old people's home; HOST = hostel; SHELT = sheltered or very sheltered housing; SGH = staffed group home; USGH = unstaffed group home; FOST = adult fostering; LODG = supported lodgings; INDEP = independent house or flat.

2 Percentages of those with a preference for another location.

The service components of care packages

As we have described, there was no simple or single model of community care, nor was provision confined to just one or two agencies. Services used by clients were neither thrown together willy-nilly nor proffered in rigidly inflexible combinations: case management and individual programme planning processes helped to ensure that support packages were tailored, as far as possible, to individual needs. The tailoring was not perfect – needs were not always accurately assessed, information was not always complete, preferred service solutions were not always available, misjudgements sometimes occurred – but there was clear evidence of close links between those client characteristics commonly associated with need, on the one hand, and the costs of care packages on the other (see Chapter 14), which encourages us to believe that there was fairly consistent responsiveness.

Community care in practice meant making continued use of some hospital-based services as well as other health care. Particularly challenging for service or case managers was the organisation of day care, support and leisure activities, and arranging for the receipt of education services. For the individual client and case manager there was the additional task of securing access to key professionals such as GPs, social workers and therapists. Through our contacts with projects over some years, and from the completed Client Service Receipt Interviews, we were able to gain a detailed picture of the service components of community care. We describe them below under a number of heads, organised by type of service or professional group. In the next two chapters we will be looking more closely at community care staffing and the organisation of service packages by case managers.

Hospital and other health services

Hospitals continued to play a variety of roles in the development of community care people with long-term needs. Not only did they supply funds and staff (see Chapters 7 and 9), but they continued to accommodate people who required short- or long-term 'retreat' from life in the community, and they offer a range of non-residential services.

In-patient admissions. Eight per cent of the 829 people who moved to the community in the research period were readmitted to hospital at some time in the first nine months. Half of them were subsequently redischarged during the research period, and some others were expected to be redischarged a little later. These readmission and redischarge figures hide huge differences between client groups (Table 8.13): 11 per cent of people with mental health problems were readmitted to hospital (of whom 71 per cent were redischarged), compared with 3 per cent of people with learning difficulties (20 per cent redischarged). The proportions were much higher for elderly people. There was also a difference in length of in-patient stay. For *all* readmissions recorded during our research (some occurring after more than nine months in the community) a fifth of the readmissions of people with mental health problems lasted less than a fortnight, nearly half less than ten weeks, and only 14 per cent had not been discharged again during our period of contact with projects (Table 8.13). Similar research in North East Thames found that, from a total of 278 people with long-term mental health problems discharged over a three-year period, 6 per cent were readmitted and not redischarged for at least one year, 3 per cent had remained in hospital for between one and 12 months, and 15 per cent spent less than a month in hospital (Dayson, 1990).

Nineteen per cent of people with mental health problems readmitted to hospital had more than one readmission, and during the research period one client had six, one had five, three had four, and two returned to hospital three times. Out of the total of 227 leavers this indicates that pilot project clients were certainly *not* becoming 'revolving door' clients (Howat and Kontny, 1982).

Table 8.13

Hospital in-patient readmissions and redischarges

	Client group[1]				
	Mental health	Learning diffs.	Elderly Phys.frail	Elderly Ment.health	All clients[2]
Clients readmitted to hospital in first nine months					
- total	24	10	27	5	66
- as % of all movers[3]	11	3	18	5	8
Clients returning to the community					
- total	17	2	11	0	30
- as % of all readmissions	71	20	41	0	45
Duration of all first readmissions[4]					
- up to 2 weeks (%)	22	7	17	0	16
- up to 10 weeks (%)	46	7	42	0	35
- up to 20 weeks (%)	58	14	44	0	42
- not discharged (%)	14	79	56	100	54
- total number[4] (%)	50	14	36	13	113
Total no. clients	226	356	147	91	826

1 There were no readmissions by the Cambridge or Glossop clients.
2 Includes Cambridge and Glossop.
3 Excluding clients for whom hospital readmission data were missing.
4 Including some readmissions which occurred after more than nine months' residence in the community. Second and subsequent readmissions are excluded. Readmissions of unknown duration (these are *not* continuing placements) are excluded from these calculations.

Note, however, Haslam's view that a low readmission rate is 'a matter of policy rather than of need' (Haslam, 1988, p.197).

Few people with learning difficulties were readmitted to hospital, but most became long-term residents, only one in five returning to the community in the research period.

Readmission rates were, as expected, much higher among elderly clients – 18 per cent for the elderly physically frail and 5 per cent for elderly people with mental health problems. About half the former were redischarged to the community, but only a small number of elderly people with mental health problems returned again to community accommodation. (These readmission rates are a lot lower than those found by Townsend et al., 1988, over a similar period of time for a *general* population of elderly people discharged from hospital.)

In a number of cases, hospital admissions for people with mental health problems were unrelated to mental illness, and most people with learning difficulties readmitted had physical health problems.

- One woman lived successfully in the community for a few months, getting on well with the three other residents of a shared house, but then started to behave aggressively towards one staff member who was expecting a baby. Challenging behaviour became more apparent both inside the home and outside, and it was soon realised that there was a history of disruptive behaviour which had not been fully appreciated when assessed for the scheme. She returned to hospital a year after she had left, because of her own unhappiness and because of the disruption to the lives of other residents. A few years she moved out of hospital.
- Another client became very distressed after the death of his mother (he did not live with her) and seriously damaged his housing association accommodation. Neighbours complained and he was threatened with eviction. He requested and was offered temporary asylum in hospital.
- A very capable woman diagnosed as suffering from schizophrenia repeatedly found it difficult to adhere to many of the codes of conduct in her hostel. After many warnings regarding smoking in her bedroom she was asked to leave the hostel as it was felt by staff that she was putting the safety of other residents at risk. With no other community options available she returned temporarily to hospital before moving to a private care home.

The need for some form of asylum or haven for some people remains clear, although the long-stay hospital ward does not look the appropriate place for it.

Out-patient attendances. A third of the 433 clients followed up in our evaluation of service receipt had at least one hospital out-patient attendance after moving to the community (Table 8.14). In some cases attendance was frequent, but generally clients either had occasional, routine attendances (to see a psychiatrist or geriatrician, for example) or attended for reasons unconnected to their original reason for hospital admission. There did not appear to be a problem of non-attendance (compare Smyth et al., 1990).

Other hospital attendances. Clients had few other links with hospitals. Fourteen per cent of clients with mental health problems returned to their previous place of residence or another hospital for industrial (or occupational) therapy, 9 per cent attended an activity centre and 2 per cent a social club. These proportions are a lot lower than in the Friern-Claybury psychiatric reprovision programme (Beecham et al., 1991b). Although some hospitals will eventually close, and although spending one or two days a week in a sheltered hospital setting does not represent integration or 'ordinary' living, it may be an important contributory factor in influencing a client's quality of life in the graduation to community living, at least in the short term and possibly for some time to come. This was illustrated by the clients of one project who missed the hospital because they had lost both their friends and the jobs which had given them status. There was virtually no opportunity for employment outside hospital. One client went back to work three days a week in the hospital library and others went back for industrial therapy. It was argued by staff that clients' wishes were respected, and that this was a preferable option to doing nothing in the community (Lyne, 1988). No member of the other client groups made any other use of hospital services. In projects for people with learning difficulties it was common for people to experience community-based day support services before leaving hospital.

Hospital contacts and managing agencies. Do people living in NHS community facilities make more use of hospitals after the move to the community? Although there was some suggestion from our interpretation of projects' practices that those led or staffed by health authorities, or using NHS community accommodation facilities, may have been less reluctant to readmit clients to hospital, there was in fact no statistical evidence in support of this.

Psychiatrists. Few elderly people, few people with learning difficulties and no-one in the Cambridge or Glossop projects consulted psychiatrists (Table 8.14). Twenty-eight per cent of clients with mental health problems consulted a psychiatrist (including domiciliary visits), this proportion being *over and above* any in-, out- or day patient sessions at hospital which included seeing a psychiatrist. Projects reported difficulties in getting psychiatrist appointments for clients, especially for people with learning difficulties.

Nurses. Obviously, many clients received nursing assistance while resident in or visiting hospital, and there were nursing staff employed in some community accommodation facilities (see Chapter 9). Over and above these inputs, just under half of all clients had used nursing services (from district nurses, community psychiatric nurses and others) in the month preceding our follow-up assessment. Sixty-one per cent of people with mental illness problems received nursing inputs – in the majority of cases from CPNs, usually including depot injections of long-acting tranquillizers. There was no clear pattern of receipt by type of accommodation or sector. Two broad patterns that *did* emerge, though weakly, were the substitutability of CPNs and field social workers, as found by Mangen et al. (1983), and the complementarity of CPNs and psychiatrists, contrary to Mangen's findings. It appeared that CPNs were working more as skilled specialist nurses than generic community workers.

Only a quarter of the sample of people with learning difficulties were receiving any nursing input in the community.

General practitioners. For some years the Royal College of General Practitioners has argued that a community care policy imposes heavy burdens on GPs. The Select Committee stressed that 'community care depends to a large extent on the continuing capacity of GPs to provide primary medical care to mentally disabled people' (House of Commons Social Services Committee, 1985, para. 188). It recommended a review of GP training in relation to psychiatry and learning difficulty, and that psychiatrists should have a better understanding of the GP's role.

Table 8.14
Services used in the community

Service	Learning diffs. %	Adoles. mult.dis. %	Phys. dis. %	Mental health %	Elderly phys.frail %	Elderly ment.hlth %	All clients %
Hospital out-patient	34	33	33	30	22	30	32
Hospital day patient	0	0	0	0	4	0	–[1]
Hosp. indus. therapy	0	0	0	14	0	0	4
Hosp. activity cent.	0	0	0	9	0	0	3
Hospital social club	0	0	0	2	0	0	1
Psychiatrists	6	0	67	28	70	85	45
Nurses	26	100	33	61	91	35	42
GPs	81	100	100	89	91	70	83
Dentists	41	0	0	25	13	48	35
Opticians	26	0	0	21	22	28	24
Psychologists	9	100	0	11	13	3	10
Education inputs	50	100	33	14	0	0	32
Field social work	35	0	67	24	9	3	27
Chiropodists	45	0	67	28	70	85	45
Physiotherapists	10	100	0	1	13	3	7
Other therapists	14	33	0	10	17	10	13
Number of clients	232	3	3	129	23	40	430

1 '–' indicates not zero but too small to record.

In the month prior to the collection of service utilisation data, 83 per cent of clients had at least one GP appointment. Bearing in mind that some clients were also returning to their previous hospitals of residence or travelling to other hospitals for day treatment or as out-patients, this is a high proportion. According to the General Household Survey, average consultation rates in the UK in 1984 were 3.2 per annum for males and 4.4 for females. By this standard, Care in the Community clients were visiting or being visited by their GPs at least two and a half times as often as the national average, and not simply in the first few weeks after leaving hospital. Differences between the client groups were not marked. Although it is well-known that GPs undertake most of the medical care of people with mental health problems (Goldberg and Huxley, 1980), it is surprisingly difficult to find evidence on GP services or consultations by former long-stay hospital patients (Wilkinson et al., 1985; Wilkinson and Pelosi, 1987; Wilkinson, 1988; CroftJeffreys and Wilkinson, 1989), making it difficult to check whether the findings from the present evaluation are out of line. The consistently high utilisation rates across all projects and places of residence suggest, however, that these are not random results.

This burden on GPs may explain, but perhaps not excuse, the occasional refusals to accept some project clients onto their lists. This problem is not peculiar to the demonstration programme, and will become particularly acute if community care facilities are grouped in 'community care ghettoes', for they then impose disproportionate demands on a few GP practices. Some projects tried to avoid this by ensuring clients were dispersed across different practices even if they all lived in the same residential setting, although this is obviously not possible everywhere. On the other hand, projects which had a single GP or practice responsible for a whole facility or group of clients found that the concentration allowed expertise, knowledge and interest to accummulate. This has to be weighed against the lack of choice and the prolongation of institutional practices.

Dentists and opticians. We noted in Chapter 5 that a sizeable proportion of the people who moved to the community were rated by interviewers (while in hospital) as having 'inappropriate' or 'unusual' glasses or teeth, reckoned by many to be a distinguishing mark of institutionalism. The need for attention from dentists and opticians was only too evident. In fact, after leaving hospital only a third of all clients consulted a dentist. Clients living in independent accommodation made less use of dental services than those living elsewhere, which may be attributable to less intensive keyworker support, although we are unable to satisfactorily standardise for need in order to examine this further. A quarter of all clients had seen an optician since leaving hospital. Securing good dental care was more problematic than gaining access to good GP services in at least two projects. Some dentists would not or could not cater for people with learning difficulties, particularly the more disabled or those with challenging behaviours. Dentists and opticians are not available for domiciliary visits, causing access difficulties for less mobile clients. Some clients therefore had to travel to a hospital to use these services.

Our evaluation could not measure dental or ophthalmic outcomes, and clinical assessments were out of the question, but we could look at the appropriateness of each client's personal presentation in the community and compare with the rating in hospital (Table 8.15). The results are not particularly encouraging: 8 per cent of clients had a 'more appropriate appearance' regarding teeth and glasses in the community than in hospital, but 16 per cent showed a deterioration in 'appropriateness'. It needs to be remembered, however, that hospital and community assessments were made in two very different social environments, overlaid with different norms and expectations. Moreover, some clients chose not to take up the opportunities offered in the community. (At least two people had been fitted with dentures but found them too uncomfortable after many years of having relied only on their gums, and so did not wear them.)

Table 8.15
Appropriateness of appearance of glasses and teeth in hospital and in the community

	Appropriateness of appearance in community compared to appropriateness in hospital - teeth and glasses only			
Client group	**Less appropriate** %	**No difference** %	**More appropriate** %	**No. of clients** N
Mental illness	11	82	7	223
Learning difficulty	25	65	10	338
Elderly physically frail	3	95	3	146
Elderly mentally impaired	10	81	9	59
Cambridge and Glossop	0	50	50	6
All clients	16	77	8	772

Psychologists. Inputs from psychologists were limited. One in ten clients consulted a psychologist in the period since leaving hospital, with few variations between client groups or projects (the exceptions being a third of the Greenwich clients and every Torbay client). The major shortage of psychologists, especially in public sector community work, was undoubtedly a contributory factor.

Day care, support and recreation

The centrality of day care, support and leisure activities (along with education and employment, which we discuss separately below) to the success of Care in the Community was recognised by some projects at the outset, but regrettably not by all. Careful daytime planning was certainly as important as getting the right accommodation. Project by project provision is detailed in Table 8.16.

If it is to be provided in accordance with the broad principles of community care described earlier, day care and support should respond to individual needs and preferences, should actively promote integration, should be provided in places used and valued by other members of society, and should offer the range of options available to other users. Yet securing *any* day support services proved difficult enough in some areas. Difficulties stemmed from poor planning, scarcity of resources, and the inappropriateness of available services. Fewer non-project resources were available than had been hoped, which left many schemes with day staff stretched on unexpected duties. Some agencies and facilities (particularly education) refused to take unaccompanied clients. Behavioural problems barred some clients from activities outside their place of residence. Korman and Glennerster found that the absence of day care for former Darenth Park residents was 'one of the major failings of the project' (1990, p.76), and the House of Commons Social Services Committee's reports of 1985 and 1990 pointed to the inadequacy and narrowness of provision. From these reports it seems probable that the Care in the Community projects achieved rather better standards of day care, support and leisure provision than was (and still is) available in the rest of the country. The clear reason for this was the ear-marking of parts of some programme grants for day service development.

Integration was deemed undesirable in cases where projects' initial appraisals of existing facilities for day care revealed woeful inadequacies. Adult training centres (ATCs), social education centres (SECs) and day centres encompass a range of different support and activity philosophies suited to clients with quite different needs. The SECs were not suitable for elderly people or those who were looking for employment. Some ATCs were too institutional, and some had managers unhappy about competition from programme clients for the limited numbers of places, and sometimes openly antagonistic to a project's aims.

Some projects set up new services in parallel with those already in existence.

- In Brent the core unit was a resource centre providing drop-in facilities and day care including informal therapy sessions and structured activities (covering 18 hours in each 24). The core unit also provided a focus for formal access to both health services and social service staff, for a relatives' support group, and for crisis intervention. Volunteer helpers assisted users of the centre by supplementing the skills of professional workers in specific areas.

Table 8.16

The provision of day care, support and education

Project	*Type of day care, support and education provided*
People with learning difficulties	
Bolton	Rural training scheme, education support tutors, other employment opportunities.
Calderdale	A resource centre. Used local college of further education and adult training centres (ATC). Access to all community resources.
Camden	Access to all community resources. Special needs programmes created.
Derby	Total range available by use of existing services.
Islington	New day care centre established, also used ATC and educational facilities.
Kidderminster	Work experience, recreational schemes and variety of diversified day services. Instructors employed from ATCs.
Liverpool	ATCs and some further education facilities
Maidstone	Tailor-made to fit individual needs. Training workshops. Self-advocacy, new resource centre, adult education, clubs, employment, social education centre (SEC).
Somerset	Three days per week at ATC or day centre.
Torbay	Within hostel. Participation in general life of community if wished. ATC, community placements.
Warwick	SECs or more appropriate care as required.
Young people with multiple disabilities	
Cambridgeshire	Clients attended local special school.
People with physical handicap	
Glossop	Ordinary community opportunities in education, work and social areas.
People with mental health problems	
Brent	Core unit (resource centre) provided 15 hours per day drop-in facility.
Bucks	30 place day centre
Chichester	Day activity centre
Greenwich	Daytime activities from project base.
Waltham Forest	Adapted shop-front community facility plus normal community facilities.
Warrington	Day centre weekdays and Sundays. Industrial therapy centre at hospital. Other community resources.
West Berkshire	New 36-place treatment unit. Other community resources.
West Lancashire	Social club, leisure centre, educational and recreational schemes. Used existing day centre.
Elderly people with physical frailty	
Coventry	20-place day centre. 7-day week, 2 care staff, voluntary workers.
Darlington	Access to community services not supplied by project.
Winchester	A warden and access to normal community services.
Elderly people with mental health problems	
Camberwell	Based on care plans, utilising volunteers, relatives and paid local people. Support and bereavement counselling for relatives.
Hillingdon	Social care to enable enjoyment of common domestic practices and experiences.
St Helens	Clients received health care from the primary health care team as used in other local old people's homes.
West Cumbria	24-hour reality orientation. Use of day centre. Relatives, neighbours and friends involved.

- The activity centre in Chichester was developed as an integral part of the core and cluster model and was used by staff, clients, volunteers and people with a mental illness already living in the community.
- The Coventry enhanced sheltered housing development, opened with the help of DHSS central funding, incorporated a 20-place day centre, planned to be open seven days a week.
- The Islington project inherited a traditional day care resource which it moulded to better meet the requirements of clients and the project philosophy. It evolved to become a client and staff base, with drop-in facilities and programmes of activities open to the wider community.

Among other projects which opened new day or resource centres or their equivalents were Bucks, Calderdale and Waltham Forest. In projects which aimed to meet clients' total needs, daytime services played a vital part.

- In Derby, the overriding philosophy was to provide services, so far as possible, in the way similar services would be delivered to 'ordinary people' – anyone in the community. This aim applied, in fact, to *all* provision including the buildings people lived in, leisure time, work, education, dress or behaviour, and the range of opportunities and choices open to them.
- The Kidderminster project employed training instructors attached to adult training centres throughout the county. They succeeded in developing new day services in the form of work experience placements, leisure and recreational activities, independent living training and home teaching programmes.
- The rural training scheme in Bolton encouraged the physical well-being and social development of people with learning difficulties by training in agricultural and horticultural skills, although with hindsight clients perhaps found this of less value in securing open employment than was hoped. The project also offered other activities.
- The Warwick Mencap project employed a leisure organiser with a development role. Warwickshire SSD was closing its ATCs and SECs, and staff became mobile resources instead.
- The Somerset core houses were used as bases from which to explore local community work, education and leisure opportunities and resources. Flexibility was built in to each network.

Employment has not been discussed here. It is considered as one of the programme outcomes in Chapter 14.

Education

Local education authorities (LEAs) were brought into joint planning arrangements with implementation of the *Health and Social Services and Social Security Adjudications Act 1983* in April 1984. The Act made it easier for LEAs to collaborate with other statutory and voluntary agencies to develop education for adults with special learning needs. Education was both an achievement in its own right for clients, perhaps more so in integrated settings, and a means to further self-development and participation in the community. It can improve self-image as well as basic self-care and other skills (Griffiths et al., 1985).

In seeking to meet the education needs of clients through appropriate provision, projects were guided by the same principles and hampered by the same constraints as applied to other services. In Calderdale, a 'Classmates' scheme developed by Stansfield View Hospital and Calder College linked people with learning difficulties to volunteers sharing the same interest. The Classmates volunteer received free sessions, and the client paid reduced fees. Normalisation and integration were preferred by some but not all. Integrated classes may be closer to the principle of normalisation, but in some areas people without 'disabilities' or 'special needs' melted away from classes when integration was attempted. Even when this did not occur, project clients were usually but a small proportion of the total number of people receiving a service and projects found it hard to negotiate full integration where LEAs themselves preferred segregation. For some people, special (segregated) education provision was necessary and preferred by clients, even though it ran the danger of reinforcing negative attitudes. For example, using the DHSS grant, the Bolton project appointed six education support tutors who each worked closely with a small group of clients both within local colleges and in domiciliary settings. They provided a successful education input into day care.

Local or accessible facilities were often unavailable, or full, or unable to make special small classes viable, or would not accept 'people with handicaps'. These and other factors led some projects to provide an education input within their own 'core' day activity provision. In Brent, for example, the resource centre offered continuing rehabilitation and therapeutic work (taking over from Shenley Hospital), and at least five Brent clients were also attending education classes or receiving assistance from a tutor.

Across the sample, a third of all clients attended education classes or college, or received tuition from a tutor at home or elsewhere (Table 8.14). These numbers *exclude* any education provided within ATCs and SECs, and education provided within the budgets of project resource centres and residential facilities. Half the clients with learning difficulties used education services in these first nine months in the community, but no elderly clients. For every user, the education input was organised and funded *outside* the residential budget and, if the project had one, the resource centre, core house or activity centre. The figures in the tables thus give the *minimum* percentages of clients receiving the service.

Other services

Field social work. Social workers comprised a large proportion of the staff of many projects' residential complements (Chapter 9), but there still remained a need for field social work support. A quarter of all clients, including a third of the clients with learning difficulties, received some field social work. Those clients living in the more independent settings (unstaffed group homes, foster or adult home finding placements, sheltered housing and independent accommodation itself) were more likely to be in contact with field social work staff. Most but not all such staff were local authority employees; the remainder were employed by voluntary agencies.

Chiropodists. Chiropody was a low-cost, occasional input to the pilot projects, fundamentally important for improving mobility, thus enhancing independence and integration. The high proportion of clients in the elderly projects who used this service was no surprise, but it was also used by 45 per cent of people with learning difficulties and 28 per cent of people with mental health problems.

Therapists. 'The basic skills necessary for mentally disabled people to live an ordinary life in the community are crucially dependent on help from professional therapists' (House of Commons Social Services Committee, 1985, para. 202). The importance of these skills were recognised by projects which included therapists on project teams (occupational therapy staff in West Berkshire and Greenwich, physiotherapy in Bolton). Physiotherapy was used by one in ten of all clients with learning difficulties and a slightly higher proportion of elderly physically frail people. Other special therapy inputs used by clients included art, speech, music and drama. Some clients with speech difficulties had never been assessed by a speech therapist until they entered the Care in the Community programme.

Service development – summary

Translating a philosophy of care into practice demanded compromise and often triggered debate. Normalisation, although essentially a value base, was sometimes misunderstood or inflexibly applied. Ideological commitments had to be tempered by client needs and wants. Service packages had to be constructed in cognisance of these issues and what could be provided within available resources. Incorporating self-determination and client choice required an element of risk-taking by both staff and clients, particularly in relation to money management, medication, life skills, friendships and sexuality. Staff had to allow some clients to make 'wrong choices' and had to accommodate conflicts between the wishes of users and professional judgements. Yet in projects such as Kidderminster, Somerset and some of those in London, self and citizen advocacy proved workable at worst, and usually enormously helpful. The Maidstone project addressed the issue head on with a client-centred case management model. Other projects involved users in planning groups or on residents' committees.

The programme intended to help people move from hospital to a variety of facilities within the community, ranging from independent living and ordinary housing to group homes and hostels. Polar opposites illustrate this. The Kidderminster project provided no accommodation itself, but gained access to residential resources across the mixed economy of provision (local authority, health authority, voluntary sector, housing association, private agency). This contrasted with Somerset, where provision was solely the responsibility of the county social services department. There were other differences. Somerset and Warwick utilised a model based on core and cluster arrangements. In Chichester, however, core and cluster came to mean a high-dependency hostel and minimum support group homes, loosely linked by staffing. The Somerset core houses provided a staff, training and resource base. Other projects such as Brent and Chichester built separate resource and activity centres into their service models, which although designed to perform a similar function, were clearly demarcated from residential facilities.

Where someone sleeps may go some way to describing the underlying philosophy of care, proscribing the costs of service packages, and determining client outcomes, but it is only one aspect of successful community care. As many people have pointed out, the planning of community alternatives to hospital too often begins and ends with residential accommodation. This chapter has hinted at the importance for client welfare of support in day activities, access to educational and leisure resources and opportunities for employment, each of which appears again later in the book. New but rather different day facilities were opened in, for example, Bucks, Brent, Islington, Calderdale, Waltham Forest and Coventry, while some of the other projects encouraged clients to use existing facilities.

Each service system contained its own frictional forces, constraints, pressures and distortions. Delivering services and moving clients within the three years of central funding proved demanding. Developing good relationships with neighbours, the local press, politicians, volunteers, police, general practitioners, schools and social security officers helped projects and their clients integrate into the community, although integration was far from easy.

What were the effects on client quality of life? We examine these in Chapters 12 to 15, but first continue our description of the processes of community care by turning to staffing.

9 Staffing community services

The key resource in social and health care is staff, and any transition of the locus of provision, as with the move of many hundreds of people from hospital to the community, obviously posed challenges for staff at all levels within the organisations involved. Some of the most difficult tasks for projects over the period of Care in the Community funding concerned staffing policies. Many staffing decisions faced projects, including:

- preparatory work with hospitals and their staff;
- the forecasting of staff numbers;
- the recruitment and selection of people to fill the posts forecasted as needed;
- the arrangement of shifts and rotas, and the general organisation of work;
- the support and supervision of staff holding demanding new responsibilities, especially with the introduction of case management and keyworker roles, and also for staff working in the comparative isolation of dispersed housing;
- the introduction and maintenance of development and training programmes; and
- the translation into practice of those broad principles set out in project plans about how high-quality care is to be provided. Since many projects set out to test innovative styles of provision, the demands on staff were likely to be considerable.

These staffing issues are considered in detail in this chapter, as is the issue of liaison between employing agencies, which cross-cuts all of the others. Table 9.1 scans the broad staffing arrangements adopted by projects. The diversity of policies and practices will already be clear, and one of the aims of this chapter is to draw insights from this multiplicity of intentions and experiences relevant to the overall development of community care.

Data on staffing policies and staff numbers, qualifications and experience, special training, attitudes, responsibilities and duties, patterns of communication and job satisfaction were gathered. Much of the data came from the four or more years of monitoring and liaison, including questions on staff in the routine annual report and end of project questionnaires. Some projects supplied us with less data than others, for operational and policy reasons, and some were simply reluctant or unable to share their experiences. We were nevertheless able to collect a complex array of staffing data, some integrated with other collections (such as the information on the inputs of different professional staff groups described in the previous chapter), but most elicited from three purpose-built instruments:

Table 9.1
Staffing

	Type of staffing	*Number of staff*	*% full-time*	*Major employer*
Bolton	Core support team, home care teams, education support tutors, rural training instructors, CMHN, SW, OT, PT, etc.	151	75	LA (94%)
Calderdale	All accommodation to have staffed support	24	83	LA (100%)
Camden	Team of project leaders and team of support workers.	34	76	VOL(100%)
Derby	Multidisciplinary teams, IPP coordinators, instructors, residential care staff.	—	—	—
Islington	Initially supported by residential social workers who may be withdrawn later. Support workers.	9	—	LA (100%)
Kidderminster	Resettlement workers. Part-time evaluation officer, training instructors, pre-discharge nurses.	25	68	LA (72%)
Liverpool	Houses have 24-hour staffing managed by a homes coordinator.	—	—	—
Maidstone	Coordinator, evaluator, resource management teams, CMHT, residential staff, part-time support workers.	54	72	LA (91%)

'—' throughout the table indicates no response.

Table 9.1 (continued)

Main source of job satisfaction	*Main source of job dissatisfaction*	*Rostering problems*	*Staff training*
Relationships with colleagues; nature of work.	Lack of opport-unity for advancement.	Difficult to cover for sickness and turnover.	Various workshops and courses staged. Induction course, training packs for care staff, profess-ionals and managers.
Relationships with colleagues, challenges, hours	Income level	—	Induction course 'Patterns for living'. In-service training courses.
Opportunity to use initiative, hours.	Supervision, opportunity for advancement.	No problems	Attended various courses, confer-ences and seminars from training budget.
Opportunity to use initiative, job security.	Public respect for job.	No problems	Training tailing off due to financial constraints. Some attendance at external courses.
Relationships with colleagues. Supervision.	Opportunity for advancement. Public respect for job.	Cover inadequate because of staffing levels.	3-week induction course and various in-service courses.
Nature of work. Own accomplish-ments.	Being set challenges. Opportunity to use own initiative.	—	In-service training seminars; a range of workshops. Secondment to external conferences and courses – BIMH, etc.
Relationships with colleagues.	Opportunity for advancement	Long shifts affect health and personal lives.	Maketon evening classes. Input by dietician.
—	—	Covering for days in recruitment. Inflexibility of volunteers.	In-service training by joint tutor, plus external courses. Team workshops.

Table 9.1 (continued)

	Type of staffing	*Number of staff*	*% full-time*	*Major employer*
Somerset	24-hour support in core houses. Some support in clusters.	24	46	LA (100%)
Torbay	24-hour staffing	8	63	VOL (100%)
Warwick	Multidisciplinary selection and staffed homes staffed by Mencap employees	—	—	—
Cambridge	Professional foster parents	5	—	LA (100%)
Glossop	24-hour support from domiciliary staff, paid volunteers, warden on site.	11	9	LA (73%)
Brent	Use of all disciplines and voluntary sector, staffed and unstaffed provision.	44	73	LA (52%)

Table 9.1 (continued)

Main source of job satisfaction	*Main source of job dissatisfaction*	*Rostering problems*	*Staff training*
Relationships with colleagues	Accomplishment. Lack of respect for job.	No problems	In-house/in-service training programmes. Plans for joint training with HA. Specialist social service MH training officer.
Hours, supervision relationships, status, opportunities to use own initiative.	—	Inadequate staffing levels. Dislike of sleep-ins.	Implementation of staff training programme. Tap into joint MI/MH programme.
Relationships with colleagues. Nature of job.	—	Sleep-ins. Covering for illness and holidays.	No project-specific strategy. King's Fund. SAUS. SSD 'living like other people' training courses. Local staff developed own packages. Open University 'Patterns for Living' material purchased.
Relationships with colleagues. Supervision by superiors.	Variety of tasks. Flexibility of hours.	Covering for illness. Shifts unpopular with staff.	Four weeks induction. In-service training in response to encountered needs, plus evaluation sessions.
—	—	Conflict between staff needs and client needs.	All staff and volunteers to train alongside nursing staff in hospital. On-going training in practical and theoretical aspects, coordinated by service coordinators.
Hours, variety.	Opportunities for advancement	Inadequate staffing	Four induction courses, various topics. Training seminars plus normal professional supervision.

Table 9.1 (continued)

	Type of staffing	*Number of staff*	*% full-time*	*Major employer*
Bucks	Mainly use of staff in group home/ hostel and day centre with a contribution from social work staff	34	71	LA (97%)
Chichester	24-hour staffing and housekeeper in core house. Visits from members of community rehab. team in clusters.	20	60	NHS (85%)
Greenwich	Varied degrees of staffed support as appropriate. Mainly 24-hour cover with visiting support.	11	100	LA (100%)
Waltham Forest	Multidisciplinary team employed by MIND, on-call service evenings and weekends, portable 'phone system.	7	100	Vol. (100%)
Warrington	24-hour staffing	10	80	Vol. (100%)
West Berkshire	24-hour staffing in hostel, multi-disciplinary teams and day treatment unit staff.	8	0	NHS / LA
West Lancashire	Community team headed by rehabilitation officer. Staff provide caring service 8 a.m. to 11 p.m.	7	86	LA (100%)

Table 9.1 (continued)

Main source of job satisfaction	*Main source of job dissatisfaction*	*Rostering problems*	*Staff training*
Challenges	Respect for job. Income.	No problems	Variety of in-service training. Formal pilot-project training and joint training just begun.
Relationships with colleagues.	Respect for job.	Cover for holidays.	Nursing courses on rehabilitation, violence, diploma in nursing, plus psychotherapy in the community, health and hygiene, social skills, first aid.
Supervisors, relationships with colleagues, security, accomplishments.	Difficulty of travel to work	Providing optimal level of care as needs change	In-house training with some attendance at external courses. Induction period, ongoing team training, support group, external courses on various topics.
Nature of work, opportunities to use initiative, skills development.	Opportunity for advancement.	Weekend work unpopular. Cover for holidays and sickness.	Staff support meetings and personal external supervision.
—	—	Sleep-ins interfere with personal life of staff.	Formal induction courses, placement in other agencies involved, on-the-job training.
—	—	—	On-site joint training planned. Attendance at seminars and workshops, visits to other hospitals.
—	—	Difficult to build in flexibility.	Induction and familiarisation period for all staff. Individually tailored programmes.

Table 9.1 (continued)

	Type of staffing	*Number of staff*	*% full-time*	*Major employer*
Coventry	24-hour staffing – care staff and daytime nursing staff.	43	14	LA (95%)
Darlington	Home care assistants provide a maximum of 9 hours per 2 clients per day.	61	93	NHS (100%)
Winchester	24-hour on-call system. Additional 4 hours care per day from care attendants	16	0	Vol. (56%)
Camberwell	Core team of health service staff to provide protection and support.	1	100	Vol. (100%)
Hillingdon	Additional staff to work in units and home care staff to help clients live at home.	32	34	LA (91%)
St Helens	Staffing will be based on the staffing levels of LA homes of 50-55 places, reflecting greater levels of dependency	52	23	LA (100%)
West Cumbria	24-hour staffing – enhanced staffing	31	10	LA (100%)

Table 9.1 (continued)

Main source of job satisfaction	*Main source of job dissatisfaction*	*Rostering problems*	*Staff training*
Security, relationships with colleagues.	Opportunity for advancement.	Staffing levels inadequate	3 day induction, monthly meeting, care assistant courses, observation days, on-the-job training, in-service training, CSS training as appropriate.
—	—	—	Home care assistants training. Assessing project management team training needs.
Supervision, relationships with colleagues, hours, opportunity to use initiative.	Variety of tasks, own accomplishments.	Complexity because of involvement of two agencies	Training according to experience/need in situ in hospital and community.
—	—	No problem	Investigating training needs
Opportunities to use initiative. Ease of travel to work.	Opportunities for advancement.	No problem	One week induction course by SSD. Day placements for staff.
—	—	No problem	Two weeks induction training plus ongoing training. Training day, team building, reality orientation.
Relationships, income job, accomplishments.	—	—	Two weeks induction to familiarise staff with philosophy of home. Individual training programmes on understanding dementia. Reality orientation. Reminiscence therapy and achievement of maximum client independence.

- *Staff Record 1*, completed by line managers for all staff funded by projects, together with other staff with a significant input even though funded from elsewhere (including volunteers);
- *Staff Record 2*, completed by individual staff, and returned direct to the PSSRU to preserve confidentiality and to encourage candid responses; and
- the *Staff Time Budget*, used in a sub-sample of ten projects, recording staff activities over a sample week (with completed instruments returned by 129 staff).

The two Staff Record forms were returned by 20 projects. Response rates were good, although lower than we hoped (Table 9.2), partly a consequence of self-completion without interview, and partly the result of the turnover of senior staff (which sometimes took away local commitment to the research) and pressure of work (leaving little time for completing 'yet another' PSSRU questionnaire). No staff forms of any type were returned by seven projects. (These included Camberwell and St Helens which had not established their community services at the time we conducted this work, and Maidstone and Darlington which were the subject of parallel evaluations, as reported by Leedham, 1990, and Challis et al., 1989.)

In June 1988, shortly after the end of DHSS funding for the second-round projects, and 15 months after funding ceased for the first-round projects, 722 staff were employed in 25 projects (we had no data for Derby, Liverpool or Warwick). Of these, 436 (60 per cent) were full-time. The boundaries between some projects and their host agencies were blurred, but these figures represent employees responsible to project managers. They were not all funded from the programme grants. Three-quarters of these staff were local authority employees, 17 per cent NHS employees and 11 per cent in voluntary organisations. Two staff in Glossop were self-employed. Agency lead helps to explain inter-project variations in employing agencies (see Chapter 11).

Table 9.2
Response rates, staff questionnaires

Client group[1]	*Numbers of responses*		
	Staff record 1	**Staff record 2**	**Staff time budget**
People with learning difficulties	280	192	57
Young people with multiple disabilities	4	5	3
People with mental health problems	67	47	6
Elderly people with physical frailty	16	26	31
Elderly people with mental health problems	49	47	32
All client groups	416	317	129

1 There were no responses from Warrington, West Berks, Maidstone, Darlington, Camberwell, St Helens or Glossop on these instruments for the reasons outlined in the text, although other information is available on staffing.

Table 9.3
Numbers of staff working in pilot projects, June 1988

Project[1]	Client group[2]	Total no. staff	Full-time staff (%)	*Employing agency (%)* DHA	LA	VOL
Bolton	LD	151	75	6	94	0
Calderdale[3]	LD	24	83	0	100	0
Camden	LD	34	76	0	0	100
Islington	LD	9	0	0	100	0
Kidderminster[3]	LD	25	68	28	72	0
Maidstone	LD	54	72	0	91	9
Somerset	LD	24	46	0	100	0
Torbay	LD	8	63	0	0	100
All LD projects		**329**	**70**	**5**	**81**	**14**
Cambridge	AM	5	100	0	100	0
Glossop[4]	PD	11	9	0	73	9
Brent	MH	44	73	34	66	0
Bucks	MH	34	71	0	97	3
Chichester	MH	20	60	85	0	15
Greenwich	MH	11	100	0	100	0
Waltham Forest	MH	7	100	0	0	100
Warrington	MH	10	80	0	0	100
West Berks[3]	MH	8	0	50	50	0
West Lancs	MH	7	86	0	100	0
All MH projects		**141**	**71**	**26**	**60**	**15**
Coventry	EPF	43	14	5	95	0
Darlington	EPF	61	93	100	0	0
Winchester	EPF	16	0	31	13	56
All EPF projects		**120**	**53**	**57**	**36**	**8**
Camberwell	EMH	1	100	0	0	100
Hillingdon	EMH	32	34	9	91	0
St Helens	EMH	52	23	0	100	0
W. Cumbria	EMH	31	10	0	100	0
All EMH projects		**116**	**23**	**3**	**96**	**1**
All projects		**722**	**60**	**17**	**72**	**11**

1 No information for Derby, Liverpool or Warwick.
2 Client group abbreviations: LD = people with learning difficulties; AM = adolescents with multiple disabilities; PD = people with physical disabilities; MH = people with mental health problems; EPF = elderly people who are physically frail; EMH = elderly people with mental health problems.
3 Information drawn from last available questionnaire (for 1986-87).
4 Two people were self-employed.

Preparation and forecasting

The first policy issues to arise were linked to the forecasting of desired staffing numbers and characteristics and liaison with hospitals. Forecasts were partly built on hospital-based assessments and expectations about client behaviour and support needs. Hospital staff often conducted these assessments and contributed generally to rehabilitation and training. During this process, if not before, some hospital staff began to consider the relative attraction of employment in community care.

Working with hospitals

The transition from hospital to community was a major change not only for clients, but also for the many nurses and specialists working in the 50 or more hospitals from which project clients were selected. Because of the clear longer-term threat to job security, there was naturally some resistance to project proposals. Where projects were part of well-publicised and previously announced hospital closure programmes, such as in Calderdale and Somerset, access to clients was less difficult. Nursing staff were better informed about future plans and had been reassured by widely-discussed personnel policies, redeployment schemes and training programmes. (Somerset's joint health and social services strategy document was in fact not circulated initially to health service staff, and there was a temporary dispute.) For many other projects, however, the approaches to nursing staff by project staff (for the purposes of client selection) were the first visible evidence of hospital rundown. Some hospital staff had no idea that beds or wards were to be closed. Some also responded critically through the local media, or by refusal to refer clients, mobilisation of campaigns of opposition by relatives, and – most commonly – constructive professional concern about the future of nursing and the appropriateness of new models of care.

Projects sought to involve hospital staff in various ways in the preparation for community care:

- In Brent hospital staff were actively involved in assessment and running community services.
- Redundancy and relocation arrangements and quotas for redeploying health service staff in community services were introduced in Somerset.
- The Warrington and Bucks projects appointed specialist coordinators to work intensively with hospital staff in order to gain cooperation, and in Somerset, a senior assistant undertook the same task.

Others launched publicity campaigns, circulating leaflets and newsletters within hospitals and holding special consultation meetings. Despite these activities the impression remained in one or two areas that community care concerned the movement of clients and services away from hospitals to the almost total exclusion of the interests of hospital staff.

Forecasting staffing needs

More than half the projects under-estimated clients' needs for staff support. Obviously, forecasting community staffing levels for the new services put in place by the programme proved especially problematic. Many difficulties arose because projects and host agencies were just starting on the community care learning curve, and because many service models were *intended* to be new and challenging. Great uncertainty concerned the identification of individual clients, what they and others would expect from community living, and how each of these aspects would evolve.

Some projects decided to aim for staff-client ratios in the community that matched those in hospital, and to leave room for manoeuvre, which was likely to have to be considerable if clients were living in small, dispersed housing settings. Support services and leisure activities were often similarly dispersed rather than on a single site, and staff spent much of their time accompanying clients who had been capable of finding their own way to work or day activities within the hospital. Where services were inappropriate or did not materialise, as was the case with the plans to offer education, work and leisure opportunities (as reported in Chapter 8), staff had to fill the service gaps.

Flexibility was built into staffing forecasts wherever possible. Projects deliberately choosing enhanced staffing with in-built flexibility benefited – in as much as deficits could be more easily covered – when they discovered their under-estimation of client needs. In Cumbria, enhanced staffing which had been planned to implement a reality orientation programme gave a margin of flexibility. Special project-related posts, such as the care coordinator in Warrington, gave key people the freedom to direct their energies into service and practice management instead of delivery, without being pulled by the demands of the host agency. The Liverpool project planned to offer clients care and support on a 24-hour basis in the first instance, to be reduced if circumstances demanded. The philosophy of the Derby Scheme was for staff as well as clients to adapt as needs and circumstances changed. In Chichester the core house was staffed 24 hours a day whereas the cluster houses were only supervised if and when the need arose. In West Lancashire a round-the-clock service for people with mental health problems used a team of rehabilitation officers and community care assistants to provide care as situations demanded. The Glossop scheme was staffed by a flexible team providing 24-hour cover, supported by a warden who lived in one of the four flats in the building. Many projects were allowed more virement between budget heads than is conventional in health and local authorities. Teamworking also helped.

Three particular lessons can be drawn from the forecasting experiences of projects. First, until service values and objectives have been defined and agreed it is not sensible to attempt to predict staffing levels. Second, special enabling and coordinating posts facilitate change and leave the post-holder free to concentrate on service development. Third, case management arrangements help to bring to individual service planning both the client's views and flexibility in service design.

Staff recruitment and selection

In their original plans, many projects set out the range of staff skills they wished to secure and the qualities they intended to recruit. Some explicitly stated that health service personnel were not expected to be suited for community work because of the inappropriateness of importing institutional or 'medical' ideas and practices to new models of care. Some others were equally explicit about their preference for nursing staff, especially in working with clients during the transition to the community. In West Cumbria the decision was taken not to recruit any care staff who had received only 'traditional' professional health or social care training, although it was difficult to adhere to this in practice. Projects planning to provide accommodation in hostels, residential homes or sheltered housing generally aimed to recruit staff with experience of such facilities, and also had few difficulties finding them. Those planning more independent housing, or new models of support (such as those which required recruitment to posts with the novel label – at the time – of case manager), tended to have greater difficulty attracting applicants. The qualities projects sought when recruiting staff are summarised below (25 projects responded):

- understanding, empathy or sensitivity (11 projects);
- commitment to project philosophy or concern (9);
- particular personality, nature or attitude (9);
- relevant work experience or background (9);
- acceptance of normalisation and individuality aims (8);
- flexibility at work (7);
- practical skills (7);
- particular qualifications or knowledge (6);
- maturity (5);
- good social, inter-personal or communication skills (4);
- team work skills, or appreciation of multidisciplinary operations (4);
- initiative or enthusiasm (4);
- a positive attitude (2);
- patience (2); and
- reliability, a non-directive approach, commonsense, tenacity, and attentiveness (each cited once).

Personal attributes were more frequently cited as relevant than previous experience or formal qualifications. In fact four projects mentioned personal attributes or attitudes to the exclusion of other considerations. There were no marked differences between projects across client groups.

In our review of projects at the end of their central funding we asked each project to reflect on the staff qualities they valued initially. Half did not see a need for change. The other projects recognised that staff needed to change and adapt with clients (with an ageing clientele, for example), that certain skills had not been recognised (skills for new assessment procedures; for chairing case conferences and meetings; for non-verbal communication with clients using sign language, and coping with stress and frustration levels). (Some inexperienced staff had particular problems coping.) Some projects were convinced that it was important to appoint on the basis of attitudes and understanding, and to develop the knowledge and skills base through a developing team culture. By contrast, one project considered it had been mistaken simply to recruit 'caring people' without regard for particular skills. Another said there was a need to accentuate previously-specified skills, and another realised that the opportunities for on-the-job or 'time-out' training were so limited (by funds and pressure of work) that skills needed to be bought in from the beginning. Other skills specified as lacking were dealing with the rigours of shift working, coping with clients' challenging behaviours, and managerial skills to enable staff to shoulder more responsibility. If there is one conclusion to draw from this it is that community care makes huge and continuing demands on staff.

Recruitment difficulties

Despite relatively high unemployment in the mid-1980s, a number of projects reported serious recruitment difficulties and consequential delays. Indeed, the unemployment situation in Cumbria was reckoned to make it unattractive for new staff to move to the area if partners also wanted employment. High-calibre personnel were particularly difficult to find. One reason was certainly superficial – the use of new and unfamiliar labels for posts (rehabilitation coordinator, care or resource coordinator, for example), which did not readily identify the tasks and responsibilities, and which may have suggested a need for specialist qualifications. Significant recruitment difficulties were undoubtedly related to the temporary nature of project posts, especially for middle management positions, although those attracted tended to be adventurous and energetic, well suited to the development of new services and systems. Advertising procedures in local authorities caused delays in at least two projects.

Projects which hoped to persuade NHS staff to move to local authority posts (or, though less common, statutory agency staff to move to the voluntary sector) found various barriers in the way – different conditions regarding retirement age, fringe benefits, mileage allowances, career progression, relocation allowances, pension rights, salary scales, traditions and principles of care practice. Community care *per se* looked unattractive, either because of the demands highlighted above, or because, after 20 years of very slow progression towards a community care policy, some professional staff were sceptical about the transition actually happening.

Staff characteristics

Who, then, were the staff recruited to projects? Using information collected by Staff Record Forms 1 and 2, data were available on 416 and 317 staff, respectively. (From those staff characteristics which were covered by the Staff Record Forms and the End of Project Questionnaire completed in June 1988, it appears that these sources of data provide consistent figures.) The workforce was predominantly young:

- 44 per cent of staff were aged under 30;
- 29 per cent were aged 30 to 39;
- 19 per cent were aged 40 to 49; and
- 6 per cent were aged 50 and over.

Forty-two per cent of staff were male.

Table 9.4 reports job titles by employing agency. Over half of the total of project staff were employed as social workers (including community social workers) or care assistants. Forty-two per cent of NHS staff had social work or care assistant job titles, suggesting a mode of 'joint-working' or cross-disciplinary provision generally hidden from view.

Staff hailed from a range of professional backgrounds representing wide working experiences. The vast majority (88 per cent) had more than five years' experience of work they considered relevant to their new job, and over half had professional qualifications although not necessarily in social work or nursing. For staff with experience in one or more of these areas, a relatively high proportion had more than five years' experience (see Table 9.5). There were marked differences between projects. For example, two-thirds or more of the staff in Winchester, West Cumbria, Liverpool and Warwick held no profession qualifications. The Cambridge, Chichester, Brent, Waltham Forest, Bolton and Derby projects had low proportions of unqualified staff. Overall, 16 per cent of staff had nursing qualifications, and a similar proportion had social work or residential care qualifications (Table 9.6).

What these statistics cannot indicate is that the programme attracted very dedicated and talented people to run and deliver services.

Table 9.4
Community care staff job titles, by employing agency

Job title	Number of staff by employing agency				
	DHA	LA SSD	Voluntary organisation	Other	All agencies
Coordination manager, coordinator, supervisor[1]	13	45	7	3	68
Social workers, care assistants[2]	36	194	9	4	243
Instructors	2	22	0	5	29
Nurses	16	1	0	0	17
Ancillary workers	0	10	0	2	12
Community workers	0	7	0	0	7
Administrators	1	6	1	0	8
Para-medical staff	13	3	0	0	16
Medical staff	1	0	0	0	1
Psychologists	3	0	0	0	3
Other	0	6	1	1	8
Total	85	294	18	15	412

1 Whatever the discipline, someone with a managerial (or similar) job title is included here.
2 Includes care assistants and community social workers.

Table 9.5
Length of previous experience, by area of activity

Area of experience	0-2 yrs %	3-4 yrs %	5-9 yrs %	10+ yrs %	All N
Hospital work	26.4	17.8	36.4	19.3	140
Residential care	43.1	16.3	29.3	11.4	123
Social work	24.4	9.8	36.6	29.3	41
Primary health care	8.3	8.3	75.0	8.3	12
Other[1]	24.0	14.6	55.2	6.3	96

Total sample size = 412.
1 Includes day care, teaching in special schools and farming (relevant in Bolton).

Work organisation, rotas and shifts

In their important study of community care staffing, Allen et al. (1988) identified considerable differences in the organisation of work between hospital and community settings, even though both were offering 24-hour cover. The hospital system was most accurately described as a shift system and involved

Table 9.6
Staff with professional qualifications

Professional qualification[1]	Learning diffs. %	Adolescent Mult.dis. %	Mental health %	Elderly phys.frail %	Elderly ment.hlth %	All projects[2] %
Nursing	14	20	30	12	11	16
Social work	15	0	6	8	2	11
Residential care	5	20	2	12	0	5
Medical degree	1	0	2	0	0	1
Psychology	0	0	2	0	4	1
Therapist	4	0	4	0	2	4
Other[3]	32	80	30	24	4	28
All respondents	186	5	47	25	46	309

1 Some staff had more than one qualification.
2 No information for Warrington, West Berks, West Lancs, Maidstone, Glossop, Darlington, Camberwell, St Helens.
3 Includes paramedical, occupational (such as accountancy), speech therapy, physiotherapy, radiotherapy, teaching and degree qualifications.

different sets of people working conventional shifts. Usually this meant, alternately, two short and two long shifts, with one waking night shift worked by different people to those employed in the day. Most members of staff were part-time and matched their working arrangements to their personal circumstances. The position in the community was quite different. The system was rotating and flexible rather than static. The same people were likely to be involved, night and day, working a mixture of short and long shifts with sleep-in duties. Some staff were offered additional remuneration for sleep-in duties although it was often considered part of the job. Staff tended to be full-time and had little choice about their working arrangements because of the small number of staff involved. Allen and colleagues found that community staff were much more likely to have worked overtime because of the pressure of staff shortages than their hospital counterparts. In contrast to the sharply defined roles and responsibilities found in large establishments, some community staff worked in loosely-structured and informally-supervised settings.

The organisation of work in the demonstration programme was similar, although we were unable to examine staffing in the same detail. Because most clients were relatively disabled and required quite high levels of staff support, all projects found they had to provide supportive care around the clock, either continuously, intermittently during the day, or on an *ad hoc* basis, depending on client need. Organising rotas to provide staff cover in the community consequently proved extraordinarily difficult, and some projects concluded that it was only possible to offer flexible, responsive support by asking staff to work constantly changing rotas. In Greenwich, by staggering the opening of new community houses, intensive staff cover (24-hour cover with two staff on duty at any time) could be provided initially, and reduced as clients gained confidence and competence. Some staff were freed for intensive cover in the next house. This process was obviously complex and required staff willing and able to regularly readjust their rotas and working conditions. It proved possible because staff were fully involved in project planning and committed to success.

Generally a careful balance had to be struck between the needs of clients and the needs and preferences of staff. A shorter and more regular working week could reduce staff stress, whereas flexibly deployed residential staff could improve service responsiveness and quality (see Wagner, 1988, and the evidence to the committee). Flexibility was easier to achieve in larger projects without compromising other objectives (such as needs-led care and client self-determination). Larger projects were also able to assemble a pool of staff to provide cover in times of sickness, annual leave and vacancies, and so created opportunities for further training. Small projects faced difficulties in organising rotas, with night duties proving particularly unpopular and making rostering problematic. It was not infrequently reported that staff were exhausted and isolated, that absenteeism and turnover were creeping up in some facilities, and that the personal or domestic lives of staff were suffering. These problems were in addition to the inadequate basic staffing levels in a few projects, and the general feeling that client needs demanded or deserved more flexibility than rotas allowed. Using bank, night or agency staff worked against continuity of care aims.

This type of care in the community is itself challenging, and staff were more likely than their hospital counterparts to be required to undertake a wide variety of tasks. Drawing the line between a positive professional relationship with a client (such as is required in keyworking) and a close friendship was often difficult. There was a tendency to under-estimate the psychological and emotional effects of support work. It was common for staff to visit their work-places on days off or during the evenings or weekends to honour social commitments with clients. These problems were exacerbated by two features of community care within the programme: the keyworker system encouraged staff to build special relationships with individual clients; and the lack of suitable day support, leisure, education and employment opportunities shifted an even greater burden onto residential-based staff.

Staff morale and turnover

There are links between staff morale or job satisfaction and quality of care, and thus to clients' quality of life. Job satisfaction is also an important predictor of labour turnover. (This is a common result from occupational psychology which has received confirmation in the community care context by Allen et al., 1990, and – less rigorously – by our findings reported here.) In our (self-complete) questionnaire (Record Form 2) we included a job satisfaction scale covering 17 aspects of employment (taken from Dyer and Hoffenberg, 1975). These items are listed in Table 9.7, together with aggregated responses. Satisfaction levels, by Dyer and Hoffenberg's criteria, were generally rated highly, with 81 per cent of staff 'very satisfied' or 'quite satisfied'. For only two areas of employment did more than 20 per cent of the 309 respondents express dissatisfaction: income (24 per cent) and promotion prospects (21 per cent). These results are fairly consistent with other studies which have found community staff to be satisfied overall, but feeling frustrated and powerless in relation to some aspects of the job (Gibson et al., 1989; Stenfert-Kroese and Fleming, 1989). The areas giving most *satisfaction* were relationships with colleagues (93 per cent), which augured well for team work, opportunities for using initiative (89 per cent), important for the development of devolved care

Table 9.7
Staff job satisfaction

Item	*Percentage of staff (all projects) indicating this satisfaction*			
	Satisfied[1] %	Ambivalent %	Dissatisfied[2] %	No. of respondents N
Income	60	16	24	299
Job security	81	12	8	293
Work hours	76	10	14	300
Flexibility of hours	74	13	13	299
Ease of travel to work	77	14	8	309
Management by superiors	74	11	16	301
Relationship with colleagues	93	6	2	306
Promotion prospects	46	33	21	294
Public appreciation	53	33	14	298
Self-satisfaction	83	11	6	304
Own skills level	77	11	12	305
Satisfaction with meeting challenges	81	11	8	302
Satisfaction with tasks (variety of)	78	11	11	306
Opportunity for initiative	89	3	8	309
Work in general	87	6	7	307
Satisfaction with tasks	81	10	10	305
All criteria	81	14	12	

1 Quite or very satisfied.
2 Quite or very dissatisfied.

responsibilities such as case management, and work in general (87 per cent). There are interesting consistencies with the findings of Allen et al. (1990), using the same instrumentation. They found relationships with fellow workers to be associated with higher satisfaction, whereas income and opportunities for advancement were associated with lower satisfaction.

There were marked differences from project to project (not tabulated). Dissatisfaction in general (and particularly with income) was greatest in the 20-34 age group, which was also the group with least experience of related work prior to appointment. There did not appear to be any systematic variation of satisfaction levels between trained and untrained staff, nor with in-service training.

Staff turnover

High and fluctuating levels of staff turnover among social workers and health care staff have long caused concern. Turnover can be disruptive and confusing for clients, and can prolong crises. Staff burn-out is also a familiar problem in the caring professions.

> 'Burn-out' is that state of disillusionment and apathy that can eventually affect any of us if our ideals and ambitions are constantly eroded by frustrations and obstacles. The various helping professions are particularly at risk concerned as they are with [difficult client groups] and working frequently with inadequate resources and insufficient acknowledgement or support. All of us under such circumstances will inevitably experience periods of emotional exhaustion from which we sooner or later recover; but for many, a state of 'burn-out' can become chronic, sometimes with considerable effects on mental and physical health and on family life. Yet training agencies make few allowances for, or take safeguards against, the phenomenon (Cane, 1983).

Surprisingly little is known about the problems of stress, burn-out and turnover in community care. Although we were unable to conduct a comprehensive study of these phenomena, we sought retrospective information on the extent of staff turnover in the End of Project Questionnaire. We also asked projects their opinions of the reasons for staff turnover. (It is important to emphasise that these data are project managers' views and not those of leavers themselves.) Almost half of all staff who left had been employed for one year or less, and 11 per cent (23 staff) had been employed for three months or less. These rates are lower than might have been expected (compare, for example, some other turnover studies, such as Knapp et al., 1981; Harissis, 1986; de Kock et al., 1987; Stenfert-Kroese and Fleming, 1989), but proved troublesome when concentrated in one house or hostel. The disruption to clients and patterns of interaction was sometimes acute.

Project managers' responses suggested the following reasons for the departure of 227 staff across the programme (and destinations if given), listed in descending order of frequency:

- staff member moved to another community care (or similar) job (12 per cent);
- moved to another job with promotion (11 per cent);
- stress, difficulty coping with job, demoralisation (9 per cent);
- personal reasons (9 per cent);
- moved to a more permanent job (8 per cent);
- moved back to previous job, almost always a social or health care post (8 per cent);
- sacked/resigned due to incident (8 per cent);
- moved to a different job, not seen as promotion (8 per cent);
- moved out of the area, new job (if any) not specified (7 per cent);
- started further education course (6 per cent);
- internal relocation within the agency (4 per cent);
- contract ended, destination not given (4 per cent);
- dissatisfaction with hours (2 per cent);
- dissatisfaction with lack of training and support (2 per cent); and
- retired (1 per cent).

There were seven other reasons mentioned once each. In two projects, a number of former hospital staff returned to hospital employment, citing problems with working arrangements and styles, and lack of support and structure as reasons for the move. Allen et al. (1990) found similar stress levels in hospital and community settings, but a higher incidence of stress-related turnover among community staff, which they explained in terms of opportunity: community staff were more mobile, having fewer family commitments and being younger. They also explained dissatisfaction with the limited variety of tasks in the community as a function of the typical 'community' employee. There was probably no greater task variety in hospitals, but because community staff were usually selected for their commitment to community care, they also had high self-development needs which required satisfaction via the challenge of additional variety.

Although our study did not incorporate a stress rating, many of the 'difficulties associated with the job' identified by respondents were consistent with the major stressors uncovered in other studies (for example, Potts and Halliday, 1988; Ward, 1989; Stenfert-Kroese and Fleming, 1989; Savage, 1990): inadequate staffing levels, lack of time, resources, training and management support, differences in service philosophy and aims, and long shifts and sleep-ins which interfered with family life. Gibson et al. (1989) identified 'lack of personal accomplishment' as a virtually omnipresent indicator of staff burn-out, and yet in the demonstration programme all but two projects scored highly on this dimension. There also appeared to be an interesting positive relationship between satisfaction and stress in relation to some aspects of employment. For example, those tasks rated most highly as sources of satisfaction, such as teaching new skills and accompanying clients on outings, were simultaneously considered to be the most stressful (compare Stenfert-Kroese and Fleming, 1989). A similar combination of stress and satisfaction was observed by Potts and Halliday (1988) who reported that staff preferred working in less institutionalised settings such as houses rather than hostels, despite greater stress. From our less structured collection of evaluative evidence from project staff it was clear that the intensive, one-to-one work required of an 'ordinary life' model of care was stressful and paramount in the decision to leave, move sideways into another care post, or simply to take time out to rest or recuperate. Often it is the cumulative impact of a large number and variety of responsibilities, none on their own particularly stressful, which is so demanding (Stenfert-Kroese and Fleming, 1989).

Thus, although staff stress was common in the Care in the Community programme, and often seemed to accompany satisfaction at managing or coping with challenging tasks, the cumulative or longer-term damage could prove considerable.

Training, development and support

Staff training

If it was not already obvious at the outset, the majority of projects soon appreciated the value of training as community services developed. Training as the dissemination of information about service change and new roles was one way to smooth the transition for staff with little or no experience of community care. It was also the best formal means of transmitting the new philosophies and models of care introduced, often requiring new ways of working, such as allowing clients to speak for themselves. Training as skills acquisition prepared staff for the many emotional and physical demands of working (sometimes *living*) with people who had spent large proportions of their lives in hospital. When client needs were uncertain, a degree of budgetary and staffing 'slack' helped projects to respond to new information and evolving circumstances. Projects also needed to establish comprehensive support and review systems for staff to reduce the risks of isolation and burn-out and, of course, to promote high-quality services. Democratic models of teamworking, peer review and inclusion in service review proved useful mechanisms for fostering involvement and a sense of ownership.

Each project utilised some mode of training programme, although some were low-key. Two projects which had moved a number of clients from hospital made virtually no progress on training in three years. Another ten were unable to provide information on training activities, although we knew that some had been instigated. Some projects targeted training in a specific area such as individual programme planning. Others, such as Bolton, set up ambitious and comprehensive programmes (Taylor and Bailey, 1988). Pulling programme-wide experience together, it is possible to distinguish four types of training activity designed as an investment in staffing:

- *Education* included staff reorientation and imparting project philosophy, often achieved through home-grown induction courses.
- On-going *staff development* in response to revealed needs, an important task for projects which deliberately sought unskilled staff, but a feature of all. Staff development programmes included secondment to acquire specific professional qualifications, and importing external resources. Career development was sometimes addressed by tapping into Open University Modules, Diploma in Management Studies courses and Certificate in Social Service courses.
- *Specific skills acquisition,* such as training staff to lift bedfast clients or learning about the aims of normalisation, usually facilitated by a mix of in-house and external resources.
- *Staff support,* needed to help employees cope with the stresses of working in community settings, provided by building appropriate supervision into project management and developing peer group support. Training courses had therapeutic value by providing a forum for discussion about care principles and practices.

Larger projects had better opportunities to address most of these training needs, although without good links with host agencies some found they had little real flexibility. The position was more serious when it proved impossible to release staff or when training budgets were cut. The Somerset project benefited from the joint training strategy initiated by health and social services. Joint training strategies obviously had the potential to aid joint working in community care (at many levels within the participating agencies). For example, the Derby project held IPP workshops, 'working together' seminars and sessions on the integration of people with learning difficulties into the community. These were open to both NHS and social services staff. The Maidstone project organised a variety of staff development and in-service training programmes from a jointly financed health and social services tutor. An outside lecturer provided training in counselling skills, and senior project staff trained newly-appointed home support staff in participative workshop sessions which also involved clients.

Fifty-five per cent of staff had received some in-service training in community care (induction courses, on-the-job learning for counselling and support, and so on) during the course of their employment in projects. In Bolton, three-week induction courses were held for all project staff, and further courses, both locally developed and bought-in, were offered. The Winchester project encouraged care attendants to spend time working alongside nurses in the community and in hospital, as well as attending courses on lifting. The

West Cumbria project organised a two-week induction course for staff, incorporating sessions on reality orientation and reminiscence therapy techniques as well as more routine activities. In Darlington, training was deemed an integral part of the preparation of staff for their new multipurpose role. After an initial induction period of two weeks, home care assistants were individually trained in the particular care tasks needed for their clients.

Across the programme, 72 per cent of staff received specialist training (nursing qualifications or particular social work skills, for example). Staff in projects for elderly people were more likely to have had specialist training than staff in other projects, but less likely to have had in-service training (see Table 9.8). Receipt of training was more likely for older staff (aged 45 or over). Voluntary organisations were much less likely than DHAs or local authorities to have provided training, especially specialist training. In-service training was more likely to have been received by those *already* possessing some professional qualifications, and was not targeted specifically at staff with less previous experience. There was, however, some association between the receipt of in-service training and expressed satisfaction about opportunities for advancement, development of personal skills, and general job satisfaction. There was no association between receipt of specialist training and the level of satisfaction expressed about development of personal skills.

What were the effects and costs of training? As well as the correlation with expressed job satisfaction, project managers certainly believed that it stimulated discussion about the key issues of providing new community care services. At the same time, however, many projects uncovered problems in running training programmes. For example, releasing staff from a service which was already under-capacity was only possible by bringing in temporary replacements or by employing peripatetic training officers to visit dispersed housing settings, but neither intrusion into clients' homes is consistent with normalisation principles. Organising *joint* training days also proved difficult in under-staffed, dispersed or small settings. Shift patterns made it difficult to

Table 9.8
Training received by staff

Client group of project	*Percentage of staff receiving:* In-service training %	Specialist training %
People with learning difficulties	52	73
Young people with multiple disabilities	75	75
People with mental health problems	67	65
Elderly people with physical frailty	75	94
Elderly people with mental health problems	55	69
All projects	55	72

organise group sessions, with reports reaching us of staff attending training sessions after long periods on shift when they were too exhausted to benefit. Training was clearly not a substitute for inadequate *numbers* of staff, and stood a much lower chance of success under such circumstances.

The other lesson learned (or relearned) by some projects, sometimes bitterly, was that training budgets and programmes are particularly vulnerable to the vicissitudes of agency funding. Those projects which did not make training an integral and protected part of their initial plans risked the enforced abandonment of key training components. The irony was that projects which (deliberately or accidentally) left open some parts of this strategy until the needs and preferences of clients and staff became apparent were penalised for their foresight!

When asked about further and continuing training needs after at least three years of operation, projects produced an extensive litany. Without describing in detail the local contexts in each of the 28 projects it is difficult to appreciate the relevance of these needs to community care. Nevertheless, the list is informative. Six projects did not detaill their needs, and three simply said 'general training'. Seven noted that staff would continue to need training related to the philosophy or objectives of care. Medically-related training (first aid and drugs management) was cited by three projects, and nine cited 'social training' (counselling, sexuality and advocacy skills, welfare rights, group work, and helping clients find employment). Another group of training needs revolved around normalisation, general rehabilitation skills, coping with aggressive and challenging behaviour, coping with stress, working with families, and suicide care work. Eleven projects noted needs of this kind. Finally, 13 projects identified requirements related to the effectiveness of working practices, such as management skills, practical skills such as lifting, inter-personal skills, assessment, teamwork, communication, instructor skills, non-directive working, report writing and financial management. These are management's interpretations. Staff themselves reported needs associated with support, client-orientated working and coping with challenging behaviours (compare Stenfert-Kroese and Fleming, 1989; Gibson et al., 1989).

Compared to their hospital counterparts, community staff were often young, unqualified and relatively inexperienced, which many managers interpreted as adding to their needs for support. As we have seen, challenging behaviours in small and dispersed housing are demanding and stressful and, unlike hospital wards, staff cannot get support by drawing staff from other parts of the establishment or system. Difficult behaviours might even be exacerbated by smaller community settings, because of the intensity of inter-personal relations. In some cases the knowledge that a house was short-staffed was said to have precipitated demanding behaviour. There were, moreover, difficulties in supporting challenging behaviours in the community because of a reluctance to isolate and because of space constraints.

Conclusion

Community care required staff with rather a different range of skills from those conventionally expected of hospital staff, and flexibility in their deployment. Multi-agency working within the Care in the Community programme meant breaking down traditional professional barriers, blurring some roles, and developing the ability to work *with* rather than *for* the client. Training was (or in some cases should have been) an integral component part of the planned process of change, and not a reaction to management or resource crisis. It was often dynamic and responsive, but often risked being aborted in the name of economy. The training experiences and challenges of the pilot projects emphasised a general feature of community care: a needs-led service asks a great deal of front-line staff, demands an unusual degree of flexibility and, without training and support, is likely to produce casualties.

10 Case management

Case management policies

It was an enlightened decision to build case management, albeit loosely, into the demonstration programme proposals drawn up in 1983. Case management is now one of the central planks of government community care policy, as spelt out in the 1989 White Paper (Cm 849) and developed in a subsequent implementation document alongside the assessment task (Department of Health, 1990).

Although case management arrangements in Britain had previously been explored in the delivery of services to elderly people, the demonstration programme offered the first chance to examine these methods for people with mental health problems, learning difficulties or physical disabilities. The Audit Commission (1989) drew on some of the programme's case management experiences when making its recommendations for the development of services for people with learning difficulties, and the White Paper (para. 3.3.3) noted that the decision to recommend the introduction of case management was influenced by the experiences in the Care in the Community programme and by other evaluative work by the PSSRU (especially the carefully evaluated experiments in Kent and Gateshead; see Challis and Davies, 1986; Davies and Challis, 1986; Challis et al., 1988, 1990). These case management experiments outside the pilot programme demonstrated how budgetary devolution to staff with smaller caseloads and comprehensive information could produce better and less costly services for elderly people. The results of these experiments encouraged both the Audit Commission (1986) and Griffiths (1988) to advocate case management as a key component of community care reform.

Case management is 'the movement of each individual client from application status to closure status' (Henke et al., 1975, p.218). It is 'the lynch-pin of an individual needs-led service' (Audit Commission, 1989, para. 49), the 'glue that binds otherwise fragmented services into arrangements that respond to the unique and changing needs' of clients (Freedman and Moran, 1984, p.23). The process can be disaggregated in different ways (Dant and Gearing, 1990), but in the UK it is now most commonly considered to comprise five core tasks (Davies and Challis, 1986):

- case finding and referral,
- assessment and selection,
- care planning and service packaging,
- monitoring and reassessment, and
- case closure.

These are the functions of case management identified in the community care White Paper. They might not all be undertaken by the same person or team, although case continuity can be desirable, especially during the traumatic stages of leaving hospital and establishing a new life in the community. Underpinning case management, and particularly the care planning and monitoring tasks, is some form of individual programme, service or care planning. In their implementation of the case management recommendation of DHSS funding, itself allowing a variety of arrangements, projects chose widely different variants and combinations of these core tasks.

Despite the centrally administered grant and the PSSRU's early role in promoting the programme and advising many potential projects, no single model of case management was laid down. Instead, applicants were simply asked to state how they expected to undertake certain tasks (see Table 10.1). The advantage of not specifying a particular model in 1983 was that diversity of interpretation, design and practice emerged; the disadvantage was that the demonstration programme was not a controlled case management experiment. For example, only the Maidstone and Darlington projects introduced decentralised budgets and expenditure limits at the case level, whereas the future planning of community care might have been better informed had there been more such attempts at replicating the successful trials with such arrangements in Kent and elsewhere. (The government's community care recommendations for the 1990s urge local authorities to consider budgetary devolution to case level.)

Case management offered a means for managing and deploying staff and other resources, for putting together combinations of services, and for setting client outcome goals. When the local case management architecture had been designed by entrepreneurial managers, it was quite naturally seen in this light. To the politician, case management offered the opportunity to mix the supply

Table 10.1

Case management questions posed to project applicants

Each potential project was asked to describe its case management intentions, addressing each of the following questions:

How will clients be identified and selected for inclusion in the project? Who will assess the clients' needs? On what basis will this be done?

Will an individual care plan for each client be an integral part of the project? If yes, how will this be drawn up? If no, in what other ways will the project meet the particular needs of individual clients?

In what ways will either individual or group care plans take account of the preferences of clients and/or their families?

Which project staff will be responsible for establishing individual or group care plans and monitoring their progress? What control will they have over the allocation of essential resources.

economy of social care without reorganising agencies. To the consumer it offered an entry point for participation and representation. All such aims and perceptions were represented in the programme. Case management was hypothesised to be one way (or *set* of ways) to improve the efficiency and equity of resource allocation, although the many parties to community care policy and practice decisions were unlikely to agree on what or whose efficiency or equity were to have priority. Fundamental design and operational questions remained to be answered.

- What emphasis should be placed on each core task?
- To what level should budgets be devolved?
- In which agency should case managers be based? To whom should they be accountable?
- What skills and backgrounds would case managers require? Do they need to be members of teams?
- Are rights of entry to other organisations and access to resources necessary?

Because of the case management variety across the programme it is possible to examine a range of approaches and experiences in addressing these questions, in the context of some very different service models, priorities and client groups.

The purpose of this chapter is to describe and interpret these case management practices in the projects. We will make reference to, but not detail, the origins and evolution of case management outside the programme, particularly in North America and Britain, nor will we immerse ourselves in theoretical discourse about case working. Interesting as they are, these would be inappropriate for a book of this kind, and have anyway been well covered elsewhere (Davies and Challis, 1986; Challis and Davies, 1986; Onyett, 1990; Beardshaw and Towell, 1990). They have also previously been examined as they relate to the pilot programme (Renshaw et al., 1988, Chaps 7 and 8). The chapter first considers each of the core tasks, with the exception of case closure, which was comparatively rare within the demonstration programme during the period of our research. (There were comparatively few client deaths or long-term hospital readmissions.) We then turn to the experiences of delivering case-managed services, and examine some of the basic building blocks of case management (such as meeting service values, cost management and user involvement). Finally we consider the influence of organisational context.

We will say little about service values or care principles in this chapter as they have been discussed already. Case management is, of course, an arterial route for getting such values and principles put into the practice of community care. Case managers as much as anyone else therefore had to demonstrate how society values individuals whatever their disabilities; had to promote normalisation or an ordinary life; had to allow clients, users or consumers (depending on the accepted terminology) the opportunity to represent themselves or be represented; had to ensure that provision met client needs and preferences, yet protected their dignity. We have noted before that a clear set of values and principles reduced ambiguity, emphasised priorities and helped to focus attention on service achievements and client outcomes. This applied as much to the practice of case management as to any other aspect of community care.

Case finding and referral

Projects worked with long-stay hospital residents. In some cases there was difficulty agreeing an operational definition for long-stay, but more often the difficulty was refining or narrowing targeting criteria to enable selection from the many eligible hospital residents. Care principles and the desire to demonstrate new styles of reprovision had some bearing on how projects set about finding people who might move to the community. For example, adoption of normalisation or ordinary life principles explicitly encouraged the pursuit of equality of opportunity, thereby prompting projects to seek people with a wide range of needs and disabilities. Bolton's starting point was 'all those with a learning difficulty living in Bolton's long-stay hospitals, whatever their level of dependency', and the Camden project sought to demonstrate that 'care in the community is appropriate regardless of medical and social characteristics'. But there were practical limitations imposed by the flexibility of facilities or the availability of funds. The Derby project's early plans stated that medical and social factors were not relevant, although people with disturbed behaviour might be excluded. Challenging behaviour excluded people in a number of other projects for people with learning difficulties. The early stage of Somerset's dehospitalisation strategy required clients to be 'continent and ambulant, without severe behaviour disorder'. The Kidderminster project targeted people in Wessex categories I and II (Kushlick et al., 1973). In all, 12 projects selected users by their level of dependency.

Like other projects for elderly people, Winchester employed explicit targeting criteria, concentrating on frail people without confusion who were in hospital because of the lack of a full time 'informal carer'. Darlington sought to rehabilitate people who were described as 'physically handicapped but mentally alert', and only those who were totally immobile or relatively confused ('as to time and place, ... or nocturnal, ... or completely disoriented, or stuperous') were deemed to be ineligible for the service established. Camberwell and St Helens focused upon elderly people 'not requiring nursing levels of care'. This was similar to plans in Bucks, although the trend with projects for people with mental health problems was to develop more specific entry criteria: Brent included 'Fairfield outcome' scores and Chichester, Greenwich and Waltham Forest had age criteria. Chichester's full criteria were 'age range late 20s to early 70s, psychotic disorder now in remittance or under control and institutionalised'. Area of origin was a criterion in many projects.

There was at least as much variability in referral processes. Six projects illustrate the range of approaches, with pragmatism figuring highly in each of them.

- The *Islington* scheme, operating in central London some distance from the hospitals involved, needed to dispatch project workers to find potential clients and match them against the criteria of the project. Clients were then referred to the various hospital resettlement boards.
- In *Brent*, clients came from the rehabilitation wards in Shenley Hospital. The rehabilitation coordinator liaised closely with the project manager, with multidisciplinary referral information built around common documentation.
- In *Somerset*, staff from health and social services met as integrated hospital review groups to coordinate referral.
- Being health authority-led, the *Winchester* project required less inter-agency liaison, although clients were initially identified by the project coordinator who requested reports from hospital social workers as well as consultants and ward staff.
- A committee was responsible for choosing clients from a preselected pool of clients in *Warrington*. The preselection had been made by the project.
- In *West Cumbria*, the project officer and officer-in-charge were involved in case finding, referral and selection which helped coordinate the whole process.

Figures 10.1 to 10.6 summarise these referral methods, although these simplified illustrations hide complex sets and flows of information. For instance, in Somerset, coordination between different professionals and groups of staff was a major task, and a forum was necessary to bring people together for decision-making. The hospital review groups to which potential clients were referred not only had to coordinate complex sets of information, but were responsible for reconsidering clients who remained in hospital (see Figure 10.7).

No definitive model for case finding and referral emerged from the programme, but the key elements of this core task of case management were illustrated (Figure 10.8), and a number of helpful pointers to good practice were seen. It certainly helped to have project leaders or managers responsible for coordinating the referral process and liaising between agencies and services, and to involve hospital staff in decision-making to ensure that information of the right kind and quality was available when needed. (The inconsistency of inputs from consultant psychiatrists in one project caused a number of difficulties.) Finally, when referral was *indeed* the first core task of case management (or keyworking) – when these staff were involved with potential clients in hospital *before* discharge, which was not the practice in every project – better continuity of care resulted.

Figure 10.1
Islington referral system

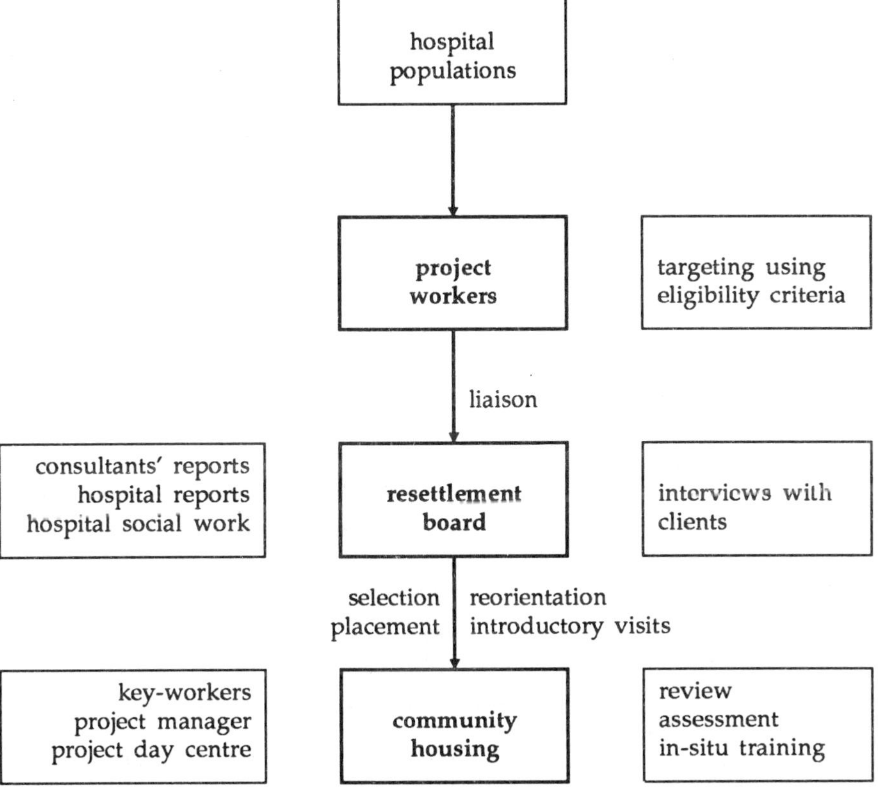

Assessment and selection

Screening for potential clients was sometimes difficult, compromises were necessary between what was desired and what was feasible, and it soon became clear that targeting criteria were overly rigid. Age, for example, does not uniquely (if at all) determine abilities, life-style or preferences. Selection criteria couched in terms of life skills were dogged by the discovery that hospital assessments (such as Wessex or NDT measures) were often of little value for gauging physical or behavioural support needs in the community, and anyway many clients improved markedly with rehabilitation and training. Projects discovered that it was both foolish to plan support services in the community

Figure 10.2
Brent referral system

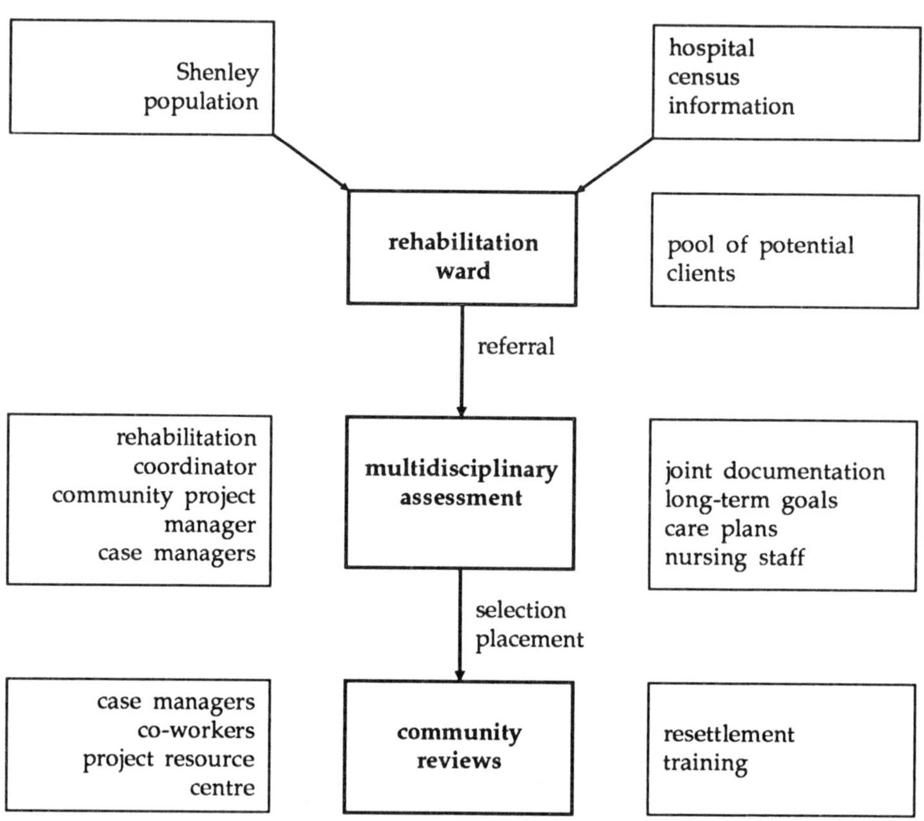

solely on the basis of information collected in hospital, and inadvisable to attempt to plan on subjective impressions alone.

Some initial targeting criteria underwent gradual evolution, as in Brent, and some became irrelevant when delays meant that the group of residents anticipated to be clients moved under other resettlement programmes, as in Islington. After central funding started, Islington produced recommendations for an operational policy, including screening criteria which were more finely tuned than those originally proposed. The age range was narrowed to between 19 and 45, and two criteria – 'no additional handicap' and 'not under legal restraint' – and one new principle – 'last in, first out' – were added. These

Figure 10.3
Somerset referral system

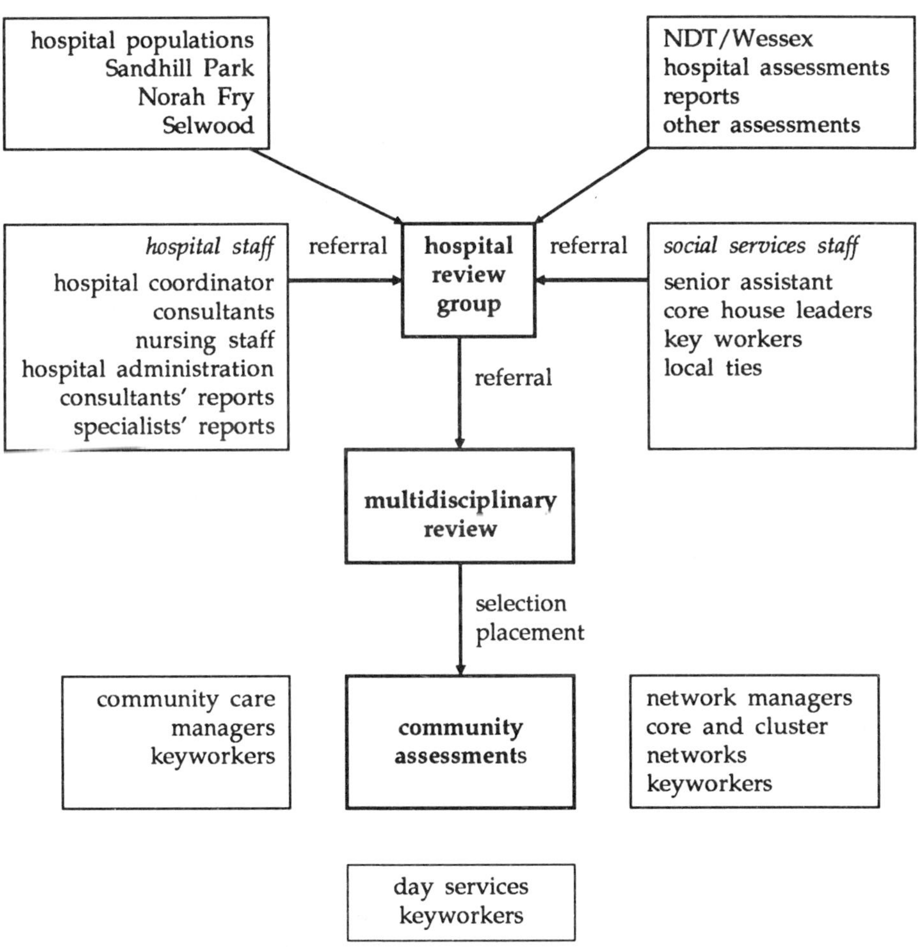

proved difficult to implement. In one case, a consultant's report failed to mention a serious physical illness, which was of critical importance to the client's support needs. Another client with strong family links in Islington was the subject of Court of Protection restrictions, but was otherwise suited to the service. In both cases clients were *successfully* placed in the community, but only after considerable difficulty.

The most demanding screening and selection procedures were based on surveys of hospital populations. From such a broad base a pool of potential

Figure 10.4
Winchester referral system

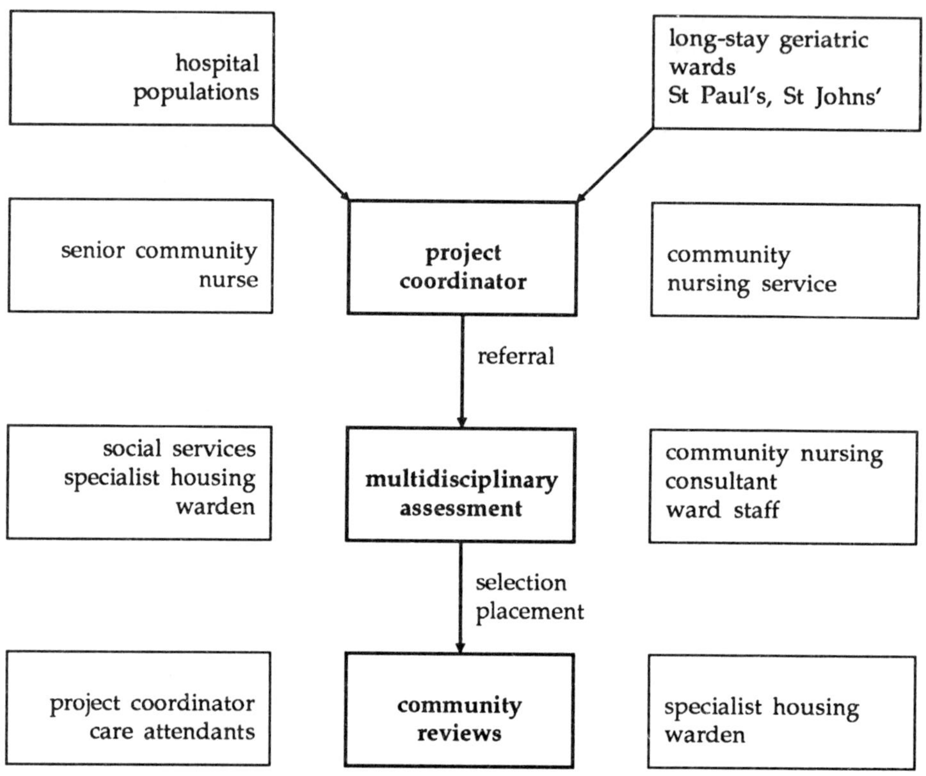

clients could be identified and more detailed assessments undertaken. In eight projects, hospital surveys of dependency and other information were conducted in this multi-stage filtering process (Calderdale, Islington, Kidderminster, Somerset, Darlington, Brent, Greenwich and Warrington). These comprehensive assessment and selection procedures were more likely in larger projects or when a project was a part of a wider strategy of hospital rundown. Smaller projects or those working in relative isolation from their host or a public service agency tended to adopt a task-oriented approach, with staff working on selection in the early days, later shifting to rehabilitation and support activities once people moved out of hospital. Nine of the 28 projects proposed named assessment instruments in their applications for funding, and most also indicated an intention to use some level of multidisciplinary

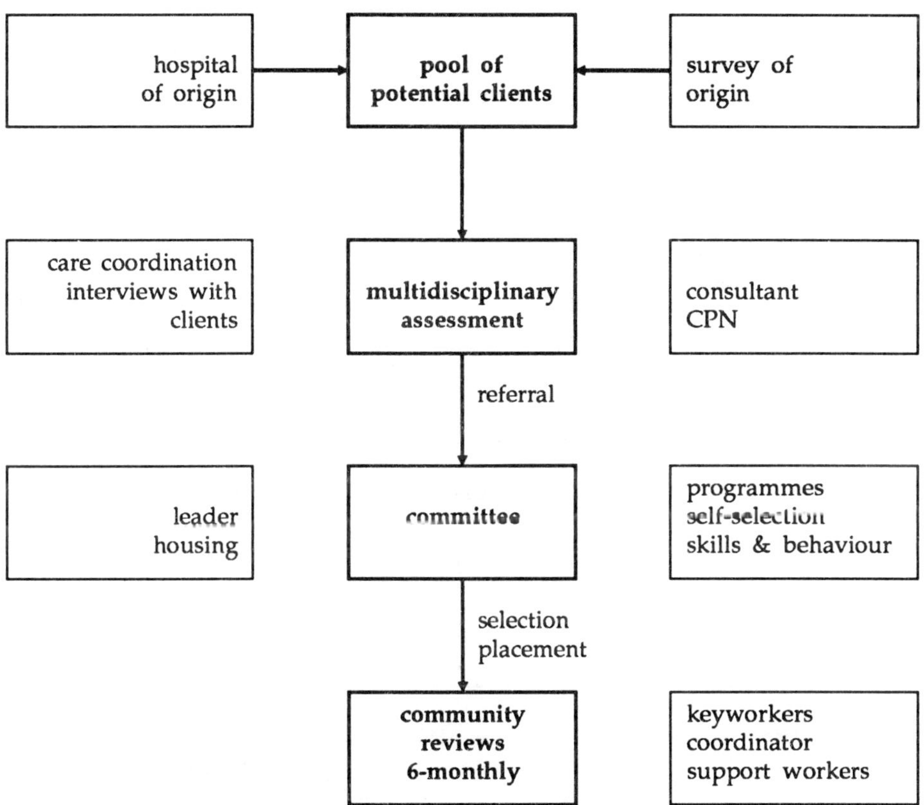

Figure 10.5
Warrington referral system

assessment for identification and selection, either by multidisciplinary teams (MDTs) or special task-orientated groups such as core teams (Bolton and Camberwell), selection panels (Islington) or hospital evaluation teams (Somerset). Hospital consultants obviously remained responsible for providing reports and key information which contributed to decisions on selection.

When it came to implementation, there were two groups of projects: those using informal methods such as observation and 'getting-to-know-you' programmes (such as Bolton, Islington, Maidstone, Greenwich and Waltham Forest), and those using off-the-shelf instruments such as HALO or PAC for people with learning difficulties (Derby, Somerset, Liverpool), REHAB and NOISE for people with mental health problems (Brent, Bucks and West Lancs), and CAPE for elderly people (West Cumbria). A few projects used semi-structured assessment techniques such as case notes or reports (Chichester),

Figure 10.6
West Cumbria referral system

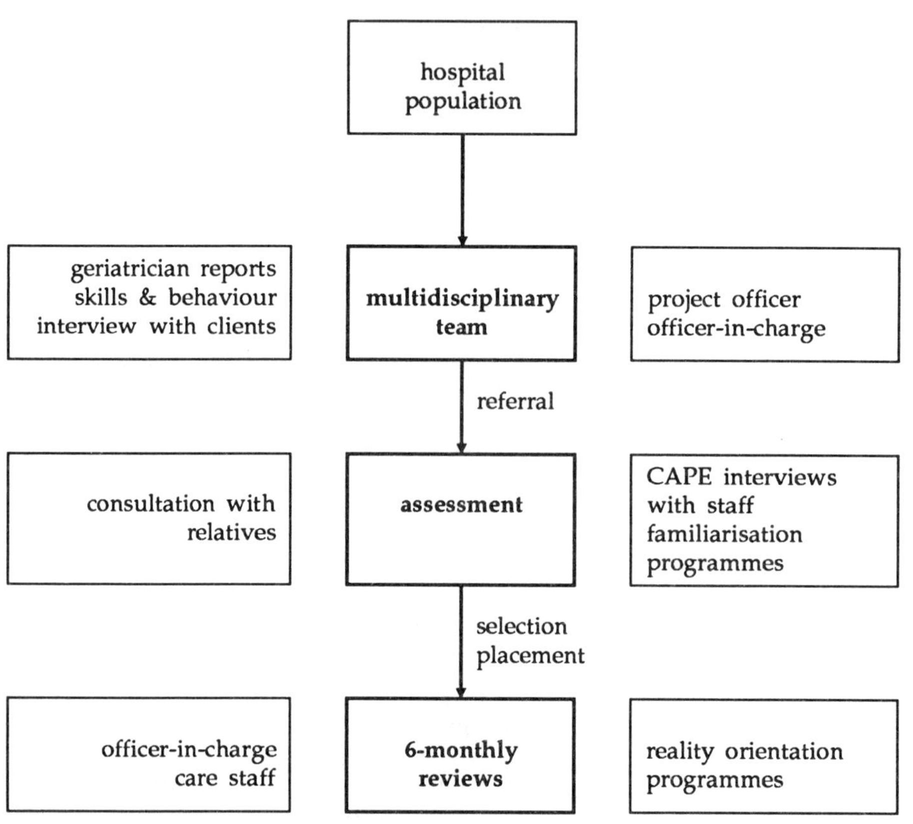

information sheets (Camden), rating sheets and getting-to-know-you techniques (Warrington) or information extracted from existing ward assessments (Kidderminster and Warwick).

What lessons were learnt? Some of the problems encountered were due more to service development difficulties than to assessment and selection *per se*. For instance, delays in getting services up and running in Derby, Islington and Chichester caused anxiety for clients. Occasional disagreements between ward staff and project workers were cited (for example in Waltham Forest). Planning the modification of targeting criteria on the basis of experience proved advantageous. Islington planned to use 'getting-to-know-you' assessments, more emphasis was being placed by Maidstone on workshop participation, Warwick found it advisable to place less reliance on Wessex and NDT

Figure 10.7
Detailed sets and flows of information for case management: initial arrangements in Somerset

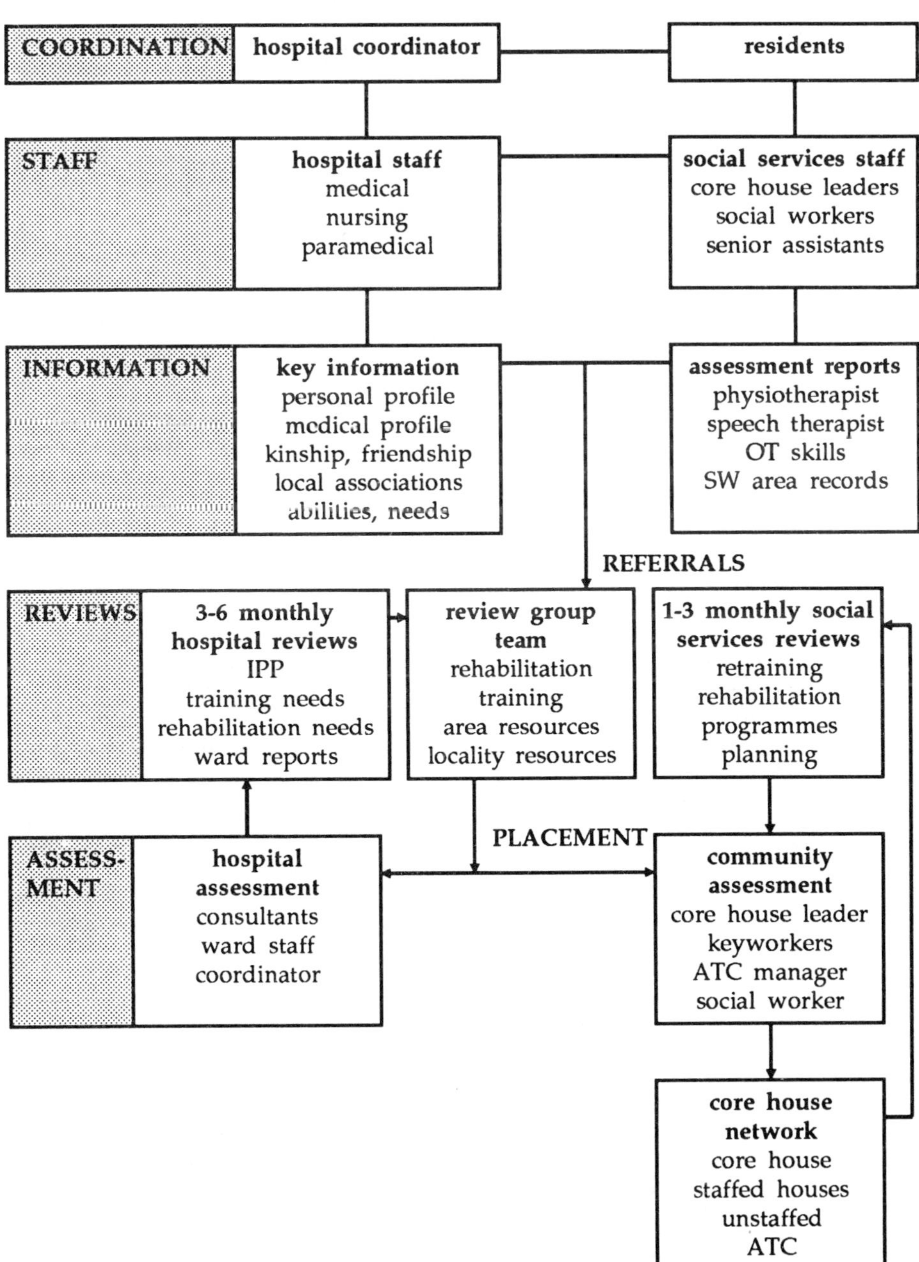

Figure 10.8
Key elements of case finding and referral

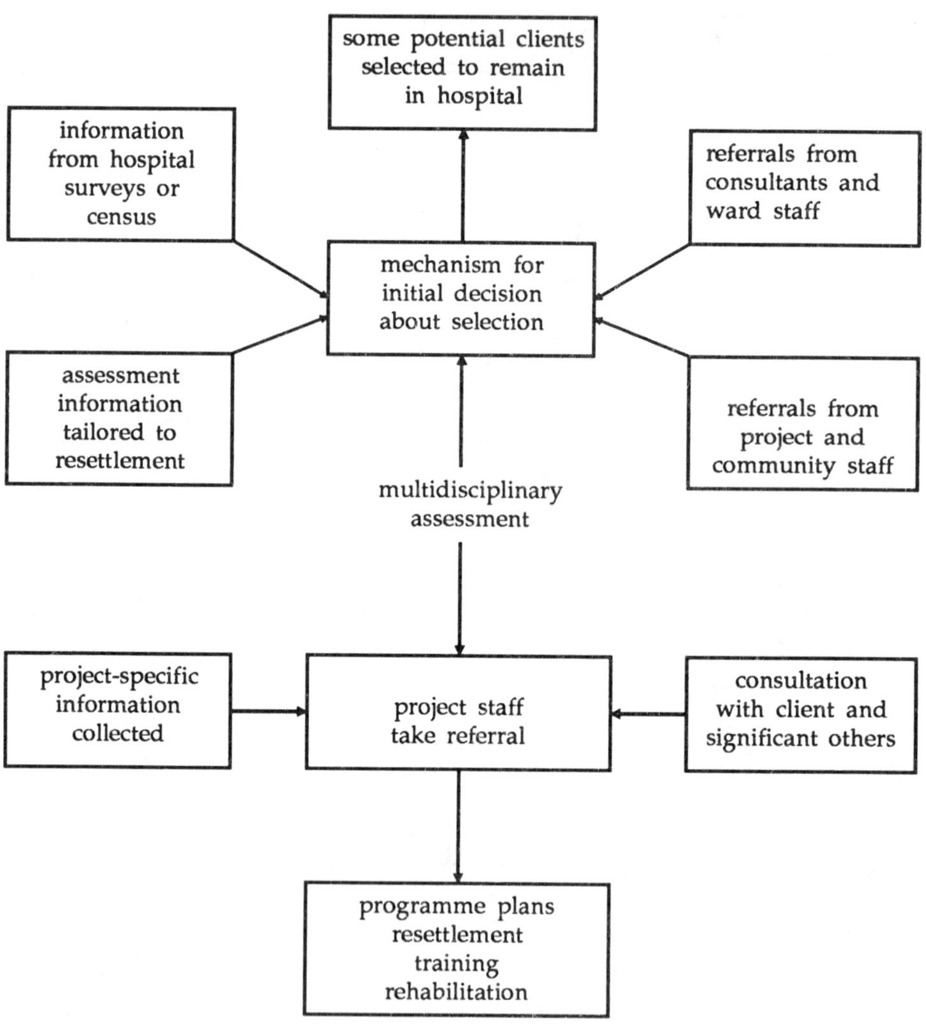

assessments, West Lancs widened selection criteria, Hillingdon relied more on multidisciplinary assessment and West Cumbria channelled referrals through one consultant. All such modifications made it possible for the assessment process to be more relevant to client and service needs. Ensuring that operational limits (service systems, professional responsibilities, and so on) were defined before moving people out of hospital avoided misunderstandings, and constructing entry criteria around the known physical limitations of services (flights of steps, distance from shops, transport services) was clearly advisable. Sometimes these physical limitations were unknown if housing was still to be acquired (see Chapter 8).

Preparing for the community

Rehabilitation training for the comparative independence of community living can be provided either before discharge from hospital, gradually making the transition to the community, or in a half-way setting, or in the community itself. Each of these options was to be found in the demonstration programme. Sometimes training was physically and operationally part of the hospital system, as in a rehabilitation ward or training unit, although, except in those projects led by health authorities (including jointly with local authorities), hospital-based rehabilitation was usually beyond the control or influence of projects, and thus needed supplementing with specially-developed facilities or extant day services. Some projects – including Brent, Chichester and Warrington – used the existing hospital rehabilitation facilities, but also developed their own programmes to take over from predischarge rehabilitation. Rehabilitation training offered somewhere between the hospital and the community made use of training units or core houses. Kidderminster used health authority halfway houses for assessment and training; Somerset provided longer-term training in core houses.

Most often, however, the main training and rehabilitation activities were undertaken in the community in the settings which clients were expected to continue to use for some time. The view taken by a majority of projects was that 'normalised training' was fundamental to good practice, and that other arrangements and facilities provided institutional or unreal social and physical environments. This view prevailed even though it was often unclear which hospital residents would most benefit from community care until rehabilitation was well underway. Introductory visits and short stays in new accommodation were the techniques commonly used to provide a gradual introduction to community living. They were often tied to leisure activities, shopping trips in the community or to more structured 'community orientation' programmes. Bolton started with day visits and moved to longer stays. Islington organised a combination of one-to-one visits with staff and interactive group activities. For people with learning difficulties or mental health problems, selected training activities were provided either in traditional day facilities such as adult training centres, social education centres or industrial therapy units or in new, custom-designed resource and activity centres. However, most work went on in people's homes, organised by residential or other social work staff.

Care planning, monitoring and reassessment

Case management is most closely associated with the two core tasks of care planning and monitoring, involving individual programme planning (IPP), individual service planning (ISP), or individual care planning (ICP). (In the absence of any obvious consistency of terminology in the literature, we shall use IPP to signify all of them.) These case review activities are intended to identify needs and plan service responses to achieve desired changes in client welfare. Where there are many different professional inputs and agencies likely to be involved, IPP and its close relatives provide the opportunity for coordination of action (Jenkins et al., 1988).

Some form of IPP system was planned and implemented in each project. Most organised IPP on a team basis, like Kidderminster's resettlement team or Chichester's community rehabilitation team, and some received assistance from community mental handicap teams (Islington, Somerset and Cambridge) or joint care planning teams (Torbay). In Chichester the project used multidisciplinary clinical reviews, case managers being health service professionals. The Brent project used a standard format for records for hospital and community care settings to avoid misinterpretations, with information coordinated and updated as an integral part of the case management process.

Location

In projects with a wide geographical spread or with placement diversity, IPP techniques varied in response to local operational and management conditions. The Bucks project used a mix of residential placements, and different practices emerged in response to the preferences of line managers and agencies managing the residential facilities. When a project was part of a broader community care programme, care planning procedures may already have been determined. This was the case in Somerset, with IPP undertaken by area fieldwork staff (although arrangements varied across the county), and in Warwickshire where local Mencap groups worked with divisional social services staff. Projects which were more self-contained, such as Cambridge, Kidderminster, Torbay and Islington, had more control over choice of planning system.

Frequency

Six-monthly case reviews were the norm (23 projects), which is much more regular than is generally to be found in local authorities. (The Audit Commission, 1989, found that over half of all local authorities conducted annual reviews, but only a third were developing individual programme plans.) In the projects with less frequent formal case reviews, supplementation came from regular informal monitoring.

- In *Maidstone,* where it was felt that the weekly contracts could respond to most changes in client needs, reviews were held only when needed.
- Ongoing assessment in *Somerset's* core and cluster model was initially supplemented with six-weekly reviews and formal annual reviews. At first there were separate reviews for day services, but these were later integrated into a review process which included inputs from keyworkers, day and residential service managers and, often, the area community care manager.
- An annual coordinating review was undertaken by social services staff at ATCs for clients in the *Warwick* project.
- In *Brent,* case reviews were undertaken every four months, with care plan coordination every six weeks.
- The *Greenwich* project held reviews more frequently (fortnightly) for clients who had recently moved out of hospital than for clients who had gained more independence (every four weeks).
- Flexibility came from a combination of frequent informal reviews and occasional formal assessments in *Waltham Forest* and *Coventry*. Both projects held quarterly reviews and weekly case meetings.

Design and structure

Existing assessment and planning systems were rarely adequate without adaptation. Differences in service principles and priorities and, of course, in local circumstances, ought to be reflected in IPP methods. Ten projects used standard packages. (An oft-voiced view across the programme was that existing assessment packages focused excessively on client weaknesses and ignored strengths.) Islington explored a range of techniques and took those components which suited its needs and principles. The Maidstone project designed a system of initial client profiles, later developed into a framework based on 'getting-to-know-you' techniques, its IPP system covering health, personal and social development, advocacy, home management, community skills, vocation and leisure, accommodation and finance. The personal component included matters relating to dress and appearance, outward behaviour, anti-social and age-inappropriate behaviour, possessions, privacy, self-care, personal hygiene, social adjustment and social awareness. These were developed from the structure and foundation provided by the initial personal profiles. Brent IPP records included one-off tasks for staff, responsibilities and outcomes, strengths and assets profiles, staff and clients' views regarding care plans, progress record sheets for task descriptions and rehabilitation activity records. Coventry, Hillingdon and Cambridge were among the projects which used the PSSRU case review form with some amendments to suit their particular needs.

Client involvement in IPP

Clients were involved or consulted in IPP in almost every project, though at different points and in different ways. Greenwich clients were invited to reviews, but if they chose not to attend they were always able to discuss services with staff. Clients in Kidderminster and Coventry sometimes attended reviews, but the main link was their keyworker who discussed reviews with them. In Brent, clients attended case review meetings if they wished, but not care coordination meetings, although their views were sought. The Glossop clients led the review process, in contrast to the Chichester clients who were consulted only if a problem arose or they specifically requested involvement. Although few would argue that it is inappropriate for clients to be involved in IPP, circumstances may not be conducive – such as when a large multi-disciplinary team is involved and it is feared that the client may feel over-whelmed – or may be constrained by the client's characteristics, such as dementia or communication difficulties. This is where citizen advocates can act on a client's behalf to express views and safeguard rights, as in the Somerset and Kidderminster projects. Relatives were also encouraged to attend case review meetings in some projects.

Delivering case-managed services

As local authorities up and down the country come to terms with their new responsibilities to introduce better care planning and assessment procedures, there will be numerous practice and policy debates about the best ways to deliver case-managed services. Some of the central issues concern teamwork, links between case managers and keyworkers, financial management and user involvement.

Case management as teamwork

Although case management was occasionally conducted in relative isolation by senior staff of hostels or group homes, it was generally a team activity. In ten projects, at least some case management work was the responsibility of a single individual, though with peer support. Cutting across the individual/team distinction was the choice between *facility-based* case management (which risks conflict between client advocacy and responsibility for provision or loyalty to colleagues) and *peripatetic* case management (which risks client iso-lation with relatively infrequent contact with the case manager). There was peripatetic case management in 16 projects, being significantly more likely as a team activity and in larger projects, and facility-based case management in 12 projects.

Teamwork in case management appeared to generate a number of advantages: it encouraged multidisciplinary working (in so far as this worked successfully); it allowed democratic management to emerge when this was desired; it facilitated peer support and the dissemination of good practice; it helped projects to agree common basic objectives and mutually agreed individual goals; and arguably it promoted innovation and introduced a measure of safety (compare Challis and Davies, 1986; Ovretveit, 1986; Onyett and Malone, 1990; West and Farr, 1990). Communication needs to be good if these advantages are to be achieved, and many projects quickly realised the need for regular team or management meetings and well-structured, open information systems. Communication outside the team was harder to develop, for example with community mental health or mental handicap teams, and experience from the programme underlines the importance of clarifying the operational mesh between CMHTs and case management teams (particularly when the latter are multidisciplinary or peripatetic).

Multidisciplinary working

Teamworking in case management made it easier for projects to fully involve the range of professional skills needed to provide specialist inputs. The mix of expertise represented on teams varied enormously, reflecting perceived service and client needs, the strength of principles such as normalisation, and the agencies represented in the original application for DHSS funding. Because of the predominance of projects initiated or led by social services departments, case management teams were rarely dominated by health professionals. Two projects had teams which recruited members solely from the health service; 15 projects had mixed health and social work teams; and 11 projects set up teams whose members were all residential social work staff.

The health-social services mix can give a misleading impression of team operation and the delivery of specialist skills. In Bolton, nurses on the team liaised with hospital staff and social workers liaised with families. (There are now no health service staff in the teams.) In Maidstone, team members who were previously working for the health authority were absorbed into a social work culture, with the advantages and potential drawbacks that implies. The community rehabilitation team in Chichester was entirely made up of health service employees, but was one of the most multidisciplinary across the programme because of the many different professions represented (nurse, CPN, occupational therapist, clinical psychologist, GP, clerical assistant, and – for a short time – a social worker). The case manager in Winchester held primary responsibility for case conduct and liaised with a loosely structured 'team' comprising care attendants, social workers, wardens of specialised sheltered housing and two consultant geriatricians. These examples span the extended and core types described by Ovretveit (1986).

Few pilot projects attempted to utilise case management as a lever into a more mixed economy. Most used it as a means to incorporate the specialist skills of individuals from different agencies, generally – as we have seen – via team organisation. For example, behavioural psychology and speech therapy were especially valuable resources for multidisciplinary teams in some projects for people with learning difficulties.

Keyworking

Keyworker systems were almost universally established across the programme, enabling clients' day-to-day needs to be monitored and support to be provided. Keyworkers assume some direct care responsibility for individual clients, whereas care managers assume more administrative and organising responsibility. Case management, therefore, tends to encompass more than keyworking (see Dant and Gearing, 1990). The detailed knowledge of clients or service users which is necessary for planning is arguably only gained through regular daily contact, and so keyworkers and case managers need to liaise closely for effective decision-making. Generally keyworkers fed this information directly into IPP and case review, though sometimes indirectly via the case manager.

The degree of separation between keyworking and case management – the extent to which case managers left direct service provision to others, as recommended by Griffiths (1988), for example – was a question each service had to face, and resolutions depended on the strength of the case management model as well as simple operational details, such as the scale of the service and the location and dispersal of residential facilities. In eight projects case managers provided some care services to clients (this was often the case in projects for elderly people), but it was more common for this to be delegated to keyworkers. Case managers performed a strategic role, and keyworkers (and co-workers and family aides) were delegated to perform some of the core tasks of case management. This was the arrangement in Brent, and was increasingly the case in Maidstone as the project was incorporated into Kent case management structure. Keyworkers also acted as 'professional advocates', working through team meetings and case review procedures, or they simply held responsibility for putting plans into practice, as in the Griffiths model of 'care management'. With this latter arrangement (which was more common in the larger projects), some case management decisions were taken without direct contact between clients and case managers. Keyworking in many projects was the responsibility of a single worker who supported clients in a range of settings. Where different keyworkers supported clients in different settings, such as residential and day services, projects moved towards integrated support and training programmes ensuring consistency through the case review process.

Inter-agency ties

Some of the arrangements found within the programme were based on the notion that case management should be independent from other activities such as resourcing or provision so as to reduce conflicts of interest or split loyalties. Projects found independent case management arrangements difficult to practise, because power usually remained in the hands of funders or providers. (Dant and Gearing, 1990, make a similar point.) A central task of case management in more independent services, including voluntary-led projects, was to connect inputs from other organisations or to provide a bridge between agencies. Providing inter-sectoral ties is an essential, though sometimes difficult, responsibility of case management. It was identified in the community care White Paper as a way to promote greater mixing of the economy of care (Cm 849, 1989, para. 3.4.3). This was done to good effect in projects run by voluntary agencies, such as Camden, Liverpool, Waltham Forest, Warrington and Camberwell, and those where voluntary agencies led and managed facilities, such as Warwick and Bucks. Here, case managers and keyworkers worked semi-independently of the statutory sector. In projects where social services adopted an enabling or coordinating role, case managers sometimes retained responsibility for arranging service packages in a 'fix-it' capacity, as with the resettlement team in Kidderminster. In Warwick, although social services coordinated resettlement, case management responsibility rested with Mencap.

Financial management

Ring-fenced funding may be out of fashion, but this aspect of Care in the Community programme grant aid forced projects to pay more attention to financial management than was usual for services at their level within health and social care agencies at the time. Although most projects tapped into mainstream public services, a number used devolved or special budgets to gain access to services provided by other agencies or individuals not usually accessible, or to keep track of specific or overall service costs for clients. Service packaging in the mixed economy requires a service menu to facilitate informed choice, together with information on availability and cost (or price). Only the Darlington and Maidstone projects introduced devolved budgets to each case manager, with a cost ceiling or micro-budget for each client. This was the arrangement later to find favour with Griffiths (1988), who suggested care management with greater budgetary autonomy, Wagner (1988), who argued for nominated social workers exercising control over financial resources, the Audit Commission (1989) and the government (Cm 849, 1989).

How did the arrangements work in Maidstone and Darlington? The Maidstone project was deliberately modelled on the wider Kent Community Care

Project (Davies and Challis, 1986), though transferring the experience to a different client group. The project's initial plans recognised that replication would not be easy.

> The needs of mentally handicapped people who have been in hospital for some time are very different from those of old people who hope to avoid hospital. Nevertheless, there will be important similarities of approach.

The project undertook detailed assessments of each client from which it was able to describe the packages of formal and informal services needed. These were bought in from appropriate agencies, and the costs monitored with the help of price information (these were mainly 'shadow prices' since money often did not change hands, for example if local social services were used or if clients attended hospital clinics). The budget ceiling was the target figure for each placement, set at two-thirds of the cost of hospital care. Community care helpers were recruited to provide direct assistance and support. Unit coordinators made bids for particular resources and service planning coordinators were responsible for overall liaison and administration of budgets. Service flexibility helped ensure resources were better matched to changing user needs, and was formalised through weekly 'contracts' between case managers and clients. (Figure 10.9 summarises such arrangements.)

The Darlington Project provided intensive domiciliary support for elderly people, setting up case management arrangements with clear budgetary control at the client level. Three service managers and a project manager controlled expenditure, again based on an average of two-thirds the cost of hospital in-patient provision. The managers also helped prepare individual care plans, which were regularly reviewed and modified. Flexibility was ensured by a mix of care, including home care assistants (providing domestic, caring and therapeutic inputs), existing health and social service provision and a range of support developed from the local community using the care budget. The scheme crossed traditional agency boundaries by using decentralised budgets. The Darlington experience supports the view that a joint agency budget at the client level can coordinate care more effectively at the level of the individual client (Challis et al., 1989).

The advantages of devolved (individual) budgets are that they give clear financial signals, which ease the task of allocating resources or buying in services from the mixed economy. They also increase the range of opportunities for service substitution, and are more likely to result in service flexibility, efficiency and equity. Autonomy in spending helps to clarify accountability and has been found to encourage creativity. On the other hand, detailed and accurate cost information is essential, which is itself costly to obtain and maintain. Cost monitoring needs to run in parallel to IPP, and although this may look less of an added disadvantage today than it was ten years ago, there is a need for an accessible management information system and case managers trained to use it. Brent and some other projects considering delegated budgets came to the view that they would compromise the professional advocacy role of case management. However, we incline to the view that, without control over resources, case management will not achieve its full potential for clients. This is the conclusion reached from a number of experimental and quasi-experimental studies in this country and elsewhere (Davies and Challis, 1986 and Renshaw et al., 1988 offer reviews; see also Callaghan, 1989; Challis et al., 1990; Dant and Gearing, 1990).

User involvement

By increasing accountability to users and by encouraging user participation, case management helped to bring users into the decision-making processes of community care. In principle, this is a more genuine or active form of user involvement than receiving information or being consulted (Croft and Beresford, 1990). The Maidstone project, for example, was developed around a *client-centred case management model*. The operational policy stated:

> Clients are supported by case managers who advocate on their behalf and counsel them through the transitional period, supporting their personal status and offering them choice by buying-in a range of service options.

In order for the service to recognise and respond to clients' wishes and needs and to enable users to fulfil obligations and exercise rights, a close *two-way* relationship between case managers and clients was seen as necessary. The operational policy also included a charter of care, which attached basic principles to residential support, to be adhered to by all staff. The charter comprised a visiting policy, and included items on accommodation, finance, health and welfare, personal and social care, money management, sexual privacy and medication. Principles stressed user involvement, choice and the importance of case management tasks such as individual service planning. The charter set a floor for a more equitable balance of power between clients and case managers, with regular contract negotiation the chosen mechanism. In a report on service outcomes, the project stressed the role of case management in this process.

> It is difficult to envisage of service planning based on individual need without case management. Case management is a vital ingredient if a service is to facilitate the needs of its clients and enable them to receive opportunities that will be responsive to individual circumstances and not service need. Clients' needs are ever changing as opportunities are provided and they respond individually to such opportunities. The ISP coordinator keeps the finger on the pulse of client development. It is their relationship with the client – one step removed from day-to-day service contact – that establishes the boundaries in which client contacts can be negotiated weekly and their response monitored.

Service users in Brent were involved in case management decisions. Realistic short- and long-term goals were set at assessment and reassessed and adjusted *in consultation with the user*. Clients were encouraged to be as involved as possible in the formation of their treatment plans as part of promoting independence. Like Maidstone, case management was central to facilitating user involvement. Even at the hospital preparation stage, each client had a named member of staff responsible for service coordination, monitoring, welfare and advocacy. Maidstone and Brent were not typical, as we saw in Chapter 3. Not every project tackled consumerism in case management as enthusiastically, some citing practical difficulties, such as the operation of the necessary mechanisms for enabling effective consumer participation, the resolution of conflicts between operational aims and user requirements, and the management of the service flexibility essential with such a system. Others remained unconvinced (at the time) that user involvement in case management was necessary.

Case management models suggested for the UK, some of them imported from North America, tend to reflect more the organisational and economic conditions of community care, particularly the health-social services split and latterly the enhanced roles of non-statutory agencies, rather than principles of consumer control or objective and informed decision-making. It is important that these are not overlooked. The concentration of responsibility in a single person (the case manager) could in fact reduce rather than improve client involvement and influence, and the auditing of local authority services by the Audit Commission and the inspections of community care by the Social Services Inspectorate will need to be alert to such dangers. Giving clients the power to change their case managers would introduce a welcome quasi-market force.

Involving relatives

Many projects involved relatives only after certain other goals had been attained:

- 'relatives informed when accommodation and services became available' (Bolton);
- 'informed after selection' (Islington);
- 'informed following discussion on attendance at day centre prior to move' (Somerset);
- 'informed in a way agreeable to client' (Waltham Forest); or
- 'involved if they showed an interest' (Buckinghamshire).

Some projects clearly anticipated a potential conflict of interest between clients and relatives:

- 'resident's choice comes before relative's choice' (Somerset); or
- 'preferences of clients are fundamental; family concerns to be considered as appropriate' (Islington).

These approaches contrast with the active encouragement of relatives' participation in Camden (which held parents' evenings), Maidstone (which involved relatives in drawing up individual profiles), and St Helens and West Cumbria (which took the wishes of relatives into account before selection). West Cumbria also sought to involve relatives directly in reality orientation programmes designed to reduce the confusion of clients.

The influence of organisational context

The design and operation of case management were inevitably influenced by local organisational and funding arrangements, particularly the extent and style of inter-agency working, the lead agency for the project, and the degree of budgetary autonomy. The multidisciplinary case management team in Brent mirrored the multidisciplinary project management arrangements between the health and social services authorities. The case managers in Bolton employed by either health or social services retained separate line management accountability, but strong joint service management ensured operational unity within a common case management framework. Simple statistical analyses of project and case management styles across the programme revealed that in single agency-led projects, management lead was correlated with lead responsibility for IPP, and in joint agency-led projects was associated with cross-agency responsibility for IPP. Some other associations will be discussed in the next chapter.

The lead agency helped determine the service model and culture for case management; for example, social services lead generally meant social work orientation to case management. The balance of joint working helped determine agency involvement and opportunities for inter- and multidisciplinary working. Case managers were more likely to be able to call on the services of a care agency if it was represented on case management teams. Lead agency responsibility for case management most often rested with social services departments (20 projects), although case management teams often had health service or voluntary sector members. Of course, this social services domination did not result in standardised arrangements, for the internal organisation of social services departments and the availability of different public, voluntary and private services had their effects.

Management and budgeting autonomy were generally welcomed by projects. Our evidence from projects with devolved budgets, particularly where devolved down to case managers, suggests that financial autonomy facilitated the creative use of resources and generated an independent culture (see Chapter 11). Case management also has a poorer chance of success when funding of key services is fragmented. In projects led by social services, mainstream financial control was the norm (as in Somerset, West Cumbria and Calderdale), except where services and budgets had *already* been devolved to areas or neighbourhoods (as in Islington and Maidstone). Jointly-managed projects usually pooled resources before reallocation to cases or facilities, which helped

Table 10.2
A typology of case management arrangements in the Care in the Community programme

Type 1 Residential social work arrangements, where keyworkers were responsible for day-to-day monitoring, with project leaders, residential managers or line managers overseeing assessment and case review, or taking responsibility for securing particular resources. Examples from the programme include Islington and Greenwich.

Type 2 Sub-area social services case management, where a senior assistant or care manager for a client group, network or patch held responsibility for most case management tasks, and coordinated inputs from a range of individuals inside and outside the agency. Examples were Somerset and Calderdale.

Type 3 Peripatetic social services case management, involving senior social work staff, some with health authority backgrounds. Service managers or coordinators were also usually team members with caseload responsibilities. Such teams were democratically managed, with accountability to principal or chief officers in divisions or headquarters. Examples from the programme include Kidderminster's resettlement team and Maidstone's integration with Kent's care management structure.

Type 4 Multidisciplinary case management, with joint health and social services teams, where case managers either retained separate line management or worked to a joint management committee. Team members had their own caseloads but also provided specialist inputs. Examples were Bolton and Brent.

Type 5 Multidisciplinary teams, though solely within the health service, taking in different specialisms, with accountability to the health authority. Liaison and coordination with voluntary organisations and social services departments does not extend to team membership. The best example from the programme was the Chichester project.

Type 6 Quasi-brokerage case management, using mechanisms such as individualised funding agreements. The Cambridge project is currently developing such an approach. Loosely linked were some micro-budgeting arrangements such as those developed by Maidstone and Darlington, and individualised budgets controlled by users themselves, as in Glossop.

Type 7 Semi-independent case management outside the public sector, with responsibility for the regular tasks of case management held by support and care staff employed by a voluntary organisation. Health, or more usually social services professionals, share some care management responsibility, gaining entry via public funding (from dowries, direct grants, top-ups for residential placements). Examples from the programme are Torbay and Warwick.

deal with splits between care and funding responsibilities, particularly between health and social services. If the voluntary sector was involved, one possible solution was to move the case management lead outside the public sector. No project developed a completely independent case management agency, although semi-independent models emerged in four areas.

Developing case management

Each project organised the delivery of case management in a different way, usually by extended or core team working. Table 10.2 suggests a basic typology, condensing the span of arrangements employed across the programme into ideal types which also reflect the location of case management in the local service economy and associated political imperatives.

We have seen how projects interpreted the core tasks of case management, building and delivering case managed services in quite different ways and a series of operational variables surfaced to intervene and modify local practice Table 10.3. Figure 10.9 models the multivariate nature of case managed community care as it occurred across the programme, summarising the variables likely to require consideration when developing case management in the 1990s.

The pilot projects have shown how case management can be used as an instrument for identifying client needs and abilities, involving service users in decision-making, translating broad care principles into practice, planning and coordinating service packages for matching resources to needs, monitoring achievements, carrying out reassessments, and introducing relevant financial information into comparatively routine community care processes. Projects' experiences also point to some of the limitations of case management outside controlled experiments. With the endorsement of the 1989 community care White Paper, case management should become nationwide practice in the 1990s. At its worst, it will simply provide social services with case review or keyworking procedures, but it is more likely to link service performance, quality and costs with IPP information, provide the opportunity to review service performance and promote cost-effective and equitable provision. Drawing out lessons for the 1990s from the diversity in the demonstration programme, we can point to those case management arrangements which appeared to increase the likelihood of good quality community care reaching clients.

- Assessment and review procedures, using IPP and its variants, need to be comprehensive and multidisciplinary for effective case management. Such procedures create opportunities for user involvement and representation.
- Devolving budgets to case managers is a basic prerequisite for cost-consciousness. Micro-budgeting is more likely than other arrangements to encourage service substitution in a way which explicitly weighs service costs against client outcomes. It forces consideration by those who make

Table 10.3
Operational variables of case management: summary

Location Peripatetic modes of delivery predominated, with team-delivered case management (16 projects) offering greater flexibility and objectivity for performing the core tasks. Facility-based case management was also represented (12 projects). In situ delivery risks comprising professional advocacy with direct support or provision.

Continuity Case management responsibilities were continuous between hospital and community settings in most projects. The Brent joint-team maintained common records and individual service planning information, whereas in Chichester and Kidderminster the rehabilitation and resettlement teams handed over most responsibility to support staff after resettlement.

Individual responsibility Case management was the responsibility of a single individual, such as a residential manager or residential team leader in ten projects and the shared or part shared responsibility of a separate team in 18 projects.

Client contact In all services case managers maintained regular formal and informal contact with clients. Six-monthly case reviews were the norm (23 projects). Projects holding less frequent reviews also used informal monitoring via keyworkers.

Keyworking In eight projects case managers provided some keyworker-like support or special training but in the majority, direct support was delegated to keyworkers.

Devolved budgets Budgetary delegation to case managers helped overcome the tendency for macro-organisation to determine service packages through set mainstream services. The White Paper recognised this when it made reference to the Kent, Gateshead and Darlington projects evaluated by the PSSRU and the few pilot projects which utilised micro-budgeting. Maidstone for instance, linked user budgets to two-thirds of the cost of hospital care, and case managers had access to shadow service costs and bought in a range of supplementary services encouraging cost-effectiveness and accountability.

Multidisciplinary working Teamworking enabled projects to incorporate a range of specialist skills which would otherwise have to be negotiated. Mixed health and social services backgrounds predominated (15 projects) although residential social work orientations were also common (11 projects).

Caseload limits In projects using micro-budgets like Maidstone or with clear case management structures like Brent and Bolton, caseloads were limited to enable intensive case management.

Providing In most services, case managers had responsibility for organising inputs from different agencies, in some cases buying in services. In some, such as Maidstone and Brent, specialist inputs were provided on a one-to-one basis or through special needs workshops. In a few, most if not all support, was provided by case managers themselves.

Professional advocacy Most case managers acted as professional advocates, although this was more objectively performed where case management was separate from direct provision or support (above). Brent considered that devolved budgets compromised professional advocacy although Maidstone used a client-centred case management model and contracts with users. Somerset and Kidderminster developed citizen advocacy schemes.

Figure 10.9
Operational variables for case-managed community care

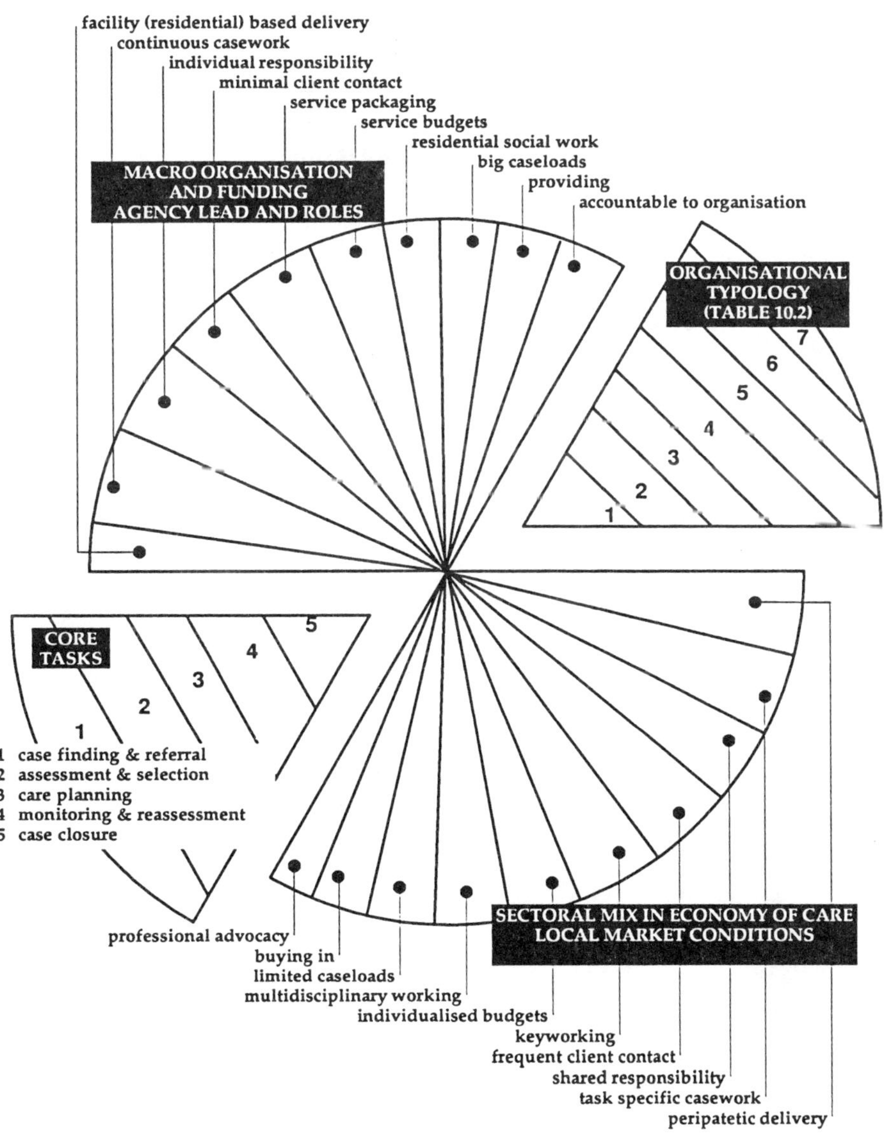

decisions about the relationships between needs, resources and outcomes. Better accountability, creativity and costeffectiveness should follow.

- Peripatetic, multidisciplinary case management delivered by teams brings practice and operational advantages which do not follow from residence-based, single agency, case management. A range of professional inputs is on tap, and agency and professional divides are more easily bridged.
- Case management which is separated from provision and keyworking increases objectivity in decision-making. It also helps to preserve the influence and power of clients, particularly if professional advocacy is seen as a case management responsibility.
- If the aim is to further mix the supply economy of community care, case management can better aid service coordination if service brokerage arrangements are introduced. A single point of contact (and contract) for users and professionals encourages more consistent and continuous support.
- Public sector case managers with advocacy responsibilities find themselves accountable to both clients and the employing agency, risking conflicts and tensions. Objectivity and professional advocacy can therefore be enhanced if case management is independent (outside the public sector) or semi-independent (with management and administrative walls built around the case management functions).

11 Joint working and service organisation

The mixed economy

With responsibilities defined and delimited along agency lines, it has long been difficult for social services and health authorities to jointly plan, coordinate and fund community care. In 1983, the Care in the Community projects found themselves caught in the implementation gap between central policy and local practice (Wistow, 1985), working under numerous organisational and funding constraints stemming from the separation of health and social care, and with no obligation to develop integrated community care plans, let alone open them for public consultation. Unlike the present community care reforms, the 1983 Circular was not very prescriptive: joint working between social services and health authorities was a core objective, but little guidance was given as to its form and extent; and although joint working was an initial condition for central funding, only limited central monitoring was possible thereafter. A further major difference between 1983 and the 1990s was the exclusion, if projects so desired, of the voluntary and private sectors.

In many areas, the joint planning and joint finance machinery of 1983 offered little assistance to authorities seeking to diversify the supply and funding of community care services. New resource exchange agreements and coalitions between agencies were needed in order to facilitate the greater mixing of the economy of care. Sometimes this resulted in organisational arrangements which themselves highlighted the inadequacies inherent in joint planning and joint finance (Webb and Wistow, 1985), and sometimes this produced a new determination to overcome disincentives to cooperation and diversification. In areas such as Somerset and Calderdale, significant progress had been made towards joint community care strategies before 1983, making it comparatively straightforward for the projects in these areas to build their plans on accumulated experience. This contrasts with the Chichester project, for example, which was led and developed by the health authority with minimal involvement from West Sussex County Council. Joint consultative committees and joint care planning teams were engaged to varying degrees and with varying success across the programme, and remained key elements in the planning set out in the *National Health Service and Community Care Act 1990*.

By no means all of the inadequacies and disincentives of the 1980s will disappear in the coming years; many will remain as challenges for some time. For example, externally-imposed controls on local authority expenditure place constraints on pilot projects just as they continue to exert a considerable influence on community care planning in today's mixed economy (Wistow et al., 1992). Rate-capping may have become charge-capping, but the effects look much the same. A second challenge for some projects, which continues to test the patience of community care planners, was the need to resolve inter-departmental differences in financial priorities and target client groups. Housing, education and finance departments have their own obligations, views and constraints. One project set up its own housing association because the supply and quality of local authority or privately rented housing was inadequate, and another gained access to local authority housing only after considerable delays, prompting a members' enquiry. Labyrinthine inter-agency negotiations were almost inevitable where local and health authority boundaries were not coterminous, or where a number of district councils were to be involved. Geographical mismatches between authorities continue to dog community care planning.

In building up joint working arrangements, projects obviously capitalised where possible on the successes of the past, taking advantage of the special features of the demonstration programme to enhance and improve upon previous ventures. Existing links with non-statutory agencies were extended or replicated, particularly those with voluntary social services organisations and housing associations. Greater use was made of dowry funds, social security coffers and regional capital programmes so as to expand the range of services, lessening the traditional resource control of health authorities. The overall result, to use today's terminology, was a greater mixing of the community care economy. For instance, social services provided more than half the community accommodation used by clients, and health authorities played only a small part, owning 5 per cent of accommodation and transferring management of half of it to other agencies. Inter-organisational links were more complex and new collaborative cultures were demanded, although some of the provision and funding arrangements now emerging in England – such as non-profit trusts to manage residential facilities and tighter contractual links between statutory purchasers and non-statutory providers – were not in evidence in the pilot programme. However, the programme did show how some of the organisational difficulties intrinsic to developing community care can be successfully confronted *without* the realignment of responsibilities and finances described by the *Caring for People* White Paper (Cm 849, 1989) and introduced by the 1990 Act. In this chapter we describe the various alliances, host and lead arrangements and joint service management agreements established within the programme.

The joint working stipulation of the Care in the Community programme was mandatory at the design stage but permissive in execution. The underlying aim was for projects to explore their own chosen ways of bringing together a variety of experiences and resources in order to move people and resources from hospital to community care. No single model for agency lead, roles or responsibilities was imposed, so one of the important qualities of the demonstration programme was its ability to explore alternative solutions to the pervasive problems of joint working. We first describe the five organisational types or models which emerged within the programme, and their key aspects of project or service management. The chapter then looks at the 'mixing of the economy' of community care, particularly the contributions of the voluntary sector, and concludes with an account of how some of the projects were integrated into mainstream provision as central government funding ended. The experiences of the pilot projects provide a window through which to view some of the difficulties and solutions likely to be encountered in organising and building community care services in the 1990s.

Organisational models

The slow and uneven development of community care stems in part from fragmentation of responsibility and accountability, horizontally across agencies and vertically between tiers of government. Not surprisingly, the suggested reforms of many commentators, including the Audit Commission (1986) and Griffiths (1988), included single agency responsibility for client groups, combined with unambiguous funding channels. Griffiths recommended social services departments to lead and coordinate care, and urged ring-fenced funding through community care grants. The *Caring for People* White Paper took a more cautious line, encouraging an enabling role for local authorities and preserving local autonomy over spending allocations. Most of the projects emerged from their pre-application discussions with social services departments taking the lead, sometimes shared with other agencies, in 20 of the 28 projects. Health authorities had lead or shared lead roles in only eight projects. More traditional functions were also performed by social services departments, including service provision (in just over half of the projects most of the services were directly provided in this way), quality monitoring and longer-term planning. In half the projects, local authorities were performing what amounted to an enabling role, with substantial purchasing of services through loosely drawn up service agreements and/or by case managers.

Reviewing the myriad organisational arrangements and styles in the pilot programme we identified five broad types or models:

- unitary agency,
- semi-independent agency,
- lead agency,
- joint agency, and
- multi-agency models (see Table 11.1).

These models, which we describe below, are summaries of a variety of project arrangements and experiences, and so inevitably gloss over some finer detail. They are not intended to be blueprints for future organisation, rather an indication of options chosen in the 1980s and still largely available in the 1990s. They are neither definitive nor mutually exclusive: other possible arrangements were not represented in the programme, and some projects

Table 11.1
Organisational models

1. Unitary agency model

Advantages
- clarity in line management, accountability and leadership
- less development work required, with minimal consultation and negotiation
- directly addresses organisational needs with control over resource inputs

Disadvantages
- narrower operational boundaries risk service isolation
- innovative services are less likely
- marginalisation of other agencies with common interests may occur

2. Semi-independent agency model

Advantages
- united by conventional operational and practice constraints, potential for innovation
- opportunities for experimental management arrangements
- potential for flexibility and choice to suit local circumstances

Disadvantages
- difficulties accessing mainstream services, with risk of isolation
- political marginalisation, making strong leadership and faithful allies essential
- unconventional use of labour resources may generate operational difficulties

3. Lead agency model

Advantages
- intentions and responsibilities clear and service co-ordination easier
- usually employed tested models of support and staff cultures
- fewer developmental risks

Disadvantages
- less flexibility for lateral or innovative development
- accountability focused, requiring strong leadership
- resource management agreements necessary

4. Joint agency model

Advantages
- common service and client goals, and joint operational procedures
- foundation for interdisciplinary working
- shared management accountability helps organisational dynamics

Disadvantages
- different organisational characteristics and priorities generate management pressures
- differential service conditions and allegiances generate conflict
- investment in negotiation with ongoing organisational effort required

5. Multi-agency model

Advantages
- greater flexibility in service design and input mix efficiency
- access afforded to a wide range of resources and skills
- mutually-agreed output objectives targeted by a single service

Disadvantages
- conflicting management and practice attitudes and priorities
- service coordination is a major task
- potential for organisational inefficiency

combined the characteristics of more than one type. In Table 11.1 we briefly note the advantages and disadvantages of each model as we observed them during the demonstration programme.

Unitary agency model

As the label we have chosen suggests, the main characteristic of the unitary agency model is single-agency responsibility for service development. However, there may have been shared planning in the first instance, and also shared provision and staffing, and ongoing responsibility for managing particular facilities or teams may be handed over to another body. When other agencies were involved in the project, therefore, their roles extended no further than the day-to-day management of particular facilities, perhaps on a contractual basis. To the exclusion or with only the token representation of other agencies, the unitary agency usually conducted the assessment and selection of clients, undertook project administration, provided specialist resource inputs, and made all strategic decisions. Although the mixed economy of community care may be extended by such arrangements, this model is not consistent with the enabling authority objectives of the 1990 Act.

Two projects fitted this model: Chichester (where the health authority was the unitary agency) and Islington (social services department). With joint working a condition of central funding, there should not, in principle, have been any examples of the unitary agency model in the Care in the Community programme. In practice, the involvement of a subsidiary organisation tailed off or never moved beyond the periphery of decision-making, and key functions simply remained with the primary agency for want of other influences.

Semi-independent agency model

In the semi-independent agency model, a single agency, usually a voluntary or special project organisation or consortium, took on responsibility for service development and management. (Recently some of the 'trusts' and not-for-profit agencies established by statutory authorities have performed these roles. There were forerunners in the programme.) The semi-independent organisation largely designed the services to their own specifications, rather than reacting to external demands, and did not necessarily seek to fill gaps in local service provision. However, the supply of clients (by definition) and longer-term funds (by convention) remained dependent on public agencies, and day care, occupational therapy, social work support and other services were often 'bought in' from other agencies. Thus full independence was never likely to have been achieved, nor would it have been deemed desirable, but semi-independence was assured by filtering the power and influence of outside organisations through managerial control, and by using social security benefits to fund revenue expenditure. It is this semi-independent agency model which has recently attracted some local and health authorities as they seek to divest themselves of some service provision responsibilities while holding on to the purse strings.

In the programme, all clients came from hospital settings of course, so the model took on a more limited form than could be the case in the current climate. Four projects exemplified this model: Liverpool (where the semi-independent agency was Mencap), Waltham Forest (Mind), Warrington (Community Care Consortium) and Camberwell (Age Concern).

Lead agency model

When a single agency set the community care objectives, steered service development and management, held control of practice decisions, and managed staff and service provision, we had the classic (pre-Griffiths) lead agency model of community care. The lead agency worked closely with the supply agency (health authority) for service planning and design and for the selection and assessment of clients, and although the health authority usually retained responsibility for important resources, redistribution was fashioned by the lead agency through its responsibility for case management and targeting. Through its service delivery activities, staff management and financial semi-independence, the lead agency was generally more powerful than the supply agency. Not all of these characteristics applied in each of the ten projects which we identified as adopting a lead agency approach – for example, some provision was delegated to voluntary organisations or housing associations – but each of the ten resembled this model more than any other. Inter-agency liaison was usually through the joint care planning team or joint consultative committee, *and* at the individual officer level.

Projects were developed some years before Griffiths put his weight behind lead agency arrangements and before the enabling authority concept developed by the White Paper, so some aspects of the Care in the Community model now appear dated. In the programme model, for example, there was rather less contracting out of services than the 1990s' version, but they resembled the later model in that the lead agency was usually the social services department (in Calderdale, Coventry, Hillingdon, Kidderminster, Maidstone, Somerset, West Berks, West Cumbria and West Lancs). In Winchester the lead agency was the health authority, although it enjoyed close links with voluntary organisations, and the housing and social services departments.

Joint agency model

The joint agency model had many of the characteristics of lead agency arrangements. Important functions such as planning were shared, and bilateral agreements over the allocation of such key responsibilities as staffing were reached. The primary difference was that agencies operated on a partnership basis, making working relationships both more equitable and accountable. Liaison and coordination between agencies needed to be strong at the practice and management levels, with the emphasis on partnership reinforced by a shared, perhaps democratic, approach to decision-making. A project committee, steering group or partnership team oversaw the joint agency models, and some projects developed a joint health-social services staff team to manage the project at the grassroots. A shared approach to case management was a notable feature of this model. Different management responsibilities and lines of accountability were retained, so that joint working priorities had to overcome or override competing organisational interests.

Six projects fitted this model: Bolton, Brent, Bucks, Darlington and St Helens (joint health and social services), and Warwickshire (joint social services and Mencap).

Multi-agency model

A marked feature of the mid-1990s may be the proliferation of provision and support activities which involve numerous agencies and sectors. In the mid-1980s it was unusual for agencies in the public sector to be working closely together, and rarer still for a voluntary organisation to be involved in a tripartite relationship. Without carefully developed community care plans to help in the identification of needs and the planning of the range and mix of services, multi-agency projects were less well placed than their counterparts should be in future years. However, the encouragement of organisational pluralism by the Care in the Community programme produced six projects which are best described as adopting multi-agency approaches to joint working (Cambridge, Camden, Derby, Glossop, Greenwich and Torbay) and which succeeded in sharing both the management and service delivery tasks, though not necessarily equally among the partners. Clarity of objectives, effective mechanisms for coordination and steering, and a workable system for project accountability were required if multi-agency projects were to meet their organisational and client-level objectives effectively.

Service management

Projects were required to set out their management plans in advance of central funding, and it was no surprise that these plans and the subsequent practice should often closely reflect management operations in the agencies involved, particularly where strong lead agency arrangements had already been established. Thus intentions were closely tied to macro-organisation, especially in relation to joint working and agency lead. For instance, the Bolton and Brent projects, both joint agency services, proposed joint management mechanisms. Calderdale, Islington, Somerset and Cumbria, led by social services, designed project management to link with existing social services line management. Chichester, which was health authority-led, proposed management through the community rehabilitation team which was comprised entirely of health care specialists. Projects where voluntary organisations shared lead responsibilities tended to plan for statutory sector representation, and some projects coordinated by social services planned to include representation from the voluntary sector in order to ensure a mix of interests in line with broader service aims. Projects which planned to move some way beyond previous local service configurations developed management mechanisms which reflected their operational complexity or isolation. In Warwickshire, for example, a management committee was planned to include two members each from health and social services and six members of the local Mencap society in each locality. The two housing components of the Winchester project were designed to be managed separately in order to reflect the organisation of each specialised sheltered housing scheme.

Service culture and structure in the lead and other agencies obviously exerted an influence: for example, the area or divisional structure in the social services department was reflected in project management arrangements in the larger projects. A general departmental restructuring in Somerset brought changes to the project, and service decentralisation in Islington on a neighbourhood basis introduced organisational change from outside. Other changes included moves from generic to specialist social work teams, altered geographical responsibilities (moving from divisional to neighbourhood or 'patch' systems), redefined client group responsibilities, and budgetary reform. In contrast, health authority organisation – itself less variable – had less influence. However, we have already noted that management reorganisation in the NHS coincided with the programme and affected a number of projects. Even where general management in the health service did not import problems of liaison and coordination between organisations, it affected lines of accountability in health authority-led projects, influencing the degree of professional and managerial autonomy in services.

Some projects remained separate or indeed marginalised, but most were incorporated into mainstream organisational structures in key respects. Integration and autonomy have their respective problems. Devolved responsibility for decision-making is an important part of the changes to community care delivery introduced by the 1990 Act, and certainly the majority view across the pilot projects was that greater autonomy in decision-making, policy formulation and budgetary control proved to be helpful. Yet before the 1990 announcement of change, few social services departments had made much progress in this direction; as the Audit Commission observed in 1989, barely 3 per cent of local authorities had achieved much decentralisation of management and budgeting control. Within the demonstration programme, most budgets were devolved at least to the service management level, and sometimes further (see Chapter 10), generating considerable (relative) autonomy.

When asked about their arrangements for delegation of responsibilities towards the end of the period of central funding, a number of projects regretted not going, or being allowed to go, further. For example:

- the Bolton project would have delegated more authority for decision-making at an earlier stage;
- Somerset would have welcomed greater financial autonomy so as to encourage flexibility and experimentation;
- Winchester would have preferred greater project involvement in the initial selection of clients;
- Hillingdon recognised certain benefits were to be gained from greater autonomy (although the project would have needed a full-time manager in the team);
- insufficient autonomy was recognised in West Cumbria, and plans were afoot to delegate more responsibility in the future; and
- staff in the Cambridge project had enjoyed a relatively high level of autonomy, with benefits for clients, and started to negotiate independent status using an independent agency-service brokerage model.

The preference for more autonomy was not universal, for some of the projects encountered the difficulties that can arise when autonomy is not backed up by access to information (on service availability, utilisation, budgets, costs and the like), clear policy guidance, or effective line-management support. The Camden project would have preferred more effective financial management, the Derby project view was that better top-down management would have avoided some of the uncertainties experienced, and in Islington the absence of policy guidelines forced the project to develop a coordination team to deal with liaison. Staff in the Maidstone project wanted the health authority to pass them more information. Because of projects' small-scale, quasi-independent funding and locally innovative modes of working, information was usually outside their direct sphere of influence. Good line management *support*, rather than *direction*, was seen as the answer in some cases; another was to involve influential individuals on steering groups, balancing central (or outside) control with service independence; and a third was to ensure that the project manager or coordinator established direct links with service managers. Service agreements, annual targets and performance indicators also helped tie projects to host agencies and to improve operational clarity.

The contributions of the voluntary sector

The 1981 Care in the Community consultative document referred to the value of a multiplicity of provision, and the 1983 Circular explicitly encouraged a mixed economy (DHSS, 1981a, 1983).

> If the fullest benefits of transferring patients from hospital to community care are to be realised, voluntary resources will have to be engaged at all levels, both when arrangements are being made for transfers and in the long-term provision of supporting services (DHSS, 1983, para. 14).

The linked imperative of good liaison was also recognised. In Chapters 2 and 3 we discussed the demonstration programme in its mixed economy context, noting that it encouraged not only joint working between health and social services authorities, but also between the statutory and non-statutory sectors. Among the voluntary organisations heavily involved in management and/or provision were Mind in Waltham Forest, Mencap in Warwickshire, the Parkview Society in Torbay, and Age Concern in Camberwell. Private (for-profit) sector care provision was limited to placements in residential homes, almost exclusively in the Maidstone and Kidderminster projects, although privately-rented accommodation and home care placements were more widely used.

As was hoped would be the case, and as will necessarily increasingly become the nationwide reality, the programme demonstrated how care and support can be provided effectively from a variety of sources within a unifying enabling structure. The roles performed by the voluntary sector, set out in Table 11.2, generally linked well with those of the three main statutory agencies – health, housing and social services departments – in large part because they were planned from the outset. As social services departments are finding today (Wistow et al., 1992), involving non-statutory bodies at an early stage is crucial to their coordinating and commissioning responsibilities, but is far from easy. Projects tapping private sector provision, by contrast, found liaison and monitoring difficult. On a more subjective level, we encountered some less-than-suitable placements in the private sector, gauged in terms of material and social environments and the levels of support provided.

We would not want to give the impression that the voluntary sector was well-integrated into project planning, service organisation or operational management in each of the 28 projects. In some areas the sector was in no position to make a contribution, and in some others its potential as supplement or substitute was overlooked. For example, despite the emphasis placed on consultation with the voluntary sector, the first priority for most statutory agencies contemplating applying for programme funding was to submit plans to meet the short application deadline, and this usually meant delaying formal consultation with the voluntary sector until after funds had been secured. A common criticism of the pilot programme from the voluntary sector was lack of consultation at this planning stage. Although strong inter-sectoral links were often established at a later stage, success was almost a lottery, dependent mainly on the voluntary sector's access to information, its energies and its contacts. This is a lesson which local authorities are likely to learn as they begin to plan services across the mixed economy in readiness for agreement of their community care plans in April 1992. With existing joint planning machinery, it will be no easy task constructing workable and agreed plans, involving district health authorities, family health services authorities, housing departments, housing associations, other voluntary organisations, consumer groups and private sector suppliers, as the projects discovered.

Collaboration and partnership between the statutory and voluntary sectors within the programme often led to the latter sharing responsibility for service management, although Table 11.2 shows that six projects with voluntary sector inputs had no representation at the planning or management levels. The most common form of involvement was housing or residential provision: eighteen projects worked with housing associations, ten under management agreements, and twelve projects worked exclusively with the voluntary sector for residential provision. The Maidstone project established its own housing association in response to a local need for flexible housing resources. In some situations it was clearly considered necessary not just to stimulate the mixed economy but to create it.

Few projects developed links with voluntary-led advocacy schemes, but the increasing importance attached to organised citizen- and self-advocacy outside case management developed midway through the demonstration programme. Such links will be important for social services departments seeking to implement the consultation and consumerism recommendations of the 1990 Act. While common use was made of volunteers across the programme as a whole, in four projects this was the *only* input from the voluntary sector. Volunteers were mainly used as befrienders, helping with leisure activities or escorting. Direct care or support from volunteers was generally felt to be inappropriate, and can be a difficult resource to manage.

Housing associations

Housing associations were centrally involved in most of the projects. A scarcity of suitable public sector housing or affordable private sector accommodation for purchase or rent made housing the most difficult resource for projects to secure. Good quality housing, linked to appropriate staffing, is fundamental to successful community care, and the character of the housing facilities obtained will constrain the pursuit of normalisation and ordinary life principles.

Table 11.2

Involvement of the voluntary sector – a simplified representation as at mid-1988

	Managed	Staffed	Represented on		Housing	Advocacy service	Day care provision	Employment opportunities	Leisure activities	Volunteers	Transport	Other services
			Planning body	Management group								
BOLTON			Through CHC representative		25% in housing association accommodation			Services of Mencap Pathway employment officer	Volunteers helping with normal use of community activities	Volunteers		
BRENT			Housing associations, Black Mental Health Project	Yes	Provided by Carr Gomm, Mental After-Care Association and others						Brent Community Transport	Secondhand furniture store and workshop facilities
BUCKS			Yes		Guidepost Trust bedsit development		Social/recreation day/placement opportunities		Friendship circles/TocH			
CALDERDALE			Yes	Yes					Clubs and centres	Volunteer bureau finding befrienders		
CAMBERWELL	Age Concern											
CAMBS			Yes							Befrienders		

	Managed	Staffed	Represented on		Housing	Advocacy service	Day care provision	Employment opportunities	Leisure activities	Volunteers	Transport	Other services
			Planning body	Management group								
CAMDEN	Managed by CSMH	Linc/ CSMH	Yes	Yes	Some provided with housing & support service of CSMH	Yes						
CHICHESTER				Local management committee	Housing developed by Stonham HA		Link (Mind Club) volunteers in activity centre			Trying to mobilise friends of activity centre		
COVENTRY										Befrienders SSD voluntary organiser	Escorts	Tuck shop trolley
DARLINGTON				Re-roof	5% of housing provided by HAs		Lunch club		Outings, Xmas shopping, church activites	Paid volunteers, MSC task force decorating, etc.	Escorts	Laundry service, specific servicers for individuals, meals-on-wheels
DERBY			Mencap Homes Foundation HA	Mencap	Over 50% provided by HA and Mencap Homes Foundation					Volunteers help in clubs and befriend clients	Volunteers escort people to pubs	

Table 11.2 (continued)

	Managed	Staffed	Represented on		Housing	Advocacy service	Day care provision	Employment opportunities	Leisure activities	Volunteers	Transport	Other services
			Planning body	Management group								
GLOSSOP					Managed by N. counties HA				1 client pursuing hobby with vol. group		Provided by volunteer bureau	
GREENWICH				Mind, National Schizo phrenia Fellowship	Maintained by Hyde, and London & Quadrant HAs		Mind day care centre available			Mind befriending scheme available		
HILLINGDON												
ISLINGTON							The Peter Bedford Trust		Use of local facilities, including the church	Propose to recruit volunteers	Will be using Bridge-in and Link	
KIDDER-MINSTER					Partnership arrangements with Mencap, Mind	Hereford & Worcester Citizen Advocacy Scheme	Mencap, Where Next					
LIVERPOOL	Managed by Mencap	Staffed by Mencap	Yes	Yes	Liverpool Housing Trust							
MAIDSTONE					Managed by HA	Self-advocacy group		To be developed		Volunteers		
SOMERSET			Yes	Yes	Mencap	Advocacy group, belongs to People First	Through church, FE, work experience		Single volunteers, use of FE courses	Volunteers	Yeovil CS, local small buses, volunteers	

	Managed	Staffed	Represented on		Housing	Advocacy service	Day care provision	Employment opportunities	Leisure activities	Volunteers	Transport	Other services
			Planning body	Management group								
ST HELENS										Volunteers		
TORBAY	Managed and staff employed by Parkview Society				Devon & Cornwall HA				Gateway club, theatre workwhop	Yes		
WALTHAM FOREST	Managed and staffed by Waltham Forest Mind – a company limited by guarantee				E. London HA: Mind managed		Mind facility and cafe	Limited	Mind facility	Proposed to recruit volunteers	Volunteers as required	Use generic services as required
WARRINGTON	Managed and staffed by Warrington Commonity Care – a consortium				Grosvenor HA		Yes		Yes			
WARWICK	Mencap	Mencap	Yes	Yes	Core & cluster – managed by Mencap		Mencap	Pathway scheme	Normal use of community facilities		Volunteer driver	
WEST BERSHIRE			Yes	Yes	1 client in Guidepost Trust Hotel		Maidenhead Association for Mental Health					
WEST CUMBRIA						Yes, 1 resident			Tea dances and other local facilities	Relatives		Fundraising
WEST LANCASHIRE			Yes, Richmond Fellowship	Yes, NW Fellowship, advocacy by families	Richmond Fellowship hostel		Skelmersdale day centre			Befriending in cooperation with W. Lancs Volunteer Bureau	W. Lances Volunteer Bureau	Decorating: WLVB & Task Force. Relatives/carers support group
WINCHESTER		Hants HA manages staff	Hampshire HA	Hampshire HA	Andover scheme: Hants Vol. HA		Exercise and craft sessions		Brownies, Red Cross Library & outings		Volunteer drivers, relatives and friends	Meals-on-wheels

In this context, housing associations offered a feasible and affordable means to meet the housing needs of clients.

In response to the Care in the Community initiative of the early 1980s, the Housing Corporation issued Circular 6/84 to all registered housing associations to give additional guidance to those interested in providing or managing facilities for long-stay hospital residents moving to the community. Three types of scheme were identified in relation to capital funding:

> The Corporation will continue to provide capital finance for schemes for elderly, mentally ill and mentally handicapped people, which may include people returning to the community. ... Health authorities may fund up to 100 per cent of the capital cost of a housing scheme. They can fund housing associations directly, and under these circumstances, the Corporation will have no involvement. ... In principle, schemes under the Care in the Community Initiative may be funded using a mixture of Corporation and health authority finance (Housing Corporation, 1984, para. 3.1).

Housing association involvement in the programme included all such arrangements. It also illustrated the potential financial and managerial complexities which can result and which certainly require clarification through joint working and community care planning procedures. Voluntary housing input was actively sought by projects, not simply because it offered additional financing, but because it improved the chances of securing flexible needs-led services which were almost immediately available. In fact, 18 projects worked jointly with housing associations, in some cases relying on them as sole providers (including the hostel in Warrington, the supported flats in Glossop, the core and cluster houses in Chichester, the staffed group homes in Liverpool, and the residential accommodation in Torbay). Eight projects illustrate the complexities of the arrangements put in place.

The *Cambridge* project was designed to provide support for three adolescents with multiple disabilities who moved from Ida Darwin Hospital. A house was rented from Cambridge City Council housing department by Cambridgeshire County Council social services department, and managed by King Street Housing Association. The social services department managed the staff. Capital funding of £10,000 from the demonstration programme covered the set-up costs of furniture and special equipment.

The project for people with mental health problems in *Chichester* worked in partnership with Stonham Housing Association to develop community-based housing in Bognor Regis. Although not clearly specified at the outset, by 1986 management responsibility for the accommodation was firmly written into the project design:

> The core and cluster houses will be managed by Stonham Housing Association. ... In order to manage the houses on a day-to-day basis a local management committee will be established which will become a local branch of Stonham Housing Association.

It was envisaged that committee members would be drawn both from senior staff at Graylingwell Hospital and lay members of the community. The health authority was responsible for purchase, with capital and upgrading costs met from project funds. This was a cooperative venture, with Stonham Housing Association owning and managing the houses and employing a 'housekeeper', and peripatetic rehabilitation nursing input provided by the health authority.

The *Glossop* scheme was developed in April 1985 after discussions with a physically disabled man living in Withington Hospital. By May 1987 three people had moved to community accommodation (four self-contained purpose-built flats, one for staff) designed by the Northern Counties Housing Association in conjunction with the local housing department, who owned the land and property. The housing association took over management responsibility, with ongoing maintenance costs met from social security allowances, and worked closely with residents to tailor accommodation to their needs.

The accommodation in *Liverpool* comprised three ordinary houses, each occupied by four people with learning difficulties who had moved from Olive Mount Hospital. Care and support was available 24 hours a day. Two of the houses opened in August 1984 and the third in May 1985, having been purchased by Liverpool Housing Trust using Housing Corporation loan facilities. The Trust converted the houses with maintenance met from rent and service charges from DSS and housing benefits to individual residents. The project aimed to show that housing associations could usefully work in conjunction with statutory agencies to provide ordinary housing for people with a learning difficulty. There was no major capital outlay from central funds (apart from £6,000 for furniture). The project was a collaborative effort involving a housing association (Liverpool Housing Trust), a voluntary body (Liverpool Mencap), Liverpool Health Authority and Liverpool social services department. Mencap and Liverpool Housing Trust assumed leadership of the project in April 1987, when central funding finished. Formally, the project was managed by a joint general management group incorporating representatives from the four agencies, although each organisation remained responsible for employing its own staff. Part of the *Warwickshire* project used a similar approach: Mencap running a hostel in Rugby which was built as a new facility alongside an existing hostel, and other local Mencap groups developing and managing units across the county, using capital allocated from central funds. The Nuneaton hostel was purchased from central funds with the Coventry Churches Housing Association responsible for administration, adaptation and renovation.

The *Torbay* project, funded from April 1984 to March 1987, was designed to provide flexible, family-type living within a caring environment where residents with learning difficulties could develop according to their individual abilities. A ten-place residential home was opened in Newton Abbot in June 1985, managed by the Parkview Society. (The Society already managed a successful group home for mentally ill people.) The property was purchased for £110,000, 90 per cent of which came from the demonstration programme grant. A top-up grant of £25,000 from the health authority financed the necessary renovation. Revenue costs were met from residents' social security benefits.

The staffed hostel in *Warrington,* which was converted from a nurses' home, offered 24-hour cover for 16 people from Winwick Psychiatric Hospital. Ownership was transferred to the Grosvenor Housing Association and management to Warrington Community Care, a consortium and company limited by guarantee. The hostel opened in November 1985. Central funding provided the initial capital with revenue from residents' board and lodging allowances. The *Registered Homes Act 1984* had a marked effect on the development and management of the scheme; after discussions between Warrington Community Care and the registration officer, changes were made, including the installation of a warden call system. Conditions of registration included flame-retardant furniture and dietary record sheets. The pilot project became a catalyst for subsequent service developments funded by the health authority and managed by Grosvenor Housing Association.

Places in the two specialised sheltered housing schemes used by the *Winchester* project were provided by Winchester City Council and the Hampshire Voluntary Housing Society in Andover. Both housing units originally allocated five places to clients. The Andover element was separately managed by a multi-agency steering group convened by the Housing Society. While the scheme as a whole was designed to extend norms of provision and test the viability of supporting very dependent elderly people (with dependency levels normally associated with long-stay geriatric admission wards), it also provided opportunities to test new cooperative management arrangements.

Housing management arrangements varied from those tightly steered by a small group in a housing association to those based on committees of users, professional workers and individuals from different agencies (councillors and community representatives, as well as from the housing association itself).

Local experience and successful ventures obviously influenced plans: for example, the impetus for the Torbay project came from the Parkview Society's success with a hostel for people with mental health problems, and the Stonham Housing Association's specialised experience in working jointly with public service agencies contributed significantly to the Chichester project. There are clear advantages in building community services on local experience. Some housing associations are particularly geared to providing special needs housing, and are perhaps skilled at obtaining the necessary capital financing. As one interviewee remarked:

> To make special needs housing work you need to be an expert in your field. It is a political area and you must be hard-nosed about it. You have to be in the driving seat. Care in the community used to be flavour of the month and there was plenty of money around, but this is no longer the case. It is impossible to plan ahead but we have managed by 'fixing' deals with the Housing Corporation and the health authority so that both promise to contribute half the money each to schemes.

As we saw in Chapter 7, securing funds for capital development proved problematic for many projects. Anticipated reliance on housing associations to secure capital funds from the Housing Corporation not always justified. For example, the original plan for the West Lancs project was to use vacant public housing stock in Skelmersdale. When this proved inappropriate, local housing associations were approached to apply for Housing Corporation finance. But this funding was restricted to localities with 'stressed area' status, and the Ormskirk area was ineligible. With additional and diverted funds, the project was eventually able to finance a hostel in conjunction with the Richmond Fellowship. These difficulties can be contrasted with Chichester's experience, where a capital component in the original application for Care in the Community funding allowed housing to be purchased and ownership transferred to the Stonham Housing Association. Liverpool and Torbay also bought properties outright from central funds, with management then passing to housing associations. Some projects were fortunate (or far-sighted) in securing ad hoc housing resources, for example where a health authority donated a property.

Further development and service integration

The pilot projects helped many people move from hospital to the community, and the chapters of Part III will describe how these moves were often successfully accomplished. We will consider the generalisability of these findings in the final chapter, but it is pertinent at this stage to examine the local positions of the projects. Following the end of the central funding period, were the projects isolated within their locales or were they integrated successfully within 'mainstream' provision and decision-making?

One of the conditions of participation in the programme was that the agencies involved would meet the continuing resource requirements of projects after central funding ceased. Once this had been assured – and not every project was supported to the degree expected after three years – the primary concern to projects was service integration. Would they be able to maintain their organisational and other characteristics? Mechanisms established for coordinating services usually became redundant after the period of central funding, having been developed to steer projects through a complex start-up phase. However, modified arrangements were retained to assist in monitoring (as in Calderdale and Darlington, for example), managing and targeting placements (Bucks), developing rolling programmes (Greenwich), or coordinating services in projects which were semi-independent of the public sector (Waltham Forest). Among the projects which found existing arrangements to be satisfactory and planned no change were Islington, Torbay, Warwick, Chichester, Warrington, West Lancashire, Camberwell, St Helens, Cambridge and Glossop. Some projects lost their (comparative) autonomy in decision-making at the end of the programme, coming under broader management umbrellas. New line managers or tighter financial or administrative systems took over, not always preserving good elements from the pilot programme period.

For most projects it was intended that health authorities would take over responsibility for funding. The second most frequent intention was a form of joint funding between health and social services, perhaps managed via the joint consultative committee (as in Camden and Brent), or by various tapering arrangements (as in Darlington, where the aim was to use health service savings after seven years of joint funding, or in West Lancashire, where financial control ceded to social services after a similar period). A minority of projects always intended to be self-supporting. In Torbay, Care in the Community programme funding was only used for capital investment, and – as in many projects – social security benefits were used to meet revenue costs (see Chapter 7).

Most projects also planned further change, including new facilities, different staffing patterns and shifts in the balance of services on offer. Bolton sought to include provision for sheltered housing, and Camden to increase choice, opportunities and specialised services. Maidstone aimed to investigate the role for contract employment groups, and Somerset the role for the voluntary sector. Warrington planned a second hostel, and Cambridge planned joint training. Staff deployment changes were planned by Camberwell, Darlington and Winchester.

Although most projects felt their service model had been successful, there were caveats. Bolton sought more integration with mainstream services, Camden the further deprofessionalisation of services, Islington wanted to develop more flexible housing, and Kidderminster wanted services for more dependent clients. Brent and Torbay recognised the need for an increased range of accommodation, with services responding to an ageing clientele with changing support needs. Projects serving each of the client groups recognised the need for strategic readjustment of resources and their deployment as a consequence of their under-estimation of client needs in the community.

As regards the wider question of service integration, we observed four types of experience.

For a small core of projects, including Somerset, Bucks and Warwick, integration into the mainstream of provision was effectively guaranteed, each project being part of a strategic service reorientation. The two core and cluster developments in *Somerset* were part of a county-wide strategy for ten such networks which would allow the closure of the three Somerset mental handicap hospitals and the discharge of over 400 patients. The social services department was also exploring ways to integrate these services with those used by clients already living in the community, estimated to number more than 600. Day care was developed alongside community units, and although priority places were reserved for clients moving out of hospital, partial integration was achieved, with fuller integration intended in the longer term. Community mental handicap teams and a new community care management structure were also developed. One aim of the latter was to promote functional integration between the two groups of users, with more equitable service access and receipt. In the short term, competition for resources was dominated by the priorities of hospital closure, but later the services established by the project were fully integrated into the broader plan. Joint staff training activities, common assessment, individual programme planning and regular monitoring and review helped in the process of integration.

The *Bucks* project, also part of a wider policy change, depended on using existing or newly-built social services hostels which also provided accommodation for non-project clients. The *Maidstone* project proved to be a useful testing ground, and was later absorbed into Kent County Council's decentralised care management structure.

Projects like *Cambridge* were in the second group. The project established one of a number of small group homes in the area. This facility was managed by the social services department, while the others were run by the health authority. Although fitting into the broader service development, the project was and remains distinctive in management and practice. As one of the original aims of the Cambridge project was to demonstrate an operational alternative to small-scale health authority provision using a residential social work (originally a professional fostering) rather than a nursing model, this distinctiveness was clearly the *sine qua non* of operational success (not to be confused with client success). After discussion of the *Caring for People* White Paper, the staff group decided to negotiate control of their complete budget, with the extension of the service to support four people already living in the community. The additional users would benefit from the skills and experience of the team, but needed appropriate accommodation or support. In a report to the social services department, the team recommended an independent support service. Using a brokerage model, the service would be managed as a not-for-profit organisation – 'Cambridge Support Service' – which could also be commissioned to provide objective assessments for the social services department.

A third group comprised those projects which were seen from the outset as the first stage of a rolling programme of community care, established without local parallels, even though the resources for the longer term may not have been committed. Replication was therefore expected, provided that the project was judged a success (on such local criteria as cost-effectiveness, and the effectiveness of case management or multidisciplinary working). Successful service development in Bolton encouraged the local authority to adopt the model for all residential provision for learning difficulty and mental health services. The aim of the *Greenwich* project was to help 16 people move from Bexley Hospital into ordinary housing with staff support. The project application noted that:

At the end of the three-year period the team will continue to support residents already settled in the community and, if possible, assist more people to leave Bexley Heath Hospital and settle into local communities ... [and] at the end of the three year period Greenwich Health Authority will transfer a negotiated sum per place to enable the local authority to continue running the project.

During the development of this project, health authority members considered expansion to provide a high-quality service to more patients moving from Bexley hospital. By the end of central funding, homes had been established in two localities, with additional housing planned in conjunction with local housing associations. Staffing comprised a project leader, occupational therapist, five residential social workers and three part-time domestic support workers. Experience in working with the first ten residents demonstrated the need for more round-the-clock staff support than was possible if the rolling programme was to develop according to plan. This was despite the fact that the support needs of the first group of residents decreased over time. Staff also had ongoing responsibility for working with patients in Bexley Hospital, helping to establish a much-needed rehabilitation ward to enable more Greenwich patients to gain the skills and confidence required for community living. The original concept of a short-term rehabilitation resource proved inappropriate, so a series of small residential units for three to five residents was developed. People moved straight from hospital and could stay in these units indefinitely, with a gradual reduction in staff cover over several years. The role of domestic support workers was phased out, with resources redirected towards additional residential social work input.

By late 1987 a funding crisis had developed in Greenwich. The regional health authority had indicated unofficially that the closure of Cane Hill Hospital was a priority. Consequently, funds would not be forthcoming for the pilot project. The regional health authority was lobbied by project staff and the director of social services. A special meeting was arranged with finance directors from the health and local authorities to confirm the status of the project and the conversion of temporary posts to permanent appointments. Also on the agenda were: the question of funding relative to individuals or places (the latter having implications for future allocation rights); the need for a team base; and proposals to change project management when the development phase was complete. It was felt that the original steering group was now inappropriate, as liaison was no longer necessary between such a large number of individuals and agencies, and a joint management group from health and social services was recommended.

The *Winchester* project successfully moved elderly people out of hospital into specialised sheltered housing. After central funding ceased the operational shift was aided by the project's integration with broader community services. There was already some operational integration as each client had a self-contained flat, sharing a housing complex with clients admitted from their own homes. The success of Winchester's wider community care attendant scheme, launched earlier by the health authority, provided care attendant visits for people in their own homes up to seven days a week. The scheme further aided integration, as project clients had enhanced care attendant input, providing support above that required by other residents. In April 1988 the community care attendant scheme became part of a social services extended home help service. Management and staffing became the direct responsibility of the housing department in January 1989.

Some elements of projects, such as day support or housing, were also seen as suitable for replication. Assessment and review arrangements proved particularly useful in this regard with programme experience helping many social services departments develop integrated or improved arrangements under the 1990 Act. Cambridge, for instance, has undertaken independent assessments of client needs and costed appropriate service packages for the social services department. Other lessons concerned advocacy and consumer participation, with the Brent, Maidstone, Somerset and Kidderminster projects making significant contributions. In Camden, individual programme planning systems were adopted elsewhere and a contract was agreed with a second health authority to set up resettlement services.

The final group of projects found themselves comparatively isolated. A small number of projects were managerially marginalised from the start, leaving them in 'organisational limbo'. Developing non-traditional services did not necessarily lead to isolation, as Camden and Greenwich illustrated, but 'maverick' projects were at a distinct disadvantage if seeking to join mainstream service provision. A different form of separation was selected by the *Glossop* project, which always intended to remain largely independent. *Torbay* and *Waltham Forest* were rather different voluntary sector projects which both planned separation from the outset. Both established financial and operational independence within their local policy contexts, one using conventional social security channels, the other using the regional health authority's psychiatric reprovision programme. Unplanned separation – in the extreme, disintegration – arose where one or more agency took the view that their long-term funding obligations had been misinterpreted by others. In the *Kidderminster* project, managerial and professional support folded. Despite meeting resettlement targets and being well regarded by the social services department, the project effectively disappeared because of the regional health authority's funding policy.

Overall, the evidence is that the programme of pilot projects was highly influential in demonstrating the feasibility of new service models within their local systems.

Part III: Outcomes and costs

12 Evaluating outcomes and costs

Does community care improve the well-being of project clients? At what cost? These disarmingly simple questions were at the core of the evaluation, and in Part III of the book we examine the outcomes and costs of the demonstration programme. This chapter introduces the outcome and cost methodologies, and considers some of the commonly-feared failings of community care policies.

Outcomes of Care in the Community

We suggested in Chapter 2 that the absence of any coherent community care policy throughout the post-war period encouraged the media, politicians and even researchers to concentrate their attention on the failures of hospital-based care. It was not surprising, therefore, that there was a parallel focus to the informal evaluation of community care in the early 1980s, with more energy devoted to what was *wrong* with community care than on what it could achieve. It was important that the evaluation of the Care in the Community programme selected a less reactive, less negative line.

The pursuit of normalisation was an objective set by many projects and now pervades national policy, although on its own it is an inadequate template for an evaluation. Normalisation is a *process* objective which correctly emphasises the rights and views of individual people with learning difficulties, mental health problems or other long-term needs. But normalisation is not the only concern of clients, nor of policy-makers, service practitioners or the general public. Moreover, in assessing whether normalisation is successful or sensible, and in considering which variant of normalisation works best and in what circumstances, an evaluation must look at client quality of life, client characteristics and client views. The acquisition or rediscovery of skills, for example, is the route to greater independence and self-determination; it can extend the range of choice and aid social integration. Moreover, an evaluation should ask clients for their views about their living environments, economic situation, social relationships and general life-styles.

In so far as there is a consensus, most people agree that community care should pursue a variety of objectives, such as meeting the material needs for shelter, security, warmth and nourishment, providing occupation or engagement in activity, facilitating social contacts, training for skills in daily living, and creating the opportunity for clients to exercise choice and control over their lives. Community care should not leave former hospital residents vulnerable to exploitation, destitution or delinquency. It should not place an unfair burden on relatives or neighbours. Generally, it should allow people to achieve their full potential and enjoy a satisfactory quality of life. Our evaluation was designed to cover these material and psychological facets of life in the community.

The outcome dimensions for the study covered:

- type of accommodation provided;
- integration and opportunities;
- choice and empowerment;
- skills;
- symptoms and behaviour problems;
- social contacts;
- activities and engagement;
- morale and life satisfaction; and
- personal presentation.

Each aspect of client quality of life and need was assessed both in hospital and after approximately nine months in the community. The different facets of outcome are interlinked, and the instruments we employed overlapped. Some dimensions are more relevant for some client groups than others, as we describe in Chapters 13 to 15. Some have already been considered in earlier chapters, such as the types of accommodation to which clients moved and their achievement of the normalisation and similar objectives set by projects and pervading national policy (Chapter 8). We have also already examined client choice and empowerment, and their integration into 'mainstream' community services and activities.

In selecting these outcome dimensions we were influenced by national and local community care objectives and previous research, and in the chapters which follow we compare and contrast our findings with these policy intentions and previous findings. The root principles of our evaluation methodology and measurement of outcomes were described in Chapter 4, and the research instruments in Chapter 5.

The failings of community care

The care objectives behind our choice of outcome dimensions are ambitious. To date, many hospital rundown programmes and community care plans, both in the UK and elsewhere, have failed famously to achieve some or indeed any of them. This has left many people distinctly uneasy about the efficacy of today's emphasis on Care in the Community and the concomitant rundown of hospitals. A number of community care *failings* have been posited, and each has attracted a huge amount of sometimes vitriolic but usually well-meaning criticism from the media and from 'community care sceptics'. Did these same failings characterise the demonstration programme?

One of the most common criticisms of hospital closure plans is a variation on the 'cycle of custody' theme. People leave hospital after many years of what may be seen as 'custodial care' to lead lives which, it is argued, are marginalised and dogged by economic and social impoverishment. In turn this leads to destitution, homelessness, minor or even major criminal acts, a recurrence of mental health symptoms or problem behaviour, and eventually a return to 'custodial care' in a hospital ward (the classic 'revolving door' status) or prison. Other people, so the argument runs, leave hospital for a residential or nursing home or other board and lodging setting, probably in the private sector, where the accommodation is barely acceptable, the staff are inexperienced and unqualified, and social security funding traps the resident in that facility. 'Custodial care' is again the result. The luckier ones move from hospital to live with relatives who, without adequate support, carry a stressful and uncompensated burden. When relatives die or can no longer cope, the former hospital resident returns to some form of 'custodial care'. 'The mentally ill', it has been claimed, 'have long wandered the streets, rotating between destitution, psychiatric hospital and prison' (Weller, 1990, p.469).

This concern is not new.

> To scatter the mentally ill in the community before we have made adequate provision for them is not a solution; in the long run not even for HM Treasury. Considered only in financial terms, any savings from fewer hospital in-patients might well be offset several times by more expenditure on the police forces, on prisons and probation officers, more unemployment benefit masquerading as sickness benefit, more expenditure on drugs, more research to find out why crime is increasing. At present we are drifting into a situation in which, by shifting the emphasis from the institution to the community – a trend which, in principle and with qualifications, we all applaud – we are transferring the care of the mentally ill from trained staff to ill-equipped staff or no staff at all (Titmuss, 1963; see also Jones et al., 1975).

The most commonly voiced fears about community care therefore concern:

- the 'dumping' of former hospital residents to 'drift' without support in the community;
- unemployment and poverty;
- destitution and homelessness;
- crime and imprisonment;
- an unacceptable burdens for relatives, neighbours and communities;
- mortality; and
- readmission to hospital.

Dumping and drifting. It is often claimed that dehospitalisation policies 'dump' people in communities without informing relatives, GPs, social services or voluntary care agencies, and without adequate health service support. The fear is that former in-patients will be inadequately prepared for their return to the community, and that little or no attempt will be made to integrate them into service systems, employment or social networks. The National

Schizophrenia Fellowship told the Select Committee on Social Services that most people with chronic schizophrenia 'are returned to their "families" if any. The rest are on park benches, in prisons, doss houses or seedy and rapacious lodgings'. Evidence to the Committee from the Society of Clinical Psychiatrists complained of policies 'turning the mentally ill and unrecovered out onto the streets, boarding houses, lodging houses, gutters and prisons' (House of Commons Social Services Committee, 1985, para. 44).

These are real and serious problems for community care, but they did *not* emerge in the demonstration programme. Most clients moved to carefully prepared community placements, with keyworkers or case managers to help them gain access to appropriate community resources. There were few accommodation changes, in contrast to experience elsewhere (Caton and Goldstein, 1984; Korman and Glennerster, 1990; Andrews et al., 1990; Allen et al., 1991). There were certainly challenges – for example, we reported in Chapter 8 the difficulties of obtaining the services of GPs and some therapists, the widespread unavailability of open education facilities, and the restrictive regimes in one or two placements – but there was no 'drifting' or loss of contact, and residential placements were not, on the whole, applying institutional practices. The demonstration programme was not guilty of a rapid over-commitment to community care before the necessary reprovision resources were in place. It did not scatter former hospital residents hither and thither to fend for themselves. It was not guilty of 'transinstitutionalisation'.

Unemployment and poverty. As well as being a source of income, employment confers many benefits, including status, identity, economic freedom, a structured day, a source of activity, and opportunities to develop friendships and acquire skills (King's Fund Centre, 1984; Fagin and Little, 1984; Porterfield, 1988). The discussion in Chapter 7 reported how few programme clients were able to secure open employment after leaving hospital, and the only source of income for most was social security payments. Many of the pilot projects sought work opportunities for clients, but faced two main obstacles. First, securing employment for someone who is relatively unskilled and has spent the last ten or 20 years in hospital is hard at the best of times; in a period of high unemployment it proved virtually impossible. General unemployment levels should be no excuse for inaction, for few employers meet the required 3 per cent quota of registered disabled people (Wertheimer, 1987), but there was a second obstacle. The loss of social security benefits when employment is found will often be greater than the net wage earned by unskilled and inexperienced former hospital residents. Neither clients nor projects could afford this.

When clients found sheltered employment (in adult training centres, social education centres, or hospital occupational or industrial therapy units), this was often boring, repetitive and possibly meaningless work. This was not peculiar either to the demonstration programme or to hospital rundown policies in general, for people with mental health problems or learning difficulties almost always face difficulties in securing competitive employment (Ford et al., 1987). Contrasting with this general tendency were efforts by a few projects to create employment opportunities with their own resources. LinC in Camden and Mind in Waltham Forest opened cafés, and some Calderdale clients worked at a salad products cooperative which had a contract with the local authority to develop 25 jobs for people with special needs alongside 25 other staff (Brandon, 1988). These efforts are closer than conventional 'stepping stone' approaches through sheltered employment schemes to the goal of supporting people in 'real jobs' (King's Fund Centre, 1984; National Development Team, 1990; House of Commons Social Services Committee, 1990, paras 132-136).

Destitution and homelessness. Although rarely in employment and with little disposable income, Care in the Community clients did not face destitution, although like most people dependent on welfare benefits they faced economic marginalisation. However, no client became homeless during the period of our research (or since, as far as we know). By contrast, destitution and homelessness appeared to follow the rapid dehospitalisation programmes in the USA (Bassuk et al., 1984; Fischer and Breakey, 1986; McCausland, 1987) and parts of Italy. In the UK, voluntary agencies have reported a high proportion of homeless people using shelters or associated services who have come from psychiatric hospitals (Gibbons, 1988; Timms and Fry, 1989). Reception centres and the 'Crisis at Christmas' provision have also encountered large numbers of former hospital residents, though not necessary former *long-stay* residents (Tidmarsh and Wood, 1972; Weller et al., 1987; Shanks, 1989).

The more encouraging results reported here stem from three features of the demonstration programme: the management of community care at the project level, management at the case level, and the committed funding of services. All three features are reproducible outside a demonstration programme, indeed all three are central planks of the community care reforms currently being laid in place across the country (Cm 849, 1989). As an American Psychiatric Association Task Force concluded for the USA, homelessness is not a *necessary* corollary of dehospitalisation; it is avoidable (Lamb and Talbott, 1986; Thornicroft and Bebbington, 1989; Tannahill et al., 1990).

Crime and imprisonment. In its first major report on community care, the Audit Commission (1986) warned that the US experience of former long-stay hospital residents being imprisoned in large numbers could be repeated in Britain. In suggesting a causal connection between hospitals running down and prisons filling up, the Commission thus joined the British Medical Association, the House of Commons Social Services Committee, and some psychiatrists in pointing to another failing of community care. But does the evidence exist? Weller and Weller (1986, 1988) presented correlations which they interpreted as proving such an association, but their findings have been criticised as methodologically unsound (Altman, 1986; Gibbons, 1988; Heginbotham, 1988). In particular, we are not aware of evidence showing that criminality and imprisonment are more likely for former *long-stay* hospital patients now living in the community than for the general population.

It is therefore not surprising that no Care in the Community client was imprisoned (on remand or under sentence) in the first nine months after leaving hospital, and few had any police contact. The most serious criminal offence within the programme was shoplifting. Similar evaluations of community care for people with long-term mental health problems in North London and New South Wales provide confirmatory evidence (Dayson, 1990; Andrews et al., 1990).

If there *is* an association between running down hospital provision and the growing numbers of people in prison it is not due to the discharging of long-stay patients but the reluctance or inability to admit people with acute mental health problems to hospital (Orr, 1978; Coid, 1988; Allen et al., 1991), or to provide intensive support work (Stein and Test, 1980; Hoult and Reynolds, 1984).

The burden on relatives. A great deal of research has documented the size of the community care burden borne by 'informal carers', usually female relatives (for example, Grad and Sainsbury, 1968; Creer and Wing, 1974; Equal Opportunities Commission, 1981; Gibbons et al., 1984; Hudson 1985; Haley et al., 1987; Qureshi et al., 1989; Ungerson, 1990; Netten and Davies, 1991). Organisations such as the National Schizophrenia Fellowship and Rescare have criticised hospital rundown for failure to offer sufficient support and relief for relatives of former hospital residents. For better or worse, the demonstration programme did not impose an unreasonable burden on relatives, as virtually no one, with the exception of clients in the Darlington project, returned from hospital to live with relatives. Indeed many clients had lost all meaningful contact with their families many years before the move from hospital (see Chapter 5). Those projects which included the possibility of return to family residence as part of their placement planning found this option largely unrealistic.

In Darlington, the project developed more closely as an alternative to hospital care for patients living at home than had been originally envisaged as a result of a change in the availability of housing between the planning and implementation stages of the project. A change of political control of the district council led to the withdrawal of the offer of public sector housing and, at the same time, funding from the Housing Corporation to the local housing association was deferred. Consequently the finance for caring and support services was available but not the housing facilities which had been planned (Challis et al., 1989). Of the 101 project clients in Darlington, 38 were discharged to live alone and 63 were discharged to live with family, relatives or 'others', 42 of whom returned to live with a spouse (25 of the 42 were male).

For the community at large, there was some opposition to the establishment of some community care facilities, but no obvious lasting opposition (see Chapter 8).

Client deaths. It has been claimed that a 'surge in suicides has been observed shortly after discharge from mental hospital care' (Weller, 1984, p.9; and see Wilkinson, 1982, and the House of Commons Social Services Committee, 1985). However, there is *no* such evidence to link hospital discharge with suicide for *long-stay* psychiatric hospital patients (Sturt, 1983; Gibbons, 1988), or for people with learning difficulties. For elderly people, relocation is known to be associated with mortality (but not suicide), the rate being higher when people are less well prepared for a move and have less control over it (Tobin and Lieberman, 1976; Schulz and Brenner, 1977; Davies and Knapp, 1981, Chap. 6; Anthony et al., 1987).

Mortality rates were low in the demonstration programme. Six per cent of the 826 people in our evaluation sample died in the first nine months after leaving hospital (see Chapter 8, Table 8.13). Most of these people were elderly, with mortality rates of 1 per cent and zero in nine months for the mental health and learning difficulty client groups, respectively. (Over the longer period of our association with projects there was only one recorded suicide and one open verdict.) These results for the younger client groups are similar to those found by Jones et al. (1986) and Dayson (1990).

The higher mortality rates in projects for elderly people (28 per cent for elderly physically frail people and 11 per cent for elderly people with mental health problems) do not appear to diverge from experience elsewhere, and none was due to neglect. For example, Townsend et al. (1988) reported a mortality rate of 19 per cent in the first year after elderly patients left hospital (from all wards, not just geriatric or long-stay) and Haslam (1988) reported that 35 per cent of elderly confused people discharged from hospital had died (period of measurement not stated). Moreover, the high mortality rate among Darlington project clients was due in part to a specifically targeted 'terminally ill group' of 14 clients, 13 of whom died within nine months of leaving hospital. Excluding terminally ill people, comparison of death rates for the Darlington project and its control group at 12 months showed no difference (Challis et al., 1991).

Readmissions to hospital. Hospital readmission rates were relatively low in the demonstration programme (Chapter 8, Table 8.13). Overall the rate was 8 per cent in the first nine months after leaving hospital, with some variation:

- 11 per cent for people with mental health problems;
- 3 per cent for people with learning difficulties;
- 18 per cent for elderly physically frail people; and

- 5 per cent for elderly people with mental health problems.

If it is national or local policy to retain some hospital capacity for people with long-term care needs it would be perverse to interpret readmission as 'failure', particularly since most are of short duration. If hospital readmission can be avoided without detriment to health or quality of life, a reduction in utilisation is welcome, but short-stay readmission may also be a positive indication of ordinary living (Linn et al., 1977; Solomon et al., 1984; Tantum, 1985). After all, hospitals should contribute to well-being. The continuing care of most people leaving long-stay hospital residence is not 'curative', which is why most outcome studies focus on quality of life dimensions rather than symptoms and health status measures, and it is therefore inappropriate to see short-term hospital readmission, and perhaps long-term readmission, as a failing of a community care policy.

Thus, the pilot projects compared well with regard to each of these oft-voiced failings of community care and hospital rundown policies. Clients were not dumped in the community, nor did they drift without health or social care support. No one was destitute or homeless, and no one was imprisoned. There was no evidence of an intolerable or inequitable informal care burden. In most projects, no clients moved from hospital to live with families and, where they did – as in Darlington – the support of families and other informal carers can substantially reduce the burden. Mortality rates were low for people with mental health problems and learning difficulties, and no higher than expected for elderly clients. Readmissions to hospital were mostly of short duration. It is the *poor resourcing* and *poor management* of community care which produces many of the failings considered here. The comparative success of the Care in the Community programme was undoubtedly attributable in part to adequate and protected levels of funding, and the careful marshalling of resources at the case and project levels.

The cost measurement methodology

There are four general rules to observe for the proper costing of health or social care services (Knapp and Beecham, 1990a). Costs should be comprehensively measured so as to range over all relevant service components of the care 'packages' under consideration. Second, the cost variations that are inevitably revealed in any empirical exercise – variations between clients, facilities, areas of the country, and so on – should not be glossed over or relegated merely to tabular or footnoted mentions of standard deviations. Handled properly, these variations offer useful policy and practice insights. These variations immediately encourage comparisons – one service is cheaper than another, one group of clients is more costly to accommodate than another group, and so on – and we must urge caution when making these comparisons. This is the third costing rule: only like-with-like comparisons have full validity, even though insights can be retrieved from less-than-perfect comparisons. Finally, cost information should not stand in isolation from other relevant evidence, and especially information on outcomes. Sole reliance on cost findings is not acceptable, just as it is wrong to *neglect* costs in policy and practice decision-making. As Griffiths wrote,

> To talk of policy in matters of care except in the context of available resources and timescales for action owes more to theology than to the purposeful delivery of a caring service (Griffiths, 1988, para. 9).

The four costing rules should have a ring of familiarity about them, for they are no different from the basic principles of any evaluation. Costs research in its intentions and execution does not require recitation of a special creed, adoption of new assumptions, or compromising of ideologies. Like most guidelines for evaluation, cost rules are far easier to state than implement. Nevertheless, they provided the formative framework for our evaluation of the costs and cost-effectiveness of the demonstration programme.

Four cost questions were distinguished early in the life of the programme:

- What are the total and component costs of community care?
- How do community care costs compare with hospital costs?
- What is the pattern of cost variation in the costs of community care, and what accounts for it?
- Finally, is there a connection between costs and outcomes?

These are essential but demanding questions to be asked of any community care initiative, and especially relevant to a programme of 28 different pilot projects, serving a number of different client groups, and managed by an almost bewildering variety of agencies, each with their own budgeting procedures.

The results of our application of the four cost rules to the four evaluation questions will be reported in the next three chapters alongside our client outcome findings. First, however, we briefly describe the basic procedures adopted for costing individual services and care packages, the breadth of that costing, and data collection in practice. These issues are addressed more fully elsewhere (Knapp, 1984; Netten and Beecham, 1992).

Costing principles

The cost figure quoted by a care agency is either total cost (aggregate spending on a service, usually over one financial year) or average cost (this aggregate divided by some measure of workload, such as the number of clients seen or the number of in-patient bed days). These are accounting costs based on reported, audited expenditures, and they do not necessarily give us all the information needed for evaluating health or social care programmes.

Economic theory advocates using *long-run marginal opportunity cost*. What does this mean in practice? By *opportunity cost* we mean that the resource implications should reflect opportunities forgone rather than amounts spent. The opportunity cost measures the true private or social value of a resource or service, based upon its value in its best alternative use. In a perfectly informed and frictionless market economy, this 'best alternative use value' would be identical to the price paid in the market. Not everything is marketed, not every market works smoothly, and information is rarely complete, with the result that observed prices and opportunity costs diverge. Thus the recorded depreciation payments on capital equipment or buildings do not usually reflect the opportunity costs of using these durable resources, nor do the (zero) payments to volunteers and informal carers usually indicate their social value. By *marginal* we mean the addition to total cost attributable to the inclusion of one more client (the production of one more unit of output in general economic parlance). By *long-run* we mean to move beyond the small-scale and immediate development of community care which could probably be achieved by using present services more intensively at very low marginal cost, and to examine the costs of creating new services. Since national policy intentions are to substitute community services for most long-term hospital places, it would hardly be credible to measure only short-run cost implications.

In application of these principles, it happens that today's (short-run) average revenue cost, plus appropriate capital and overhead elements, is close to the long-run marginal cost (LRMC) for most services we encounter. In making this assumption we are following precedent (see, for example, Jones et al., 1980; Mangen et al., 1983; Knapp, 1984; Davies and Challis, 1986; Wright, 1987).

Comprehensive cost measures

Most community care clients use more than one care or support service, often from more than one public or independent agency. A resident of a local authority hostel, for example, may have regular visits from a community psychiatric nurse (CPN), may go to a voluntary sector day centre, may have occasional hospital out-patient appointments with a psychiatrist, and may receive benefit payments from the Department of Social Security. Any evaluation of local authority hostels, CPNs, voluntary sector day care, hospital psychiatry or social security support programmes which seeks to address the resource dimension should, in principle, include every one of these service inputs. Certainly, any evaluation of community care which chose to ignore one or more cost component would need convincing justification. The planning of community care in the 1990s should be multi-agency, the voluntary and private sectors will often be involved, and the burdens of informal care need to be recognised and hopefully eased. Furthermore, the combinations of services used by any one person should not be thrown together randomly, but planned carefully and jointly by case managers, clients and others (Cm 849, 1989).

Without sight of the full costs of all care options, policy-makers cannot be sure that community care policies will take health and social care systems towards cheaper options, and – more importantly – without parallel evidence on client and other outcomes they cannot be sure of a more equitable, efficient or efficacious allocation of available resources. Even if some hidden costs are not readily expressed in monetary magnitudes there is no reason why they should not be included in an evaluative study and taken into account in the policy process. Good community care is likely to be comprehensive in addressing clients' needs and wants; good community care *costings* should comprehensively measure the resource implications of doing so.

Incanting comprehensiveness is fine, but there are practical limits to any empirical exercise. It is common, for example, to concentrate on costs in a single year, even though the need for support may continue for much longer and service decisions are usually intended to have lifespan effects. Indeed, many cost and outcome implications of community care decisions outlive the clients immediately affected by them, as with the permanent closure of a hospital or the investment in new community accommodation. In the present study, the time-scale and period for the evaluation were externally determined, and we concentrated on each client's first nine months in the community. (However, we will soon also have data on the costs and outcomes for people with learning difficulties five years after they left hospital.)

Perpendicular to the time dimension is the question of which services, activities and expenditures to include. We included and costed every identifiable service used by clients, whether funded from public or other budgets, whether provided by an agency or an individual, whether sold in the market or offered free of charge. Local property rates (as they then were) which were not paid at all or in full by voluntary and some private sector facilities were included, for the costs fall to local authorities. Capital costs were included, calculated from replacement cost estimates rather than actual depreciation payments made, plus costs for land, professional fees and transitional elements (each treated as a fixed or durable element), and spread as an annuity over 60 years at 5 per cent rate of discount. Volunteer and informal care inputs were included, the former costed as equivalent to home helps because of the task that many appeared to perform, ranging from day-to-day direct financial support and loss of earnings, to losses of leisure time and general psychological strain (Challis et al., 1991). Holidays and in-patient hospital stays for community care clients were included.

We did not include any cost for forgone earnings or associated losses in (national) productivity of people with long-term needs not in the labour force. The productivity benefits flowing from the Training in Community Living programme developed in Madison, Wisconsin, and replicated elsewhere were an important and manageable component of the evaluation of that innovative service for people with acute mental health problems (Weisbrod et al., 1980). In the UK, Ginsberg and Marks (1977) and Jones et al. (1980) are among those who have used earnings as a proxy measure for productivity. In our case, however, we considered it unnecessary to attach a cost since *no* client was in open employment. It thus made no difference for any comparative purpose what cost value we assumed. (Even when conducting 'cost of illness' studies, such as those by Fein, 1958; Davies and Drummond, 1990; or Croft-Jeffreys and Wilkinson, 1989, it is dubious practice to attach a cost to lost earnings or productivity. See Shiell et al., 1987, and Hurst, 1988.)

Another exclusion was the set of transfer payments, which are those transfers of money not made in return for goods or services. The best examples are social security benefits, which move purchasing power from taxpayers to benefit recipients. The 'cost' to one group is exactly offset, bar the administrative burden, by the gain to the other. In the aggregate costing of community care for society it would make no difference if benefit levels were doubled or halved, and there would anyway be the problem of double-counting, on the one hand the benefits received either by clients or (on their behalf) by residential facilities and, on the other, the expenditures by clients or facilities on the normal requirements of daily living. We *do*, however, need to collect information on these benefits, partly because it is a dull study which confines itself to global aggregates of efficiency and ignores the distributional consequences of community care, and partly because the funding channels between the health, social care, housing and income maintenance agencies create incentives and disincentives for particular courses of action. (It was of course the perversity of some of these incentives which prompted some of the financial and organisational reforms in the *National Health Service and Community Care Act 1990*.) As well as these distributional and efficiency reasons for an interest in social security transfer payments, there was a practical reason. In the absence of information on household expenditure, social security payments can been used as proxy measures for the 'living' expenditures of some clients, since most had no other source of income and the amounts received were not sufficient to allow savings to be accrued. (Their general validity for this task can be seen by comparing these amounts with household spending levels recorded in the annual Family Expenditure Survey, although actual benefit receipts are superior for research purposes.)

The inputs of senior management overheads of care agencies were not costed, although middle management and project-specific overheads were included. The higher-level overheads could not be estimated without a special costing exercise, and they would anyway account for a only a minute proportion of the total cost of care when set alongside the direct costs of service packages. Moreover, they would probably not be greatly different for the different types of provision covered by the programme (including hospital).

Cost data collection in practice

To describe how we moved from these principles to evaluation in practice consider again the four cost evaluation questions.

Total and component costs. Community care's rich tapestry cannot be fully appreciated, nor can community care practices be properly evaluated, without looking at the experiences of individual clients. Individualised costings were therefore imperative. Data on services used were collected in the Client Service Receipt Interview for 430 clients after nine months in the community (Beecham and Knapp, 1992). Long-run marginal opportunity costs were attached to all services used. Where possible, the costs of accommodation, day services, hospital services (in-, out- or day patient) and project overheads were based on local, facility-specific figures. These services were expected to make the largest contributions to aggregate community care costs, and also tend to display too much inter-facility variation in purpose, clientele and cost for national averages to be sufficiently accurate. To approximate costs to their long-run levels, all residential and day facility costs were based on the expected long-run average annual occupancy. All other services, including peripatetic professional inputs, were costed at national price levels. Expenditure on travel and other revenue and capital overheads was taken into account and an amount was allocated to each client to reflect the level of direct contact with the service. Using this methodology we could maintain our focus on the individual; that is, we could calculate the cost of supporting each individual client in the community.

The price base for all cost calculations and analyses was 1986-87, chosen because of the large number of clients moving from hospital during that period and because of the availability of accounts data. (To inflate the costs reported here to 1990-91 levels apply a multiplier of roughly 1.3.)

Hospital-community cost comparisons. Although we were more interested in cost differences between community settings and arrangements, the demonstration programme afforded the opportunity to look at cost differences between hospital and the community. The costs of in-patient care fall mainly to health authorities, who provided us with the accounts for 56 hospitals spread across the 14 English regional health authorities. In addition there were social security, social care and voluntary organisation inputs to in-patient care. On the basis of work in a small number of hospitals, these were found to amount to about 4 per cent of the total cost. Capital costs estimates were added, based on the sale value of sites, premises and equipment (using local land price indicators and data on site size and utilisation). It was not feasible to disaggregate hospital costs down to ward level when working with so many establishments, although ward costings were undertaken in a small number of cases (see

Sussex, 1986; Knapp et al., 1987; Haycox and Brand, 1991), and we discuss their implications when interpreting the cost findings in subsequent chapters.

In comparing the costs of hospital and community services there are at least two time frames to be considered. The first is the longer-term, 'steady state' time frame when community services have worked through their transition phase and are compared with hospital residence, the costs of which are not distorted by the process of rundown. The other time frame is the transition period itself, when it is pertinent to ask about the speed with which hospital costs fall as resident numbers decline. Both will be considered with empirical data below, and we also report multivariate analyses of psychiatric hospital costs as their resident numbers fall (see Chapter 14).

Patterns of cost variation. The costs of service packages are unlikely to be invariant with respect to the characteristics of service users, and so comparisons between care settings should be cognisant of possible differences between client populations. As we saw in Chapter 5, the first groups of clients moved by projects were generally less 'dependent' in terms of skills, challenging behaviours and so on than those who remained behind in hospital. The hospital care formerly received by 'movers' will be costing rather less than the hospital average. Across projects there were also differences in client characteristics which may have had cost implications. An important task in the examination of patterns of community cost variations, therefore, was to make like-with-like comparisons.

Given the necessary data, the most informative way to examine such patterns is to estimate a statistical cost function, preferably taking individual clients as the 'data points'. (Knapp, 1984, Chap. 9 offers a description of this technique and its utilisation in social care contexts.) Two series of such functions were estimated, one for people with learning difficulties and one for people with mental health problems, and we shall say more about the methodology below (see Chapters 13 and 14).

Cost-outcome connections. Costs and outcomes are not measured in identical units, and so there is no possibility whatsoever of reaching conclusions of the form 'the costs of community care in project X exceeded the benefits'. What we can do, however, is compare the costs of achieving given levels of outcome (or effectiveness) in different projects or placement types. In short, we can conduct cost-effectiveness but not cost-benefit analyses. In this way we can ask whether *for whom* and *under what circumstances* was community care more cost- effective than hospital care, or was one community care arrangement more cost-effective than another. Because of the focus on individuals, we are able to move away from grand generalisations and reliance on broad averages, to consider individual clients and their needs, as well as the consequences for different agencies. Proper recognition is accorded to the diversity of individual circumstances and their implications for service systems in general, and for costs and client outcomes in particular.

The costing methodology employed in the Care in the Community evaluation was developed from previous research by the PSSRU and, of course, by numerous other researchers. It was informed by appropriate economic principles, but the exigencies of a large, dispersed and complex demonstration programme sometimes meant that pragmatic considerations had to dominate theoretical niceties. The result was a comprehensive costing which compares well with other work in similar fields, and which is congruent with our outcome research.

Chapters 13 to 15 now apply the outcome and cost methodologies described in this chapter to three client groups. In Chapter 13 we look at the projects for people with learning difficulties and the Cambridge project for young people with multiple disabilities. In Chapter 14 our attention turns to the projects for people with mental health problems, and in Chapter 15 we report the outcome and cost evaluations for elderly people and people with physical disabilities supported by the Glossop project.

13 Outcomes and costs for people with learning difficulties

The evaluation of the Care in the Community programme sought answers to a variety of outcome and cost questions. What, for example, was each client's quality of life in the community? Did they express satisfaction with their places of residence and their life-styles generally? Were they able to undertake self-care tasks with little or no support from staff? In these and other respects, were they better off in the community than in hospital? Did some people fare better in the community than others? Were differences in outcome systematically related to accommodation type, or case management organisation, or the age, gender, or other characteristics of clients? On the cost side, what were the full and component costs of community care, and how did they compare with hospital? Were costs associated with client characteristics, needs or outcomes?

The evaluation of client outcomes and costs was based primarily on interviews and assessments using structured questionnaires, but also on more than three years of formal and informal contacts with staff and clients. With few exceptions, the interview schedules were common to all client groups. In this chapter we concentrate on people with learning difficulties, although we say relatively little about the three young adults in this client group (from the Cambridge project) because of data limitations. The mental health and elderly client groups are considered in Chapters 14 and 15.

Three hundred and fifty-six people with learning difficulties moved to the community during our evaluation period. Nine months after leaving hospital the majority were living in staffed group homes or hostels (see Chapter 8, Table 8.3). When assessed in hospital prior to discharge, many were identified as needing intensive staff support in the community due to problem behaviours or difficulties with self-care or life skills (see Chapter 5 for full descriptions).

Although not every client was included in every aspect of the outcome and costs work for the logistical and timetabling reasons explained in Chapter 4, we obtained sufficient data for most analytical purposes. Outcomes along most dimensions were defined as the differences between the two assessments made for each client, in hospital and in the community. We were interested in both absolute and relative welfare or outcomes, that is, to return to our algebraic notation, (T2-T1) and (T2-T1)/T1. Welfare measures covered *skills* (essentially a measure of adaptive behaviour), *behavioural problems* (maladaptive behaviour), *satisfaction with social interaction* (the Interview Schedule for Social Interaction developed by Henderson, 1981), *depression* (from the inventory of Snaith et al., 1971), and *morale* (from the Psychosocial Functioning Inventory of Feragne et al., 1983, and from the life satisfaction 'ladder' of Cantril, 1965).

We also looked at these quality of life dimensions using a qualitative, less structured approach, giving us insights which might otherwise have been missed. We made little use of quantitative methods, for instance, when looking at activities, levels of engagement and social networks. For most clients for whom we obtained outcome data we also examined service utilisation in the community and related costs.

The numbers of clients for whom we gathered quantitative data on the key dimensions of outcome are given in Table 13.1.

Table 13.1
Outcome and cost research instruments, sample sizes for people with learning difficulties

Research instrument[1]	*Numbers of clients*[2]	
	Baseline	**Movers**
Skills	373	196
Behavioural problems	373	196
Satisfaction with services questions	247	139
Schedule for Social Interaction	220	129
Depression Inventory	149	81
Psychosocial Functioning Inventory	170	103
Personal presentation	325	170
Client Service Receipt Interview	–[3]	235
Costs	197	197

1 Each instrument is described in the text.
2 The effective number for some analyses will be smaller because of missing information on some component items for some clients. Totals include Cambridge project clients.
3 Hospital of residence was known for every client, but service utilisation data in hospital were not collected. Hospital costs were estimated *only* for those clients for whom we also had community costs data.

Client outcomes

We now turn to the skills, behavioural problems, activities, social contacts, morale and life satisfaction of clients in the community, and hospital-community differences. We conducted a variety of statistical tests, which are introduced as we use them, and we employ the following terminological conventions when reporting the results:

- $p < 0.001$ (0.1 per cent level) indicates a *highly significant* difference; there is only a very small chance (less than one in 1,000) that the hospital-community difference occurred by chance (this is reported as $p = 0.000$);
- $0.001 < p < 0.01$ (1 per cent level) indicates a *significant* difference;
- $0.01 < p < 0.05$ (5 per cent level) indicates a *borderline* difference; and
- $0.05 < p$ indicates *no significant difference.*

Skills

Some of the most commonly-used indicators of the success of community care are skill level, role performance and behaviour. Indicators of integration into the community and level of independence include self-care, performance of everyday tasks such as shopping, and getting along with others. Abilities may well improve following rehabilitation or training, or with widening experience of community living, but usually not without staff support. The extent to which the skills of people with learning difficulties can be expected to improve after leaving hospital is still a matter of some debate. Different opportunities for demonstrating abilities present themselves in new situations, but some research has shown that some people have developed only marginally since leaving hospital (see below).

In interviews with staff in hospital and community settings we collected information on clients' skills and behaviour. The staff who were interviewed knew clients well and were asked to assess a broad range of self-care activities, domestic skills, physical health and mobility, mental functioning and behaviour. Schedules to measure skills and behaviour were developed from the Social Behaviour Scale and the Disability Assessment Schedule (see Chapter 5). We first examine skills.

The aggregate scores on the skills instrument are reported in Table 13.2. (Individual project averages ranged from 61 to 73.) The improvement in client skills levels between hospital and community is highly significant overall, and for no project did we find a deterioration attaining statistical significance. The three Cambridge project clients had relatively few skills, but still achieved marked changes after leaving hospital. (Mean T2 score was 50, mean difference 15.) These general skills improvements for the learning difficulty clients are encouraging. The potential for skills acquisition (improvements in adaptive behaviour) by people with learning difficulties leaving hospital was never doubted, but it was important for the pilot projects to demonstrate the superiority of community living over hospital residence found in some previous community care programmes (see, for example, Clark and Hermelin,

Table 13.2
Skills of clients with learning difficulties in the community, and community-hospital differences

Skills score and difference	Mean	Standard deviation	Sample[1]
Skills score in community (T2)	64.3	9.6	196
Community-hospital difference (T2-T1)	3.2	7.4	196
Community-hospital difference significance:		p = 0.000	

1 Excludes Cambridge clients.

1955; Tizard, 1964; Smith et al., 1980; Robinson et al., 1984; Conroy and Bradley, 1985; Felce et al., 1985; Davies, 1988; Eastwood and Fisher, 1988). We are not suggesting that skills acquisition was a foregone conclusion, for Aanes and Moen (1976), among others, have shown how a change in place of residence *alone* is insufficient to generate significant changes. For this reason we explored inter-client differences in levels and changes in skills, as we report below.

It is instructive to look at the component skills included in our assessments (Table 13.3). Particular skills which improved significantly (as indicated by the Wilcoxon test) were: conversation and social mixing with other clients; initiation of conversation or interaction with other clients; doing their fair share of collective tasks; participation in decisions regarding roles; dressing; cooking and getting meals alone; basic housework and care of clothes; shopping alone; finding their way around the neighbourhood; using amenities in the community, such as churches and pubs; writing; numeracy and handling money; looking after their own clothes and possessions; and appearance if left to their own devices. On each of these items, the group of clients performed significantly better in the community than in hospital. For only a few items – vision, eating habits at meal-times, missed opportunities to use community facilities, and needing staff encouragement to undertake these community activities – were average skills levels *lower* in the community than in hospital.

Behaviour

The questions on behavioural problems covered a number of dimensions conventionally found in 'maladaptive behaviour' scales, including challenging behaviours problematic for the individual or for others. Previous research has established a clear association between challenging behaviours, carer difficulties and the individual remaining in or moving to a more restrictive placement, like a hospital (Emerson et al., 1987; Turner and Turner, 1985; Borthwick-Duffy et al., 1987). This applies particularly to destructive and disruptive behaviour patterns such as aggression and self-injury. Challenging behaviours can make the individual highly conspicuous, thus militating against community presence, respect and participation. Fewer challenging behaviours, indicated by higher scores on our instrument, can aid independence, self-determination and choice.

As a group, clients with learning difficulties showed no deterioration in behaviour between hospital and community, although there was a statistically significant increase in the intensity or frequency of behavioural problems in two projects (Table 13.4). In five component items of behaviour, there were significant deteriorations between hospital and the community: odd gestures and mannerisms; attention-seeking behaviour; obsessional behaviour; objectionable behaviour at night; and wakefulness at night. Landesman (1987) has reported that maladaptive behaviour deteriorates when people move from

Table 13.3
Changes in clients' skills since leaving hospital, people with learning difficulties

Item description[1]	Worse %	Same %	Better %	Sig. changes[2] p	+/–
Vision[1]	14	81	5	0.026	–
Hearing[1]	5	89	6		
Mobility	11	82	7		
Conversation, social mixing with other clients	14	57	29	0.012	+
Initiation of conversation/interaction with other clients	18	52	30	0.003	+
Non-verbal communication	20	56	24		
Length of conversations	10	75	15		
Clarity of speech	15	72	13		
Eating habits at mealtime	26	57	17	0.063	–
Does fair share of collective tasks	16	56	28	0.059	+
Task-sharing with other clients	22	54	24		
Argues with other clients	24	46	30		
Participation in decisions re. roles	10	51	39	0.000	+
Washing and bathing self	15	63	23	0.085	+
Dressing	12	64	25	0.007	+
Cooking and getting meals alone	11	47	42	0.000	+
Basic housework and care of clothes	16	52	32	0.020	+
Shopping alone	13	51	36	0.000	+
Manages own financial affairs	19	62	20		
Finds way around	10	57	33	0.000	+
Uses amenities in community (church, pub, ...)	7	43	50	0.000	+
Has missed opportunities in last month to use these facilities[3]	26	61	13	0.010	–
Do staff encourage client to use these facilities?[3]	21	67	12	0.077	–
Do staff stop client doing things, reducing independence?[3]	24	53	23		
Independently plans/organises weekly activities	17	60	23		
Understanding communication	9	77	14		
Reading	7	80	13		
Writing	7	78	16	0.030	+
Counting and handling money	13	67	20	0.039	+
Looking after own clothes and possessions	21	51	28	0.040	+
Appearance if left to own devices	19	49	32	0.005	+
Sample size[4]		197			

1 All except items indicated by note 3 have three categories of response.
2 Using the Wilcoxon test we examined the significance of changes between hospital and community. 'p' indicates significance level; +/– indicates whether the change was for the better (improvement since leaving hospital) or worse (deterioration since leaving hospital). Only significant differences are reported.
3 Item required Yes/No responses.
4 Missing values varied from item to item, ranging from 0 to 40. In most cases missing assessments arose because hospital residents did not have opportunities to test these particular skills.

Table 13.4
Behavioural problems of clients with learning difficulties in the community, and community-hospital differences

Behavioural problems score and difference	Mean	Standard deviation	Sample[1]
Behavioural problems score in community (T2)	67.1	5.8	194
Community-hospital difference (T2-T1)	-1.1	6.8	194
Community-hospital difference significance:		p = 0.126	

1 Excludes Cambridge clients.

hospital to the community, but Conroy and Bradley (1985) could find no difference. The deterioration for Care in the Community clients may have resulted from greater demands or stress encountered in community settings, for projects had successfully raised clients' skills and self-care capabilities. It may have followed changes in medication, or may simply have been associated with a major change in life-style and experience. There were also different norms and expectations in some hospitals compared to community placements, and challenging behaviours were certainly less obtrusive and usually more readily tolerated in some hospital wards than in relatively intense and public settings such as small staffed group homes or hostels.

In the Bolton Neighbourhood Network Scheme (part of the demonstration programme) the difficulties of overcoming this problem were noted.

Something that people who once lived in long-stay institutions often have to learn is not to demand attention using attention-seeking behaviour. Helping people to unlearn the skills of deploying attention-seeking behaviour is something that Neighbourhood Care Workers do not always find easy. One possible way of helping people to learn this skill, is to substitute an alternative understanding, that is to ask them quietly to wait their turn. Since it is not common practice to make such an understanding implicit and not all adults adhere to such noble principles in everyday situations, the form appropriate guidance should take poses one of many dilemmas for care workers. On the one hand, overt attention-seeking behaviour is generally inappropriate as it usually results in the least favourable impression being attributed to the attention-seeker, on the other hand, some form of assertiveness if desirable, is admired and is to be encouraged. To strike the right balance in a learning situation is difficult (Bolton Community Health Council, 1987, p.12).

Activities and engagement

A large stream of research in the learning difficulty field has built up around the concept of *engagement* in activity. A person is said to be 'engaged' if they are

Table 13.5
Changes in clients' behavioural problems since leaving hospital, people with learning difficulties

Item description[1]	Worse %	Same %	Better %	Sig. changes[2] p	+/–
Depression or weeping	16	67	17		
Suicidal preoccupations	4	95	1		
Anxiety, panic, phobias	19	67	14		
Slowness of movement	17	64	19		
Underactivity	20	58	22		
Overactivity	16	72	12		
Elated or euphoric behaviour	16	72	12		
Odd gestures, mannerisms	33	46	21	0.071	–
Acting out delusions, hallucinations	6	89	5		
Attention-seeking behaviour	29	56	15	0.016	–
Agressive or violent behaviour	22	57	21		
Obsessional behaviour	19	71	10	0.086	–
Self-injury	8	86	6		
Stealing (e.g. food, cigarettes)	11	75	14		
Collecting, hoarding meaningless items	12	72	16		
Shouting, swearing, offensive, screaming	29	51	20		
Incontinence during the day	11	79	10		
Incontinence at night	12	79	9		
Confused	24	60	17		
Objectionable at night	16	76	8	0.050	–
Awake at night	27	60	13	0.007	–
Accuses others of doing harm, stealing	16	66	18		
Wanders or runs away (if not supervised)	6	87	7		
Stereotyped repetitive activities, echolalia	20	64	16		
Sexually offensive behaviour	4	89	7		
Any other problems	19	54	27		
Sample size[3]		197			

1 All except items have three categories of response.
2 Using the Wilcoxon test we examined the significance of changes between hospital and community. 'p' indicates significance level; w/b indicates whether the change was for the better (improvement since leaving hospital) or worse (deterioration since leaving hospital). Only significant differences are reported.
3 Missing values varied from item to item, ranging from 0 to 40. In most cases missing assessments arose because hospital residents did not have opportunities to test these particular skills.

interacting with materials or with people in a manner which is likely to maintain or develop ... skills and abilities. A highly-engaged person is constantly doing things ... can be seen to be interacting with materials or people (Blunden and Kushlick, 1974, p.5).

Engaged activity has been defined in empirical studies as 'all client interactions with people, materials, furniture or fittings and a small group of other defined activities such as watching television. Disengagement consists of all other observations' (Felce et al., 1980, p.16). Many empirical studies have relied on intensive regular time-sampling – Felce and colleagues made minute-to-minute observations, for example. We were unable to undertake such intensive data collection across the demonstration programme, but parallel research in a few projects for people with learning difficulties produced mixed results. In Calderdale, an intensive diary study revealed *lower* engagement levels in the community when compared to hospital (Leedham, 1989), while in Derby activity levels appeared to be higher.

Across the whole programme, we asked 215 clients living in the community about their preferences for activities. There were few differences between hospital and community responses:

- 70 per cent expressed a liking for outdoor activities (compared to 72 per cent in hospital);
- 83 per cent for indoor activities (89 per cent in hospital);
- 92 per cent for social activities (82 per cent in hospital);
- 97 per cent for passive activities (92 per cent in hospital); and
- 74 per cent for other activities such as attending church and looking after pets (57 per cent in hospital).

Another question asked if they 'had enough to do'. Eighty-one per cent expressed satisfaction in the community compared to 68 per cent in hospital.

Social contacts

One of the fundamentally important dimensions of quality of life in the community is participation and social contacts. Social isolation is often described as a classic feature of an impoverished institutional life. Almost every policy and practice document includes this aspect of well-being, and it is a key component of normalisation, accomplishment and ordinary life approaches to supporting people with long-term needs (Wolfensberger, 1972; King's Fund, 1982; O'Brien, 1986). In the discussion document *Ties and Connections*, the King's Fund (1988) identified eight types or sources of inter-personal connections:

- '*Friendship*: having friends, relationships, including a 'best friend' ...
- *Acquaintance*: having a network of acquaintances.
- *Membership*: being a member of associations and organisations.
- *Keeping in touch*: with trends and movements of interest; subscribing to them; belonging to 'social worlds'.
- *Being part of a family*: having an active connection with family life.
- *Having a partner*: or someone to whom a long-term commitment has been made.
- *Being a neighbour*: living next door to, or at least near to someone – down the street or across the road.
- *Knowing or being known in a neighbourhood*: using the resources of a neighbourhood (usually the area within easy walking distance from where you live) and recognising and being recognised by others who use them too' (King's Fund, 1988, p.4).

As the authors of the discussion document noted, these ties and connections assume different degrees of importance for different people, are of different durations, can sometimes be intense or intimate, and offer opportunities for reciprocity.

In the design of our evaluation we sought information on social contacts from both staff and clients, including frequency and nature of contacts with friends, relatives, people in the local community and care professionals, although we could not address the full range of inter-personal connections listed above. We also elicited clients' views on the importance and quality of their social contacts and friendships.

Staff of community accommodation facilities were asked about clients' social contacts over a two-week period, and clients living independently were asked to complete their own record forms. Staff reports of clients' *outings* from their place of residence, which were considerably more frequent in the community than in hospital, were discussed in Chapter 8. The pattern was repeated for visitors *received by* clients. For the 74 community care clients for whom we had data, the average number of visits was 2.4 per fortnight. We could not make direct comparisons with hospital because the samples did not overlap. Staff respondents opined that clients were generally satisfied with their level and quality of social contact, but two-thirds of clients would appreciate more.

A more meaningful picture emerged from clients' own views, although we could not include the views of those who were unable to communicate. Using Henderson's (1981) Interview Schedule for Social Interaction, which is one of the few social network schedules to ask about both the frequency and quality of contacts, and restricting attention to those people whose views we obtained in both hospital and the community, a number of changes are evident (Table 13.6). Fewer clients saw family or relatives in the community than in hospital (54 per cent compared to 76 per cent), and they reported having fewer friends. Conversely, clients reported having more confidants, and 90 per cent had someone they considered they knew very well. Overall scores on the Schedule for Social Interaction showed borderline increases ($p = 0.025$). We will report in later chapters how people in other client groups reported generally much larger increases in social contacts, but without a parallel increase in *satisfaction* with these contacts.

In hospital, most clients were free to walk around the buildings and grounds, meeting and making friends. Community settings tend to impose greater restrictions. Some are remote. Sometimes staff are reluctant to take risks and therefore restrict some activities outside the place of residence. Sometimes staff support is not forthcoming for social activities if staff are hard pressed meeting more immediate demands. Or it may simply take people a long time to build new social networks after moving from one place of residence to another. A study by Bolton Community Health Council (1987) included a detailed examination of social contacts, friendships and integration. Their findings suggest that the Bolton clients had active social lives, with plenty of activities organised

Table 13.6
Social contacts – the views of clients with learning difficulties

Questions and overall instrument score[1]	Percentage responses Hospital	Community
Do you ever see your family or relative?		
Yes	76	54
How many friends do you have?		
None	11	12
1 or 2	33	54
3 to 5	19	24
6 to 10	19	3
more than 10	17	7
How many friends could you go to if you were upset or wanted help?		
None	31	15
1 or 2	29	76
3 to 5	28	6
6 to 10	1	0
more than 10	1	1
Is there anyone who knows you very well?		
Yes	85	90
Overall score on Schedule for Social Interaction – mean[2]	3.7	4.2
Sample size	100	100

1 Taken from the Schedule for Social Interaction.
2 The community-hospital difference (mean –0.2, standard deviation 2.3) was not significant ($p = 0.709$).

for and by them, but that their social contacts were mainly restricted to other people with learning difficulties:

Even though people are going out daily, they are gaining little experience of community life and come into contact with few people who are neither part of the service for mental handicap nor are handicapped. ... Apart from family contact, contact with neighbours and tradespeople such as taxi drivers, people working in local shops, and a delivery man, little evidence was seen of contact with people in the local non-handicapped community outside the Bolton Neighbourhood Network Scheme. ... [This shows] how difficult is the task of integrating people with a mental handicap into the community. Therefore, to look for quick and easy results would be totally misleading (Bolton Community Health Council, 1987, pp.15,25).

However, although fewer community contacts were found in Bolton and elsewhere when compared to hospital, they were more highly valued by clients. Community participation has been found to be less than satisfactory in some previous studies for this client group (Birenbaum and Re, 1979; MRC Social

Psychiatry Unit, 1986; Schalock and Lilley, 1986; Cattermole, 1987; Wing, L., 1989). In the demonstration programme, however, a more encouraging picture emerged.

Morale and life satisfaction

Subjective ratings of well-being, grouped under the general heading of morale and life satisfaction, were central to the Care in the Community evaluation. We placed a high priority on eliciting clients' views. A client interview was conducted to find out about feelings, likes and dislikes, worries and aspirations. It was difficult to discover the opinions of some people, especially when their ability to communicate was limited, and although it was originally intended to rely on non-verbal cues with attempts to back up observations with other measures, this did not prove possible.

Few previous studies attempt to measure the morale or satisfaction of people with mental illness or learning difficulties. As described in Chapter 5, we used questions or scales borrowed from Seltzer and Seltzer's (1983) satisfaction questionnaire, Wykes' (1982) assessment of satisfaction with services, the global morale measure offered by Cantril's ladder (1965), the entire morale sub-scale of the Psychosocial Functioning Inventory (Feragne et al., 1983), the Depression Inventory of Snaith et al. (1971), as well as Henderson's (1981) Interview Schedule for Social Interaction, the results from which we have just described. Scores on the three complete scales are reported in Table 13.7. It is clear that people with learning difficulties rated their morale more highly in the community than in hospital on each of these scales. The result for the PFI sub-scale looks broadly consistent with the findings on client affect in similar hospital discharge services (Cattermole, 1987; Conroy and Bradley, 1985). Analyses of variance revealed differences of borderline significance between projects on the changes in scores on Cantril's ladder and the PFI, but no differences between accommodation types.

The Cambridge clients were unable to participate in our interviews.

Table 13.7
Morale and life satisfaction of clients with learning difficulties in the community, and hospital-community differences

	Comm. score			*T2-T1 difference*			
Instrument	M	SD	N	M	SD	N	p[1]
Cantril's ladder	5.1	1.5	67	1.2	3.0	50	0.011
Depression Inventory[2]	9.2	7.1	84	-2.8	8.9	56	0.027
Psychosocial Functioning Inventory	40.9	6.4	97	3.1	6.9	75	0.000

1 M = mean; SD = standard deviation; N = sample size; p = significance of test of difference between hospital and community scores.
2 Lower scores on the Depression Inventory indicate greater morale (lower depression).

Exploring client outcome variations

These client outcome results apply to the group of clients with learning difficulties as a whole, and there were obviously variations around the averages. Some of those variations were related systematically to community accommodation type and project (Table 13.8). For example, the general finding that clients' skills levels improved significantly over the period since leaving hospital masks the fact that there were large differences within the programme. The analyses of variance support the view of Shaw et al. (1986), who argued

> Quality of life for people with a mental handicap is improved in smaller homes or units as more opportunities are created for activities and increased staff resident interactions. Staff are able to give more attention to appropriate behaviours, thus strengthening them, and stimulating further developments of adaptive skills. Longer-term follow-up research has shown significant improvements in residents' adaptive skills as a result of teaching programmes and increased staff resident interactions. Small homes help increase participation in activities, and increase the control individuals have over their own lives (p.50).

Our evidence implies that people with learning difficulties moving to *other* and larger community placements also develop their (adaptive) skills.

What we have not yet done, however, is standardise these skills differences or other inter-project and inter-facility differences for the various factors likely to exert an influence, such as client background, social and physical environments, service inputs and so on. In other words, the broad brush findings of improved client welfare in the community need to be examined in more detail, with a focus on individual variations. A framework for such an examination – the production of welfare approach – was introduced in Chapter 4, where we emphasised the need for a comprehensive, flexible but theoretically sound methodology. Production of welfare theory helps by suggesting a framework for the synthesis of previous research, an agenda for new evaluative research, and a set of empirical tools. With suitable refinement, an estimated production

Table 13.8

Analyses of variance of community scores, and community-hospital differences, by project and facility, for people with learning difficulties

	T2 scores		*(T2-T1) differences*		*(T2-T1)/T1 ratios*	
	Between projects	**Between facilities**	**Between projects**	**Between facilities**	**Between projects**	**Between facilities**
Skills Scale	0.000	0.002	ns	0.001	0.048	0.006
Behaviour Scale	0.005	ns	0.005	ns	0.004	ns
Schedule for Social Interaction	ns	ns	ns	ns	ns	ns
Cantril's ladder	ns	ns	ns	ns	0.039	ns
Psychosocial Functioning Inventory	ns	ns	ns	ns	ns	ns
Depression Inventory	ns	ns	ns	ns	ns	ns

'ns' indicates not significant ($p > 0.05$).

function, which follows logically from this theoretical approach, provides not only the means to standardise client outcomes for the influences of factors extraneous to the evaluation, but also a route to test hypotheses about the quality and efficacy of care for people with long-term needs. The approach also helped in the interpretation of cost differences in community care, as we describe later.

It will be recalled from our discussion of methodology in Chapter 4 that the organisational, financial and political forces at play during the gestation and infancy of the Care in the Community pilot programme ruled out the use of a randomised controlled trial design for the evaluation, even assuming that such a design would have been sufficient for our purposes. The quasi-experimental design reliant on statistical controls has some advantages, particularly the pressure it exerts to examine the range of possible influences on the criterion variables (in our case outcomes and costs), but it has the disadvantage of requiring large samples of clients and good data on hypothesised influences. These requirements constrained our examination of outcome variations, although they did not prevent the exploration of some relevant issues in the care and support of people with learning difficulties.

We were able to conduct statistical work tantamount to the estimation of 'production functions' for four outcome dimensions: client skills, behaviour, morale measured by the Psychosocial Functioning Inventory (PFI) and client satisfaction with social interaction measured by the Schedule for Social Interaction. (Note that responses on the PFI and Social Interaction Schedule were limited to people with good cognitive and communication skills; moreover, there were few inter-project or inter-facility differences in these aspects of quality of life.)

Ideally, an analysis of multiple outcomes would examine all dimensions of client welfare simultaneously. This could either be accomplished by collapsing the various dimensions into a single scale, suitably incorporating trade-offs between dimensions, such as an improvement in skills against a deterioration in relation to maladaptive behaviour problems, or by examining multiple outcome measures. An example of the single outcome approach is the Quality Adjusted Life Year (QALY) measure, currently restricted largely to somatic health (reviewed by Baldwin et al., 1990). Although some progress has been made in the development of QALYs for use in mental health evaluations (Wilkinson et al., 1990), and although the approach has considerable merit in making explicit many of the judgements which are otherwise fudged or hedged, there remain too many difficulties for it to be employed in our evaluation (Donaldson et al., 1988; Williams, 1989). The dimensions of client outcome were too numerous, each dimension was itself multidimensional (for example, the skills score subsumes a huge variety of abilities and accomplishments), and the alternative 'positions' of people along these dimensions can be difficult to describe in a way which permits raters to begin to make the necessary inter-dimension trade-offs. It is possible to pursue the alternative – the examination of multiple outcome measures – by estimating multiple outcome production functions (multivariate estimation of a single equation which models trade-offs between both inputs and outcomes), but these were too complex econometrically and too data-hungry for the present study. The approach we selected was to examine variations in each outcome dimension in turn. Causal and contemporaneous links between outcomes were entertained in conducting the statistical analyses. (To take one example, a client's skill level may help to explain their behavioural attributes and satisfaction with the living environment.)

Bolstered by hypotheses suggested by care principles and the evaluative literature on services for people with learning difficulties, we examined inter-client differences in well-being by estimating series of multiple regression equations linking scores in the community (T2) to:

- client characteristics prior to leaving hospital (the T1 scores on all measures for which there were sufficient data);
- background data on client age at admission to hospital and at discharge, duration of hospital residence, number of previous admissions to hospital, gender and 'severity of handicap' (as assessed in hospital);
- experience of hospital readmissions during the post-discharge period (of which there were few);
- social and physical environmental features of community accommodation; and
- cost, as a summary measure of resource inputs to care.

We also examined the effects of type of community accommodation (hostel, unstaffed group home, and so on), style of case management, and organisational features of projects (DHA versus LA lead agencies, for example), but introduced these factors at a second stage. There were numerous specification, interpretation and inter-correlation problems associated with these factors.

This is a far from exhaustive list of the factors suggested or proven to influence the welfare and quality of life of people with learning difficulties, nor could our statistical analyses capture the complexity of their inter-relationships. (Despite an ambitious and comprehensive design, Conroy and Bradley concluded that their five years of research and analysis 'did not produce any final list of things that *really matter*', 1985, p.158. Leedham, 1989, has a useful review of much of the literature.) Nevertheless, the data provided by the demonstration programme allowed us to explore some of the reasons for the observed differences between clients.

For each of the four aspects of client welfare – skills, behaviour, morale and satisfaction with social interaction – we explored numerous representations of the 'outcome production function'. Table 13.9 reports the four 'best' equations on the conventional criteria of statistical significance, parsimony and interpretability. The overall explanatory power of three equations is good: 74 per cent of observed variation in clients' skills levels in the community is 'explained' statistically, as is 42 per cent of variation in behaviour and 54 per

Table 13.9
Outcome 'production functions' for clients with learning difficulties

	Client skills		*Behaviour*		*Morale*		*Social interaction*	
Explanatory variables	**B**	**sig.**	**B**	**sig.**	**B**	**sig.**	**B**	**sig.**
Constant term	24.98	.00	-27.90	.52	305.3	.04	-1.02	.78
Male[1]					5.93	.01		
Age at admission to hospital	0.33	.01	-0.09	.03				
Age at start of programme			0.08	.05			0.27	.12
Age at start, squared (÷ 100)	-0.24	.16					-0.33	.10
Years in hospital, squared	0.01	.04						
Skills score at T1	0.64	.00						
Behaviour score at T1			2.94	.03	-8.36	.06		
Behaviour at T1, squared			-0.02	.05	0.06	.07		
Size of community accom. (places)	-0.84	.00			2.76	.01		
Size of community accom., squared			-0.02	.02	-0.11	.04		
Domesticity of exterior of accom.	-1.85	.03	-2.70	.05				
Domesticity of exterior x size of accom.			0.25	.08				
Pleasantness of interior of accom.	0.80	.09						
Domesticity of interior of accom.					1.27	.09		
Domesticity of interior x size of accom.			-0.13	.01				
Age-inappropriate possessions not encouraged[1]	2.81	.02	4.30	.00	-7.59	.02	-1.45	.12
Staff actively encourage client activities[1]	2.35	.15			-3.73	.08		
Sample size	101		99		30		42	
R^2 and $\bar{R}^2$	.74	.71	.42	.36	.54	.37	.11	.04
F and sig.	28.59	.00	7.02	.00	3.09	.02	1.60	.21

1 Dummy variable taking value 1 for the characteristic noted, and 0 otherwise.

cent of variation in morale. Inter-client differences in satisfaction with social interaction remain largely unexplained.

The significant influences on client welfare fall into three groups: basic characteristics such as age, gender and duration of hospital residence; client welfare in hospital (the T1 scores on some scales); and the physical and social environmental characteristics of community accommodation settings. We consider them in turn, although it is the complex *interplay* of personal attributes and environmental features which has such a marked effect on outcomes. Of course, while environmental variables can be manipulated by service providers, clients' own characteristics are fixed or predetermined, and thus of less immediate relevance to policy-makers unless they specifically and energetically pursue a policy of matching resources to needs.

Clients' basic characteristics. There was little evidence of a gender difference (only found for morale), but there were marked age effects. Clients older at the date of admission to hospital (which was often 30 or more years before they left hospital again) appeared to have better skills levels ('adaptive behaviour', including self-care capabilities), but more behavioural problems. Age at the beginning of the funding round (a standardised measure of age at the time of their inclusion in the programme) was also relevant: older clients had fewer skills but also fewer behavioural problems. Both results are obtained *after* standardising for T1 scores on the relevant variables; that is, younger clients had higher skills levels in the community relative to their skills levels in hospital.) Duration of hospitalisation had no impact on behaviour in the community, but was positively associated with skills levels, although its absolute impact was small.

What is the significance of these results? We know that it was the younger hospital residents who were more likely to move to the community under the demonstration programme. In the longer term, therefore, future cohorts of leavers will be much less skilled – and will therefore require more staff support and hence greater expenditure levels. They are also likely, it would seem, to pose fewer behavioural problems, which implies, as we demonstrate in the section on cost variations, that this too will push up costs of future cohorts of community care clients.

Clients' welfare in hospital. The skills and behavioural characteristics displayed by clients in the community were found to be directly related to their skills and behavioural characteristics, respectively, in hospital. This would be expected. For example, Raynes and Sumpton (1986) found that predischarge adaptive and maladaptive behaviours (similar to our skills and behavioural problems measures) were key predictors of their respective post-discharge behaviours, and Eyman et al. (1979) found that older, less-disabled clients improved more than others in all aspects of adaptive behaviour given the stimulation and opportunities of a positive, normalised environment. In our case, the effect of behavioural problems is nonlinear: clients with more behavioural problems in hospital improved more in the community than those with fewer problems. A similar conclusion was reached by Eyman et al. (1979) and others. Unlike Landesman (1987), we did not find that clients with more behavioural problems at T1 got worse over time, and unlike Borthwick-Duffy et al. (1987), we did not find that maladaptive behaviour prompted readmissions to hospital.

Hospital skills levels had no impact on behavioural characteristics in the community, and hospital behaviour had no influence on community skills.

Physical and social environmental characteristics. The Care in the Community evidence appears not to support a conclusion reached by Conroy and Bradley (1985, p.150) that 'program and environmental variables appeared to be relatively weak in predicting, or explaining, variations in individual growth' when compared to unchangeable individual characteristics. The characteristics of community environments made significant contributions to the outcomes for individual clients.

Using information gathered by the PSSRU interviewers during their visits to community residential facilities, we were able to obtain some descriptors of physical and social environments. The environmental features were described in Chapter 8, and were subsequently used in the examination of variations in client outcomes. In this latter use, we found it helpful to collapse the many features into six indicators, five of which proved to be significant predictors of client welfare in the community. Higher scores on each of the indicators describe environments which are 'more normalised/ordinary', or less institutional. The normalisation arguments predict that client welfare will be higher when environments are more domestically scaled, furnished and decorated, and when staff behave in a less intrusive or dominant manner. For example, it has been suggested that a greater degree of physical and social integration into the community and more client-oriented and appropriate support and management practices will be associated with improved social relationships and community participation, themselves facets of quality of life and predictors of improvements in affect and morale. Thus, moving from a 'less' to a 'more normalised' setting – such as from hospital into a good community placement – has been found to improve *adaptive behaviour* (Conroy and Bradley, 1985; Felce et al., 1985; Turner and Turner, 1985; Shaw et al., 1986; Thomas et al., 1986; Davies, 1988; Eastwood and Fisher, 1988; and many other studies), *engagement in activities* (Felce et al., 1985, 1986; Sperlinger, 1987), *morale and life satisfaction* (Conroy and Bradley, 1985; Cattermole, 1987) and *maladaptive behaviour* (Conroy and Bradley, 1985; Turner and Turner, 1985; Thomas et al., 1986).

The normalisation approach gains mixed support from the demonstration programme. Larger community facilities – those with more residential places (generally residential homes and hostels, as we have defined them) – were found to have less beneficial effects on clients' abilities to acquire skills and to be associated with more behavioural problems. Lorna Wing (1989) found that, among former Darenth Park Hospital residents, those 'in small houses experienced the most improvement in personal independence within the home, taking part in decisions and using community services' (p.102), a result broadly consistent with ours. Of course, facility scale is not *itself* important as a determinant of client welfare, but tends to be correlated with other social and physical environmental features which are important (see, for example, King et al., 1971, and libraries of research since then).

In the placements which encouraged clients to retain or acquire age-inappropriate possessions (and behaviours) were more likely to 'de-skill' clients and generate more behavioural problems, other things being equal. Active encouragement to participate in activities – which could variously be seen as intrusive or good care – raised skill levels and left behaviour unchanged. The pleasantness of the interior environment was associated with higher skills scores, but a domestically designed *exterior* was significantly associated with lower skill levels and worse behaviour problems. Also, the domesticity of the interior environment had a small (scale-mediated) influence on behaviour.

Together we interpret the scale and environmental effects as offering support for the normalisation preference among carers and some policy-makers, but the evidence is not overwhelming. This conclusion allows for the correlation between clients' predischarge characteristics and community placements (see Chapters 5 and 10).

Costs. We describe the costs of community care below. In examining variations in client well-being in the community we introduced the cost of each client's comprehensive community care package as a potential predictor. Although there was some indication of a significant effect in the early analyses, cost proved to be unimportant in the final reckoning.

Community facility type. Three sets of possible influences on client outcomes were introduced at a second stage in the statistical analyses. Community facility type (residential home, hostel, and so on) was likely to be highly correlated with some of the environment indicators, by dint of its definition (see Chapter 6), and case management style and certain organisational features were measured at the project (not client) level, and were thus highly multicollinear (as well as having links with client welfare that could only work through a number of mediating factors). No association was found between placement type and client outcomes, once other factors (as in Table 13.9) had been taken into account.

Case management arrangements. The dimensions of case management and keyworking were discussed in Chapter 10, from which a number of simple dichotomous variables were defined. For example, one variable indicated whether or not clients were involved in case management decisions, and another indicated whether case management was a team or individual responsibility. By including these variables in the regression equations, and alternatively by conducting analyses of variance on the residuals from the equations reported in Table 13.9, we found a small number of significant associations with outcome:

- Clients' scores on our measures of skills and behaviour in the community were higher when case management was allocated to teams rather than individual staff members ($p < 0.001$ in most analyses).

- Skills and behaviour outcomes were also better when case management involved clients as active participants ($p < 0.001$). Because the analyses take into account clients' skills in hospital, this is probably *not* reflecting the opposite causal connection between abilities and invitation to become involved in decision-making.
- Clients' had higher skills levels when case managers were delegated greater autonomy and authority to purchase or create service packages on behalf of (or with) clients, similar to the delegation recommended in the community care reforms ($p < 0.01$).

These should be seen as very tentative conclusions about the different case management arrangements found in the demonstration programme, for the data, sample size and evaluation design employed in this study are short of the ideal for testing their effects on the well-being of clients.

Organisational features. The same sentiment applies to the interpretation of the small number of statistically significant links between client skills and behaviour outcomes in the community and certain features of the organisation of projects and agencies. Standardising for clients' characteristics in hospital and the environmental features of community accommodation, projects organised along multi- or unitary-agency lines appeared to perform better than those with lead-, joint- or semi-independent agency models. (See Chapter 11 for definitions.) The *operational* significance of this finding is not clear, although the questions it raises need to be answered in planning the organisation and management of community care.

Costs

Comprehensive costs

The total costs of the care services used by clients, expressed in 1986-87 prices and based on the methodology set out in the previous chapter, are summarised in Table 13.10. Average hospital costs are also reported, estimated as the full costs of the hospitals in which clients previously resided. For the three Cambridge project clients, accommodation accounted for 70 per cent of the total community care cost of £583 per week, education 22 per cent, and community social care 6 per cent. We were not given access to hospital cost data for these clients.

The most readily identified and often largest financial item is the running cost of each residential facility, but it is obvious from Table 13.10 that the full cost of community care includes rather more. Indeed, some seemingly small costs may loom disproportionately large for individual service suppliers. A good example is the burden of provision by GPs whose practices take on a large number of former hospital residents, all living in the same area of a town or city. Overall, the hidden or indirect non-residential costs of community care were considerable. They represented a smaller proportion of observed or direct (accommodation) costs in smaller, generally more domestic, settings.

Fragmented funding and multiple lines of management responsibility are two pressing reasons why community care policies need to be built on a platform of comprehensive and accurate cost information. Prior to the reforms in the *National Health Service and Community Care Act 1990* no single public agency or tier of government had the power to shift the balance of provision on its own. The distribution of costs across a number of services and agencies illustrated in Table 13.10 was not fully typical of the time: on the one hand,

Table 13.10

Community care costs, by place of residence, for people with learning difficulties (excluding Cambridge clients)

Community care component	Pecentage of total package cost by place of residence in the community[1]							
	RESID %	HOST %	SGH %	SHELT %	USGH %	INDEP %	FOST %	All %
Accommodation and living expenses[2]	62	75	58	50	33	36	42	63
Project overheads[3]	26	8	22	29	33	34	31	18
General practitioner	1	0	0	1	1	0	0	0
Day activity services	2	10	4	5	4	8	12	7
Education	2	5	8	3	0	7	7	6
In-patient hospital	1	0	1	0	5	0	0	1
Out- and day patient hospital	0	0	0	1	1	0	0	0
Community health care[4]	2	0	3	2	1	0	4	2
Community social care	4	0	3	10	22	14	3	3
Other[5]	0	1	0	0	0	0	1	0
Total (%)	100	100	100	100	100	100	100	100
Sample size	6	86	67	14	6	6	9	194
Community cost[6]	332	364	457	349	312	330	410	398
Hospital cost[6]	423	343	342	353	280	308	315	341

1 Accommodation codes are: RESID = residential home; HOST = hostel; SGH = staffed group home; SHELT = sheltered housing; USGH = unstaffed group home; INDEP = independent accommodation; FOST = adult fostering.

2 Includes staff costs where staff are employed solely at place of residence and included in accommodation budget.

3 Inclusions vary from project to project, usually covering some immediate managerial support and some peripatetic staff support.

4 Includes community nursing, medical practitioners not attached to hospital or family practices, miscellaneous community health paramedic services (chiropody, dietary services, incontinence service, and so on).

5 Includes police, travel not covered elsewhere and miscellaneous minor services.

6 Costs expressed in pounds at 1986-87 price levels per client per week.

projects' own overhead budgets sometimes reduced the need to bring services in from outside, which may have reduced the number of agency sources, while on the other hand the introduction of case management may have secured more services for clients than conventional community care provision. Nevertheless, within the programme there was still the need to painfully negotiate and then manage flows of funds and responsibilities across agencies.

Hospital costs and community costs

Despite the fact that financial considerations have been so important in affecting politicians' attitudes to deinstitutionalisation, it is surprising how little hard economic evidence there is (Korman and Glennerster, 1990, p.144).

It is the expected savings from running down hospitals which will allow the development of community care, and the figures for this client group clearly show that these savings will be insufficient on their own. The House of Commons Social Services Committee warned of this in its 1985 report.

A decent community-based service for mentally ill or mentally handicapped people cannot be provided at the same overall cost as present services. The proposition that community care could be cost-neutral is untenable. ... The Victorian hospitals in which thousands of mentally ill or handicapped people still live, in visibly inadequate conditions, will either have to continue to be shored up, at growing capital and revenue expense, or demolished and replaced by more appropriate housing at even greater expense. ... Proceeding with a policy of community care on a cost-neutral assumption is not simply naive: it is positively inhumane. Community care on the cheap would prove worse in many respects than the pattern of services to date. ... We recommend that the Government now accept that genuine community care policies are achievable only in the context of some real increase over a period of years in expenditure on services for mentally handicapped and mentally ill people (House of Commons Social Services Committee, 1985, para. 21).

Our cost findings for the other client groups and from other research suggest this may have been unduly pessimistic (see Chapters 14 and 15), but for people with learning difficulties the average cost of community care exceeds the average cost of hospital care by £57 per client per week (1986-87 prices). On average, community care therefore cost 17 per cent more than hospital. It was more than 50 per cent more costly than hospital for a quarter of the sample. By contrast, community care cost *less* than hospital for 42 per cent of clients, and the Audit Commission's conjecture that 'these care programmes do *not necessarily* require more money' (1987, para. 61; our emphasis) gains empirical support. As a group, demonstration programme clients were among the more able, less dependent residents of the hospitals they left behind, so that the cost comparisons made here may be misleading. In-patient hospital costs are known to vary with patient characteristics, as demonstrated by Wright and Haycox (1984), Johnes and Haycox (1986) and, for one of the hospitals involved with the demonstration programme, by Haycox and Brand (1991). The hospital costs in Table 13.10, which are averages for all in-patients, may therefore be higher than those actually relating to Care in the Community clients, and the true hospital-community cost difference may therefore be even larger than suggested.

The community cost differences between and within projects will be analysed more thoroughly below. Without standardising for differences in client characteristics it appears that staffed group homes were relatively costly, although three projects provided this service at a cost little different to hospital. Adult fostering was a lot less expensive than hospital in two areas and a lot more in two others.

There has been comparatively little previous costs research on community services for people with learning difficulties. Conroy and Bradley (1985), in a US study, reported like-with-like comparisons between a large hospital setting and a range of community units, the latter being cheaper. Across different community settings, it was the smaller units (akin to staffed group homes as defined here) which proved the more costly, although these researchers did not study individual clients. Three well-executed UK studies found community care to be more costly than hospital. Wright and Haycox (1984) concluded that the long-term costs in community units (run by the NHS) were 22 per cent greater than hospital costs in 'matched wards', and 75 per cent higher than short-term marginal savings. Davies (1988) looked at three settings in the Bristol area, and concluded that a staffed group home was more costly than hospital, in turn more costly than three private residential homes/hostels. From their evaluation of the Darenth Park hospital closure, Korman and Glennerster (1990) concluded that care in the community cost 50 per cent more than hospital provision, with the 'larger, more institutionalised NHS hostels' being less costly than the 'more intensively staffed group homes' (p.153). This result is the most important to date for the learning difficulty client group for two reasons. First, parallel work by Lorna Wing (1989) found community provision to be no worse than hospital, and second, Korman and Glennerster are the only researchers to have costed a *complete* hospital closure. (In the next chapter we will draw on work from outside the demonstration programme, using cost function extrapolations, to predict the costs of full rundown of two psychiatric hospitals, but the Korman and Glennerster study works with observed rather than predicted costs.) Two studies, one in Wessex (Felce, 1986) and the other in Sheffield (Dalgleish, 1983), have concluded that community care for people with learning difficulties costs less than hospital, but both appeared to employ less-than-comprehensive cost definitions.

Exploring variations in cost

One of the inherent difficulties in the calculation and examination of cost data is variation between clients, settings, facilities and areas, and it is partly this variation which prompted the type of quasi-experimental design chosen for the evaluation. Cost variation is of more than passing interest to policy-makers as they seek to provide efficient and equitable community care. Did the variation in cost between individuals reflect different achievements in relation to client welfare? Were the higher costs of some London services attributable solely to higher prices and wages within the metropolis? Did staffed group homes have higher costs than, say, hostels, because they were accommodating clients with greater needs for support? Were the lower costs observed for residential homes attributable to an inherently cheaper service or were more independent clients placed in those settings? Was voluntary sector provision of accommodation less costly than public sector provision? Each of these questions needs to be addressed with other things held equal. In terms of analytical technique, we need to conduct multivariate statistical analyses which included a wide range of possible cost-raising factors.

These statistical analyses were constructed on the basis of cost function theory, a natural corollary of the production of welfare approach (Knapp, 1984, chap. 9). We will describe the cost function approach in more detail in Chapter 14. We did not have data for every factor which the theory of cost variations would suggest should be examined, and we were also hampered by missing observations on some key variables. However, there were sufficient observations to permit estimation to proceed, with the sample size generally around 109 clients. A range of functions was fitted using ordinary least squares (OLS) regression throughout, with average cost per week as the dependent variable. (Average cost was normally distributed, and the other assumptions necessary to validate the OLS estimates held true.) We report a single equation in Table 13.11, this being the best representation of the cost function obtained. Compared to the cost functions estimated for people with mental health problems reported in the next chapter, the overall explanatory power (23 per cent) is disappointing, even though the cost function makes some interesting suggestions about community care for this client group. The results are probably more important for the questions they stimulate than for the answers they provide. (We have not found any previous research which has examined cost differences between individual *clients* with learning difficulties, and so we do not know how well our analyses compare in their overall ability to 'explain' variations, or in their modelling of constituent cost determinants. Conroy and Bradley, 1985, claim to have 'explained' 48 per cent of the observed average cost variation by reference to staffing levels and staff-client ratios, but this is simply stating a tautology with limited policy relevance. Furthermore, by including staff levels or ratios, the effects of the *true* determinants of cost variations are masked.)

Table 13.11
Cost function estimates for clients with learning difficulties

Dependent variable = average cost per week, 1986-87 prices (£)

Variable	Coefficient	Sig.
Constant term	506.44	0.00
Behaviour score in community, squared (÷ 100)	3.24	0.01
Skills score in community, squared (÷ 100)	-1.12	0.17
Personal presentation in community	-6.58	0.03
Size of community accommodation (no. of places)	-19.16	0.01
Number of places (squared)	0.55	0.11

N = 109, R^2 = 0.229, $\bar{R}^2$ = 0.192, F = 6.133 ($p < 0.001$)

Analysis of residual costs

Residence type	Mean residual	s.d.
Residential home	-15.18	96.00
Hostel	-0.92	81.74
Staffed group home	30.03	116.07
Sheltered housing	-69.54	136.43
Unstaffed group home	105.61	46.27
Independent living	-100.12	108.97
Foster placement	-68.57	109.87

Between groups F = 4.11 (p = 0.001); within groups eta squared = 0.13

Sector of residence management	Mean residual	s.d.
LA social services department	32.72	95.27
District health authority	55.30	79.12
Voluntary organisation	-72.24	92.14
Housing association	-163.84	66.52
Independently managed	-96.53	71.41
Private care agency	-82.40	44.90

Between groups F = 15.30 ($p < 0.001$); within groups eta squared = 0.31

There are links between costs and client needs. Higher scores on the behaviour, skills and personal presentation dimensions in the community indicate fewer needs, and the second and third of these are associated with lower costs. On the other hand, clients with fewer behavioural problems (higher scores on the behaviour rating) received community care packages which were *more* costly. This relationship can be interpreted in two ways, both valid in this case. First, clients with fewer behaviour problems were more likely to take part in social and employment activities outside the place of residence and to lead fuller lives. Second, the causal connection may run from cost (which measures expenditure on services, and therefore service volume) to behaviour score in the community or behaviour *change*. Korman and Glennerster (1990) tabulate costs which suggest a similar link, for the costs of community care for 'socially impaired' clients were often lower than the costs for 'sociable' clients.

The equation in Table 13.11 also provides evidence of economies of scale in accommodation facilities. (The dependent variable in the analyses was not, of course, solely a measure of accommodation cost, but Table 13.10 illustrates how accommodation accounts for a large proportion of total community care cost.) Thus, larger facilities are less costly than smaller facilities, but were previously seen to be less successful in achieving favourable client outcomes along some of the dimensions of quality of life.

In addition to the variables reported in the table we examined the cost-raising properties of a variety of other client characteristics – including ratings of morale and social interaction in both hospital and community, age, gender, duration of hospital residence prior to the move, previous hospitalisation experience, and overall severity of 'mental handicap' – but none proved consistently significant.

At the foot of Table 13.11 we report the results of analyses of variance of residual costs against accommodation type and the sector of management of accommodation. Other things being equal, costs were significantly lower in the more independent accommodation settings (unstaffed group homes, independent living, sheltered housing and foster placements). Within the programme, staffed group homes and hostels were the most commonly-used accommodation facilities for people with learning difficulties, and the cost results now imply that the former are more costly, *ceteris paribus*, although the difference does not attain statistical significance. (It is equivalent to only 7 per cent of average weekly cost). Staffed group homes had a number of features which our outcome variations analyses showed to be associated with favourable client outcomes, and would be preferred on these grounds to hostels. Leedham's (1989) more focused study of the Maidstone and Calderdale demonstration projects reached the same conclusion. Moreover, looking back at Table 8.5 shows that, in terms of their hospital characteristics, the clients who moved to hostels and staffed group homes were virtually indistinguishable.

The analysis of variance of residual cost against sector indicates that the voluntary and private sectors were delivering less costly services than either of the two public sectors, again standardising for client needs and facility scale. This is a result which mirrors our findings for mental health services, both within the Care in the Community programme (see the next chapter) and elsewhere (Beecham et al., 1991a). We found no significant outcome differences between sectors.

Summary

The evaluation of outcomes and costs for people with learning difficulties has produced some clear results.

The cost of community care was higher than the cost of hospital for more than half the sample. Across the range of community settings, higher costs were partly attributable to supporting people with greater needs and partly associated with scale of accommodation, although much of the variation remained unexplained.

We have seen both in this chapter and in Chapter 8 that some projects successfully established care settings which approached a 'normalisation' ideal and which encouraged and valued autonomy and independence.

- Clients acquired many new self-care skills since leaving hospital, particularly in relation to dressing, preparing meals, shopping, generally finding their way around, undertaking basic housework, taking care of clothes and personal possessions, writing and counting.
- They were offered greater choice about their daily activities, including leisure pursuits, and far more clients were reported to be actively participating in decision making about their own lives.
- They made greater use of ordinary community amenities than had been possible when they lived in hospital, although activity levels *generally* were no different. Of some concern must be the finding that integration into community life was far from complete for the vast majority of clients. Most difficulties were reported in the areas of education and employment, where access to 'open' (competitive) places or positions was limited.
- Social contacts were fewer in the community than in hospital, but clients were rated as significantly more highly skilled at social mixing and at initiating conversations and interactions than they had been in hospital. They themselves expressed greater levels of satisfaction with their social networks.
- The evidence from those people able to express their views points to higher levels of satisfaction with life in the community than in hospital.
- In one important area there were indications from the evaluation of a *deterioration* in quality of life. In two of the 11 projects, clients exhibited significantly more behavioural problems after they had moved, while elsewhere there was sometimes a slight but not significant deterioration. The characteristics which showed up as particularly troublesome for the client group as a whole were odd gestures and mannerisms, attention-seeking and obsessional behaviour, and disturbances at night. It must be stressed that these latter behavioural problems were not extreme or socially offensive. Nevertheless, whether this proves to be a short-term phenomenon caused by a fundamental change in life-style, including changes in medications and an active integration policy in some projects, or a more lasting effect, it clearly has implications for staff recruitment and training.

These outcome findings apply to the group of clients with learning difficulties *as a whole* and there were exceptions to this general tendency to improve. Looking at the variations in outcome we concluded that smaller, more domestic community accommodation settings – particularly group homes and independent living – were associated with better client outcomes. The multivariate analysis of costs led us to conclude, *inter alia*, that staffed group homes were not significantly more costly than hostels, these being the most commonly used community facilities in the programme. We know from other parts of our evaluation that staffed group homes presented numerous staffing and managerial problems (Chapter 7), but they have now been shown to be better for clients and not more costly than their principal alternative. Higher costs for agencies and community care staff bought better quality care and better quality of life for clients.

14 Outcomes and costs for people with mental health problems

Psychiatric hospital closures and the plight of homeless people on the streets of Britain's cities have been newsworthy items for more than a decade. To many people, the two are inextricably linked. Care in the community sometimes looks tarnished even before it starts. As an article in *The Economist* noted

> So debased has the phrase 'in the community' become that the flippant young use it as a euphemism for 'behaving oddly' (20 April 1991, p.28).

Central and local community care policies and the closure of long-stay hospital beds affect all client groups, yet most attention focuses on the psychiatric population. Even though in recent years the reduction of mental handicap hospital accommodation has easily outpaced the reduction of psychiatric hospital accommodation (a 39 per cent fall in the number of residents of mental handicap hospitals between 1979 and 1989, compared to a 27 per cent fall in psychiatric hospital residents, House of Commons Social Services Committee, 1990, Table 2), most of the 'popular opposition' – from media reports to local acts of vitriol – appears to have concentrated on people with mental health problems. There may be more popular opposition to community care today than when the demonstration projects started to plan their services in the mid-1980s, but this atmosphere of suspicion and outright opposition caused them understandable anxiety and occasional difficulty.

In fact, as we demonstrated in Chapter 12, some aspects of popular opposition to care in the community were based on mistaken assumptions and the occasional mischievously distorted anecdote masquerading as research evidence. Some other concerns proved unfounded for clients of the Care in the Community programme, even though they may have validity for some other groups of people. For example, although over 200 former hospital residents with long-term mental health problems moved from hospital during our evaluation period, no one was 'dumped' in the community, each had a case manager or keyworker, and each had a planned and supported place to live. The accommodation arrangements meant that there was virtually no informal care burden. No one was homeless, destitute or imprisoned. Deaths and readmissions to hospital were few.

From our examination of community services in Chapter 8 we saw that the clients with mental health problems enjoyed many improvements in life-style after they moved from hospital. Many lived in ordinary housing, either in groups of three or four, or independently. They expressed more positive attitudes about their places of residence and their access to community facilities.

Although falling short of projects' and clients' aspirations, many people made regular and full use of community services and resources, whether for education, leisure or to meet their health and social care needs. In these and other areas, clients were able to exercise choice in more areas than had been possible in hospital, even if the constraints imposed by staffing levels and low incomes frustrated full integration and empowerment.

In the pursuit of 'process' or 'intermediate' objectives, therefore, the pilot projects generally succeeded in providing clients with good quality care, and with opportunities and possibilities previously unavailable to them in hospital. But, as we have argued on numerous occasions in this book, process and input indicators are not sufficient in the evaluation of community care. Too many research studies in decades past concentrated on the failings of hospitals and gauged the success of community care by the same yardstick: avoiding the failings was implicitly taken as sufficient evidence of success. There was a second inhibition in much previous research in the mental health field.

> It was also argued that because chronic health problems, morbidity and mortality are insensitive variables, and are seemingly unrelated to health care changes in the short term, the use of input and process indicators as proxy measures for outcome was justified (Jenkins, 1990, p.501).

The evaluation of the Care in the Community programme paid particular attention to client outcomes. How successful, then, were the projects in meeting their, the Department of Health's, and clients' outcome objectives, and at what cost? This is the focus of the present chapter.

Client outcomes

In the paper quoted above, Jenkins (1990) helpfully reviews some of the needs for, approaches to the measurement of, and drawbacks associated with, systems of outcome indicators for mental health care. After discussing mortality, morbidity, subjective health indicators, direct measures of health and social functioning, and measures of need, she suggests input, process and outcome indicators for the major categories of mental illness. For example, she offers as indicators of outcome for people with schizophrenia: prevalence of schizophrenia; rates of hospital admission and readmissions; employment; suicide and standardised mortality; and extent of homelessness. These are administrative indicators amenable to collection by health and local authorities. They lend themselves naturally to the monitoring and strategic planning functions of these and other agencies. They are not, however, typical of the outcome indicators most commonly employed in smaller-scale, focused and generally time-limited evaluations of psychiatric services. They are also rather heavily weighted towards positive symptomatology, relapse, recidivism and failure. They are not as sensitive to change as some policy or practice questions would require. For example, employing only the Jenkins dimensionality would lead us to conclude that there were *no* differences between the eight Care in the Community projects, for homelessness, mortality, hospital readmission and employment rates showed no variation, and scores on the symptoms and behavioural problems instrument did not register significant inter-project differences. Yet on some other outcome dimensions, inter-project variations were considerable and statistically significant. Administrative indicators also give no opportunity for service users to express their views about services and quality of life generally (Lehman, 1983). Our point is not to criticise any suggestion for better *routine* statistics on the performance of mental health services, but to stress the need for more searching indicators of outcome in *non-routine* evaluative enquiries.

A scientific group convened in 1989 by the World Health Organisation to select criteria for evaluating 'the effectiveness of treatment of schizophrenic disorders' produced a list which is typical of outcome dimensionalities now employed in evaluations. They recommended the examination of: overall functioning, including adaptation in vocational, residential and recreational roles; dependence/autonomy; presence and severity of negative symptoms; social skills; side and toxic effects of pharmacological treatments; and patients' and families' perceptions of overall quality of life (de Girolamo, 1990). In evaluating deinstitutionalisation programmes, similar outcome dimensions have been employed. The most ambitious evaluation of the movement of long-stay psychiatric hospital residents to the community in the UK is being conducted by the Team for the Assessment of Psychiatric Services led by Professor Julian Leff. People leaving Friern and Claybury hospitals under North East Thames Region's psychiatric reprovision scheme have been interviewed and assessed in hospital, and again 12 months after discharge. Outcome dimensions include an examination of the 'failings' of community care similar to our discussion in Chapter 12, and the assessment of mental health status (including symptoms and behaviour), physical health, basic everyday living skills, social networks, clients' attitudes and living environments (TAPS, 1990).

By comparison to these other studies, the outcome evaluation of the Care in the Community programme spans the dimensions most often discussed and employed. (As well as the work cited above, see the reviews by Braun et al., 1981, and Avison and Speechley, 1987.) We have already reported our findings on the quality of living environments, philosophy of care, social integration, homelessness, mortality, hospital readmissions, choice and empowerment, and we now consider the programme's impact on skills, symptoms and behavioural problems, activities, social contacts, and morale and life satisfaction.

The broad methodology for our outcome evaluation was described in Chapters 4 and 12, and some of the practical considerations were discussed when we reported outcomes for people with learning difficulties in the previous chapter. The instrumentation chosen for the evaluation has also been introduced, this being the same for both the learning difficulty and mental health client groups. It is therefore not necessary to repeat earlier accounts of our approach to outcome evaluation. Table 14.1 provides an overview of response rates for the main quantitative instruments employed in the evaluation. With fewer projects serving people with mental health problems than learning difficulties, it was inevitable that sample sizes would be smaller although, because of fewer comprehension and communication difficulties, we had a higher response rate when interviewing clients with mental health problems.

Table 14.1
Outcome and cost research instruments, sample sizes for people with mental health problems

	Numbers of clients[2]	
Research instrument[1]	**Baseline**	**Movers**
Skills	319	153
Symptoms and behavioural problems	319	153
Satisfaction with services questions	293	152
Schedule for Social Interaction	287	150
Depression Inventory	267	142
Psychosocial Functioning Inventory	275	148
Personal presentation	313	151
Client Service Receipt Interview	-[3]	130
Costs	130	130

1 Each instrument is described in the text.
2 The effective number for some analyses will be smaller because of missing information on some component items for some clients.
3 Hospital of residence was known for every client, but service utilisation data in hospital were not collected. Hospital costs were estimated *only* for those clients for whom we also had community costs data.

Skills

Hospital and community-based rehabilitation training programmes set great store by the skills needed for the basic activities of daily living. Even though many leavers will first move to sheltered or well-supported community accommodation, the ability to cook, carry out basic housework, shop, handle money, use public transport, and look after one's clothes and possessions will have considerable bearing on the type and success of clients' long-term placements. 'Personal and social skills' comprise one of the two areas of functioning in the MRC Needs for Care Assessment, for example (Brewin et al., 1987). Social skills acquisition has been found to be a predictor of successful rehabilitation (Linn et al., 1977; Presly et al., 1982), and so it was clearly important to monitor each client's skills attainments.

The skills scale used in the evaluation included items taken from the Social Behaviour Scale and the Disability Assessment Schedule. Scores can run from 31 to 90. The mean community score for the 121 people with mental health

Table 14.2
Skills of clients with mental health problems in the community, and community-hospital differences

Skills score and difference	Mean	Standard deviation	Sample
Skills score in community (T2)	73.8	6.8	121
Community-hospital difference (T2-T1)	-0.5	6.2	121
Community-hospital difference significance		p = 0.372	

problems for whom we had both hospital and community ratings was 74, and the mean difference between the two assessments virtually zero, and certainly not statistically significant (see Table 14.2). On only three of the component items of the skills instrument were there significant differences between hospital and community for the full sample: in relation to eating habits, task-sharing and taking opportunities to use community facilities, clients were performing worse in the community (Table 14.3). When comparing the assessments of skills in hospital we found that people with mental health problems were better skilled than people with learning difficulties (see Chapter 5); this difference persisted into the community (compare Tables 14.2 and 13.2).

Looking at each of the eight projects for this client group singly, none registered a significant skills improvement or deterioration. Although community skills scores were significantly different between projects (ranging from 70 to 79; $p = 0.023$), there was no inter-project difference in the *change* in skills score ($p = 0.125$). Looking at the different accommodation facilities, people living in residential homes and hostels appeared to perform less well than those living elsewhere, although the differences were not statistically significant (compare Segal and Moyles, 1979).

Our finding that the skills levels of people with long-term mental health problems neither deteriorated nor improved is consistent with results from the ongoing TAPS (1990) research for a similar cohort of former hospital residents, but is in contrast to some other findings. For instance, Wykes (1982) looked at 25 'new long-stay patients', 15 of whom remained in hospital and ten who moved to a hostel. Using the earliest version of Wykes's Social Performance Scale (most items of which were incorporated in our instrument), he concluded that the movers had more problems with self-care and lacked self-confidence. Hyde et al. (1987) reached a similar conclusion, whereas Gudeman et al. (1981) found community clients to be *more* skilled than a comparable group of hospital residents.

When they learned of our finding that clients' skills showed no significant improvement after nine months in the community, some project staff expressed surprise and disappointment. This may simply be a perception problem, for the marked improvements of some clients may be remembered and the deteriorations of others overlooked. A nine-month follow-up period is quite

Table 14.3
Changes in clients' skills since leaving hospital, people with mental health problems

Item description[1]	Worse %	Same %	Better %	Sig. changes[2] p
Vision	7	84	9	
Hearing	4	91	5	
Mobility	7	91	2	
Conversation, social mixing with other clients	23	59	19	
Initiation of conversation/interaction with other clients	19	58	23	
Non-verbal communication	26	55	20	
Length of conversations	14	74	12	
Clarity of speech	8	85	7	
Eating habits at mealtime	17	76	7	0.059
Does fair share of collective tasks	22	59	20	
Task-sharing with other clients	30	62	8	0.002
Argues with other clients	24	59	17	
Participation in decisions re. roles	25	43	31	
Washing and bathing self	18	69	13	
Dressing	13	69	18	
Cooking and getting meals alone	25	54	22	
Basic housework and care of clothes	20	58	22	
Shopping alone	22	59	19	
Manages own financial affairs	24	56	20	
Finds way around	18	70	12	
Uses amenities in community (church, pub, ...)	19	54	17	
Has missed opportunities in last month to use these facilities[3]	27	62	12	0.010
Do staff encourage client to use these facilities?[3]	21	66	13	
Do staff stop client doing things, reducing independence?[3]	16	64	20	
Independently plans/organises weekly activities	26	43	31	
Understanding communication	3	96	1	
Reading	4	88	8	
Writing	18	72	10	
Counting and handling money	7	87	6	
Looking after own clothes and possessions	18	58	24	
Appearance if left to own devices	18	58	23	
Sample size[4]		121		

1 All except items indicated by note 3 have three categories of response.
2 Using the Wilcoxon test we examined the significance of changes between hospital and community. 'p' indicates significance level. Only significant differences are reported. All four significant changes were deteriorations.
3 Item required Yes/No responses.
4 Missing values varied from item to item, ranging from 0 to 20. In most cases missing assessments arose because hospital residents did not have opportunities to test these particular skills.

short when compared with the duration of hospitalisation that preceded it, and clients may have acquired further skills after we had completed our evaluation. It must not be forgotten that skills levels were already high before clients left hospital, for the movers had more self-care and other skills than the stayers, and our instrument may have been insufficiently sensitive to recognise some client improvements. These can only remain as untested hypotheses.

Symptoms and behavioural problems

It was natural that the evaluation of community care for people with mental health problems should monitor any changes in symptomatology and behavioural problems, although it was recognised that some characteristics were deep-seated and unlikely to change, especially over the short period we had for the evaluation follow-up (Brown et al., 1966). The research resources were not available to allow the use of an instrument like the Present State Examination (PSE) or some other direct interviewer rating of a client's psychiatric symptoms. Our more modest aim was to gather information in an interview with a staff member who knew the client well. The interview asked about the presence and seriousness of 26 characteristics, symptoms and behaviours commonly found in people with long-term mental health problems. Each item was rated on a three-point scale, from serious behavioural problem or symptom (score 1) to no behavioural problem (score 3). The total score could therefore run from 26 to 78. For the 121 clients assessed in both hospital and community, the mean community score was 69, marginally but not significantly lower than in hospital (Table 14.4).

Although there was no evidence of any overall change in symptoms or behaviour nine months after leaving hospital, there were statistically significant deteriorations along two dimensions – waking at night, and a miscellaneous problems item – and changes on two other items (depression or weeping, and suicidal preoccupations) almost attained significance (Table 14.5). There were no differences between the eight projects or between the different accommodation types on either the aggregate symptoms/behaviour score in the community, or the hospital-community difference.

Table 14.4

Symptoms and behavioural problems of clients with mental health problems in the community, and community-hospital differences

Behavioural problems score and difference	Mean	Standard deviation	Sample
Behavioural problems score in community (T2)	68.8	5.2	121
Community-hospital difference (T2-T1)	-0.9	5.4	121
Community-hospital difference significance:		p = 0.168	

Table 14.5
Changes in clients' behavioural problems since leaving hospital, people with mental health problems

Item description[1]	Worse %	Same %	Better %	Sig. changes[2] p
Depression or weeping	17	74	9	0.072
Suicidal preoccupations	8	89	3	0.087
Anxiety, panic, phobias	17	67	16	
Slowness of movement	20	64	17	
Underactivity	23	57	20	
Over-activity	15	74	11	
Elated or euphoric behaviour	10	82	8	
Odd gestures, mannerisms	18	61	21	
Acting out delusions, hallucinations	12	64	24	
Attention-seeking behaviour	17	71	12	
Agressive or violent behaviour	12	74	14	
Obsessional behaviour	15	78	8	
Self-injury	2	97	1	
Stealing (e.g. food, cigarettes)	4	91	5	
Collecting, hoarding meaningless items	9	79	12	
Shouting, swearing, offensive, screaming	20	69	11	
Incontinence during the day	6	92	3	
Incontinence at night	5	91	4	
Confused	17	70	13	
Objectionable at night	10	84	6	
Awake at night	34	54	12	0.001
Accuses others of doing harm, stealing	14	76	10	
Wanders or runs away (if not supervised)	5	88	7	
Stereotyped repetitive activities, echolalia	16	73	11	
Sexually offensive behaviour	8	89	3	
Any other problems	39	39	21	0.038
Sample size[3]		121		

1 All except items have three categories of response.
2 Using the Wilcoxon test we examined the significance of changes between hospital and community. 'p' indicates significance level. Only significant differences are reported. All four significant changes were deteriorations.
3 Missing values varied from item to item, ranging from 0 to 20. In most cases missing assessments arose because hospital residents did not have opportunities to test these particular skills.

These experiences of the demonstration programme clients – no changes in symptomatology or general manifestations of mental ill health – appear to be consistent with what has been found elsewhere. In North London, TAPS (1990) found no difference between hospital and community scores on the PSE or on their measure of social behaviour (which also has its roots in the work of Wykes, 1982), nor were there inter-temporal differences between the leavers and a matched sample of people who remained in hospital.

Activities

Wing and Brown's (1970) classic study found a link between mental health symptoms and the amount of time that hospital residents spent engaged in activities. A common aim and a common disappointment for the eight projects for people with mental health problems was to help clients to find employment in the community. A number of factors conspired to keep clients unemployed – a depressed labour market, the 'benefits trap' (which penalised earnings by cutting the social security payments to clients and facilities), insufficient numbers of staff if clients needed to be accompanied to their workplace, lack of confidence, skills and relevant experience, and the negative attitudes of some potential employers (see Chapter 8).

The evaluation did not ask clients directly for their views on employment opportunities, although 81 per cent said they were happy with how they spent their days (compared to 78 per cent hospital), and 89 per cent said they had enough to do with their time (compared to 74 per cent in hospital). All four percentages relate to 120 clients. When asked about their preferences for activities:

- 61 per cent expressed a liking for outdoor activities such as walks, sports, cycling and gardening (compared to only 34 in hospital);
- 86 per cent for indoor activities such as painting, sewing, playing games, cooking and reading (69 per cent in hospital);
- 74 per cent for social activities such as visiting friends and social clubs (65 per cent in hospital);
- 94 per cent for passive activities, including listening to the radio or records, or watching TV (86 per cent in hospital); and
- 44 per cent for other activities such as going to church and looking after pets (only 17 per cent in hospital).

These percentages were based on interviews with 196 clients. The move to the community apparently opened up new vistas for people with mental health problems in ways that were not found for the other client groups but which have precursors in the psychiatry literature. For example, Gibbons and Butler (1987) also found a significant increase in participation in activities by the 15 'new' long-stay patients who had moved to a hospital-hostel from a district general hospital unit and a psychiatric hospital.

Social contacts

Social isolation and distorted social contacts and activities have been described as classic features of an impoverished institutional life. We planned to obtain information on clients' social contacts using a diary record over a two-week period, covering the frequency and nature of contacts with friends, relatives, members of the local community and care professionals. It proved very difficult to get this information. Clients living independently were asked to complete their own records, but in the main staff supplied our data. Completed social contacts records were obtained for only 38 people in the community, indicating that clients had an average of 3.6 visitors per fortnight (compared to the average of 1.0 for 101 hospital residents). However, most of these visitors were now professional staff, whereas previously the modal group was family members.

Clients' reports of their social networks were included in our interviews with them in both the community and hospital (employing the Interview Schedule for Social Interaction developed by Henderson, 1981). These reports provide less detailed indications of social contacts, but they were available for a much larger sample of people. A summary of the responses from 114 people who moved to the community and who had also been interviewed in hospital is given in Table 14.6. A higher percentage of clients reported contact with their families in the community than in hospital (74 per cent compared to 52 per cent), but *fewer* had friends, defined as 'people who you go and see or who come to see you'. In hospital, a third of the clients had no confidant and three-

Table 14.6
Social contacts – the views of clients with mental health problems

Questions and overall instrument score[1]	*Percentage responses*	
	Hospital	**Community**
Do you ever see your family or relatives?		
Yes	52	74
How many friends do you have?		
None	28	58
1 or 2	20	22
3 to 5	14	12
6 to 10	32	4
more than 10	7	4
How many friends could you go to if you were upset or wanted help?		
None	33	63
1 or 2	50	29
3 to 5	12	7
6 to 10	4	2
more than 10	1	0
Is there anyone who knows you very well?		
Yes	77	87
Overall score on Schedule for Social Interaction – mean[2]	4.9	4.7
Sample size	114	114

1 Taken from the Schedule for Social Interaction.
2 The community-hospital difference (mean 0.5, standard deviation 2.9) was significant at $p = 0.709$ level.

quarters no intimate friends; in the community, both proportions had increased noticeably.

We conclude, therefore, that there was an increase in clients' social contacts after leaving hospital, as reported by both staff and themselves, and clients were more likely to have established close friendships. This is a different conclusion from that reached by TAPS (1990), who reported no widening of social networks for long-stay residents leaving Friern and Claybury hospitals. However, their sample included some people who were more disabled and less socially skilled than the Care in the Community cohort, and there is research evidence from elsewhere that the most important determinant of social network size is social competence (Denoff and Pilkonis, 1987). Unlike Murphy and Datel (1976), we did not find that people who moved from hospital to foster placements became increasingly isolated and, unlike Lehman et al. (1982) and Gibbons and Butler (1987), we did not find that clients had limited contacts with relatives and friends. Honig et al. (1987) argued that 'the social network surrounding many chronic patients often becomes diminished and is taken over by therapists and their services' (p.307; and see Speck and Attneave, 1973). A similar danger was there for some Care in the Community clients.

Scores on the aggregate Schedule for Social Interaction were not significantly different between hospital and community, and neither community scores nor changes between hospital and community varied significantly between projects or community accommodation types.

Morale and life satisfaction

Six different instruments were used to gauge clients' morale and life satisfaction globally and in a few key component areas. Like most research studies today, we placed considerable emphasis on this aspect of our evaluation, although our instrumentation was not as comprehensive as the specially focused Quality of Life work of Lehman (1983), Thapa and Rowland (1989), Levitt et al. (1990) and others. Some of the views expressed by clients were described in Chapters 5 and 8. The scale scores computed from the interviews in the community and the differences between hospital and community scores can be seen from Table 14.7. Apart from a borderline improvement in the global rating provided by Cantril's ladder, there were no significant changes over time. There were no differences between projects or community accommodation types.

As some other research enquiries have found, people with long-term mental health problems moving from hospital often express positive views about life in the community, even if the overall ratings do not amount to significant changes (Dickey et al., 1986; Gibbons and Butler, 1987; Hyde et al., 1987; Drake and Wallach, 1988).

Table 14.7
Morale and life satisfaction of clients with mental health problems in the community, and hospital-community differences

Instrument	*Comm. score*			*T2-T1 diff.*			
	M	SD	N	M	SD	N	p[1]
Cantril's ladder	3.9	1.7	109	0.5	2.1	101	0.027
Depression Inventory[2]	11.2	8.1	111	0.7	6.7	103	0.255
Psychosocial Functioning Inventory	39.2	6.7	115	0.6	6.1	111	0.121

1 M = mean; SD = standard deviation; N = sample size; p = significance of test of difference between hospital and community scores.
2 Lower scores on the Depression Inventory indicate greater morale (lower depression).

Exploring client outcome variations

Table 14.8 summarises the results of our tests of inter-project and inter-facility differences in the community scores, and hospital-community differences and ratios, for the main quantitative indicators. Few of these differences were significant, for there were comparatively few variations between clients. Nevertheless, we examined whether these small inter-client variations in outcomes could be interpreted by reference to client characteristics, accommodation, service input, case management and other effects. Our approach and methodology followed those used to explore outcome variations among clients with learning difficulties (Chapter 13). The statistical analyses offered no insights: not one of the multiple regression analyses produced a statistically robust, easily interpretable result. The reasons were obvious – limited inter-client variations in the community scores and small overall changes on each of the dimensions.

Costs

> Community care is a matter of marshalling resources, sharing responsibilities and combining skills to achieve good quality modern services to meet the actual needs of real people, in ways those people find acceptable and in places which encourage rather than prevent normal living. ... This requires the better use of that proportion of ... resources which is now locked up in the hospitals. A good quality community-orientated service may well be more expensive than a poor quality institutional one. ... The aim is not to save money: but to use it responsibly (Cmnd 9674, 1985, pp.1-2).

The question of the comparative costs of hospital and community provision for people with long-term needs has often been posed but rarely answered. Most of the answers suggested have been tentative not because of the

Table 14.8
Analysis of variance of community scores, and community-hospital differences, by project and facility, for people with mental health problems

	T2 scores		*(T2-T1) differences*		*(T2-T1)/T1 ratios*	
	Between projects	**Between facilities**	**Between projects**	**Between facilities**	**Between projects**	**Between facilities**
Skills Scale	0.023	ns	ns	ns	ns	ns
Symptoms/behaviour scale	ns	ns	ns	ns	ns	ns
Schedule for Social Interaction	ns	ns	ns	ns	ns	ns
Cantril's ladder	ns	ns	ns	ns	0.040	0.031
Psychosocial Functioning Inventory	ns	ns	0.039	ns	0.020	ns
Depression Inventory	ns	ns	ns	ns	ns	ns

'ns' indicates not significant ($p > 0.05$).

complexities of cost measurement, but because of the difficulties of cost *interpretation.*

Costs were measured comprehensively in both hospital and community settings for 130 people with mental health problems. Hospital cost calculations were based on average revenue expenditures for whole establishments (later adjusted for inter-ward and other differences), with the addition of a capital element (site and durable resources sale valuation, annuitised over 60 years at 5 per cent) and a small proportion to reflect non-hospital service inputs such as social work provided by a local authority. Community costs ranged over every public, voluntary, private and personal budget concerned, with calculations guided by opportunity costing principles. Thus, group accommodation and day centre costs were based on facility-specific revenue costs plus a replacement value for capital. In each case, as described in Chapter 12, we chose cost figures to be as close as possible to expected long-run marginal costs.

The full costs of community and hospital care are given in Table 14.9 for 130 clients, arranged by type of community accommodation. All costs are expressed at 1986-87 price levels. (Inflating them by 28 per cent will give an indication of costs at 1990-91 prices.) Differences between community and hospital costs – which have not yet been adjusted for differences in client characteristics between settings – suggest that community care is less costly than hospital. These cost differences are broadly in line with previous research on community mental health services for people with long-term needs moving from hospital. Studies in the USA (Murphy and Datel, 1976; Segal and Kottler, 1989), Canada (Cassel et al., 1972) and the UK (Stilwell, 1981; Hyde et al., 1987; Knapp and Beecham, 1990a, 1991) concluded that costs were lower in the community (variously defined). Community care was not the less expensive option for *every* client; for 18 of the 130 it was greater, and for eight of them

Table 14.9
Community care costs, by place of residence, for people with mental health problems

Community care component	Pecentage of total package cost by place of residence in the community[1]							All places
	RESID	HOST	SGH	USGH	INDEP	FOST	SUPP	
	%	%	%	%	%	%	%	%
Accommodation and living expenses[2]	66	71	68	42	62	60	57	61
Project overheads[3]	0	4	6	12	7	0	11	6
General practitioner	0	0	0	1	0	0	1	0
Day activity services	12	16	14	21	22	31	19	17
Education	0	1	0	1	3	3	1	0
In-patient hospital	15	1	6	1	0	0	0	3
Out- and day patient hospital	0	2	2	1	0	0	0	1
Community health care[4]	6	2	3	5	1	1	2	3
Community social care	0	2	2	17	4	3	6	10
Other[5]	0	0	0	0	0	0	0	0
Total (%)	100	100	100	100	100	100	100	100
Sample size	11	52	13	40	6	5	3	130
Community cost[6]	374	269	325	243	222	260	181	271
Hospital cost[6]	386	330	380	363	362	354	359	354

1 Accommodation codes are: RESID = residential home; HOST = hostel; SGH = staffed group home; USGH = unstaffed group home; INDEP = independent accommodation; FOST = adult fostering; SUPP = supported lodgings.
2 Includes staff costs where staff are employed solely at place of residence and included in accommodation budget.
3 Inclusions vary from project to project, usually covering some immediate managerial support and some peripatetic staff support.
4 Includes community nursing, medical practitioners not attached to hospital or family practices, miscellaneous community health paramedic services (chiropody, dietary services, incontinence service, and so on).
5 Includes police, travel not covered elsewhere and miscellaneous services.
6 Costs expressed in pounds at 1986-87 price levels per client per week.

it was more than 25 per cent greater. Again, this result has parallels, such as in the Mannheim study of people suffering from schizophrenia (Häfner, 1987; Häfner and an der Heiden, 1989b). Häfner correctly concluded that 'certain patients require such intensive care that it is more economical to treat them in in-patient than extra-mural services' (1987, p.123), but there are times when it may be more *cost-effective* to select the more expensive alternative.

On average, Care in the Community provision cost less than residence in the hospitals which the 130 clients left nine months earlier. This prompts five questions.

- Where does the cost burden fall?

- Is the relatively low cost in the community simply a consequence of 'skimming' the most independent hospital residents for community care?
- Should we therefore expect the costs of future cohorts of discharged hospital residents to be significantly higher?
- At what rate do hospital costs decline as beds are closed? That is, how quickly can funds be released for developing community services?
- Do higher community care costs result in better client outcomes?

The distribution of costs

The cost figures in Table 14.9 show how the aggregated costs are distributed across services and agencies. A number of agencies which contribute to the support of former hospital residents are not compensated financially for their contributions. For example, even though the contribution of GP services to total package costs is very small, the burden on individual practices can be large, particularly with the growing tendency for homes to be grouped in areas of towns with appropriate housing and within reach of day or resource centres. Dowry transfers do not always compensate local authorities for their social care support of former hospital residents (see Chapter 7), yet it is the role of the case manager to identify client needs and to coordinate services from wherever they can be obtained. The new Mental Illness Specific Grant and the forthcoming joint health-local authority community care plans should, in principle, help to overcome some of the problems of perverse incentives and coordination in the fragmented care system.

Despite projects' concerns that they were unable to provide all the day activities for clients they had hoped (see Chapter 8), a comparison of the percentages in Table 14.9 with equivalent data from *outside* the demonstration programme (Knapp et al., 1990) shows that they had much greater success.

The 'skimming' of hospital residents

Project clients were among the more able, less dependent residents of the hospitals from which they moved. We could not undertake separate ward-costing exercises in each of the 60 or more hospitals involved in the programme, but careful work in one large psychiatric hospital from which many clients moved revealed that the mean ward-level cost for clients had been £338 (median £330) at 1986-87 prices. This was 93 per cent (median 91 per cent) of the overall hospital average. That is, even though this project – in common with others – selected people for the move to the community who were less dependent (as a group) than the hospital average, these people had previously been accommodated on wards where costs were not *greatly* different from the hospital average. Hospitals which adopted a more 'functional' allocation of residents to wards were likely to display wider inter-ward differences. For example, the equivalent percentages in an earlier hospital cost disaggregation indicated that mean hospital cost for the 'matched controls' of a cohort of leavers was 85 per cent of overall hospital cost, median 89 per cent (Knapp et al., 1987). Thus, although projects were 'skimming' some less dependent people from hospital, the adjustment to average hospital cost needed to validate the comparisons with community costs is small. Only if programme clients had been living in wards whose costs were 77 per cent of the hospital average would their community care have been the more costly option.

Research has shown that both hospital and community costs are higher for people who are more disabled or dependent (see below for evidence on community cost variations). Leaving to one side the medium-term transitional problems of shifting resources from hospital to community use, the extent to which hospital savings can adequately finance community care in the long-term depends on the difference in the cost-dependency gradients for the two settings. Because the typical hospital rundown policy resettles the less dependent people first, and because these people are often more dependent than other people with mental health problems already in the community, the 'average level of dependency' and the average cost will increase in both settings. Policy-makers may be disappointed to observe inflated costs – (the House of Commons Social Services Committee, 1990, Table 2, reports that hospital costs have increased by 47 per cent at constant prices over ten years) – especially if the hospital rundown policy was supported in part on the grounds of economy, but the aggregate cost of provision will have fallen.

One caveat should be entered here: hospital costs in 1986-87 may not have reflected the 'steady state' costs of in-patient care had a policy of community care not been implemented. For example, the Scottish Home and Health Department (1984) noted that £26 million of urgent repairs were needed to Scottish psychiatric hospitals. The difficulty that this poses for research is that psychiatric hospitals have been running down their resident places for as much as 50 years, and a 'steady state' may not have existed for some time.

Future community care costs

We cannot put figures on the likely costs of community care for the more dependent hospital residents who had not moved to the community with the help of demonstration programme provision, but evidence from the evaluation of the rundown of Friern and Claybury hospitals provides useful information (Knapp et al., 1990). The Team for the Assessment of Psychiatric Services collected information on all long-stay residents of the two hospitals who, if aged over 65, did not have a current diagnosis of dementia. (Almost 1,000 people were assessed using a comprehensive battery of instruments.) The PSSRU cost study of the psychiatric reprovision services established for leavers from the two hospitals allowed these hospital characteristics to be examined alongside community care costs. A prediction equation was estimated by multiple regression analysis, 'explaining' 38 per cent of the observed community cost variation by reference only to clients' characteristics in hospital. (We carried out the same exercise for the Care in the Community clients, obtaining similar results, but did not have the full hospital baseline data to take the next step.) The prediction equation was then applied to the baseline data for *all* hospital residents. In this way we were able to predict the cost of transferring the care of every long-stay hospital resident to the community. The TAPS research had also shown that client quality of life was at least as good in the community as in hospital (TAPS, 1990).

The projected future cost of community care for hospital residents who had not yet moved was calculated to be £332 per week (19 per cent higher than the average of £270 for the first cohorts of leavers). For the full hospital long-stay populations the average weekly community care cost was £321. (These are all London costs, quoted at 1986-87 price levels.) These predicted costs cover everything expected to be needed in the community, and they take account of the fact that future cohorts of leavers will have greater needs for support. (The prediction equation includes negative psychiatric symptoms, social behaviour, social networks, length of time in hospital and age among the determinants of cost.) Making an adjustment for the lower costs of long-stay wards (compared with acute and psychogeriatric wards), the predicted community cost was probably marginally smaller than the cost of in-patient care in each of the two hospitals at the time the reprovision programme commenced.

The replacement of hospital with community services does *not* appear to require the injection of substantial additional sums of money if patient quality of life is to be at least maintained. This does not mean that the locus of care can be shifted without difficulty, for there are potential problems with the speed with which resources can be transferred and, as we saw above, the distribution of the community cost burden.

The prediction equation developed from our Friern-Claybury research can also be used for national predictions (Knapp et al., 1991). Using information on the 24,000 psychiatric hospital residents in England in 1989 who had been in residence for at least one year and who did not have a diagnosis of dementia, we predicted that community care for these people would cost approximately £11,100 each year, 12 per cent of which (£1,367) would be revenue expenditure borne by local authorities in the provision of social care, without social security or other compensation. These costs are expressed at 1986-87 price levels. This is considerably in excess of the amount currently set aside for the new Mental Illness Specific Grant.

Cost savings by hospitals

Arrangements for the transfer of money from hospital to community care to facilitate the development of the latter, introduced in 1983, are generally tied to the closure of beds. Some of the advantages and problems associated with these dowries were discussed in Chapter 7. One of the principal concerns of health authorities, unit general managers and hospital staff has been to prevent the transfer of money out of hospital budgets before savings are reaped. A common argument is that hospital costs change only slowly in response to falling bed numbers because of the fixed overheads that have to be carried, at least until whole wards or whole establishments close.

Using data for every psychiatric hospital in ten of the 14 English health regions for each of three years, we fitted an average cost function in order to estimate (after some differential calculus) the *marginal cost* of hospital in-patient care. This would give an indication of marginal savings as hospitals run down their long-stay provision. Data were limited – there were no patient profiles or case mix information, for example – but the analyses provided an indication of the *average* speed with which hospital costs fell. With one exception, previous British studies of the costs of psychiatric hospital care do not permit a comparison with the results described below (Stern and Stern, 1963; McKechnie et al., 1982; Mercer, 1975). The exception is the unpublished doctoral dissertation of Casmas (1976) whose finding that average and marginal costs are similar in magnitude mirrors our finding here.

Ordinary least squares estimation was used to fit a cost function with average revenue cost per in-patient day as the dependent variable. (Out-patient and day patient costs were omitted, as were all capital cost elements and any costs falling outside the hospital budget.) The potential explanatory variables were the number of in-patient days, the proportion of available beds occupied over the year and regional location (since regions have different policies for their long-stay hospital beds and face different labour supply prices). The best representation of cost function gave the marginal cost as:

$$MC = 46.00 - 43.32 \times (\text{change in occupancy, 85/6 to 86/7}) + \text{regional effects}$$

Taking the mean change in occupancy across the 119 hospitals in the sample, marginal cost (averaged across regions) was £43 per in-patient day, or £298 per week, at 1986-87 prices. Yet the mean average cost per in-patient day for these same hospitals was £368. Across the full sample, marginal cost – the cost of one additional or one fewer in-patient – was 81 per cent of average revenue cost, and the estimated function indicates that this marginal cost will be higher in hospitals which are quicker to adjust their available beds to falling patient numbers. This is exactly as one would expect. Hospitals which have 'closed' beds (or whole wards or wings) as patients have moved out or died have smaller year-on-year changes in their occupancy proportions and therefore higher marginal savings.

From this estimation exercise, therefore, we conclude that, *on average*, as much as 81 per cent of a hospital's revenue costs per patient are saved in the short term as in-patient numbers decline. This function assumes *smooth* cost adjustment, when the reality is a stepped process, but many hospitals are now running down bed numbers at a speed that easily allows the annual closure of a whole ward, should this be acceptable on care grounds and to residents.

We do not propose that dowry transfers should be governed by results of the kind presented here, but these estimates give a perspective on the financial implications for hospitals as they move towards long-term in-patient targets. They also offer evidence on economies of scale suggesting that the Victorians were clearly practising sound financial management when they built the huge asylums, although then, as today, patient welfare and other non-monetary considerations were also important in shaping services.

The cost-outcome relationship

Costs are not identical for everyone, and the question then arises whether differences in cost reflect differences in needs and outcomes.

Exploring cost variations

It is reasonable to hypothesise that the costs of community care services received by individual clients will vary in response to or be associated with differences in levels of need and *changes* in need, the latter measuring the principal outcomes of an intervention. These associations will be mediated through such other factors as scale and organisation of service delivery agencies, regional location and so on, each of which may be of interest in its own right. Hypotheses were tested through the estimation of a series of cost functions.

Client-specific measures were used as predictors of cost differences in the cost function analyses, along with measures of various mediating factors. The analyses were complicated by the fact that some background information was not available for all clients, and because there were several sets of potential mediating factors which could be included in different ways. It was therefore necessary to look at more than one series of estimates in order to draw conclusions about cost-outcome associations. The regression equations are not reported here (they are detailed in Knapp and Beecham, 1990b), and instead Table 14.10 provides a summary of the results from *six* separate series of analyses.

Community care costs were sensitive to most of the client features for which measures were developed. Costs were higher for people displaying greater needs along the dimensions measured, and the relationship between these

Table 14.10
Summary of cost function results, clients with mental health problems

Variable	Sign	Significance range[1]
Age	+	.000 to .004
Duration of hospitalisation before discharge[2]	-	.000 to .032
Original diagnosis: organic brain disorder	+	.001 to .053
Age at onset of mental illness	-	.001 to .001
Skills score in community	-	.017 to .017
Behavioural problems score in community[2]	-	.000 to .141
Schedule for Social Interaction in community	-	.015 to .034
Psychosocial Functioning Inventory in community	+	.029 to .106
Cantril morale score in community	-	.025 to .114
Behaviour change: absolute or relative	+	.000 to .015
Cantril change: absolute	+	.001 to .001
Depression Inventory change: absolute	+	.003 to .039
Client readmitted to hospital[3]	+	.018 to .086
Size of community accommodation (no. of places)	+	.001 to .001
Case management delegated to keyworker	-	.017 to .064
Clients involved in case management	+	.000 to .000
Project managed at strategic not local level	-	.005 to .005

1 Range of significance of t-tests in the 'best' equations coming from each cost function series. In some equations variables did not enter the 'best' functions, or were excluded on the basis of *a priori* restrictions (see Knapp and Beecham, 1990b).
2 Variable appears in non-linear form.
3 Two variables (incidence and duration) were employed in the analyses with mixed effects, generally indicating that post-discharge in-patient stays push up costs.

scores and costs gave an indication of the responsiveness of care resources and agencies to the health and social welfare needs of clients. This is what one would hope to observe from an integrated and carefully planned system of care services, but England does not yet have such a system, and the consistency must be attributable in large measure to the case management practices which were adopted by the projects. One dimension of client welfare deviated from this general finding: higher scores on the morale sub-scale of the Psychosocial Functioning Inventory were associated with *higher* costs, which we interpreted as a causal linkage running from service utilisation to contentment. Overall, client needs are significant determinants of cost, although many other factors intervene between the need-cost relationship (compare Taube et al., 1984).

Changes in client characteristics played only a small role in the explanation of cost variations. Both absolute and relative differences in well-being scores were examined, but the effects were small, even though statistical significance was achieved after standardising for differences in client background, hospital-based assessments of need, and some organisational features of the different projects. Higher costs were associated with the attainment of greater or better outcomes in relation to behavioural problems, symptoms, morale, personal presentation and depression. The effects are again as we would have hoped or expected on the basis of deductive reasoning or anecdote, though not on the basis of previous research, because there appears to be little evidence to confirm or deny such suppositions. (The only similar is our own work on the rundown of Friern and Claybury hospitals which produces very similar findings. See Beecham et al., 1991a.) It is interesting to note, therefore, that although client welfare improvements were modest at an aggregate level, once we delved into inter-client variations we uncovered significant positive associations with cost.

Higher community care costs were therefore not only attributable to higher levels of observed need in the community, but also with greater achievements in reducing this need. We can conclude that higher levels of spending on community care *will* generate further improvements in quality of life.

The link between costs and outcomes is of primary interest, but other cost-raising factors have relevance for policy. A small number of indicator ('dummy' or 'zero-one') variables describing organisational characteristics of the demonstration projects and their case management arrangements were introduced into some of the cost function explorations. The results are summarised in Table 14.10. Strategic (area level) rather than localised planning appeared to be associated with lower costs, other things being equal, and consumer involvement in decision-making appeared to be associated with higher costs. With the small number of different service systems covered by this analysis, we should not make hurried generalisations from these two findings.

We also looked at each client's accommodation in the community. Service packages were tailored to individual needs and circumstances, but not perfectly, and for the purposes of planning some typology of community arrangements which cuts through this individual variability is often needed. The most common basis for such a typology is residential accommodation, even though it is widely recognised that places of residence cannot (and perhaps ought not to) meet the full range of needs of people with long-term, mental health problems. A key policy question, then, is whether and how the costs of complete community care packages vary between accommodation types. This question was examined by testing for a statistical association between the residual (unexplained) costs from the cost functions and the types of accommodation occupied by clients. The analyses revealed few significant associations between costs and accommodation type; tentatively we conclude that residential care homes and staffed group homes are more expensive than other settings, having standardised for differences in client characteristics and outcomes, and independent living arrangements are less expensive.

Summary

These outcome and cost results are robust, but their generalisability needs careful consideration. Ongoing research in North East Thames Region paints a similar picture: some improvements in quality of life and no deteriorations, and care services which are less costly than the hospitals they are intended to replace.

For the programme we found:

- Integration into 'ordinary' community life-styles was not complete, but most people were regularly using shops, churches or pubs, and there was much more activity outside the confines of the place of residence than had been enjoyed in hospital.
- Twice as many people expressed positive attitudes about activities in the community compared to their activities in hospital.
- Most people had more choice about how they spent their time and the activities they engaged in, although more generously pitched social security benefits or the greater availability of 'real' jobs would significantly have improved the situation.
- Even though it took time for people to build up social networks, reported social contacts were slightly greater in number in the community than in hospital.
- Skill levels, behavioural problems and symptoms (as reported by staff) were no different between hospital and community, although staff in bigger congregate care settings, such as residential homes and large hostels, were sometimes less active in encouraging skills acquisition than staff supporting more independent living arrangements.
- Self-reported indications of satisfaction with the environment, psychosocial functioning, depression, satisfaction with social interaction, and general morale revealed some borderline improvements between hospital and community.

Were these favourable social and individual outcomes the result of a Rolls-Royce service at a Rolls-Royce cost? The comprehensive costs of the community care packages, based on the best economic principles of long-run marginal opportunity costing, were in fact found to be *lower* than the full costs of in-patient hospitalisation, even after adjustment for the tendency of projects to take clients who were less dependent than the hospital average. Higher community care costs reflected greater needs and better client outcomes.

15 Outcomes and costs for elderly people and people with physical disabilities

Nationally, elderly people make up the vast majority of community care clients. Through either physical frailty or mental health problems, some slight and some severe, about four million elderly people require support and care from informal carers, as well as from the more visible public, voluntary and private sector agencies (Cm 849, 1989). However, only a small fraction of these elderly people become community care clients after a prolonged period of residence in hospital, even though community care as an alternative to care in 'institutions' has been a long-standing policy aim. A much more common challenge for informal carers and social and health care agencies is the support of elderly people in their own homes in order to delay or prevent admission to, or long-term residence in a residential home, nursing home or hospital; and a much more common experience for elderly people who *do* take up long-term residence in hospital is that they spend the rest of their days there. The seven Care in the Community projects for elderly people – four for people who were physically frail and three for elderly people with mental health problems, principally dementia – were therefore offering an unusual community care service, both in terms of policy demonstration and potential value to the people who were able to move from hospital.

The only project supporting younger people with physical disabilities was set in a similar context. Within the community care debate, considerably more attention has been concentrated on the wishes and needs of people who have *not* been long-stay hospital residents than on those rehabilitated from care in institutions. As with elderly people, comparatively few people with physical disabilities living in hospital have the opportunity to leave.

All but two of the seven projects for elderly people were funded in the second of the two rounds. This is important for at least two reasons. First, it allowed the outcome instrumentation to be better tailored to the needs, expectations and concerns of elderly people. For example, we substituted the Clifton Assessment Procedures for the Elderly (CAPE) Behaviour Rating Scale and the Philadelphia Geriatric Center (PGC) morale scale for some of the instruments reported in the previous two chapters for younger client groups. Second, fewer data were available for the evaluation than for other client groups. In fact, our research timetable meant that we were not able to examine client outcomes at all for the Camberwell and St Helens projects, both of which had experienced delays in developing community accommodation.

The Darlington project was the subject of a separate evaluation, which allowed its innovative service and case management arrangements to be studied in rather more detail than in most other projects. The findings of that evaluation are summarised later in the chapter (and see Challis et al., 1989, 1991a,b). Because a slightly different set of research instruments was employed in Darlington, the numbers of elderly people for whom we have consistently measured client characteristics along some dimensions are small (see Table 15.1). Among other implications this did not allow the kind of multivariate analyses of outcomes and costs performed for the younger client groups. Nine months after leaving hospital, all of the elderly clients with mental health problems were living in residential homes and all of the physically frail elderly clients outside Darlington were accommodated in specialised sheltered housing, whereas most Darlington clients were in domiciliary care settings.

The Glossop project helped three people with physical disabilities to move into self-contained, purpose-built flats. Information on the characteristics, preferences and needs of the three clients was collected, as well as service utilisation data, allowing some descriptive analyses of outcomes and costs, but obviously the findings cannot be generalised from only three people.

There are three main sections to this chapter. The first gives a brief account of our findings from the Glossop project. We then turn to the elderly clients of the programme and their outcomes, and finally we examine costs.

Table 15.1
Outcome and cost research instruments, sample sizes for elderly people

	Numbers of clients[1]			
	Elderly physically frail		*Elderly mental health*	
Research instrument[2]	**Baseline**	**Movers**	**Baseline**	**Movers**
CAPE Behaviour Rating Scale	134	115	40	37
Satisfaction with services questions	52	46	34	33
Schedule for Social Interaction	50	46	28	27
Depression Inventory	43	40	25	24
PGC Morale Scale	113	112	24	24
Client Service Receipt Interview[3]	–	23 [4]	–	40
Costs	23 [4]	23 [4]	40	40

1 The effective number for some analyses will be smaller because of missing information on some component items for some clients.
2 Each instrument is described in the text.
3 Hospital of residence was known for every client, but service utilisation data in hospital were not collected. Hospital costs were estimated *only* for those clients for whom we also had community costs data.
4 Darlington clients were included in a separate evaluation. See text for details.

Outcomes and costs for people with physical disabilities

With only one project and three clients, we could draw comparatively few conclusions from the quantitative indicators of client well-being and quality of life for the clients with physical disabilities. Table 15.2 summarises the data gathered for the Glossop project. None of the improvements recorded along the various dimensions attain statistical significance. The weekly costs of community care were around £250 for two clients, but much larger at £625 per week for the third because of the considerable amount of staff support needed in the self-contained (sheltered) flats to which clients moved. (The details are given in Table 15.6.)

Table 15.2
Summary outcome indicators for people with physical disabilities

	Comm. score[1]		*T2-T1 diff.*[1]	
Instrument	M	N	M	N
Skills scale	79.3	2	2.3	2
Behaviour scale	74.5	2	0.5	2
Schedule for Social Interaction	7.9	2	3.9	2
Cantril's ladder	3.5	2	0.5	2
Depression Inventory	6.0	2	1.0	2
Psychosocial Functioning Inventory	41.5	2	3.0	2

1 M = mean; N = sample size. None of the differences between hospital and community scores was significant.

Outcomes for elderly people

The concerns often voiced about the possible 'failings' of hospital closure programmes and concomitant community care plans have less relevance for elderly people than for other client groups. As we have just noted, dehospitalisation remains a comparatively rare experience for elderly people, and when it occurs it very often involves a move into relatively well-supported, well-funded proximate or congregate care settings. The Care in the Community projects bore this out: with the exception of the Darlington clients, every elderly client moved into a residential home or a sheltered housing complex. In Darlington, a variety of accommodation placements were used, with many people in supported ordinary home care settings. There was therefore little risk of homelessness, lack of support, destitution or imprisonment, or of mortality or hospital readmission through neglect. There is always a danger that congregate community care accommodation may establish or preserve institutionalism among residents, but our examination of social and physical environments and our interviews with clients gave no evidence of this. A better degree of community integration was also achieved after the move (see Chapter 8 for evidence on both).

The other dimensions of quality of life for elderly people – the basis for the assessment of client outcomes – are reported in this chapter under four heads: skills and behaviour, activities and engagement, social contacts, and morale and life satisfaction. A number of factors conspired to keep sample sizes down for this client group, including unavoidable building delays, over-representation in the second round of programme funding and the parallel evaluation in Darlington. To these must be added the higher mortality rates compared with younger client groups: 28 per cent in the first nine months after hospital discharge among elderly people with physical frailties, and 11 per cent for elderly people with mental health problems. Most of our outcome findings relate only to those people still alive at the time of the follow-up assessment.

Skills and behaviour

Using the CAPE Behaviour Rating Scale developed by Pattie and Gilleard (1979), interviews were conducted with staff in hospital and community settings in order to assess clients' skills and behavioural problems. The interviewees knew the clients well and were asked about a range of characteristics and abilities under four heads: physical disability, apathy, communication and social disturbance.

Because higher scores indicate higher dependency, negative differences indicate an *improvement* in skills or *lessening* of behavioural problems. It can be seen from Table 15.3 that there was only one significant difference between hospital and community: on average, the sample of 86 elderly people with physical frailties were rated as more socially disturbed in the community than they had been in hospital ($p = 0.020$). For both elderly client groups together there were significant differences between projects on the aggregate CAPE Behaviour Rating Scale score ($p = 0.001$), and differences between facilities which attained borderline significance ($p = 0.031$), but these were *entirely* due to the client group effects; within client groups there were no differences.

Activities and engagement

Traditionally, many of the needs of people living in residential homes are met within the facility, although clients in specialised sheltered housing tend to draw on a wider range of outside services such as home helps, care attendants and community nurses. Projects therefore sought to work with clients' relatives and friends to increase the range of social opportunities. As we noted in Chapter 8, across the whole programme and all client groups, projects were frustrated in their attempts to gain access for clients to some community resources and

Table 15.3
CAPE Behaviour Rating Scale scores in the community, and community-hospital differences, elderly people

CAPE BRS dimensions	Client group[2]	Comm. score[1] M	SD	N	T2-T1 diff.[1] M	N	p
Physical disability	EPF	5.9	2.1	88	0.3	82	ns
	EMH	4.9	2.6	20	-0.1	11	ns
Apathy	EPF	5.3	2.2	73	-0.5	64	0.075
	EMH	6.0	2.2	25	-1.1	14	ns
Communication	EPF	0.4	0.9	89	0.0	85	ns
	EMH	0.6	0.9	29	-0.2	25	ns
Social disturbance	EPF	1.1	1.4	88	0.4	86	0.020
	EMH	2.3	2.0	28	0.7	26	ns
Total CAPE BRS score	EPF	12.9	4.9	71	0.4	60	ns
	EMH	13.9	6.1	17	-0.2	11	ns

1 M = mean; SD = standard deviation; N = sample size; p = probability that observed differences between hospital and community occurred by chance; ns = not significant ($p > 0.05$).
2 EPF indicates elderly people with physical frailty. Three projects are included here: Coventry, Darlington, Winchester. EMH indicates elderly people with mental health problems. Two projects are included here: Hillingdon and West Cumbria.

activities. It is always the case in the care and support of elderly people that staff have to balance a client's right to choose to do little or nothing against the therapeutic and other benefits of overcoming initial reluctance to take up opportunities to participate in organised or informal activities. Reports of participation by elderly clients of the demonstration programme suggested marginally increased levels of participation in activities, although our data did not permit rigorous testing of these staff impressions.

Clients' self-reported preferences for activities offered a better basis for looking at activities and participation. For both elderly client groups together:

- 25 per cent expressed a liking for outdoor activities such as walks, sports and gardening (compared to 26 per cent in hospital);
- 90 per cent for indoor activities such as painting, drawing, sewing, playing games, cooking and reading (compared to 89 per cent in hospital);
- 86 per cent for social activities such as visiting friends and attending social clubs (compared to 89 per cent in hospital);
- 92 per cent for passive activities such as watching TV or listening to the radio (compared to only 48 per cent in hospital); and
- 8 per cent for other activities such as attending church (compared to a rather larger 29 per cent in hospital).

Thus, in contrast to the younger clients with mental health problems (see Chapter 14), there were few differences between hospital and community.

When asked whether they 'had enough to do' with their time, 92 per cent elderly clients with physical frailties responded with positive remarks (compared to 78 per cent in hospital; sample of 25 clients). For elderly people with mental health problems the respective figures were 82 per cent and 88 per cent (sample of 34). Only 57 per cent of those with physical frailties expressed satisfaction with how they spent their day, a lower overall rating than the 65 per cent recorded during our interviews with the same people in hospital nine or more months earlier. For elderly people with mental health problems responses on this same question revealed a marked improvement in perceived satisfaction (66 per cent in hospital to 83 per cent in the community).

Social contacts

Social contacts were found to be higher in the community than in hospital for elderly clients, even though it took many people some time to develop new social networks, and despite the constraints imposed by staffing levels and the difficulties in gaining access to some 'ordinary' community facilities.

The evaluation asked clients their views about social contacts, based on the Interview Schedule for Social Interaction of Henderson (1981). The responses in both hospital and community for the 41 people from whom we collected some information in both settings are summarised by client group in Table 15.4. There were no differences in family contact (which were high in both settings), some indication of smaller numbers of friends in the community but considerably more friends whom clients felt they could turn to when in need of comfort or help. Respondents were less likely to have someone 'who knows you very well' in the community. The aggregation of responses on these different questions, using the weighting of items suggested by Henderson (1981), gives virtually identical scores in hospital and community. There were no significant differences between projects or facilities.

Morale and life satisfaction

Morale and life satisfaction measures have been central to social and psychological gerontology research for more than three decades, and certainly were commonplace in research on elderly people long before they came to be recognised as relevant or valid in work with other long-term client groups. Generations of gerontologists have developed good morale and life satisfaction instruments (Davies and Knapp, 1981, Chap. 2). Gaining clients' own views was a fundamental aim of the Care in the Community evaluation, and it was natural, therefore, to build into our instrumentation a well-regarded morale

Table 15.4
Social contacts – the views of elderly clients

Questions and overall instrument score[1]	Percentage responses: Hospital	Community
Do you ever see your family or relatives?		
Yes	93	97
How many friends do you have?		
None	12	24
1 or 2	12	18
3 to 5	19	8
6 to 10	5	9
more than 10	51	42
How many friends could you go to if you were upset or wanted help?		
None	50	16
1 or 2	31	8
3 to 5	8	71
6 to 10	4	2
more than 10	7	4
Is there anyone who knows you very well?		
Yes	90	69
Overall mean score on Schedule for Social Interaction[2]	5.7	5.8
Sample size	41	41

1 Taken from the Schedule for Social Interaction.
2 The community-hospital difference (mean 0.1) was not significant ($p = 0.920$).

scale from this gerontology literature. The Philadelphia Geriatric Center Morale Scale developed by Lawton (1975) had previously been 'anglicised' by Challis and Knapp (1980). The PGC scale was used alongside Cantril's (1965) global morale measure and the Depression Inventory of Snaith et al. (1971).

Our findings are summarised in Table 15.5. Higher scores on the PGC and Cantril measures and lower scores on the Depression Inventory indicate higher subjective well-being. The only significant difference is a sizeable leap in the mean PGC morale score between hospital and community. Unlike Anthony et al. (1987) we found no evidence of increased depressive behaviour after the move from hospital.

Outcomes for clients of the Darlington project

The Darlington project deviated from the general pattern of provision within the Care in the Community programme in some important respects, particularly in its specific aim to support elderly people in their own homes, with the

Table 15.5
Morale and life satisfaction of elderly clients in the community, and community-hospital differences

Instrument	Client group[2]	Comm. score[1] M	SD	N	T2-T1 diff.[1] M	SD	N	p
Cantril's ladder	EPF	4.2	1.4	20	-0.3	2.4	14	ns
	EMH	4.3	1.8	12	-0.7	2.7	6	ns
Depression Inventory	EPF	9.3	6.4	19	0.6	0.1	19	ns
	EMH	10.8	9.3	22	2.2	11.7	15	ns
PGC Morale Scale	EPF	11.0	3.9	76	1.6	4.1	63	0.002
	EMH	10.9	5.1	25	-0.5	4.3	17	ns

1 M = mean; SD = standard deviation; N = sample size; p = probability of difference between hospital and community scores; ns = not significant ($p > 0.05$).
2 EPF indicates elderly people with physical frailty. Three projects are included here: Coventry, Darlington, Winchester. EMH indicates elderly people with mental health problems. Two projects are included here: Hillingdon and West Cumbria.

expectation that the local authority or a housing association would provide accommodation where necessary. Problems later emerged when public housing was withdrawn (following district council elections) and Housing Corporation funding was deferred. The majority of clients moved from hospital to ordinary domiciliary settings, and some moved back to their own homes. For a number of reasons it was more likely that these hospital residents had a spouse or had retained a home in the community to which they could return. Admission to hospital had been comparatively recent when contrasted with all of the other demonstration projects – median length of stay was one month and only 4 per cent had been in hospital for more than two years. The project was designed to help people who were physically frail but mentally alert.

Trained home care assistants carried out both domestic and personal care tasks, including nursing auxiliary tasks, in order to avoid duplication and reduce the number of different people involved. Case managers coordinated, but did not necessarily themselves perform, the core tasks of case finding and screening, assessment, care planning, monitoring and review (Challis and Davies, 1986), and were given service price and other relevant information and a caseload budget.

The evaluation results of the Darlington project are given in Challis et al. (1989, 1991a,b). An examination of client and carer outcomes six months after hospital discharge found lower levels of apathy and depressed mood, and higher levels of morale, social activity and general quality of care, when compared to a control group of hospital patients selected from a similar health authority in the same region. Informal carers experienced fewer difficulties than both the carers of elderly patients in hospital and the informal carers of another group of elderly clients receiving conventional packages of community care, and levels of well-being were higher on some indicators of psychological burden and malaise. These project outcome results were obtained for the same or slightly lower cost.

Some of the service configurations found in Darlington will not easily be replicated in other 'dehospitalisation programmes', because of the continuing links that Darlington clients were able to maintain during their relatively short stay in hospital. However, the service model established has wider currency. In particular, the case management practices that were adopted, built on the very successful models in Kent and Gateshead, are certainly transportable and warrant close examination. As we note below, the case management experiences of the demonstration programme as a whole, together with the Kent Community Care and Gateshead projects before them, had a major influence on the *Caring for People* White Paper (Cm 849, 1989). Moreover, the Darlington project – like some of the projects for other client groups – shows how services can be purposively planned and successfully delivered for dependent people.

Costs of community care for elderly people

The most easily identified cost of community care is the residential accommodation budget and, excluding the Darlington project, it proved to be the largest cost element for elderly people in the programme: 55 per cent of total weekly cost for elderly people with physical frailties for whom we had cost data (all of whom were living in sheltered housing) and 95 per cent for elderly people with mental health problems (all accommodated in residential homes). Community social care support for those in sheltered housing accounted for most of the remaining costs (see Table 15.6).

On average, community care was considerably less costly than hospital care, basing the latter on the actual costs of clients' former hospital of residence. For only four of the 21 elderly people with physical frailties for whom we had cost data, and only one of the 39 elderly people with mental health problems, were community care costs greater than hospital costs. However, some care needs to be taken in this comparison, for our estimates of the hospital costs for the clients in two projects were high because some people moved from general hospitals (with a wide range of specialties) for which we were unable to conduct disaggregated ward costings. It happened, however, that the community costs in these two projects were also just about the *lowest* across the programme, so although the differences in cost were misleadingly large, there was little doubt that community care was less expensive than hospital. Again, this conclusion is consistent with the results of the better comparative cost studies in Britain (Mooney, 1978; Wright et al., 1981).

Table 15.6
Community care costs for elderly people and people with physical disabilities

Community care component	Elderly with physical frailty[1]	Elderly with mental health problems	People with physical disabilities
Accommodation and living expenses[2]	55	95	30
Project overheads[3]	1	0	0
General practitioners	1	2	0
Day activity services	3	0	4
Education	0	0	2
In-patient hospital	5	1	2
Community health care[4]	6	1	0
Community social care	29	0	62
Total (%)	100	100	100
Sample size	23	40	3
Community cost[5]	296	207	380
Hospital cost[5]	386	515	387
Community accommodation type[6]	Sheltered housing	Residential home	Sheltered housing

1 Excludes Darlington.
2 Includes staff costs where staff are employed solely at place of residence and included in accommodation budget.
3 Inclusions vary from project to project, usually covering some immediate managerial support and some peripatetic staff support.
4 Includes community nursing, medical practitioners not attached to hospital or family practices, miscellaneous community health paramedic services (chiropody, dietary services, incontinence service, and so on).
5 Costs expressed in pounds at 1986-87 price levels per client per week.
6 Only one community accommodation type was represented for each client group.

For the clients of the Darlington project, aggregated community care costs were approximately £242 per week on average, compared with £277 for the control group of residents in a geriatric hospital (Challis et al., 1991b).

Most of today's community care policies for elderly people, at both central and local levels, focus on diversion away from long stays in hospital and residential care rather than the decanting of residents. The demonstration programme was rather differently directed. With the exception of the plans for Darlington, the projects for elderly people helped elderly people to move to residential homes or specialised sheltered accommodation, in each setting with case managed organisation of services in response to needs and preferences.

The evaluation of client outcomes and costs shows that quality of life in the community for elderly people was certainly not inferior to, and in some respects was better than life in hospital. Skills and behaviour levels had not deteriorated, satisfaction with activities and social contacts was no lower, and overall ratings of morale had improved. Coupled with our earlier account of how projects provided more pleasant physical environments, and were often able to widen the choices and opportunities available to clients, and to achieve all of these things at lower cost than in hospital, we would conclude that the demonstration programme had provided cost-effective services for this client group.

Part IV

16 Demonstration and extrapolation

Introduction

It will be several years before the effects of the reforms introduced in the *NHS and Community Care Act 1990* can be properly evaluated. Will 1990 prove to be the turning point in community care, the reforms achieving their stated intentions, or will we witness another failed attempt to impose greater order and rationality on an inefficient, inequitable collection of fragmented, underfunded services?

The proposals contained in the Act were obviously shaped in part by the experiences of the 1980s. Particular problems emerged during the decade: the uncompensated and unpredictable burden on community care agencies as a consequence of precipitate hospital rundown; the perverse incentives of social security funding on the balance between residential and domiciliary care; the almost unregulated, explosive growth of the private sector; the dominance of suspicion over support in financial and other links between some health and social services authorities; and the hypothesised connections between hospital rundown, widespread homelessness, unemployment and general social and economic marginalisation. However, some positive lessons emerged from the Care in the Community demonstration programme, and also had their-influence, as the *Caring for People* White Paper (Cm 849, 1989, para.3.3.3) and subsequent implementation documents acknowledged.

In this book we have described the aims and resources of the 28 pilot projects, the people who moved from hospital to community, and the service systems and care packages established to enable change and provide individual support. Our evaluation of client outcomes and costs is probably the most comprehensive empirical examination of community care for former hospital residents yet conducted in the UK. The demonstration programme was also rather different from mainstream provision of the time, and those differences warrant special attention given the new arrangements for community care.

In many respects, pilot projects were attempting to do exactly the things demanded by the new legislation. It is therefore vital that the successes and failures of such experience are not overlooked, but rather incorporated into future expectations. The projects offer a window through which to view some of the future difficulties and opportunities of community care.

This book does not aim to be prescriptive, and it would be naive and patronising to think that something as complex as community care could be addressed in such terms, but lessons are there to be learnt. Aspects of the programme included, for example: the planned development of community care to replace hospital provision; protected funding to set key services in place; service delivery in response to needs, coordinated via case or care management in its various forms and guises; rational approaches to joint working and service management between the two public sector agencies, and with other organisations in the active pursuit of well-defined goals; and a commitment to local monitoring and broader performance evaluation. The insights to be gained from the programme might not address every issue now facing community care, but the programme offers interesting and informed pointers for the 1990s.

In providing funding for a programme of pilot projects to assist the rehabilitation of long-stay hospital residents, the DHSS expected projects to explore different models of community care, thereby revealing the more successful arrangements. This was the first nationwide programme funded by central government to examine and encourage the policy of replacing long-stay hospital accommodation with supported and managed places in the community. The scale of the programme – central government grants amounted to £25 million at today's prices – was itself impressive. Our evaluation was therefore not a test of a single, small scheme, but of 28 very different projects and the resettlement of over 900 people in different geographical, social and service contexts.

Principles and practices

Service orientations and philosophies were cemented in care practices developed locally or imported from outside. Care management, some interpretation of normalisation, and a commitment to user involvement were among the widely adopted principles which shaped local innovations. Implementing normalisation sometimes proved difficult, particularly when ill-conceived, misunderstood, inflexibly applied, or running contrary to the expressed preferences of clients. Allowing clients to take risks and make the 'wrong choices' had to be tempered by public expectations of staff responsibility and professional accountability. If some of the underlying principles of care proved unworkable or at least disappointing in implementation, they nevertheless encouraged staff to strive to achieve the best for clients, and challenged the narrow preconceptions of others.

Putting their various care principles into practice required adequate funding, some influence over resources owned or managed by provider agencies, and the willingness and imagination at both individual user and management levels to link service responses to identified needs and expressed wants. In these respects the pilot projects were no different from other community care services at the time or now, but they certainly did not face difficulties of the same intensity or doggedness. The grants from central government gave them both more generous funding than might otherwise have been expected, as well as a high degree of both financial and operational independence through protected funding. The funds made available included help with capital outlays, providing double funding for the period when hospital cost savings were negligible, and usually meant that resources could be established in the community before clients left hospital. The conditions of central funding ensured that joint liaison and planning were at least attempted, and they generally succeeded, as we saw in Chapter 11. Another recommendation – the use of some form of care management – helped to raise the 'target efficiency' of community care. How the planning and care management components of the current reforms succeed in reorganising community care is less certain.

Finances

The significance of social security payments in the successful operation of the projects needs to be made forcefully, and in this our findings are consistent with much other evidence and anecdotal experience. Interestingly, the shortcomings of reliance on such funding were also evident. There was, for example, a thin dividing line between flexibility and instability: social security funds reduce the constraints often imposed by agency budgets, but are themselves subject to unexpected changes of value and eligibility. A second difficulty was that the income from benefits was not always adequate to provide desired standards of care, let alone compensate for the paucity of social contacts, employment opportunities and personal belongings that so often accompany former hospital residents. However, by introducing care management responsibilities, most projects were at least able to help clients claim the benefits to which they were entitled. A third problem – the inappropriateness of some benefits – also emerged. By subsidising costs from central grants, the programme clearly reduced the disincentives standing in the way of appropriate care. (Projects still found it financially less attractive to offer domiciliary rather than residential care in order to maximise benefit receipts.)

What emerged from the programme was a greater mix of community provision than was generally to be seen at the time, but a mix which represented the resolution of the same pressures: the desire to establish good quality, 'ordinary' services versus the pursuit of local or self-interested financial prudence. But what are the implications for the 1990s? Will social security continue to play a crucial role (other than in relation to residential care), and if so will effective use of the benefits system be a key aspect of care management? Or does the new framework remove the creative potential of benefit entitlement, and does it replace it with an effective alternative?

Similar issues relate to dowries, double-running costs and the protection of funding. Do future arrangements allow for the sort of practice which has taken place within the demonstration programme? Has the depressed property market and the falling value of hospital sites removed the most tangible benefit of hospital closure and the major source of funding for new community care capital projects?

Pilot projects enjoyed protected funding for three years, with mainstream health or social services funding promised thereafter. Despite this privileged financial status, some projects encountered problems in negotiating ongoing funding packages from health authorities. The most serious difficulties arose in Camden where, almost five years after leaving, some Care in the Community clients returned to their previous hospitals of residence – a consequence of the underfunding of an ambitious service model and, to a lesser extent, the resistance of neighbours. Although this was outside the period of our evaluation, it serves as a warning for community care in the 1990s. The isolation of voluntary providers in a complex web of funding and management responsibilities and interests generated confusion and mistrust.

Staffing

Through lack of experience, hampered by poor information, or simply because of overoptimistic assumptions, many projects underestimated the support needs of people in the community. This left some of them with inadequate numbers or types of staff, and inadequate funds to meet the costs of overtime, promotions and pay settlements. These difficulties were piled on top of a more general and pervasive conclusion from the research: community care makes considerable and continuing demands on staff. If such demands are not to prove too much, training and support must be taken seriously.

Some community care arrangements need staff with different skills from those conventionally expected of hospital staff. They also need flexibility in their deployment. The challenge, therefore, is to ensure that training strategies produce the right mix of abilities, the right blend between 'therapeutic' and 'basic' skills, and the right balance between professional abilities and simple caring attitudes. In the multi-agency community care systems envisaged by the 1990 Act, conventional professional needs and boundaries may not survive.

Some of the staffing difficulties in the programme were undoubtedly the result of what was perceived by some people as a short-term initiative. The difficulties of recruitment and retention of staff in some projects may well reappear in the new mixed economy if the links between purchasers and providers are dominated by comparatively short contracts.

Accommodation and services

Between them, the projects offered many different accommodation and day support arrangements, though most were to run up against constraints and inadequacies in their locales. For example, while accommodation included residential homes, sheltered housing facilities, hostels, staffed group homes, core and cluster networks, supported lodgings, home care (foster) placements and independent living, in only a handful of projects were clients given such a wide range of choice. The finding that most people were offered more choice than they had come to expect in hospital should not disguise the fact that there is a long way to go before one of the core aims of the 1989 White Paper – enhanced user choice – can be achieved. The availability of the right kind of housing proved, and will continue to prove, a major constraint.

Accommodation plans and practices were often strongly influenced by a desire to emphasise the contrast with hospital. Even if normalisation was not an overt objective, domesticity, integration and 'ordinary living' were commonly-held objectives for community living settings. Consequently there *were* large differences between the physical and social environments of the hospital wards that clients had left and the community placements to which they moved. Indeed, by every one of the criteria of either normalisation or institutionalisation which we were able to examine, accommodation in the community was better than hospital.

There were also better standards of day care, support and leisure provision. Difficulties arose in achieving the degree of community integration and participation that many projects sought, especially in relation to education services and employment. Integration in the community is often a matter of chance – the availability of the right kind of housing in the right area, vacancies in adult education classes, a buoyant labour market – so that community care agencies can often have only limited influence. But this should not divert attention from the commonly experienced difficulties of overcoming inertia and negative or obstructive attitudes. Projects which established free-floating *welfare entrepreneurs* probably had greater success in overcoming adverse external influences.

Service organisation

The service systems set in place within the programme share many features with the organisation of community care which is likely to emerge during the coming years. Some variant of care management was employed, occasionally with devolved budgets, but without any other organisational split between purchasers and providers of the kind envisaged in the *Caring for People* White Paper. There was the widespread improvement of joint working relations between health and local authorities, and occasionally joint purchasing. (The Somerset purchaser/provider split separated health and social services authorities.) When projects employed what might now be called community care brokers, they were beginning to behave like enabling agents within a quasi-market.

Care management

There had been case or care management experiments in Britain before the launch of the demonstration programme, but confined to services for elderly people, so that the programme offered a chance to examine this mode of case-level organisation in new applications. (It was, of course, the successes of these earlier experiments which had encouraged the DHSS to include case management in the programme specification in the first place.) Because the programme was not prescriptive, a variety of styles emerged, each giving slightly different emphases to the five core tasks of case finding and referral, assessment and selection, care planning, monitoring, and case closure. Common to each of the styles was the hope that care management would help to improve the efficiency and equity with which resources were allocated, although, naturally, many different (implicit) definitions and priorities were attached to these two criteria.

Devolution of responsibility for decision-making is central to the community care changes introduced by the 1990 Act. The majority view from the projects was that benefits flow from greater autonomy in decision-making, policy formulation and budgetary control. The organisational challenge of giving autonomy to a time-limited pilot project is somewhat easier than the wholesale restructuring of a social services department, but the findings from the demonstration programme might encourage local authorities to set the necessary information and management systems in place.

Joint working

The programme contained five models of joint working between health and social care agencies. These we have called the unitary agency, semi-independent agency, lead agency, joint agency and multi-agency models. The Social Services Inspectorate's recent guide for managers on case management and assessment uses this categorisation (SSI/DH, 1991).

Although laid down as a condition of programme funding, joint working was welcomed by most projects as an opportunity to improve local inter-agency cooperation. Even within the lead agency model, it was essential to coordinate planning and service monitoring. The voluntary sector was involved rather less in community care planning than many would have wished, and the private sector was only really involved as a provider of residential care.

Some familiar organisational experiences came to light. Clarity of roles and responsibilities – for example, through joint documents, strategies, transfer agreements and personnel policies – helped avoid inter-agency and purchaser-provider conflicts. Existing joint planning machinery (JCPTs or JCCs) often proved useful for arbitration, advice and steering. Reorganisation, where it occurred in social services departments or the health service, proved demoralising and distracting. Geographical isolation required special liaison to prevent services becoming managerially remote. Devolved responsibilities and budgets helped to promote accountability and flexibility, and made services more responsive to individual needs and local circumstances. Case review was better conducted outside residential or day care settings, and on an integrated basis. Access to policy-making processes and to information on finance and budgeting helped generate positive working attitudes and staff commitment.

A mixed economy

The successful establishment of a mixed economy of provision and management owed more to chance and tradition than to the intentions and structures of the demonstration programme. Commonly, success seemed to depend mainly on the voluntary sector's access to information, its energies and its contacts. Moreover, as other research has revealed (Wistow et al., 1992), numerous obstacles block the path to a greater mixing of the social care economy, even when the political and professional wills are in concert.

The enabling authority, as set out in the community care White Paper, will adopt a more strategic role with specific responsibilities for planning, coordinating services and monitoring quality. Establishing care management and devolving budgets takes an authority some way towards this enabling role, and more than half of the pilot projects illustrated some of the benefits of contracting with voluntary agencies for the provision of certain services. These benefits may not easily be extrapolated to the wider community care field, for there are numerous supply, organisational, managerial and economic hurdles to overcome: the (quasi-) market may be elusive.

Service users and outcomes

The people who moved from hospital to the community were, in various respects, likely to need less care support in the community than the 'typical' long-stay hospital resident. Programme clients with learning difficulties generally had fewer needs for assistance in self-care tasks and fewer behaviour problems than those who remained behind in hospital. Clients with mental health problems generally had fewer symptoms of ill health and more basic skills than others in psychiatric hospitals. When gauged in terms of achievements of new life-styles and improvements in well-being, the successes of the programme must therefore be generalised carefully to those people with greater needs who are likely to be leaving hospital later in the hospital rundown process. As would be expected of a well-targeted community care system, we found evidence that greater needs as assessed in hospital prior to discharge, and also as assessed in the community some nine months later, were associated with the receipt of more care support and higher costs.

Although less 'dependent' on average than those people who remained in hospital, the clients of the programme posed many challenges for community care agencies and staff. Most of the clients exhibited the familiar characteristics of institutionalisation, having spent many years in hospital, sometimes with only limited outside contact. A majority of the elderly physically frail clients had lost contact with their families and friends. Almost all clients had some underdeveloped life skills, and most clients with learning difficulties demonstrated behaviours which required special management or support. Very few had more than a minimum of personal possessions.

Outcomes

Hospital closure generates numerous anxieties, often well-founded, about the consequences for those people discharged into an unfamiliar, hostile community. One of the simplest but most important achievements of the Care in the Community programme was the successful resettlement of a large number of long-stay hospital residents. The projects also established support systems which were able to counter the widely-feared failings of dehospitalisation. Leavers were not dumped in the community without care support or access to social security benefits. They were not homeless. No one spent any time in prison or a police cell. Rates of mortality and hospital readmission were no higher than would be expected of a general population with these characteristics. It was the distinctive approach of the programme which provided safeguards and contributed to success. The common failings of community care are often due to poor resourcing and poor management. The future success of community care will be conditional upon the availability of adequate and protected funding, and upon effective use of those funds through rigorous care management.

Improvements in quality of life and well-being after leaving hospital were very marked for most of the people with learning difficulties included in the evaluation. Statistically significant improvements were found along numerous dimensions. The cost of community care was higher than the cost of hospital for more than half the sample, but higher costs bought better quality care and better quality of life. Smaller and more domestic community accommodation settings were associated with better client outcomes: in other words, a policy of normalisation appeared to work. The fundamental policy question suggested by these results is whether local agencies are able or prepared to incur the higher costs of community care in order to reap these marked client outcomes.

Clients with mental health problems enjoyed many improvements in lifestyle after leaving hospital. Some moved to ordinary housing. Integration into the community was by no means complete, but was an improvement over hospital. More positive attitudes were expressed, and clients were exercising more choice than had previously been possible. Low incomes and low levels of staffing nevertheless often severely limited projects' and clients' options. Although there were few noticeable changes in quality of life or clients' characteristics, there were on average no deteriorations, and costs were lower. For this group of people with mental health problems, community care was therefore no lower in quality but significantly lower in cost than hospital. When community care costs rose above the average this tended to reflect greater needs and better client outcomes.

Quality of life in the community for elderly people was certainly no worse, and was in some respects markedly better, than life in hospital. There was no deterioration in skills and behaviour, nor in satisfaction with activities and social contacts, while client self-reported morale had improved. Clients moved to better physical surroundings, and were given more choice and greater opportunities. Community care costs were lower than in hospital. The programme therefore demonstrates the scope for resettling elderly people within the community after long-term residence in hospital. The successes in Darlington, however, also point to the benefits of elderly people being able to return to their former homes, which is an option usually only open to people who have spent comparatively short periods in hospital.

The evidence we have accumulated from the Care in the Community demonstration programme, both descriptive and analytical, system-related and client-focused, personal and financial, has shown that it is possible to organise community care so as to make better use of resources – either spending less than before (elderly people, and those with mental health problems), or spending more but reaping better client outcomes (people with learning difficulties) – and to target services effectively at needs. Moreover, the ways in which these successes have been achieved resemble some aspects of the new processes of organisation and delivery of community care envisaged by the *NHS and Community Care Act 1990*.

In demonstrating the possibilities and potential of community care, this book has also sought to highlight the recurring policy and practice challenges for service users, staff, agencies and governments. We have argued that the political, personal and financial commitments evident in most of the 28 pilot projects are necessary for the success of this policy, but whether they prove to be sufficient remains to be seen.

References

Aanes, D. and Moen, M. (1976) Adaptive behavior changes of group home residents, *Mental Retardation*, 14:4, 36-40.

Abrahamson, D. and Brenner, D. (1982) Do long-stay psychiatric patients want to leave hospital?, *Health Trends*, 14, 95-7.

Allen, C., Beecham, J. and Knapp, M.R.J. (1991) Community care for people with schizophrenia, Discussion Paper 716, PSSRU, University of Kent at Canterbury.

Allen, P., Pahl, J. and Quine, L. (1988) *Staff in the Mental Handicap Services: A Study of Change*, Health Services Research Unit, University of Kent at Canterbury.

Allen, P., Pahl, J. and Quine, L. (1990) *Care Staff in Transition*, HMSO, London.

Altman, D.G. (1986) Letter, *British Medical Journal*, 292, 340.

Anderson, J. (1990) The TAPS project: I. Previous psychiatric diagnosis and current disability of long-stay psychogeriatric patients, *British Journal of Psychiatry*, 156, 661-70.

Andrews, G., Teesson, M., Stewart, G. and Hoult, J. (1990) Follow-up of community placement of the chronic mentally ill in New South Wales, *Hospital and Community Psychiatry*, 41:2, 184-8.

Antebi, D. and Torpy, D. (1987) Patient preferences: a study of the accommodation choices of long-stay psychiatric residents, *British Journal of Clinical and Social Psychiatry*, 5, 13-18.

Anthony, K., Proctor, A.W., Silverman, A.M. and Murphy, E. (1987) Mood and behaviour problems following the relocation of elderly patients with mental illness, *Age and Ageing*, 16, 355-65.

Appleby, L. and Desai, P. (1985) Documenting the relationship between homelessness and psychiatric hospitalization, *Hospital and Community Psychiatry*, 36:7, 732-5.

Apte, R.Z. (1968) *Halfway Houses: A New Dilemma in Community Care*, Bell, London.

Atkinson, D. (1988) Mentally handicapped, in I. Sinclair (ed.) *Residential Care: The Research Reviewed*, National Institute for Social Work/HMSO, London.

Audit Commission (1986) *Making a Reality of Community Care*, HMSO, London.

Audit Commission (1987) *Community Care: Developing Services for People with a Mental Handicap*, Occasional Paper No. 4, Audit Commission, London.

Audit Commission (1989) Developing community care for adults with a mental handicap, Occasional Papers No. 9, Audit Commission, London.

Audit Inspectorate (1983a) *Social Services: Provision of Care for the Elderly,* HMSO for the Department of the Environment, London.

Audit Inspectorate (1983b) *Social Services: Care of Mentally Handicapped People,* HMSO for the Department of the Environment, London.

Avison, W. and Speechley, K. (1987) The discharged psychiatric patients: a review of social, social-psychological, and psychiatric correlates of outcome, *American Journal of Psychiatry,* 144, 10-18.

Baldwin, S., Godfrey, C. and Propper, C. (eds)(1990) *Quality of Life: Perspectives and Policies,* Routledge & Kegan Paul, London.

Barton, R. (1959) *Institutional Neurosis,* Wright, Bristol.

Bassuk, E., Rubin, L. and Lauriat, A. (1984) Is homelessness a mental health problem?, *American Journal of Psychiatry,* 141, 1546-50.

Bayley, M. (1973) *Mental Handicap and Community Care,* Routledge & Kegan Paul, London.

Beardshaw, V. and Towell, D. (1990) *Assessment and Case Management: Implications for the Implementation of Caring for People,* King's Fund Briefing Paper No. 10, London.

Beecham, J. and Knapp, M.R.J. (1990) Dowries, Discussion Paper 711, PSSRU, University of Kent at Canterbury.

Beecham, J. and Knapp, M.R.J. (1992) Costing psychiatric interventions, in G.J. Thornicroft, C.R. Brewin and J.K. Wing (eds) *Measuring Mental Health Needs,* Royal College of Psychiatrists, London, forthcoming.

Beecham, J., Knapp, M.R.J. and Fenyo, A. (1991a) Costs, needs and outcomes: community care for people with long-term mental health problems, *Schizophrenia Bulletin,* 17:3, 188-208.

Beecham, J., Fenyo, A. and Knapp, M.R.J. (1991b) The mixed economy of mental health care, *Bulletin No. 8,* PSSRU, University of Kent at Canterbury, 8-9.

Belknap, I. (1956) *Human Problems of a State Mental Hospital,* McGraw-Hill, New York.

Birenbaum, A. and Re, M.A. (1979) Resettling mentally retarded adults in the community: almost four years later, *American Journal of Mental Deficiency,* 83:4, 323-9.

Blatt, B. and Kaplan, F. (1966) *Christmas in Purgatory: A Photographic Essay on Mental Retardation,* Allyn & Bacon, Boston, Massachusetts.

Blunden, R. and Kushlick, A. (1974) Research and the care of elderly people, Research Report 110, Health Care Evaluation Research Team, Winchester.

Bolton Community Health Council (1987) *Living in Bolton: A Study of the Lives of Mentally Handicapped People Supported by the Bolton Neighbourhood Network Scheme,* Bolton Community Health Council, Bolton.

Borthwick-Duffy, S.A., Eyman, R.K. and White, J.F. (1987) Client characteristics and residential placement patterns, *American Journal of Mental Deficiency*, 92:1 24-30.

Boydell, K.M., Trainor, J.N. and Pierri, A.M. (1989) The effect of group homes for the mentally ill on residential property values, *Hospital and Community Psychiatry*, 40, 957-8.

Brandon, D. (1988) Growing away from crafts – to crops, *Community Living*, October, 17.

Braun, P., Kochansky, G. and Shapiro, R. (1981) Overview: deinstitutionalization of psychiatric patients: a critical review of outcome studies, *American Journal of Psychiatry*, 136, 736-49.

Brewin, C.R., Wing, J.K., Mangen, S.P., Brugha, T.S. and MacCarthy, B. (1987) Principles and practice of measuring needs in the long-term mentally ill: the MRC Needs for Care Assessment, *Psychological Medicine*, 17, 971-81.

Brimacombe, M. (1986) Dumping the mentally ill, *ROOF*, November/December, 21-5.

Brown, G.W., Bone, M., Dalison, B. and Wing, J.K. (1966) *Schizophrenia and Social Care*, Oxford University Press, Oxford.

Bulmer, M. (1987) *The Social Basis of Community Care*, Allen & Unwin, London.

Callaghan, J.J. (1989) Case management for the elderly: a panacea?, *Journal of Aging and Social Policy*, 1:1/2, 181-95.

Cambridge, P. and Knapp, M.R.J. (1988) *Demonstrating Successful Care in the Community*, PSSRU, University of Kent at Canterbury.

Campbell, D. (1957) Factors relevant to the validity of experiments in social settings, *Psychological Bulletin*, 54, 297-312.

Campbell, D. and Stanley, J. (1963) Experimental and quasi-experimental designs for research, in N. Gage (ed.) *Handbook of Research on Teaching*, Rand McNally, Chicago, Illinois.

Cane, F. (1983) The artist in each of us, Craftsbury Common VT, Art Therapy Publications.

Cantril, H. (1965) *The Pattern of Human Concerns*, Rutgers University Press, New Brunswick, New Jersey.

Casmas, S.T. (1976) Inter-hospital and inter-local authority variation in patterns of provision for the mentally disordered, PhD thesis, University of Manchester Institute of Science and Technology, Manchester.

Cassel, W.A., Smith, C.M., Grunberg, F., Boan, J.A. and Thomas, R.F. (1972) Comparing costs of hospital and community care, *Hospital and Community Psychiatry*, 23, 197-200.

Caton, C. and Goldstein, J. (1984) Housing change of chronic schizophrenic patients: a consequence of the revolving door, *Social Science and Medicine*, 19, 759-64.

Cattermole, M. (1987) *Changes in Quality of Life Perceived by People with a Mental Handicap Moving Into the Community: A Longitudinal Study* , paper presented at the British Psychological Society Conference, Brighton.

Challis, D.J. and Darton, R.A. (1990) Evaluation research and experiment in social gerontology, in S.M. Peace (ed.) *Researching Social Gerontology,* Sage, London.

Challis, D.J. and Davies, B.P. (1986) *Case Management in Community Care,* Gower, Aldershot.

Challis, D.J. and Knapp, M.R.J. (1980) An examination of the PGC Morale Scale in an English context, Discussion Paper 168, PSSRU, University of Kent at Canterbury. Reproduced as Appendix IV of E.M. Goldberg and N. Connelly (eds)(1982) *The Effectiveness of Social Care for the Elderly,* Heinemann Educational Books, London.

Challis, D.J., Chessum, R., Chesterman, J., Luckett, R. and Woods, B. (1988) Community care for the frail elderly: an urban experiment, *British Journal of Social Work,* 18, Supplement, 13-42.

Challis, D.J., Darton, R.A., Johnson, L., Stone, M., Traske, K. and Wall, B. (1989) *Darlington Community Care Project: Supporting Frail Elderly People at Home,* PSSRU, University of Kent at Canterbury.

Challis, D.J., Chessum, R., Chesterman, J., Luckett, R. and Traske, K. (1990) *The Gateshead Community Care Scheme: Case Management in Social and Health Care,* PSSRU, University of Kent at Canterbury.

Challis, D.J., Darton, R.A., Johnson, L., Stone, M. and Traske, K. (1991a) An evaluation of an alternative to long-stay hospital care for frail elderly clients. Part I: The model of care, *Age and Ageing,* 20, 236-44.

Challis, D.J., Darton, R.A., Johnson, L., Stone, M. and Traske, K. (1991b) An evaluation of an alternative to long-stay hospital care for frail elderly clients. Part II: Costs and effectiveness, *Age and Ageing,* 20, 245-54.

Clark, A.D.B. and Hermelin, B.F. (1955) Adult imbeciles: their abilities and trainability, *Lancet,* 2, 337-9.

Clifford, P., Charman, A., Webb, Y. and Best, S. (1991) Planning for community care: Long-stay populations of hospitals scheduled for rundown or closure, *British Journal of Psychiatry,* 158, 190-96.

Cm 849 (1989) *Caring for People: Community Care in the Next Decade and Beyond,* HMSO, London.

Cmnd 4683 (1971) *Better Services for the Mentally Handicapped,* HMSO, London.

Cmnd 6233 (1975) *Better Services for the Mentally Ill,* HMSO, London.

Cmnd 9674 (1985) *Community Care: Government Response to the Second Report from the Social Services Committee,* HMSO, London.

Cochran, W.G. (1983) *Planning and Analysis of Observational Studies,* Wiley, New York.

Coid, J.W. (1988) Mentally abnormal prisoners on remand: I. Rejected or accepted by the NHS? and II. Comparison of services provided by Oxford and Wessex regions, *British Medical Journal*, 296, 1779-82 and 1783-4.

Conroy, J.W. and Bradley, V.J. (1985) The Pennhurst Longitudinal Study: a report of five years of research and analysis, Human Services Research Institute, Boston and Developmental Disabilities Center, Temple University, Philadelphia, Pennsylvania.

Cournos, F. (1987) The impact of environmental factors on outcome in residential programs, *Hospital and Community Psychiatry*, 38, 848-52.

Creed, F., Anthony, P., Godbert, K. and Huxley, P. (1989) Treatment of severe psychiatric illness in a day hospital, *British Journal of Psychiatry*, 154, 341-7.

Creer, C. and Wing, J.K. (1974) *Schizophrenia at Home*, National Schizophrenia Fellowship, Surbiton.

Croft, S. and Beresford, P. (1990) *From Paternalism to Participation: Involving People in Social Services*, Open Services Project/Joseph Rowntree Foundation, London.

Croft-Jeffreys, C. and Wilkinson, G. (1989) Editorial: Estimated costs of neurotic disorder in UK general practice 1985, *Psychological Medicine*, 19, 549-58.

Curson, D.A., Patel, M., Liddle, P.F. and Barnes, T.R.E. (1988) Psychiatric morbidity of a long-stay hospital population with chronic schizophrenia and implications for future community care, *British Medical Journal*, 297, 819-21.

Dalgliesh, M. (1983) Assessments of residential environments for mentally retarded adults in Britain, *Mental Retardation*, 21, 204-8.

Dant, T. and Gearing, B. (1990) Keyworkers for elderly people in the community: case managers and care co-ordinators, *Journal of Social Policy*, 19:3, 331-60.

Davies, B.P. (1977) Needs and outputs, in H. Heisler (ed.) *Fundamentals of Social Administration*, Macmillan, London.

Davies, B.P. and Challis, D.J. (1986) *Matching Resources to Needs in Community Care*, Gower, Aldershot.

Davies, B.P. and Knapp, M.R.J. (1981) *Old People's Homes and the Production of Welfare*, Routledge & Kegan Paul, London.

Davies, B.P. and Knapp, M.R.J. (eds)(1988a) *The Production of Welfare Approach: Evidence and Argument from the PSSRU*, Vol. 18 Supplement, published for the British Journal of Social Work by Oxford University Press.

Davies, B.P. and Knapp, M.R.J. (1988b) Costs and residential social care, in I. Sinclair (ed.) *Residential Care: The Research Reviewed*, HMSO, London.

Davies, L.M. (1987) Quality, costs and an ordinary life, King's Fund Centre, London.

Davies, L.M. (1988) Community care – the costs and quality, *Health Services Management Research*, 1:3, 145-55.

Davies, L.M. and Drummond, M.F. (1990) The economic burden of schizophrenia, *Psychological Bulletin*, 14, 522-5.

Dayson, D. (1990) The administrative outcome of the long-term mentally ill, in TAPS (1990) *Better Out Than In?*, Team for the Assessment of Psychiatric Services, North East Thames Regional Health Authority, London.

de Girolamo, G. (1990) Evaluation of psychiatric treatment methods for schizophrenia: conclusions of the WHO Scientific Group and their relationship with problems of cost, presented to the meeting on 'The Cost of Schizophrenia', Venice, October.

de Kock, U., Felce, D., Saxby, H. and Thomas, M. (1987) Staff turnover in a small home service: a study of facilities for adults with severe and profound mental handicaps, *Mental Handicap*, 15:3, 97-101.

Denoff, M.S. and Pilkonis, P.A. (1987) The social network of the schizophrenic: patient and residual determinants, *Journal of Community Psychiatry*, 15, 228-44.

Department of Health (1990) *Caring for People: Community Care in the Next Decade and Beyond*, Policy Guidance, HMSO, London.

DHSS (1981a) *Care in the Community: A Consultative Document on Moving Resources for Care in England*, Department of Health and Social Security, London.

DHSS (1981b) *Care in Action*, HMSO, London.

DHSS (1983) *Care in the Community*, HC(86)3, LAC(83)5, HMSO, London.

Deutscher, I. (1973) *What We Say, What We Do: Sentiments and Acts*, Scott, Foresman & Co., Glenview, Illinois.

Dickey, B., Berren, M., Santiago, J. and Breslau, J.A. (1986) Patterns of service use and costs in model day hospital-inn programmes in Boston and Tucson, *Hospital and Community Psychiatry*, 41:4, 1136-43.

District Auditors (1981) The provision of child care: a study at eight local authorities in England and Wales, Final Report, District Auditors, Bristol.

Donaldson, C., Atkinson, A., Bond, J. and Wright, K. (1988) Should QALYs be programme-specific?, *Journal of Health Economics*, 14, 229-56.

Drake, R. and Wallach, M. (1988) Mental patients' attitudes toward hospitalization: a neglected aspect of hospital tenure, *American Journal of Psychiatry*, 145, 29-34.

Dyer, J. and Hoffenberg, M. (1975) Evaluating the quality of working life, in L. Davies and A. Cherns (eds) *The Quality of Working Life*, Vol. 1, Macmillan/Free Press, New York.

Eastwood, E.A. and Fisher, G.A. (1988) Skills acquisition among matched samples of institutionalized and community-based persons with mental retardation, *American Journal of Mental Retardation*, 93:1, 75-83.

Emerson, E., Toogood, A., Mansell, J., Barrett, S., Bell, C., Cummings, R. and McCool, C. (1987) Challenging behaviour and community services: 1. Introduction and overview, *Mental Handicap*, 15:4, 166-9.

Equal Opportunities Commission (1981) *Caring for the Elderly and Handicapped: Community Policies and Women's Lives*, Equal Opportunities Commission, London.

Etzioni, A. (1960) Two approaches to organizational analysis: a critique and a suggestion, *Administrative Science Quarterly*, 5, 257-78.

Eyman, R.K., Demaine, G.C. and Lei, T.-J. L. (1979) Relationship between community environments and resident changes in adaptive behavior: a path model, *American Journal of Mental Deficiency*, 83:4, 330-8.

Fagin, L. and Little, I. (1984) *The Forsaken Families*, Penguin, Harmondsworth.

Falloon, I. and Marshall, G. (1983) Residential care and social behaviour: a study of rehabilitation needs, *Psychological Medicine*, 13, 341-7.

Fein, R. (1958) *The Economics of Mental Illness*, Basic Books, New York.

Felce, D., Kushlick, A. and Mansell, J. (1980) Evaluation of alternative residential facilities for the severely mentally handicapped in Wessex: client engagement, *Advances in Behavioural Therapy Research*, 3, 13-18.

Felce, D., de Kock, U., Saxby, H. and Thomas, M. (1985) Small homes for severely and profoundly mentally handicapped adults, Health Care Evaluation Research Team, University of Southampton.

Felce, D., de Kock, U. and Repp, A.C. (1986) An eco-behavioral analysis of small community-based houses and traditional large hospitals for severely and profoundly mentally handicapped adults, *Applied Research in Mental Retardation*, 7, 393-408.

Feragne, M.A., Longabaugh, R. and Stevenson, J.F. (1983) The Psychosocial Functioning Inventory, *Evaluation and the Health Professions*, 6:3, 25-48.

Firth, J. (1987) *Report of the Joint Central and Local Government Working Party on Public Support for Residential Care*, HMSO, London.

Fischer, P. and Breakey, W. (1986) Homelessness and mental health: an overview, *International Journal of Mental Health*, 14, 6-41.

Ford, M., Goddard, C. and Lansdale-Welfare, R. (1987) The dismantling of the mental hospital? Glenside Hospital Surveys 1960-1985, *British Journal of Psychiatry*, 151, 479-85.

Freedman, R.I. and Moran, A. (1984) Wanderers in a promised land: the chronically mentally ill and deinstitutionalization, *Medical Care*, 22:12, Supplement.

Freeman, H. and Farndale, J. (eds)(1963) *Trends in the Mental Health Service*, Pergamon Press, Oxford.

Gibbons, J.S. (1988) Mentally ill, in I. Sinclair (ed.) *Residential Care: The Research Reviewed*, National Institute for Social Work/HMSO, London.

Gibbons, J.S. and Butler, J.P. (1987) Quality of life for 'new' long-stay psychiatric in-patients: the effects of moving to a hostel, *British Journal of Psychiatry*, 151, 347-54.

Gibbons, J.S., Horn, S.H., Powell, J.M. and Gibbons, J.L. (1984) Schizophrenia patients and their families, *British Journal of Psychiatry*, 144, 70-77.

Gibson, F., McGrath, A. and Reid, N. (1989) Measures of stress, *Social Work Today*, 20 April.

Gilbert, J.P., Light, R.J. and Mosteller, F. (1975) Assessing social innovations, in C.A. Bennett and A.A. Lumsdane (eds) *Evaluation and Experiment*, Academic Press, New York.

Ginsberg, G. and Marks, I. (1977) Costs and benefits of behavioural psychotherapy: a pilot study of neurotics treatment by nurse-therapists, *Psychological Medicine*, 7, 685-700.

Glenarther, Lord (1986) Introduction and current developments, in G. Wilkinson and H. Freeman (eds) *The Provision of Mental Health Services in Britain: The Way Ahead*, Gaskell, London.

Goffman, I. (1961) *Asylums: Essays on the Social Situation of Mental Patients and other Inmates*, Penguin, Harmondsworth.

Goldberg, D. (1990) Cost-effectiveness studies in the treatment of schizophrenia: a brief review, paper presented to the conference on 'The Cost of Schizophrenia', Venice, October.

Goldberg, D. and Huxley, P. (1980) *Mental Illness in the Community: The Pathway to Psychiatric Care*, Tavistock, London.

Gollay, E., Freedman, R., Wyngaarden, M. and Kurtz, N.R. (1978) *Coming Back: The Community Experiences of Deinstitutionalized Mentally Retarded People*, Abt Books, Cambridge, Massachusetts.

Goodwin, S. (1989) Community care for the mentally ill in England and Wales: myths, assumptions and reality, *Journal of Social Policy*, 18:1, 27-52.

Grad, J. and Sainsbury, P. (1968) The effects that patients have on their families, *British Journal of Psychiatry*, 114.

Griffiths, M., Wyatt, J. and Hersov, J. (1985) Further education, adult education and self-advocacy, in M. Craft, J. Bicknell and S. Hollins (eds) *Mental Handicap: A Multidisciplinary Approach*, Bailliere Tindall, Eastbourne.

Griffiths, R. (1988) *Community Care: Agenda for Action*, HMSO, London.

Gudeman, J.E., Dickey, B., Rood, L., Hellman, S. and Grinspoon, L. (1981) Alternative to the back ward: the quarterway house, *Hospital and Community Psychiatry*, 32:5, 330-34.

Gudeman, J.E., Dickey, B., Evans, A. and Shore, M.F. (1985) Four-year assessment of a day hospital-inn programme as an alternative to inpatient hospitalisation, *American Journal of Psychiatry*, 142:11, 1330-33.

Häfner, H. (1987) Do we still need beds for psychiatric patients?, *Acta Psychiatrica Scandinavica*, 75, 113-26.

Häfner, H. and an der Heiden, W. (1989a) The evaluation of mental health care systems, *British Journal of Psychiatry*, 155, 12-17.

Häfner, H. and an der Heiden, W. (1989b) Effectiveness and cost of community care for schizophrenic patients, *Hospital and Community Psychiatry*, 40:1, 59-63.

Haley, W.E. and associates (1987) Psychological, social and health consequences of caring for a relative with senile dementia, *Journal of the American Geriatrics Society*, 35, 405-11.

Hall, J. and Baker, R. (1983) *REHAB: A Users' Manual*, Vine Publishing, Aberdeen.

Hargreaves, W.A. and associates (1984) 'Restrictiveness of care among the severely mentally disabled, *Hospital and Community Psychiatry*, 35, 706-9.

Harissis, K. (1986) Staff turnover and wastage in the personal social services: a statistical approach, unpublished PhD thesis, University of Kent at Canterbury.

Harris, M., Bergman, H. and Bachrach, L. (1986) Psychiatric and non-psychiatric indicators for rehospitalisation in a chronic patient population, *Hospital and Community Psychiatry*, 37, 630-31.

Haslam, M.T. (1988) Letter: community-based programmes on intervention in mental illness, *Bulletin of the Royal College of Psychiatrists*, 12, 196-8.

Haycox, A. and Brand, D. (1991) *Evaluating Community Care: A Case Study of Maidstone Community Care Project*, North Western Regional Health Authority, Manchester and Social Services Inspectorate, London.

Heginbotham, C. (1988) Shelter from the storm, *Health Service Journal*, 9 June, 644-5.

Henderson, S. with Byrne, D.G. and Duncan-Jones, P. (1981) *Neurosis and the Social Environment*, Academic Press, Sydney.

Henke, R.O., Connolly, S.G. and Cox, J.G. (1975) Caseload management: the key to effectiveness, *Journal of Applied Rehabilitation Counselling*, 6:4, 217-27.

Holmes, N., Shah, A. and Wing, L. (1982) The disability assessment schedule: a brief screening device for use with the mentally retarded, *Psychological Medicine*, 12, 879-90.

Honig, A., Radstake, S., Romme, M.A.J. and Breuls, M.G.G.J. (1987) Problem analysis: an instrument in the rehabilitation of chronic psychiatric patients in the community, *International Journal of Social Psychiatry*, 33:4, 303-11.

Hoult, J. and Reynolds, I. (1984) Schizophrenia: a comparative trial of community oriented and hospital oriented psychiatric care, *Acta Psychiatrica Scandinavica*, 69, 359-72.

House of Commons Social Services Committee (1985) *Community Care*, HCP 13-1, Session 1984-85, HMSO, London.

House of Commons Social Services Committee (1990) *Community Care: Services for People with a Mental Handicap and People with a Mental Illness*, Session 1989-90, Eleventh report, HMSO, London.

Housing Corporation (1984) Circular 6/84, Housing Corporation, London.

Howatt, J.G. and Kontny, E.L. (1982) The outcome for discharged Nottingham long-stay in-patients, *British Journal of Psychiatry*, 141, 590-94.
Hudson, R. (1985) A 'people' approach to day services, *Health and Social Services Journal*, 21 November, 1474.
Hurst, J. (1988) Report of a meeting held in July 1987 at the Institute of Psychiatry, in I. Marks, J. Connolly and M. Muijen (eds) *New Directions in Mental Health Care Evaluation*, Institute of Psychiatry, London.
Hurst, R. (1990) Who's afraid of community care?, *Search*, 7 November, 39-40.
Hyde, C., Bridges, K., Goldberg, D., Lowson, K., Sterling, C. and Faragher, B. (1987) The evaluation of a hostel ward: a controlled study using modified cost-benefit analysis, *British Journal of Psychiatry*, 151, 805-12.
Jay, P. (1979) *Report on Mental Handicap, Nursing and Care*, HMSO, London.
Jenkins, J., Felce, D., Toogood, S., Mansell, J. and de Kock, U. (1988) *Individual Programme Planning: A Mechanism for Developing Plans to Meet the Specific Needs of Individuals with Mental Handicaps*, BIMH Publications, Kidderminster.
Jenkins, R. (1990) Towards a system of outcome indicators for mental health care, *British Journal of Psychiatry*, 157, 500-514.
Johnes, G. and Haycox, A. (1986) Cost structures in a large hospital for the mentally handicapped, *Social Science and Medicine*, 22:6, 605-10.
Jones, D. (1989) The selection of patients for reprovision: moving long-stay psychiatry patients into the community. First results, TAPS Fourth Annual Conference Report, North East Thames Regional Health Authority, London.
Jones, K. (1972) *A History of the Mental Health Services*, Routledge & Kegan Paul, London.
Jones, K. (1981) Re-inventing the wheel, in Mind *The Future of the Mental Hospitals: A Report of Mind's 1980 Annual Conference*, Marshallarts Print Services, Brighton.
Jones, K. and Poletti, A. (1985) Understanding the Italian experience, *British Journal of Psychiatry*, 146, 341-7.
Jones, K. and Poletti, A. (1986) The Italian experience reconsidered, *British Journal of Psychiatry*, 148, 144-50.
Jones, K. with Brown, J., Cunningham, W.J., Roberts, J. and Williams, P. (1975) *Opening the Door: A Study of New Policies for the Mentally Handicapped*, Routledge & Kegan Paul, London.
Jones, K., Robinson, M. and Golightley, M. (1986) Long-term psychiatric patients in the community, *British Journal of Psychiatry*, 149, 537-40.
Jones, R., Goldberg, D. and Hughes, B. (1980) A comparison of two different services treating schizophrenia: a cost-benefit approach, *Psychological Medicine*, 10, 493-505.
Jowell, T. (1988) A force for change, *Insight*, 20 May, 20-21.

Jowell, T. and Wistow, G. (1989) Give them a voice, *Insight*, 28 February, 22-4.

Kay, A. and Legg, C. (1986) *Discharged into the Community*, Good Practices in Mental Health, London.

Kendell, R.E. (1989) The future of Britain's mental hospitals, *British Medical Journal*, 18 November, 299, 1237-8.

King, R., Raynes, N. and Tizard, J. (1971) *Patterns of Residential Care: Sociological Studies in Institutions for Handicapped Children*, Routledge & Kegan Paul, London.

King's Fund Centre (1982) *An Ordinary Life*, King's Fund, London.

King's Fund Centre (1984) *An Ordinary Working Life*, Project Paper No. 50, King's Fund, London.

King's Fund Centre (1988) *Ties and Connections: An Ordinary Community Life for People with Learning Difficulties*, King's Fund, London.

Kirk, S. and Therrein, M. (1975) Community mental health myths and the fate of former hospitalized patients, *Psychiatry*, 38, 209-17.

Knapp, M.R.J. (1980) *Production Relations for Old People's Homes*, Unpublished PhD thesis, University of Kent at Canterbury.

Knapp, M.R.J. (1984) *Economics of Social Care*, Macmillan, London.

Knapp, M.R.J. and Beecham, J. (1990a) Costing mental health services, *Psychological Medicine*, 20, 893-908.

Knapp, M.R.J. and Beecham, J. (1990b) The cost-effectiveness of community care for former long-stay psychiatric hospital patients, in R. Scheffler and L. Rossiter (eds) *Advances in Health Economics and Health Services Research*, AI Press, Greenwich, Connecticut.

Knapp, M.R.J. and Beecham, J. (1991) Mental health service costs, *Current Opinion in Psychiatry*, 4, 275-82.

Knapp, M.R.J., Beecham, J., Anderson, J., Dayson, D., Leff, J., Margolius, O., O'Driscoll, C. and Wills, W. (1990) Predicting the community costs of closing psychiatric hospitals, *British Journal of Psychiatry*, 157, 661-70.

Knapp, M.R.J., Beecham, J. and Gordon, K. (1991) Social care in the community for people with mental health problems: cost predictions for England, Discussion Paper 750, PSSRU, University of Kent at Canterbury.

Knapp, M.R.J., Beecham, J. and Renshaw, J. (1987) The cost-effectiveness of psychiatric reprovision services, Interim report submitted to North East Thames Regional Health Authority, Discussion Paper 553/2, PSSRU, University of Kent at Canterbury.

Knapp, M.R.J., Harissis, K. and Missiakoulis, S. (1981) Who leaves social work? A statistical analysis, *British Journal of Social Work*, 11, 421-44.

Korman, N. and Glennerster, H. (1990) *Hospital Closure*, Open University Press, Milton Keynes.

Kunze, H. (1985) Rehabilitation and institutionalisation in community care in West Germany, *British Journal of Psychiatry*, 147, 261-4.

Kushlick, A., Blunden, R. and Cox, G. (1973) A method for rating behaviour characteristics for use in large-scale surveys of mental handicap, *Psychological Medicine*, 3, 466-78.

Lamb, R. and Talbott, J. (1986) The homeless mentally ill, *Journal of the American Medical Association*, 156, 498-501.

Landesman, S. (1987) The changing structure and function of institutions: a search for optimal group care environments, in S. Landesman and P. Vietze (eds) *Living Environments and Mental Retardation*, American Association on Mental Retardation, Washington, DC.

Lawton, M.P. (1972) The dimensions of morale, in D.P. Kent, R. Kastenbaum and S. Sherwood (eds) *Research Planning and Action for the Elderly*, Behavioral Publications, New York.

Lawton, M.P. (1975) The PGC Morale Scale: a revision, *Journal of Gerontology*, 30, 85-9.

Leedham, I. (1989) From mental handicap hospital to community provisions: a study of changing service patterns and the production of client welfare, unpublished PhD thesis, PSSRU, University of Kent at Canterbury.

Lehman, A.F. (1983) The well-being of chronic mental patients, *Archives of General Psychiatry*, 40, 369-73.

Lehman, A.F., Ward, N. and Linn, L. (1982) Chronic mental patients: the quality of life issue, *American Journal of Psychiatry*, 139, 1271-6.

Leibrich, J. (1988) *An Outside Chance*, New Zealand Department of Health, Wellington.

Leighton, J. (1988) *Mental Handicap in the Community*, Woodhead-Faulkner, Cambridge.

Levene, L.S., Donaldson, L.J. and Brandon, S. (1985) How likely is it that a district health authority can close its large mental hospitals?, *British Journal of Psychiatry*, 147, 150-55.

Levitt, A.J., Hogan, T.P. and Bucosky, C.M. (1990) Quality of life in chronically mentally ill patients in day treatment, *Psychological Medicine*, 20, 703-10.

Linn, M.W., Caffey, E.M., Klett, C.J. and Hogarty, G. (1977) Hospital versus community (foster) care for psychiatric patients, *Archives of General Psychiatry*, 34, 78-83.

Locker, D., Rao, B. and Weddell, J.M. (1981) Changing attitudes towards the mentally handicapped: the impact of community care, *Apex*, 9, 92-103.

Lyne, D. (1988) The Warrington mental illness project: development and operational considerations, in P. Cambridge and M.R.J. Knapp (eds) *Demonstrating Successful Care in the Community*, PSSRU, University of Kent at Canterbury.

Mangen, S.P., Paykel, E.S., Griffith, J.H., Burchall, A. and Mancini, P. (1983) Cost-effectiveness of community psychiatric nurse or out-patient psychiatrist care of neurotic patients, *Psychological Medicine*, 13, 407-16.

Martin, F.M. (1984) *Between the Acts: Community Mental Health Services, 1959-1983*, Nuffield Provincial Hospitals Trust, London.

McCausland, M.P. (1987) Deinstitutionalization of the mentally ill: over-simplification of complex issues, *Advances in Nursing Science*, 9:3, 24-33.

McKechnie, A.A., Rae, D. and May, J. (1982) A comparison of in-patient costs of treatment and care in a Scottish psychiatric hospital, *British Journal of Psychiatry*, 140, 602-7.

Mercer, A.D. (1975) A model for nursing cost, *Hospital and Health Services Review*, 71:6, 194-5.

Mills, J. (1988) An uncaring community, *New Society*, 12 February.

Ministry of Health (1962) *A Hospital Plan for England and Wales*, Cmnd 1604, HMSO, London.

Mooney, G. (1978) Planning for balance of care of the elderly, *Scottish Journal of Political Economy*, 25, 149-64.

Morris, P. (1969) *Put Away: A Sociological Study of Institutions for the Mentally Retarded*, Routledge & Kegan Paul, London.

MRC Social Psychiatry Unit (1986) Evaluation of new services to be provided for residents of Darenth Park hospital, fifth annual report, MRC Social Psychiatry Unit, London.

Murphy, J.P. and Datel, W.E. (1976) A cost-benefit analysis of community versus institutional living, *Hospital and Community Psychiatry*, 27:3, 165-9.

Murray, H.A. (1938) *Explorations in Personality*, Oxford University Press, New York.

National Development Team (1990) Memorandum of evidence to the House of Commons Social Services Committee, HMSO, London.

National Federation of Housing Associations/Mind (1989) *Housing: The Foundation of Community Care*, NFHA/Mind, London.

Netten, A. and Beecham, J. (eds)(1992) *Costing Community Care: Theory and Practice*, Avebury, Aldershot, forthcoming.

Netten, A. and Davies, B.P. (1991) The social production of welfare and consumption of social services, *Journal of Public Policy*, 10, 331-47.

Nihira, K., Foster, M., Shellbass, M. and Leland, H. (1974) *AAMD Adapative Behavior Scale*, American Association on Mental Deficiency, Washington, DC.

Normand, C. (1986) Transfer of mental handicap patients into the community: RHA policies on the transfer of resources, York Health Economics Consortium, University of York.

Normand, C. and Taylor, P. (1986) The decline in patient numbers in mental handicap hospitals: how the cost savings should be calculated, Discussion Paper 26, Centre for Health Economics, University of York.

O'Brien, J. (1986) *A Guide to Personal Futures Planning*, mimeo, Responsive Systems Associates, Atlanta, Georgia.

O'Brien, J. (1987) A guide to life-style planning: using *The Activities Catalog* to integrate services and natural support systems, in B. Wilcox and G.T. Bellamy (eds) *A Comprehensive Guide to The Activities Catalog: An Alternative Curriculum for Youth and Adults with Severe Disabilities*, Paul H. Brookes Publishing, Baltimore, Maryland.

O'Brien, J. and Tyne, A. (1981) *The Principle of Normalisation: A Foundation for Effective Services*, Campaign for Mental Handicap, London.

O'Connor, G. (1976) *Home is a Good Place: A National Perspective of Community Residential Facilities for Developmentally Disabled Persons*, Monograph of the AAMD No. 2, Washington, DC.

O'Grady, T.J. (1988) Community psychiatry: a changing locus of rejection?, *Perspectives in Biological Medicine*, 31, 325-40.

Onyett, S. (1990) *Case Management in Mental Health*, Chapman and Hall, London.

Onyett, S. and Malone, S. (1990) Making the teamwork work, *Clinical Psychology Forum*, 28, August, 16-18.

Orr, J.H. (1978) The imprisonment of mentally disordered residents, *British Journal of Psychiatry*, 133, 194-9.

Ovretveit, J. (1986) *Organising Multidisciplinary Community Teams*, Working Paper, Health Services Centre, Brunel Institute of Organisational and Social Studies.

Passfield, D. (1983) What do you think of it so far? A survey of twenty Priory Court residents, *Mental Handicap*, 11, 97-9.

Pattie, A. and Gilleard, C. (1979) *Manual of the Clifton Assessment Procedures for the Elderly*, Hodder & Stoughton, Sevenoaks.

Peterson, C. (1986) Changing community attitudes toward the chronic mentally ill through a psychosocial program, *Hospital and Community Psychiatry*, 37, 180-82.

Pfeiffer, S.I. (1990) An analysis of methodology in follow-up studies of adult inpatient psychiatric treatment, *Hospital and Community Psychiatry*, 41:12, 1315-21.

Pilkington, E. (1990) Student hardship in bleak houses, *Search*, 7 November, 5-7.

Porterfield, J. (1988) Promoting opportunities for employment, in D. Towell (ed.) *An Ordinary Life in Practice: Developing Comprehensive Community-based Services for People with Learning Disabilities*, King's Fund, London.

Potts, M. and Halliday, S. (1988) Hostel to house: measuring the effects of change, paper presented at the DCP birthday conference, York.

Presly, A.S., Grubb, A.B. and Semple, D. (1982) Predictors of successful rehabilitation in long-stay patients, *Acta Psychiatrica Scandinavica*, 66, 83-8.

Qureshi, H., Challis, D.J. and Davies, B.P. (1989) *Helpers in Case-Managed Community Care*, Gower, Aldershot.

Raynes, N.V., Pratt, M. and Roses, S. (1979) *Organisational Structure and Care of the Mentally Retarded*, Croom Helm, London.

Raynes, N.V. and Sumpton, R.C. (1986) Follow-up study of 448 people who are mentally handicapped, final report, Hester Adrian Research Centre, University of Manchester.

Renshaw, J., Hampson, R., Thomason, C., Darton, R.A., Judge, K. and Knapp, M.R.J. (1988) *Care in the Community: The First Steps*, Gower, Aldershot.

Ritchie, J., Keegan, J. and Bosanquet, N. (1983) *Housing for Mentally Ill and Mentally Handicapped People*, HMSO, London.

Rivera, G. (1972) *Willowbrook: A report on how it is and why it doesn't have to be that way*, Random House, New York.

Robinson, J.W., Thompson, T., Emmons, P. and Graff, M. with Franklin, E. (1984) Towards an architectural definition of normalisation: design principles for housing severely and profoundly retarded adults, Center for Urban and Regional Affairs, University of Minnesota, Minneapolis.

Roethlisberger, F.J. and Dickson, W.J. with Wright, H.A. (1939) *Management and the Worker: An Account of a Research Program Conducted by the Western Electric Company, Hawthorne Works, Chicago*, Harvard University Press, Cambridge, Massachusetts.

Rossi, P.H. and Freeman, H.E. (1982) *Evaluation: A Systematic Approach*, 3rd edition, Sage, Beverly Hills, California.

Ryan, J. and Thomas, F. (1980) *The Politics of Mental Handicap*, Penguin, Harmondsworth.

Savage, D. (1990) Some major factors leading to increase of stress levels in professional carers, unpublished working paper, Bolton Health Authority, Bolton.

Schalock, R.L. and Lilley, M.A. (1986) Placement from community-based mental retardation programs: how well do clients do after 8 to 10 years?, *American Journal of Mental Deficiency*, 90:6, 669-76.

Schulz, R. and Brenner, G. (1977) Relocation of the aged: a review and historical analysis, *Journal of Gerontology*, 32, 322-33.

Scottish Home and Health Department (1984) *Scottish Health Building Programme*, Scottish Office.

Scull, A. (1984) *Decarceration: Community Treatment and the Deviant: A Radical View*, 2nd edition, Polity Press, Cambridge.

Segal, S.P. and Kottler, P. (1989) Community residential care, in D. Rochefort (ed.) *Mental Health Policy in the United States*, Greenwood Press, New York.

Segal, S.P. and Moyles, E.W. (1979) Management style and institutional dependency in sheltered care, *Social Psychiatry*, 14, 159-65.

Segal, S.P., Silverman, C. and Baumohl, J. (1989) Seeking person-environment fit in community care placement, *Journal of Social Issues*, 45:3, 49-64.

Seltzer, G. and Seltzer, M.M. (1983) Satisfaction questionnaire, Paper presented at the AAMD annual meeting on Residential Satisfaction and Community Adjustment, AAMD, Washington, DC.

Seltzer, M.M. (1985) Public attitudes toward community residential facilities for mentally retarded persons, in R.H. Bruininks and K.C. Lakin (eds) *Living and Learning in the Least Restricted Environment*, Paul H. Brookes Publishing, Baltimore, Maryland.

Shadish, W.R. and Bootzin, R.R. (1984) The social integration of psychiatric patients in nursing homes, *American Journal of Psychiatry*, 141:10, 1203-7.

Shanks, N.J. (1989) Previously diagnosed psychiatric illness among inhabitants of common lodging houses, *Journal of Epidemiology and Community Health*, 43, 375-9.

Shaw, G., Naidoo, S., Wise, S. and Bateman, S. (1986) A home of their own, *Nursing Times*, 12 November, 50.

Shepherd, G. (1990) Rehabilitation and the long-term mentally ill, *Current Opinion in Psychiatry*, 3, 278-83.

Shepherd, M. (1989) Primary care of patients with mental disorder in the community, *British Medical Journal*, 9 September, 299, 666-9.

Shiell, A., Gerard, K. and Donaldson, C. (1987) Cost of mental health studies: an aid to decision-making? *Health Policy*, 8, 317-23.

Sigelman, C.K., Schoenrock, C.J., Winer, J.L., Spanhel, C.L., Hromas, S.G., Martin, P.W., Budd, E.C. and Bensberg, G.J. (1981) Issues in interviewing mentally retarded persons: an empirical study, in R.H. Bruininks, C.E. Meyers, B.B. Sigford and K.C. Lakin (eds) *Deinstitutionalization and Community Adjustment of Mentally Retarded People*, AAMD Monograph No. 4, American Association of Mental Deficiency, Washington DC.

Sinclair, I. and Clarke, R. (1981) Cross-institutional designs, in E.M. Goldberg and N. Connelly (eds) *Evaluative Research in Social Care*, Heinemann Educational Books, London.

Smith, J., Glossop, C. and Kushlick, A. (1980) Evaluation of alternative residential facilities for the severely mentally handicapped in Wessex, *Advances in Behavioural Therapy Research*, 3, 5-11.

Smyth, M., Vostanis, P. and Dean, C. (1990) Psychiatric out-patient non-attenders: a cause for relief or concern?, *Psychiatric Bulletin*, 14, 147-9.

Snaith, R.P., Ahmed, S.N., Mehta, S. and Hamilton, M. (1971) Assessment of the severity of primary depressive illness, *Psychological Medicine*, 1, 143-9.

Social Services Inspectorate/Department of Health (1991) *Case Management and Assessment: Managers' Guide*, HMSO, London.

Solomon, P., Gordon, B. and Davis, J. (1984) Assessing the service needs of the discharged psychiatric patient, *Social Work in Health Care*, 10:1, 61-9.

Speck, R.V. and Attneave, C.L. (1973) *Family Networks: A New Approach to Family Problems*, Vintage Books, New York.

Sperlinger, A. (1987) Service evaluation of a staff house for young people in Greenwich with learning disabilities, Presentation at 'Quality of Life' assessment meeting, 3 June, Friern Hospital, London.

Stanton, A.H. and Schwartz, M.S. (1954) *The Mental Hospital: A Study of Institutional Participation in Psychiatric Illness and Treatment*, Basic Books, New York.

Stein, L. and Test, M. (1980) Alternatives to mental hospital treatment, *Archives of General Psychiatry*, 37, 392-7.

Stenfert-Kroese, B. and Fleming, I. (1989) Staff's attitudes and working conditions in community-based groups of homes of people with learning dificulties, unpublished paper, School of Psychology, University of Birmingham.

Stern, B.E. and Stern, E.S. (1963) Efficiency of mental hospitals, *British Journal of Preventive and Social Medicine*, 17, 111-20.

Stewart, G. (1988) Maintaining people with mental health disabilities in the community, in S. Baldwin, G. Parker and R. Walker (eds) *Social Security and Community Care*, Avebury, Aldershot.

Stilwell, J. (1981) Mental health: shifting the balance of care, *Public Money*, 1:2, 31-4.

Sturt, E. (1983) Mortality in a cohort of long-term users of community psychiatric services, *Psychological Medicine*, 13, 441-6.

Sussex, J. (1986) A preliminary cost-effectiveness evaluation of the transfer of mentally handicapped adults from Lenham Hospital to the Maistone Community Care Project, mimeo, PSSRU, University of Kent at Canterbury.

Szmukler, G.I. (1990) Alternatives to hospital treatment, *Current Opinion in Psychiatry*, 3, 273-7.

Talbott, J. (1984) The need for asylum, not asylums, *Hospital and Community Psychiatry*, 35, 209.

Tannahill, M., Wilkinson, G. and Higson, P. (1990) Beyond mental hospital sites, *Psychiatric Bulletin*, 14, 399-401.

Tantum, D. (1985) Alternatives to psychiatric hospitalisation, *British Journal of Psychiatry*, 146, 1-4.

TAPS (1988) *Basic Everyday Living Skills Schedule*, Team for the Assessment of Psychiatric Services, Friern Hospital, London.

TAPS (1990) *Better Out than In?*, Team for the Assessment of Psychiatric Services, North East Thames Regional Health Authority, London.

Taube, C., Lees, E.S. and Forthofer, R.N. (1984) DRGs in psychiatry: on empirical evaluation, *Medical Care*, 22, 597-610.

Taylor, P. and Bailey, A. (1988) Joint working and the development of the Bolton project for people with learning difficulty, in P. Cambridge and M.R.J. Knapp (eds) *Demonstrating Successful Care in the Community*, PSSRU, University of Kent at Canterbury.

Thapa, K. and Rowland, L.A. (1989) Quality of life perspectives in long-term care: staff and patient perceptions, *Acta Psychiatrica Scandinavica*, 267-71.

Thomas, M., Felce, D., de Kock, U., Saxby, H. and Repp, A. (1986) The activity of staff and of severely and profoundly mentally handicapped adults in residential settings of different sizes, *British Journal of Mental Subnormality*, 32:1, 82-92.

Thornicroft, G. and Bebbington, P. (1989) Deinstitutionalisation: from hospital closure to service development, *British Journal of Psychiatry*, 155, 739-53.

Tidmarsh, D. and Wood, S. (1972) Psychiatric aspects of destitution, in J.K. Wing and A.M. Haley (eds) *Evaluating a Community Psychiatric Service*, Oxford University Press, Oxford.

Timms, P.W. and Fry, A.H. (1989) Homelessness and mental illness, *Health Trends*, 21:3, 70-71.

Titmuss, R. (1963) Community care: fact or fiction?, in H. Freeman (ed.) *Trends in the Mental Health Services*, Pergamon Press, London.

Tizard, J. (1964) *Community Services for the Mentally Handicapped*, Oxford University Press, London.

Tobin, S. and Lieberman, M.A. (1976) *Last Home for the Aged*, Jossey-Bass, San Francisco, California.

Torrey, E.F. (1988) *Nowhere To Go*, Harper & Row, New York.

Townsend, J., Piper, M., Frank, A.O., Dyer, S., North, W.R.S. and Meade, T.W. (1988) Reduction in hospital readmission stay of elderly patients by a community-based hospital discharge scheme: a randomised controlled trial, *British Medical Journal*, 297, 544-7.

Trute, B. and Loewen, A. (1978) Public attitude toward the mentally ill as a function of prior personal experience, *Social Psychiatry*, 13, 79-84.

Turner, F.J. and Turner, J.C. (1985) Evaluation of the five-year plan for closure of mental retardation facilities: southwest region, Province of Ontario, Southwestern Region, Ontario.

Ungerson, C. (ed.)(1990) *Gender and Caring: Work and Welfare in Britain and Scandinavia*, Harvester Wheatsheaf, London.

Wagner, G. (1988) *Residential Care: A Positive Choice*, National Institute for Social Work/HMSO, London.

Walker, A. (1982) *Community Care: The Family, the State and Social Policy*, Blackwell, Oxford.

Wallace, M. (1986) A caring community? The plight of Britain's mentally ill, *Sunday Times Magazine*, 3 May, 25-36.

Ward, L. (1989) An ordinary life: the early views and experiences of residential staff in the Wells Road Service, *Mental Handicap*, 17, 6-9.

Webb, A. and Wistow, G. (1985) Social services, in S. Ransom, G.W. Jones and K. Walsh (eds) *Between Centre and Locality*, Allen and Unwin, London.

Weisbrod, B., Test, M.A. and Stein, L.I. (1980) Alternatives to mental hospital treatment: economic benefit-cost analysis, *Archives of General Psychiatry*, 37, 400-405.

Weller, B.G.A., Weller, M.P.I., Coker, E. and Mahomed, S. (1987) Crisis at Christmas 1986, *Lancet*, 7 March, 553-4.

Weller, M.P.I. (1984) Memorandum of evidence to the House of Commons Social Services Committee, HMSO, London.

Weller, M.P.I. (1989) Mental illness: who cares? *Nature*, 339, 249-52.

Weller, M.P.I. (1990) Letters to the editor: Care in the community, *The Lancet*, 24 February, 335, 468-9.

Weller, M.P.I. and Weller, B.G.A. (1986) Crime and psychopathology, *British Medical Journal*, 292, 55-6.

Weller, M.P.I. and Weller, B.G.A. (1988) Mental illness and social policy, *Medical Science and Law*, 28:1, 47-53.

Wertheimer, A. (1987) Towards a normal working life: new directions in day services, *Community Living*, April, 8-9.

West, M.A. and Farr, J.L. (eds)(1990) *Innovation and Creativity at Work: Psychological and Organisational Perspectives*, John Wiley, Chichester.

Wilkinson, D.G. (1982) The suicide rate in schizophrenia, *British Journal of Psychiatry*, 140, 138-41.

Wilkinson, G. (1988) I don't want you to see a psychiatrist, *British Medical Journal*, 297, 1144-5.

Wilkinson, G. and Pelosi, A.J. (1987) The economics of mental health services, *British Medical Journal*, 294, 139-40.

Wilkinson, G., Falloon, I. and Sen, B. (1985) Chronic mental disorders in general practice, *British Medical Journal*, 291, 1302-4.

Wilkinson, G., Croft-Jeffreys, C., Krekorian, H., McLees, S. and Falloon, I. (1990) QALYs in psychiatric care?, *Psychiatric Bulletin*, 14, 582-5.

Williams, A. (1989) Comment on 'Should QALYs be programme specific?', *Journal of Health Economics*, 8, 485-7.

Wing, J.K. (1960) The measurement of behaviour in chronic schizophrenia, *Acta Psychiatrica Scandinavica*, 35, 245-54.

Wing, J.K. (1961) A simple and reliable subclassification of chronic schizophrenia, *Journal of Mental Science*, 107, 1070-77.

Wing, J.K. (1986) The cycle of planning and evaluation, in G. Wilkinson and H. Freeman (eds) *The Provision of Mental Health Services in Britain: The Way Ahead*, Gaskell, London.

Wing, J.K. (1989) The measurement of 'social disablement', *Social Psychiatry and Psychiatric Epidemiology*, 24, 173-8.

Wing, J.K. (1990) The functions of asylum, *British Journal of Psychiatry*, 157, 822-7.

Wing, J.K. and Brown, G.W. (1970) *Institutionalism and Schizophrenia*, Cambridge University Press, Cambridge.

Wing, L. (1989) *Hospital Closure and the Resettlement of Residents: The Case of Darenth Park*, Gower, Aldershot.

Wistow, G. (1983) Joint finance and community care: have the incentives worked?, *Public Money*, 3, September, 33-7.

Wistow, G. (1985) Community care for the mentally handicapped: disappointing progress, in A. Harrison and J. Gretton (eds) *Health Care UK 1985*, Policy Journals, London.

Wistow, G. and Hardy, B. (1986) Transferring care: can financial incentives work?, in A. Harrison and J. Gretton (eds) *Health Care UK 1986*, Policy Journals, London.

Wistow, G., Knapp, M., Hardy, B. and Allen, C. (1992) From providing to enabling: local authorities and the mixed economy of social care, *Public Administration*, 70, forthcoming.

Wolfensberger, W. (1970) The principle of normalization and its implications to psychiatric services, *American Journal of Psychiatry*, 127, 291-7.

Wolfensberger, W. (1972) *The Principle of Normalization in Human Services*, National Institute on Mental Retardation, Toronto.

Wright, K. (1987) Cost-effectivness in community care, Centre for Health Economics, University of York.

Wright, K. and Haycox, A. (1984) Public sector costs of caring for mentally handicapped persons in a large hospital, Discussion Paper 1, Institute for Research in the Social Sciences/Centre for Health Economics, University of York.

Wright, K., Cairns, J. and Snell, M. (1981) Costing care, mimeo, Joint Unit for Social Services Research and Community Care, University of Sheffield.

Wykes, T. (1982) A hostel for 'new' long-stay patients: an evaluative study of a 'ward in a house', in J.K. Wing (ed.) *Psychological Medicine*, Monograph Supplement, 57-97.

Wykes, T. and Sturt, E. (1986) The measurement of social behaviour in psychiatric patients: an assessment of the reliability and validity of the SBS schedule, *British Journal of Psychiatry*, 148, 1-11.

Wykes, T., Sturt, E. and Creer, C. (1982) Practices of day and residential units in relation to the social behaviour of attenders, in J.K. Wing (ed.) *Evaluating a Community Psychiatric Service: Experience in a London Borough, Psychological Medicine* Monograph Supplement, 2, 15-27.

Author index

Subject index